Functional Assessment
Strategies to Prevent and Remediate Challenging Behavior in School Settings

Lynette K. Chandler
Northern Illinois University

Carol M. Dahlquist
*School Association for Special
Education in DuPage County*

Merrill
Prentice Hall

D0907267

Upper Saddle River, New Jersey
Columbus, Ohio

Library of Congress Cataloging-in-Publication Data

Chandler, Lynette K.

   Functional assessment: strategies to prevent and remediate challenging behavior in school settings / by Lynette K. Chandler and Carol M. Dahlquist.

      p. cm.

   Includes bibliographical references and index.

   ISBN 0-13-015675-2 (pbk.)

   1. Behavioral assessment. 2. Handicapped—Functional assessment. 3. Problem children—Diagnosis. 4. Behavior modification. I. Dahlquist, Carol M. II. Title.

LB1060.2.C43 2002
370.15'3—dc21   2001042592

Vice President and Publisher: Jeffery W. Johnston
Executive Editor: Ann Castel Davis
Editorial Assistant: Keli Gemrich
Production Editor: Sheryl Glicker Langner
Production Coordination: Marilee Aschenbrenner, Carlisle Publishers Services
Design Coordinator: Diane C. Lorenzo
Cover Designer: Thomas Mack
Cover art: VSA arts of Maine/David Wheaton
Production Manager: Laura Messerly
Director of Marketing: Kevin Flanagan
Marketing Manager: Amy June
Marketing Coordinator: Barbara Koontz

This book was set in Novarese by Carlisle Communications, Ltd. It was printed and bound by Maple Vail Book Manufacturing Group. The cover was printed by Phoenix Color Corp.

Pearson Education Ltd., *London*
Pearson Education Australia Pty. Limited, *Sydney*
Pearson Education Singapore Pte. Ltd.
Pearson Education North Asia Ltd., *Hong Kong*
Pearson Education Canada, Ltd., *Toronto*
Pearson Educación de Mexico, S.A. de C.V.
Pearson Education—Japan, *Tokyo*
Pearson Education Malaysia Pte. Ltd.
Pearson Education, *Upper Saddle River, New Jersey*

Merrill
Prentice Hall

10   9   8   7   6   5   4   3   2   1
ISBN: 0-13-015675-2

From Lynette

To Roger, who introduced me to behavior analysis,
who continues to keep me thinking and analyzing everyday,
and who believed this book was possible,
and to my parents for their guidance and example as educators.

From Carol

To my Mom, who loved children and encouraged me to be a teacher.
To my husband John, who listens to my stories of teaching children.
To my own children, who taught me so much.

Foreword

Educators, administrators, and parents of students with and without disabilities identify challenging behavior as one of the most significant and demanding problems in our schools today (Cangelosi, 1993). Challenging behaviors often create major problems in school settings. Challenging behaviors require inordinate amounts of educators', parents', and administrators' time and effort; decrease the amount of time available for teaching academic skills and promoting appropriate behaviors; pose barriers to social development and positive self-esteem; and may result in the prescription of medication in order to reduce behavior or referral for intensive interventions or more restrictive placement.

Many educators and family members do not have adequate training in the prevention and remediation of challenging behavior (Cangelosi, 1993; Carr, Langdon, & Yarbrough, 1999; McMahon & McNamarra, 2000; Nelson, Roberts, Mathur, & Rutherford, 1998; Watkins & Durant, 1992). As a result, they often fail to address challenging behavior or they employ intensive punishment procedures or ineffective strategies after the challenging behavior is well established (Iwata, Dorsey, Slifer, Bauman, & Richman, 1982/1994; Walker, Colvin, & Ramsey, 1995). Although numerous strategies are available to address challenging behavior, as described in the applied behavior analysis and special education literature, few guidelines exist to assist educators and families in selecting specific interventions to address specific challenging behaviors. Often educators employ the strategies with which they are most familiar or strategies that seem to be the easiest to use in classroom settings. This may or may not be effective at addressing the challenging behavior of individual students (Chandler, Dahlquist, Repp, & Feltz, 1999; Mace, 1994). Educators need an effective and efficient approach that they can employ in school settings to prevent and remediate challenging behavior.

This book describes functional assessment, a positive and proactive approach for addressing challenging behavior within school settings. Functional assessment is generally recognized as a critical component of effective behavior change programs (Carr, Levin, McConnachie, Carlson, Kemp, & Smith, 1994; Reichle & Wacker, 1993; Repp, 1999). Numerous studies have documented the effectiveness of functional assessment on reducing the challenging behavior of students of all ages and across a variety of behaviors (e.g., Arndorfer, Miltenberger, Woster, Rortvedt, & Gaffaney, 1994; Chandler et al., 1999; Iwata, Dorsey, et al., 1982/1994; *Journal of Applied Behavior Analysis*, 1994; Kern & Dunlap, 1999; Repp & Karsh, 1990; Vaugn, Hales, Bush, & Fox, 1998; Wacker, Cooper, Peck, Derby, & Berg, 1999).

The effectiveness of functional assessment resulted in its inclusion in the 1997 amendments to the Individuals with Disabilities Education Act. These amendments require an educational team to develop a functional behavioral assessment and behavioral intervention plan for students with disabilities and challenging behaviors who are subject to discipline other than the short-term 10-day suspension (Armstrong & Kauffman, 1999; Bateman & Linden, 1998; Maloney, 1997; National Association of State Directors of Special Education, 1997; Turnbull & Cilley, 1999).

The various approaches to functional assessment include carefully controlled experimental analysis in classroom settings, analogue analysis in experimental or clinical settings, and naturalistic functional assessment in classroom and home settings. The functional assessment and intervention model described in this book is a team-based approach that has been used to prevent and remediate challenging behavior in school and home settings. Our approach to functional assessment is based on the naturalistic functional assessment model (Repp, 1999). It is a very practical model that can be implemented by educators and parents in natural settings such as school classrooms, gyms, playgrounds, and homes. Our model helps teams identify the variables that set the occasion for and that support challenging behavior and appropriate behavior. Assessment information is used to identify the function of both challenging and appropriate behavior. The model then guides the selection of positive interventions that address the function of challenging behavior and that teach and support appropriate behaviors to replace challenging behavior.

Although numerous articles and several texts address theories of functional assessment, we have found that they often provide little in the way of practical examples for pre-service and in-service educators. Our goal in this text is to translate theoretical and often technical information into easily understandable and applicable material. We wrote this book for teachers, therapists, administrators, and family members who are interested in guidelines and procedures for conducting functional assessment and addressing challenging behavior in school settings. Using technical terms or jargon only when necessary, we have tried to explain the concepts clearly and to illustrate them with school- or home-based examples.

Functional assessment can be used in conjunction with other methods to address challenging behavior such as counseling or cognitive mediation or it can be employed in isolation. The functional assessment and intervention model described in this book can be implemented successfully by individual educators. However, our experience has been that it is more efficient and successful when it is employed by teams that include the individuals who work with a student or group of students. The team approach facilitates a shared understanding among team members concerning why a challenging behavior is occurring and what interventions must be implemented in order to address the challenging behavior. A team approach also promotes consistency across professionals who apply intervention strategies.

The functional assessment and intervention model can be applied to individual students who exhibit challenging behavior or it may be applied at a class-wide level in order to affect the behavior of many students within a setting (Chandler et al., 1999). We have used functional assessment to address the challenging behavior of students

1. with and without disabilities,
2. of all ages,
3. within a variety of settings (e.g., classroom, gym, playground, cafeteria, home),
4. during a variety of activities (e.g., individual work, group work, lecture, transition, lunch),
5. with different types of disabilities (e.g., autism, sensory integration problems, attention deficit hyperactivity disorder, learning disabilities),
6. with a range of severity of disabilities (i.e., mild, moderate, and severe), or
7. who exhibit a range of severity and frequency of challenging behavior (e.g., infrequent severe behavior or frequent moderate behavior).

This book includes case study examples of students with challenging behavior in several types of school settings. The case studies describe students across a variety of ages and include students with and without disabilities. When you read the case studies we hope that you will think about the students or individuals that you currently work with, students you intend to work with, or students you have worked with in the past. Although the students, behaviors, and settings vary across examples, the concepts and principles are applicable to all individuals with challenging behavior. It is your responsibility to apply the principles and concepts to your students, their behaviors, and their unique situations. We hope that you will learn as much from reading this book as we did from writing it.

Preface

We have conducted workshops, university courses, and in-service training in functional assessment for more than 15 years. We also have extensive experience conducting functional assessment in a variety of settings, across a variety of ages of students, and with students with and without disabilities. We wrote this book because we needed a practical and easily understood model of functional assessment that dealt specifically with school-aged populations and settings. When we conducted workshops and taught courses in functional assessment, students and participants often asked if there was something published that they could give to other educators, parents, or administrators or that they could read as they tried to apply functional assessment. This book is a result of their requests. This book turns theory and research into practical applications in school settings and situations.

We present a comprehensive and positive approach to the prevention and remediation of challenging behavior using functional assessment. The book is written for special and regular educators and consultants who work in school settings.

This book is divided into four sections that take the reader through the process of conducting functional assessment and implementing interventions based on the function of behavior:

- Part One (Chapters 1 to 3) provides an introduction to challenging behavior and functional assessment. It presents the rationale for addressing challenging behavior, common misconceptions about the causes of challenging behavior, and it provides a rationale for using functional assessment and describes the assumptions and goals of functional assessment.
- Part Two (Chapters 4 and 5) describes the process of conducting functional assessment in school settings and identifying the function of behavior.
- Part Three (Chapters 6 to 11) presents suggestions and tips for selecting and implementing function-based interventions. It also presents specific intervention strategies by behavior function: positive reinforcement, negative reinforcement, and sensory regulation/sensory stimulation increase and decrease. Finally, it provides suggestions for implementing strategies to prevent the development of challenging behavior.
- Part Four (Chapters 12 and 13) provides guidelines for program implementation and consultation. It discusses common problems encountered in conducting functional assessment and in providing consultation to educators. It then provides strategies to prevent and remediate those problems. Part Four also includes problem-solving case studies.

These case studies allow the reader to practice functional assessment and to develop intervention plans to address challenging behavior.

This book contains numerous examples of functional assessment as it is employed in school settings. Examples cover all ages of students (preschool through high school), both regular and self-contained special education settings as well as other school and home settings, a variety of challenging behaviors, and students with and without disabilities. The examples also include a variety of team members who conduct the assessment and implement intervention strategies.

ACKNOWLEDGMENTS

We wish to thank the following individuals:

Alan Repp, Kathy Karsh, and Peggy Williams from the Educational Research and Services Center in DeKalb, Illinois, for their guidance, encouragement, collaboration, and friendship.

Barbara Truels and the staff and students at the Early Childhood Education Center in Wooddale, Illinois, for allowing us in their programs and collaborating with us as we tested and retested our model.

The many children and students, families, educational staff, and colleagues who have collaborated with us, participated in workshops and classes, participated in functional assessment, and who help us learn everyday.

The reviewers who provided feedback and suggestions for this book: David W. Anderson, Bethel College; Dan Fennerty, Central Washington University; Carol Moore, Troy State University; and W. George Scarlett, Tufts University.

Ann Davis, our editor at Merrill/Prentice Hall, for her encouragement and guidance.

Finally, we would like to thank our families for their support and encouragement throughout the years: Roger Lubeck, Sam and Ruth Chandler, John Dahlquist, John Dahlquist, Jr., David Dahlquist, and Tim Dahlquist. Your encouragement and support made this possible!

Discover the Companion Website Accompanying This Book

THE PRENTICE HALL COMPANION WEBSITE: A VIRTUAL LEARNING ENVIRONMENT

Technology is a constantly growing and changing aspect of our field that is creating a need for content and resources. To address this emerging need, Prentice Hall has developed an online learning environment for students and professors alike—Companion Websites—to support our textbooks.

In creating a Companion Website, our goal is to build on and enhance what the textbook already offers. For this reason, the content for each user-friendly website is organized by topic and provides the professor and student with a variety of meaningful resources. Common features of a Companion Website include:

For the Professor—

Every Companion Website integrates **Syllabus Manager**™, an online syllabus creation and management utility.

- **Syllabus Manager**™ provides you, the instructor, with an easy, step-by-step process to create and revise syllabi, with direct links into Companion Website and other online content without having to learn HTML.
- Students may log on to your syllabus during any study session. All they need to know is the web address for the Companion Website and the password you've assigned to your syllabus.
- After you have created a syllabus using **Syllabus Manager**™, students may enter the syllabus for their course section from any point in the Companion Website.
- Clicking on a date, the student is shown the list of activities for the assignment. The activities for each assignment are linked directly to actual content, saving time for students.
- Adding assignments consists of clicking on the desired due date, then filling in the details of the assignment—name of the assignment, instructions, and whether it is a one-time or repeating assignment.

- In addition, links to other activities can be created easily. If the activity is online, a URL can be entered in the space provided, and it will be linked automatically in the final syllabus.
- Your completed syllabus is hosted on our servers, allowing convenient updates from any computer on the Internet. Changes you make to your syllabus are immediately available to your students at their next logon.

For the Student—

- **Topic Overviews**—outline key concepts in topic areas
- **Characteristics**—general information about each topic/disability covered on this website
- **Read About It**—a list of links to pertinent articles found on the Internet that cover each topic
- **Teaching Ideas**—links to articles that offer suggestions, ideas, and strategies for teaching students with disabilities
- **Web Links**—a wide range of websites that provide useful and current information related to each topic area
- **Resources**—a wide array of different resources for many of the pertinent topics and issues surrounding special education
- **Electronic Bluebook**—send homework or essays directly to your instructor's email with this paperless form
- **Message Board**—serves as a virtual bulletin board to post—or respond to—questions or comments to/from a national audience
- **Chat**—real-time chat with anyone who is using the text anywhere in the country—ideal for discussion and study groups, class projects, etc.

To take advantage of these and other resources, please visit the *Functional Assessment: Strategies to Prevent and Remediate Challenging Behavior in School Settings* Companion Website at

www.prenhall.com/chandler

Contents

7 Intervention Strategies Related to the Positive Reinforcement Function 101

8 Intervention Strategies Related to the Negative Reinforcement Function 121

10 *Specific Intervention Strategies Related to the Increase and Decrease Sensory Regulation/ Sensory Stimulation Functions*   167

11 *Prevention Strategies and Strategies to Promote Generalization and Maintenance of Behavior*   191

PART FOUR   Functional Assessment Within School Settings   213

12 *Guidelines for Program Implementation and Consultation*   215

Part One

Introduction to Challenging Behavior and the Functional Assessment and Intervention Model

CHAPTER 1

The Importance of Identifying and Addressing Challenging Behavior

This chapter provides an overview of how to define challenging behavior and determine if that behavior warrants functional assessment and intervention. It also discusses the incidence of challenging behavior among individuals with disabilities and among school-aged students with and without disabilities. Finally, we discuss the negative effects of challenging behavior on students, peers, educators, and families.

One of the first decisions the educational team will need to make is whether a student's behavior should be identified as challenging and whether that behavior requires functional assessment and intervention. At least two perspectives should be considered when dealing with challenging behavior. The first is that of the student who is engaging in the behavior. The team should recognize that, even if the behavior is identified as challenging, for the student the behavior is in fact very functional and effective; it produces an outcome that is desirable to the student (Carr, Langdon, & Yarbrough, 1999; Foster-Johnson & Dunlap, 1993). For example, when 12-year-old Ronald uses profanity his peers look at him and laugh—his profanity produces desired attention from peers. Or when 16-year-old Sarah rips her math worksheet she is sent to the principal's office. Sarah's behavior of destroying her worksheet results in her leaving the math instructional period and not having to complete the worksheet. The challenging behaviors that Ronald and Sarah exhibit produce desirable outcomes for each of them. Ronald receives peer attention and Sarah escapes or delays math work. From each student's perspective, the behaviors are very logical and very effective (O'Neill, Horner, Albin, Storey, & Sprague, 1990). Unfortunately, many of the behaviors that produce desirable outcomes for students like Ronald and Sarah are identified as challenging behaviors by educators, peers, and family members. This leads to the second perspective that we should consider when identifying challenging behavior.

The second perspective to consider is the perspective of those individuals who identify the behavior as challenging. When we say that a student engages in appropriate behavior, we usually mean that the student's behavior is acceptable and conforms to our expectations or to the requirements of the setting. When we say that a student engages in challenging behavior, we usually mean that the student's behavior does not conform to our expectations or to the requirements of the setting and that we would like his or her behavior to change. From our perspective, the behavior is challenging and should be changed. One of the problems with this second perspective is that there is considerable variability across individuals' perspectives and different settings concerning which behaviors to identify as appropriate and which to identify as challenging. Therefore, some guidelines might help us identify when a behavior is challenging and should be changed.

When we identify behavior as challenging we should consider issues that directly affect the student as well as peers, adults, and family members. Three factors are important to examine when identifying challenging behavior: learning, social relationships, and safety. These factors are included in our definition of challenging behavior. We define challenging behavior as behavior that (1) interferes with the student's learning or the learning of other individuals, (2) hinders positive social interactions and relationships, or (3) harms the student, peers, adults, or family members (Bailey & Wolery, 1992). In the fields of special education, applied behavior analysis, and developmental disabilities, many terms commonly are used to identify the behavior that we wish to change. These include inappropriate behavior, maladaptive behavior, interfering behavior, misbehavior, and aberrant behavior. We use the term *challenging behavior* because we find it descriptive. Challenging behavior presents a challenge to learning and development. This relates back to our definition of challenging behavior and consideration of the impact of that behavior on the student and others in the classroom. Behavior that serves as a barrier to optimal learning and development or that may harm the student or others may be identified as challenging behavior.

Students may engage in many types of challenging behavior, ranging from mild to severe behavior. Severe challenging behaviors often are very disruptive, destructive, or dangerous. Severe challenging behaviors also often result in harm to the student or to other individuals. This may include behaviors such as throwing chairs, self-injurious behavior, hitting peers, tantrumming, and running from the classroom. Severe challenging behaviors are fairly easy to identify and often are the behaviors that result in referral for intervention.

Mild and moderate challenging behaviors can be more difficult to identify because they may not be unduly destructive, disruptive, dangerous, or harmful. Mild and moderate challenging behaviors may include behaviors such as sleeping, refusing to participate, inattentiveness or being off task, tardiness, refusing to complete worksheets or homework, and passive noncompliance. Mild and moderate behaviors such as these may not always result in referral for intervention.

Severity alone should not be used to determine if a behavior is challenging or if a behavior should be addressed through functional assessment. To determine whether a behavior should be identified as challenging, we should consider several factors. First, we should consider the impact of the behavior on the student and other individuals. Instead of doing this, we often focus on the type of behavior employed such as aggression. Or we focus on the topography or the physical features of behavior (e.g., hitting or kicking) and on the severity or intensity of challenging behavior (Berkson & Tupa, 2000; Derby et al., 2000; Nielsen, Olive, Donovan, & McEvoy, 1998). The danger in doing this is that we may ignore the more mild challenging behaviors that, although they are not disruptive or dangerous, also have a negative effect on learning and development.

A more useful strategy to use when determining whether a behavior is challenging is to examine the impact of the behavior on the student and other individuals. Here we refer to our definition of challenging behavior. Behaviors that harm other individuals or the student or that interfere with learning and social relationships should be identified as challenging behaviors, regardless of the severity of the behavior. For example, a student who is throwing chairs in the classroom clearly is not learning appropriate behavior or academic skills and may harm other individuals. Obviously, this severe challenging behavior must be addressed. Consider, however, a student who wanders about the classroom during seatwork activities. This student, like the student who throws chairs, also is not learning appropriate behavior or academic skills and may distract other students. Behaviors such as this that fall within the mild end of the continuum also must be addressed in order to maximize this student's and other students' learning opportunities. It is our responsibility as educators to identify and address challenging behaviors across the continuum (mild–moderate–severe) that have a negative impact on the student and on others.

In addition to severity, another variable to consider in identifying behavior as challenging is the frequency of behavior. Many infrequent behaviors such as yelling, pushing, tardiness, or tantrums may not need to be addressed through functional assessment and behavior management plans (Alberto & Troutman, 1999). For instance, all students occasionally have bad days in which they may refuse to participate or they yell at their peers. In these types of situations, you can probably address the student's behavior using strategies that are already part of your classroom management tactics (e.g., remind the student to use her words instead of tantrumming or hitting, or redirect the student's behavior). However, behaviors that occur frequently (e.g., Naomi hits peers several times each day) or behaviors that occur infrequently but predictably (e.g., Scott is disruptive and aggressive on the Monday following his monthly visit to his father in jail) should be addressed through functional assessment—provided that they are behaviors that interfere with learning and social relationships or that harm the student or other individuals).

Educators must also consider the developmental or age appropriateness of the student's behavior. Many mild and moderate behaviors that are appropriate for the student's age probably should not be considered as challenging behaviors that warrant functional assessment. The majority of these behaviors will change through learning experiences and maturation. For example, most infants engage in behaviors such as mild head banging and body rocking during the first year or two of life. These behaviors naturally decrease across time and are absent in most children by age 3 (Berkson & Tupa, 2000). These behaviors are not considered challenging behaviors in very young children. Likewise, it is developmentally appropriate for a 3-year-old child to take toys from peers and to refuse to share with peers or for a 5-year-old child to solve peer disagreements through aggression. However, if a 7-year-old engages in head banging during morning circle, a 10-year-old consistently experiences problems with sharing art materials, or a 15-year-old consistently resolves disagreements through aggression, we should consider the behavior of these students to be challenging and conduct a functional assessment in order to develop interventions to address their behaviors.

Finally, before identifying a behavior as challenging, we need to think about behaviors that are annoying or that "just drive us crazy." This is a difficult issue. Great variability is seen in tolerance of behavior across educators, across subject-specific environments (e.g., science versus physical education), and across family members (Strain & Hemmeter, 1997). One educator may identify a behavior as acceptable, whereas another identifies it as challenging. Consider the following example. During the Individualized Educational Plan meeting, Ms. Crutchfield, the language arts teacher, requests behavioral consultation to deal with Lloyd's poor seatwork behavior. She says that during individual work activities, Lloyd sits at his desk on one leg, moves his body constantly in his seat, and wiggles his fingers. Even though Lloyd finishes his work on time and gets good grades, Ms. Crutchfield says that this behavior is "driving her crazy." She requires students to sit still when they work. She thinks that Lloyd's behavior is disrespectful and she defines his behavior as challenging behavior. Mr. Boyd, the science teacher, has a different opinion. He is not bothered by Lloyd's behavior and does not think it should be addressed.

In this example, it is helpful to return to our definition of challenging behavior. Sitting on one leg, moving in his seat, and wiggling his fingers does not interfere with Lloyd's learning. In fact, as is true for many students, movement may facilitate learning for Lloyd (Colby Trott, Laurel, & Windeck, 1993). Lloyd's behavior also is not disruptive to the other students. The other students are used to Lloyd doing this and they are not distracted by his behav-

Two perspectives of behavior

ior; his behavior does not interfere with their learning. In this example, Lloyd's behavior should not be considered a challenging behavior and does not warrant intervention, even though Ms. Crutchfield finds it annoying. In fact, if we were to implement interventions to restrict Lloyd's movement, we might reduce his ability to learn during seatwork time.

Now, consider the case of Karl and his family. Three-year-old Karl frequently pokes his teenage sister, Jody, with his fork during dinner. When he does this, Jody yells and screams at him. In a loud voice Ron, the father, tells Jody to stop yelling at her brother and he tells Karl to stop poking his sister. Betsy, the children's stepmother, tells Ron not to shout at the children. Ron tells Betsy that he will discipline his children as he sees fit. Meanwhile, Karl continues to poke Jody and Jody continues to yell at Karl. Eventually Ron sends Jody to her room and scolds Karl. None of the family members have finished their dinner. Karl's behavior fits within our definition of challenging behavior. Although Karl is not really harming Jody by poking her with his fork, his behavior disrupts dinner night after night and reduces opportunities for positive social interactions between all family members. Karl's behavior is very annoying to his sister, father, and stepmother. His behavior is considered challenging because of the negative impact on social relationships. Karl's challenging behavior should be, and can easily be, addressed through functional assessment.

For example, assessment indicated that Karl poked his sister because this resulted in attention from her and Karl's parents. When Karl ate quietly, he received little to no attention from his family. This assessment led to an

A typical dinner at the Williams' home

intervention in which Jody, Ron, and Betsy turned away from Karl when he poked Jody with his fork. They did not make eye contact with Karl nor talk to him when they were turned away from him. However, when Karl ate appropriately or engaged in appropriate behavior during dinner, his family now interacted with him and they did so frequently. Karl's fork poking behavior decreased to zero after 3 days of intervention.

In summary, the determination that behavior is challenging and must be changed should not be made arbitrarily. As educators we must consider the impact of behavior on the student and others in terms of safety, social relationships, and learning. Table 1–1 provides a list of questions that should be considered when deciding if a behavior should be identified as challenging and if functional assessment is warranted.

After determining that a behavior should be identified as challenging, it is important to address that behavior in order to decrease its negative impact on the student and other individuals and to reduce the prevalence of challenging behavior within school settings. We next discuss the incidence of challenging behavior and its negative effects on all involved.

Researchers have documented the prevalence and incidence of challenging behaviors among individuals with disabilities for many years. They have reported that individuals with disabilities of all ages exhibit challenging behaviors at a higher rate and intensity than do typically developing individuals. However, considerable variability exists across studies based on the characteristics of the population reviewed (e.g., age, severity and type of disability), the behaviors examined (e.g., self-abuse, noncompliance, or off-task behaviors), and the settings selected for study (e.g., clinics, schools, and institutions) (Berkson & Tupa, 2000; Kern & Dunlap, 1999). For example, prevalence studies have indicated that 14% to 38% of individuals with disabilities engage in destructive or aggressive behaviors such as hitting, throwing furniture, or biting; 40% to 60% engage in stereotypical behaviors such as hand flapping, repetitive vocalizations, or rocking; 6% to 40% engage in self-abusive behaviors such as hand biting, head banging, and eye gouging; 47% of individuals

TABLE 1–1

Factors to consider before identifying a behavior as challenging

1. Does the behavior interfere with the student's learning?
2. Does the behavior interfere with other students' learning?
3. Does the behavior interfere with or impede social relationships?
4. Does the behavior have a negative impact on the student's self esteem?
5. Is the behavior harmful or dangerous to the student?
6. Is the behavior harmful or dangerous to other individuals?
7. Does the behavior occur frequently or infrequently?
8. Is the behavior age appropriate?

living in institutions exhibit severe behavior problems; and an estimated 25,000 individuals with disabilities exhibit severe forms of self-injurious challenging behavior in the United States (Borthwick, Meyers, & Eyman, 1981; Borthwick-Duffy, Eyman, & White, 1987; Corbett & Campbell, 1981; Fidura, Lindsey, & Walker, 1987; Griffen, Williams, Stark, Altmeyer, & Mason, 1986; Hill & Bruniks, 1984; Mace & Mauk, 1999; Oliver, Murphy, & Corbett, 1987; Paisey, Whitney, & Hislop, 1990; Repp & Barton, 1980; Sprague & Horner, 1999). One study reported that estimates of challenging behavior increased from a low of 1% for infants and toddlers to a high of 50% to 70% for teenage students (Berkson, McQuiston, Jacobson, Eyman, & Borthwick, 1985).

The higher prevalence and incidence of challenging behavior for individuals with disabilities also has been documented for school-aged students (Kern & Dunlap, 1999; McGee & Daly, 1999; Shores, Wehby, & Jack, 1999; Tobin & Sugai, 1999) and is specifically addressed through federal and state laws and regulations. The 1997 amendments to the Individuals with Disabilities Education Act included provisions concerning challenging behavior for individuals who receive special education services. These amendments require the educational team to conduct a functional behavioral assessment and develop behavioral intervention plans for students with disabilities within 10 days of suspension or removal to an interim educational placement (Armstrong & Kauffman, 1999; Bateman & Linden, 1998; Katsiyannis & Maag, 1998; Maloney, 1997; National Association of State Directors of Special Education, 1997; Turnbull & Cilley, 1999).

Although students with disabilities are at greater risk for exhibiting challenging behavior, challenging behavior is not just a special education problem. In fact, the majority of violent acts in schools are not committed by students who receive special education services (Council for Exceptional Children, 1999). Brandenberg, Friedman, and Sliver (1990) estimated that 14% to 20% of typically developing students exhibit challenging behavior. Other estimates of the prevalence of challenging behavior for typically developing school-aged students range from 2% to 30% (Guevremont, 1991; Reichle et al., 1996; Rhode, Jenson, & Reavis, 1992; Walker & Bullis, 1991). Children and youth are engaging in violent behaviors at younger and younger ages (Walker, Colvin, & Ramsey, 1995). In one school district with which the authors are affiliated, 26% of the yearly referrals for behavioral intervention were for typically developing students attending general education classrooms. Rhode and her colleagues (1992) stated that educators in general education classes (which include students with or without disabilities) should expect to have a minimum of two students per classroom per year who exhibit frequent challenging behavior.

Students with and without disabilities display challenging behavior in school settings. Challenging behaviors occur across all grade levels (beginning with preschool) and types of classrooms (general and special education classrooms). They also occur across gender and across all ability levels (gifted to severe disabilities), socioeconomic status (low to high income), and family demographics (e.g., age of parents, number of parents, ability level of parents, etc.) (Repp, 1999; Rhode et al., 1992; Walker & Walker, 1991).

Many educators have a low tolerance for challenging behavior and have insufficient training in the prevention and remediation of challenging behavior (Cangelosi, 1993). Some educators feel that their efforts to address challenging behavior will not be successful or they are skeptical about the possibility of change and the "latest fad in behavior strategies" (Blair, Umbreit, & Bos, 1999; Soodak & Podell, 1993). As a result they often resort to intensive punishment procedures, manual and chemical restraint, and referral for more restrictive placement (Kern, Childs, Dunlap, Clarke, & Falk, 1994; Schloss, Miller, Sedlacek, & White, 1983; Strain & Hemmeter, 1997; Walker et al., 1995). The most frequent reason cited for referral for special education services, behavioral interventions, and more restrictive placement (in both schools and homes) is challenging behavior (Carta et al., 1994; Soodak & Podell, 1993; Sprague & Horner, 1999).

General educators and special educators, as well as other members of the educational team, should have the skills necessary to prevent and remediate the challenging behavior of all students. Special education and general education teachers identify challenging behavior as one of their primary sources of stress and as a critical factor that influences decisions to leave the teaching profession (Reynaud, 1999; Rhode et al., 1992). The need for educators who have the skills necessary to address challenging behavior is recognized by administrators and educators who have identified challenging behavior within school-based settings as a priority area for training and in-class consultation (McMahon & McNamarra, 2000; Stephenson, Linfoot, & Martin, 2000). Meeting this need is critical if we are to reduce the prevalence of challenging behavior and decrease its negative effects on those students who engage in challenging behavior and on other individuals within school settings.

Challenging behavior can produce both short-term and long-term negative outcomes for the students who engage in it. Challenging behavior also often has corresponding negative effects on peers, educators, and family members.

Students who exhibit challenging behavior often do not obtain maximum or optimal benefits from educational placements (Will, 1984). This is because challenging behavior often is incompatible with engagement and academic learning. Students often cannot engage in appropriate behavior and challenging behaviors simultaneously (Paisey et al., 1990; Polsgrove & Reith, 1983; Repp & Karsh, 1990). For example, throwing spitballs is incompatible with taking a test or copying lecture notes; tantrumming is incompatible with listening to a story. The student who is throwing spitballs or who is tantrumming is not benefiting from his or her educational setting. Likewise, students exhibiting challenging behavior also miss learning opportunities when they are not in the classroom. Students in special education classes, especially those with social-emotional disorders, who exhibit challenging behavior have been expelled or suspended at higher rates than students in general education (Tobin & Sugai, 1999). Unexcused absences from school range from 1% to 22% per year (Guevremont, 1991). Rhode, Jenson, and Reavis (1992) estimated that as many as 65% of students with severe and frequent challenging behavior drop out of high school. Clearly, students who drop out of school, who are truant or absent, or who are expelled and suspended also are not obtaining maximal benefits from their educational setting.

In addition to not benefiting from the educational environment, students who exhibit challenging behavior often are avoided or rejected by peers (Abrams & Segal, 1998; Walker, 1998; Wehby, Symons, & Shores, 1995). As a result they have fewer opportunities to learn from peers during group work and leisure activities (e.g., recess, lunch). Lost opportunities for learning also occur when interventions result in exclusion from classroom activities such as when students are placed in time-out, sent to the principal's office, or physically restrained (Kern, Childs, et al., 1994; McGee & Daly, 1999; Repp & Karsh, 1990).

Our goal as educators is to provide quality education to all students. This goal is compromised when challenging behavior disrupts or prevents learning within the classroom (Reynaud, 1999). Peers may have decreased opportunities for learning if (a) a student's challenging behavior is disruptive or distracting, (b) they reciprocate with aggression or other forms of challenging behavior (e.g., yelling at or hitting the student who displayed challenging behavior), or (c) they imitate the challenging behavior that they observe. For example, Peter uses a superhero's voice when asked to read a passage from the textbook. As he begins to read, the other students laugh instead of listening to the reading and they also use the superhero's voice when they are called on to read. Peter's challenging behavior interferes with reading practice for him and also has collateral negative effects on peers as they attend to him instead of the lesson and when they imitate his challenging behavior.

In school settings, challenging behavior often requires excessive time and effort for educators as they react to challenging behavior when it occurs and then as they develop and implement interventions to remediate well-established challenging behavior. This results in decreased time and effort devoted to teaching academic skills and promoting appropriate behavior for all students (Chandler, Dahlquist, Repp, & Feltz, 1999; Hains, Fowler, & Chandler, 1988; McGee & Daly, 1999; Polsgrove & Reith, 1983). Students with challenging behavior often have poor relationships with educators who avoid, blame, or are afraid of the student. Teachers interact less often with students who engage in challenging behavior and they spend less time focused on academic lessons when students are engaged in challenging behavior (Carr, Taylor, & Robinson, 1991).

Challenging behavior also may result in negative outcomes for students and their families (Boulware, Schwartz, & McBride, 1999; Timm, 1993). Challenging behavior often interferes with the development of positive social relationships and interactions with family members. Parents, siblings, and caregivers may avoid or reject the child with challenging behavior, reciprocate with aggression or aversive interactions, employ punishment procedures, place the child on medications to control challenging behavior, or refer the child for more restrictive or less naturalistic living arrangements such as foster care and institutionalization (Munk & Karsh, 1999; Soodak & Podell, 1993). This is especially probable when self-injurious and aggressive behaviors physically harm the child and others through bleeding, bruising, tissue damage, and so on (Repp & Karsh, 1990).

The effects of challenging behavior can be lifelong. Without intervention, challenging behavior usually does not improve, nor does it disappear with age. Berg and Sasso (1993) estimated that children who were referred to their clinic for behavioral interventions had engaged in challenging behavior for an average of 10 years prior to referral. Challenging behavior that is not addressed typically will become more severe and frequent with age (Berkson et al., 1985; Kern & Dunlap, 1999; Reid & Patterson, 1991). For example, the preschooler who throws toys and hits his mother may become the teenager who throws his desk out the window and attacks his teacher. Challenging behavior also may continue into, and have a negative effect on, adulthood. Oppositional, defiant, and aggressive child behaviors are strong predictors of subsequent criminal behavior and recidivism, substance abuse, unemployment, referral to state institutions, and psychiatric disorder diagnosis (Mehas, Boling, Sobeniak, Sprague, Burke, & Hagan, 1998; Reid & Patterson, 1991).

SUMMARY

As stated by Don Baer (1970), "Not to rescue a person from an unhappy organization of his behavior is to punish him, in that it leaves him in a state of recurrent punishment" (p. 246). Although challenging behavior produces an immediate preferred or desired outcome for the student (e.g., when Jerry is sent to time-out for being disruptive, he does not have to participate in the activity), it also produces both short- and long-term negative outcomes that may include punishment, avoidance by others, poor relationships with others, low self-esteem, lost opportunities for learning, termination of employment, administration of medication and restraint, and more restrictive placements. When we identify challenging behavior we should consider the impact of the behavior on the student and other individuals in terms of opportunities for learning, social relationships, and issues of safety. After challenging behavior has been identified, we then need to address challenging behavior in order to reduce the negative effects that result from engaging in challenging behavior and to prevent its future occurrence.

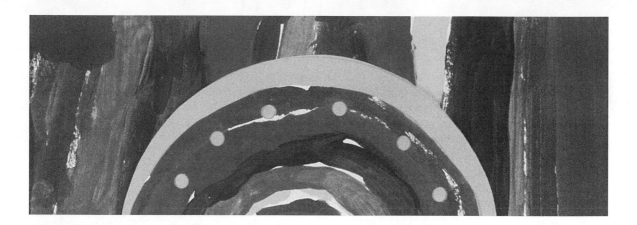

2

Identifying Why Challenging Behavior Occurs

The question "Why does challenging behavior occur?" is one that educators and parents often seek, and should seek, to answer. This should be the first step in functional assessment (Repp, 1999). Unfortunately, the answers to this question or the explanations that we provide are often based on myths or misguided beliefs regarding the causes of behavior (Skinner, 1953, 1971; Strain & Hemmeter, 1997; Sulzer-Azaroff & Mayer, 1991). These faulty explanations are not useful. They often cause us to look for someone or something to blame instead of identifying strategies to address the challenging behavior.

Faulty explanations do not help us identify the current supports for challenging behavior (i.e., variables that trigger and strengthen or maintain challenging behavior) and they seldom lead to effective positive intervention strategies. This is because our beliefs about why behavior occurs determine the interventions we select (Kauffman, Mostert, Trent, & Hallahan, 1993; Walker & Shea, 1999). If our beliefs about why challenging behavior occurs are misguided or wrong, then the interventions we select will be misguided, and the likelihood is that they will be unsuccessful in changing challenging behavior (Kauffman et al., 1993; Repp & Karsh, 1990; Repp, Karsh, Munk, & Dahlquist, 1995).

In our experience, the five most common misbeliefs about the causes of challenging behavior are (1) the bad child, (2) the disability, (3) the bad family, (4) the bad home, and (5) previous trauma or experience. In this chapter, we discuss each of these misguided beliefs or faulty explanations, identify why each belief is not helpful and indeed may be harmful, and present an alternative behavioral perspective about why challenging behavior occurs.

THE BAD CHILD

Sometimes when a student engages in challenging behavior we assume he or she is doing the behavior on purpose, that the challenging behavior is the student's fault, or that the student is the problem (Council for Exceptional Children, 1999). When we make this assumption we believe that the problem resides within the (bad) child (Alberto & Troutman, 1999; Cangelosi, 1993; Epstein & Skinner, 1982; Skinner, 1989; Sulzer-Azaroff & Mayer, 1991; Walker & Shea, 1999). You may hear teachers or parents who believe this explanation make statements such as "She does it just to make me mad," "He's been this way all his life, he's got a mean streak," or "It's just part of his personality".

This myth or explanation assumes that the child is bad or that the child has a bad personality trait; in other words, something within the student is the cause of the challenging behavior (Powers & Osborne, 1975). In some cases, blaming the student allows us to be angry with the student, to retaliate against the student, or to ignore the student. In other cases, when we assume that the student is inherently bad or has a bad personality trait, we will not even try to address the student's challenging behavior because "You cannot change a bad child or a child's personality." Or we may employ intensive punishment techniques in an attempt to make the student stop the behav-

The BAD Child

ior. We also may seek to remove the student from our classroom (i.e., to a more restrictive placement), again because of the belief that we cannot change a bad student or his or her personality (Kern, Childs, Dunlap, Clarke, & Falk, 1994; Soodak & Podell, 1993; Sprague & Horner, 1999; Strain & Hemmeter, 1997).

None of these outcomes are desirable or productive. A functional assessment view would argue that the student is not inherently bad and that there is no reason to blame the student or the student's personality. Rather, the student's *behavior* is challenging and that challenging behavior can be changed by altering the environmental variables that support it.

Consider the example of Henry who often slept or stared out the window when students were asked to complete math worksheets and he never completed his math homework. Henry's teacher, Mr. Maxie, described him as a lazy student (i.e., he had a lazy personality trait) and said that if Henry was too lazy to do his work then he could just fail the class. Mr. Maxie attributed Henry's challenging behavior to his personality and gave up on him. Yet, observations of Henry in other subjects and during recess and after school showed a student who played football, talked in class, joked with peers, and so forth. In other words, Henry was very active in some situations. In this example it is not helpful to attribute Henry's math-related behavior to a "lazy" personality. He sometimes displayed the behaviors that Mr. Maxie termed "lazy" but he only displayed those behaviors in certain situations. Therefore, he does not have a lazy personality. Rather, he exhibits challenging behavior when instructed to complete math assignments.

Using the functional assessment perspective, our first step would be to identify the behaviors that led Mr. Maxie to describe Henry as lazy such as sleeping, staring, and not completing math homework. Then we would directly address those behaviors; not his personality. Through functional assessment we would identify the triggers and supports for his challenging behaviors and use that information to develop interventions to change those behaviors. For example, we might find through conversations with Henry and his family that Henry stays up late each night, which accounts for his fatigue during math (the first period of the day). We also find that when asked, Henry tells his parents that he does not have homework. Observations of Henry in the classroom might indicate that Henry is delayed in math skills and that he does not complete worksheets that are too difficult for him to do. This information allows us to develop an intervention that addresses the real reasons for Henry's challenging behaviors. For example, we might develop a homework notebook that is signed daily by the teacher and Henry's parents. Or like some schools, we might post homework assignments on the school's web site. Henry's parents also could impose a sleep schedule so that Henry goes to bed at a reasonable time. In school, Mr. Maxie could provide assistance during math or pair Henry with a peer so that Henry is able to complete the activity successfully. Intervention strategies such as these directly address Henry's challenging behaviors—sleeping, staring, and incomplete homework assignments. Nothing is gained by referring to his personality as the cause of his challenging behaviors.

THE DISABILITY

Students who have disabilities are at high risk for also exhibiting challenging behavior. When this happens, we often assume that the challenging behavior occurs because of the disability (Powers & Osborne, 1975). In other words, we make the assumption that the challenging behavior is a characteristic of the disability or that it is directly caused by the disability. We frequently attribute challenging behavior to disabilities such as autism, behavior disorders, attention deficit hyperactivity disorder, or learning disabilities. For example, Hank repeatedly runs in the room and often knocks over the projects of his peers. When Hank's teacher was asked to speculate why he did this she said it was because he had attention deficit hyperactivity disorder (ADHD).

The disability explanation for the cause of challenging behavior, just like the bad child explanation, is not useful. If we attribute challenging behavior to a disability or a syndrome, we will have little reason to intervene because we cannot change the fact that the student has a particular disability. Individuals who attribute challenging behavior to a disability assume that behavior cannot be changed and so they often do not attempt to address challenging behavior, thus allowing it to continue (Blair, Umbreit, & Bos, 1999).

A functional assessment perspective would assume that the disability does not cause the challenging behavior. Even though a particular disability may be identified, it does not follow that any specific form of challenging behavior is a direct result of that disability (Alberto & Troutman, 1999).[1] Rather, a functional assessment perspective proposes that challenging behavior for students with and without disabilities occurs because it produces a desirable outcome for the student. In Hank's case, running around the room may provide movement and knocking over peer projects may result in stimulating attention from peers or teachers. We have no reason to attribute his challenging behavior to his disability. This does not mean, however, that knowing that a student has a disability is not important. In some cases it can be very helpful.

When dealing with challenging behavior, knowledge that a child has a disability is relevant only to the extent that it allows us to identify characteristics associated with the disability. Knowing that a student has a particular disability does not tell you how to address that student's challenging behavior (Martin & Pear, 1999). However, knowing that a student has a particular disability may help us understand variables that will trigger and maintain challenging behavior. For example, if we know that Hank has ADHD then we know that, like many students with ADHD, he may need increased sensory input through movement, touch, vocalizations, and so forth. But, how he obtains that increased sensory input is not part of his disability. The topography of his challenging behavior is *not* caused by his disability. Not all students with ADHD will run in the classroom and knock down peer projects. A functional assessment view would assume that Hank could learn other

---

[1] A small number of syndromes are specifically associated with self-injurious behavior such as Leach-Nyhan, Cordelia de Lange, and Riley-Day (Shore & Iwata, 1999).

Jenny's mother, father, and teacher assume they will just have to put up with Jenny's behavior since she has attention deficit hyperactivity.

The DISABILITY

more appropriate means of obtaining sensory input such as taking a note to the principal's office or assisting the teacher during a lesson.

In another example, Mr. Gains referred Joey, who has autism, for behavioral intervention because Joey exhibited severe tantrums several times each week. It was helpful for Karen, a behavior specialist on the instructional strategies team, to know that Joey had autism because she knew that children with autism often have problems with changes in schedules or routines. This knowledge guided her initial observations so that she examined whether his tantrums were related to unexpected changes in the classroom setting and routines. Karen's observations did indicate that Joey tantrummed every time the class visited the library and gym and when the bus was late. She then developed interventions to teach Joey more appropriate ways to communicate to others his discomfort or apprehension and to alert Joey, when possible, of upcoming changes in the schedule. In this example, it is important to point out that Joey's tantrums might easily have occurred for other reasons that have nothing to do with the characteristics often associated with autism. Thus, Karen must do more than simply observe during schedule changes. For example, Joey may have tantrummed when asked to do a task that he disliked or when a peer stole his lunch money.

Knowing that a student has a particular disability can be helpful in guiding our observations, but we need to remember that it is just one piece of information about the student and that it is not the cause of the student's challenging behavior. Regardless of the diagnostic label or disability, it is the challenging behavior that causes concern and it is that behavior that needs to be addressed (Martin & Pear, 1999).

THE BAD FAMILY OR POOR PARENTING AND DISCIPLINE

Another misbelief that many people have about the causes of challenging behavior is that students engage in challenging behavior in schools because their parents (or primary caregivers) have poor parenting skills and do not use effective discipline. In this case, we are blaming challenging behavior on extraneous variables such as the child's family (McGee & Daly, 1999). This assumption is based on a belief that if the student's parents were doing a better job at home, then the student would not engage in challenging behavior at school. We have often heard team members exclaim "Those parents need to set some limits" or "His parents need to teach him to respect others," or "No wonder she hits at school—look at her parents and you know where she learned it." This attitude causes the team to blame the parents, to be angry with the parents, and to assume that the parents must change before the student's behavior will change. Clearly, this is not an effective approach because it does not focus on the behavior in the classroom setting and also allows the challenging behavior to continue.

A functional assessment view would acknowledge that many students do live in dysfunctional homes and have parents with poor parenting skills. In fact, many children have learned challenging behaviors at home and are reinforced

Mrs. Standish wishes Eddie's parents would discipline him at home
and wonders if she should refer Eddie's parents for parent education classes.

The BAD Family

for using them by their parents and other family members (Patterson, 1982; Wahler & Dumas, 1986; Wahler & Fox, 1981; Walker & Sylwester, 1998). From a functional assessment perspective, however, the student's challenging behavior occurs at school because it produces a desirable outcome at school. Regardless of where or how a challenging behavior was initially learned, it would not continue to be exhibited at school if it did not work at school (Kazdin, 2001). For example, a student who learned to hit at home through parent example, now hits at school because hitting is effective at school.

This does not mean that we should ignore poor parenting or other family-related variables. In fact, family variables can and do affect student behavior as will be discussed in subsequent chapters. When we can, we should address family variables. For instance we may provide parenting classes, make referrals for counseling, work with parents to change morning routines, and so on (Wielkiewicz, 1986). Families can be the school's greatest allies in addressing challenging behavior, but they alone are not the solution to changing challenging behavior. We also need to address the challenging behavior in the setting in which it occurs; that is, in the classroom, lunchroom, playground, and so forth.

To illustrate this point, consider three potential outcomes of addressing family variables for the student who hits at school. First, we refer the family for counseling and parent education classes. The family refuses these services. The student still hits at school. Or we refer a family for counseling and parent education classes and they begin services. In the meantime, while they are receiving services, the student hits at school. Finally, a student's family has completed parent education classes. They have stopped using physical punishment at home and now use more positive discipline strategies. The student also stops hitting at home and yet continues to hit at school.

In each of these scenarios we assume something is wrong with the family and that the family needs to change. We attempt to address the student's behavior by changing the family's behavior. One family refuses to change, one is in the process of change, and one has changed. Yet, in each example the student's behavior continues at school. We should not be surprised by this outcome—the student's behavior continues at school because it is effective at producing an outcome at school. We also should not be surprised if the student stops hitting at home after the parents have completed their classes and begin to use positive discipline strategies at home and yet the student continues to hit at school. Students learn to behave differently in different situations (Wielkiewicz, 1986; Zirpoli & Melloy, 2001). Even if hitting is no longer effective at home, we must assume that it still is effective at school if it continues to be used in that setting. Intervention must address behavior in the settings in which it occurs (Kazdin, 2001). Even in cases where parents refuse to be involved, intervention should still be implemented at school (Wielkiewicz, 1986). A functional assessment approach would focus on the student's behavior at school by identifying the supports for the challenging behavior at school (and at home if the behavior occurred at home) and developing interventions to change those supports (Walker & Sylwester, 1998).

THE BAD HOME SITUATION

In addition to looking at the family when challenging behavior occurs, we sometimes attribute challenging behavior to a student's home or living circumstances. We frequently attribute challenging behavior to the home environment when students are from low-income settings, live in chaotic environments, have parents who are divorcing or fighting, or are experiencing multiple and changing family members and/or friends in the student's home. We also do this when the home includes individuals who abuse drugs and alcohol and when students are homeless.

This explanation, like the bad family explanation, causes us to look for solutions to challenging behavior outside of the current environment, in this case, within the student's home. We assume that the home situation must change before the student's behavior can change. An obvious problem with

While the rest of the class was taking the test, Sam, whose parents
were going through a nasty divorce, gets some attention from a peer.

The BAD Home Situation

this is that we cannot effectively change many of the serious home-related
variables such as divorce, drug abuse, or homelessness.

Another problem with the bad home explanation for challenging behavior
is that we often automatically assume that students who live in disadvantaged environments will engage in challenging behavior. This may cause us
to have lower or different expectations for the academic skills and behavior
of these students. Cangelosi (1993) cautions educators to "not apply the ag-
gregate results from demographic studies in judging individuals" (p. 9). Not
all children who live in disadvantaged home environments or who have parents with poor parenting skills will engage in challenging behavior. Cangelosi
suggests that our expectations for these students (academically and behaviorally) should reflect the students' abilities rather than the type of environment from which they come.

A functional assessment perspective would acknowledge that students do
live in poor home situations and that these variables may have an influence on
the student's challenging behavior. Increasingly children come to school from
poor home environments and circumstances (Reynaud, 1999). When possible
and welcomed by the family, we should address the home situation through referral, talking with families, providing parent education and parent support
groups, and providing referrals and linkages to resources. However, the most
important and immediate place to address the student's behavior is in the
classroom. This is illustrated in the example of Johnny, his mother, and his

school. Johnny was diagnosed with autism, mental retardation, and ADHD. Johnny was referred to the instructional strategies team because he displayed severely aggressive and disruptive tantrums when instructed to begin academic tasks. Johnny lived in a low-income household with his mother, Judy, a single parent. Judy had been diagnosed when she was in school as having a learning disability and being socially-emotionally delayed. Home visits indicated a very chaotic home environment including inconsistent discipline, cluttered and dirty rooms, multiple safety hazards, and unpredictable daily routines. Judy indicated that Johnny "ruled the household" and could do whatever he wanted, whenever he wanted. Efforts to assist Judy in addressing Johnny's behavior at home were only mildly successful. Judy did not follow through with suggestions related to discipline, establishing daily routines, safety proofing and cleaning the home, or referral for assistance to public agencies. Fortunately, efforts to address Johnny's behavior at school were more successful. Johnny learned to follow directions, to complete academic tasks, and to communicate his desires to his teacher and other adults. Even though Johnny continued to live in a less than optimal home situation, his behavior at school changed because the variables that supported his behavior at school changed.

Although we must address challenging behavior in the settings in which it occurs, it is helpful to know when there are home circumstances that may be affecting a student's behavior. One reason for this is that it may guide our interventions. For example, we may alter our expectations for students (when appropriate) and provide additional individualized support to help these students in the classroom or other school settings. Two examples illustrate this point. First, one teacher told us that in order to address the problem of a large number of incomplete homework assignments, her school opens one classroom an hour before school starts and closes that classroom an hour after classes end. This provides space to complete homework for those students who are not able to work at home (e.g., students who are homeless or who live in crowded, noisy homes). Teachers in this school volunteer to work in the homework room on a rotating schedule.

Second, several preschools in our area have food available throughout the day (not only during a preset snack time) because many of their students are from very low income homes and do not receive proper nutrition at home. These preschool teachers reported a decrease in tantrumming and peer aggression following implementation of this strategy. In both of these examples, students come from adverse home situations that are not easily changed through our educational system. The school-based interventions, however, were able to decrease challenging behavior at school (incomplete homework, aggression, and tantrums) by reducing the effect of the home-related factors on the students.

PREVIOUS TRAUMA AND EXPERIENCE

The final misguided explanation we often ascribe to is the belief that current challenging behavior is caused by something traumatic or distressing that occurred in the student's past such as sexual, emotional, or physical abuse. Or we assume that challenging behavior is a result of unconscious variables (e.g., id and ego) or a fixation at an early stage of psychological development (Alberto & Troutman, 1999; Epstein & Skinner, 1982; Malott, Malott, & Trojan, 2000; Skinner, 1989; Sulzer-Azaroff & Mayer, 1991; Zirpoli & Melloy, 2001). For example, 7-year-old Elizabeth displayed severe self-abuse and aggression each time her teacher tried to provide one-to-one instruction. The team knew that Elizabeth had been sexually abused when she was 3 years of age by her uncle. They assumed that her aggression and self-abuse occurred because of the previous sexual abuse. They speculated that she must be afraid of adults. They referred Elizabeth to the school counselor and stopped trying to provide individualized instruction.

The problem with attributing current challenging behavior to previous trauma, as was done with Elizabeth, is that we do not directly address the challenging behavior—we assume that we cannot change the previous trauma, so the challenging behavior is allowed to continue to occur. We often attempt to indirectly address the challenging behavior by referring students for counseling or other similar services. The hope is that counseling will help the student adjust to previous traumatic experiences and through that adjustment, the student will change his or her current challenging behavior. Referral for therapeutic counseling is a good first step. However, most educators want the behavior to change *now* and considering the negative impact of challenging behavior on the student (e.g., lost learning opportunities, rejection from peers), it may not be reasonable to *wait* for therapy to work. A functional assessment perspective would acknowledge that counseling could be very beneficial for students who have experienced trauma. However, the behavior that the student displays now serves a purpose that is maintained in the current setting, regardless of the initial causes of the behavior (Alberto & Troutman, 1999; Skinner, 1953).

Kazdin (2001) refers to early problems or trauma as original causes or influences on behavior and he notes the importance of finding out about original causes. However, he also points out that the primary question in determining intervention is "What are the current influences on behavior and how can they be changed in order to change behavior?" The original conditions that led to acquisition of the challenging behavior probably are not the conditions that maintain it today. Kazdin states that "The years of factors that influenced the current problem cannot be erased, but something can be done now" (p. 5). In Elizabeth's case, observation revealed that when she was self-abusive and aggressive the teacher stopped working with her. She then was allowed to select her own tasks and did not have to work on teacher-directed tasks. Although Elizabeth's behavior may have been acquired when she was sexually abused at 3 years of age, the original cause was not the current maintaining variable. Escape from teacher-directed tasks maintained her behavior in the current environment. The possibility exists that Elizabeth may successfully complete counseling and continue to be self-abusive and aggressive in the classroom. Functional assessment and a focus on current supports for behavior is necessary in order to reduce her challenging behavior in the classroom.

Please note that we are not saying that knowledge of original causes is not important. For example, knowledge of original causes such as abuse or neglect can be used to prevent future occurrences of abuse and neglect (Kazdin, 2001). Please note that we also are not saying that services such as counseling, play therapy, peer group therapy, and family counseling are not warranted and would not be helpful for these students. For many students and families such services are very appropriate. But they should not be done in lieu of functional assessment and they should not delay or prevent the implementation of positive behavioral interventions. Functional assessment and counseling services should be implemented simultaneously.

SUMMARY

Functional assessment seeks to answer the question "Why does challenging behavior occur?" It does not attribute challenging behavior to the misleading explanations discussed in this chapter. These explanations do not help us understand why challenging behavior is occurring, they do not help us address challenging behavior, and in some cases they may prevent us from addressing challenging behavior. They also can cause us to blame the student, other individuals, or family and home situations, and thus interfere with developing timely, proactive interventions to address challenging behaviors.

A functional assessment approach assumes that most challenging behavior is learned and that it continues to occur because it produces a desirable outcome for the student. The focus is on identifying the current variables that support the behavior, not on determining why the behavior originally developed. The present circumstances are considered in addressing challenging behavior, not the past. A functional assessment approach identifies the variables that are present in the current setting(s) in which the challenging behavior occurs. Intervention then changes the variables that directly influence challenging behavior in those settings.

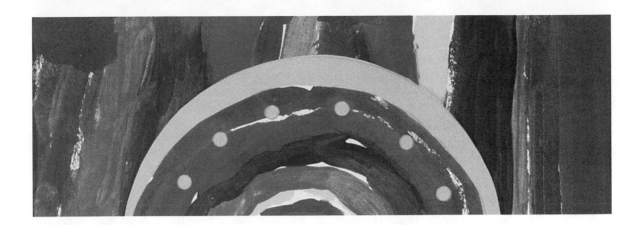

CHAPTER 3

Assumptions and Goals of Functional Assessment

The functional assessment and intervention model is built on a core set of assumptions concerning the development and maintenance of both appropriate and challenging behaviors. These assumptions guide the identification of the supports for challenging behavior and the interventions that are developed to address challenging behavior. These assumptions are as follows (Chandler, 1998; Chandler & Dahlquist, 1994, 1995, 1999a, 1999b; Repp, 1999; Repp & Karsh, 1994; Repp, Karsh, Dahlquist, & Chandler, 1994):

1. Challenging behavior and appropriate behavior are supported by the current environment.
2. Behavior serves a function.
3. Challenging behavior can be changed using positive interventions that address the function of behavior.
4. Functional assessment should be a team-based process.

ASSUMPTION 1: CHALLENGING BEHAVIOR AND APPROPRIATE BEHAVIOR ARE SUPPORTED BY THE CURRENT ENVIRONMENT

The first assumption is based on a belief that challenging and appropriate behaviors are developed and maintained through the same processes. Both challenging and appropriate behaviors are learned and maintained by the current environment (Arndorfer & Miltenberger, 1993; Cangelosi, 1993). A functional assessment perspective assumes that most behaviors are triggered by current environmental events and are strengthened or weakened by the consequences that follow behavior (Kazdin, 2001; Repp, 1999; Zirpoli & Melloy, 2001). Behaviors that produce positive outcomes are strengthened and continue to occur and behaviors that produce aversive or punishing outcomes are weakened and do not continue to occur.

When we wish to change challenging behavior we must examine the current environment within which the behavior is occurring in order to first identify variables that occur prior to or are concurrent with the challenging behavior. These variables are identified as antecedents. Antecedents set the occasion for behavior and affect the probability of its occurrence. We often describe antecedents as triggers for behavior (Chandler & Dahlquist, 1995, 1999b; Repp, 1999).

The next step is to identify the consequences that follow the behavior (Iwata, Dorsey, Slifer, Bauman, & Richman, 1982/1994). Intervention should not be developed until an assessment of antecedents and consequences is completed (Carr, 1977; Repp, 1994). This is because the interventions that will be developed will focus on changing the variables that trigger the challenging behavior and/or changing the consequences for the behavior. Intervention also will focus on introducing and/or altering antecedents that will trigger appropriate behavior and providing consequences to support appropriate behavior.

When we wish to change challenging behavior we must examine the environment that supports appropriate as well as challenging behavior (Kazdin, 2001). This often will result in the identification of a different set of antecedent triggers and/or consequences for each type of behavior. The example of Suzanne illustrates this point. When the teacher attends to other students (antecedent trigger), Suzanne uses profanity (challenging behavior). The teacher then scolds Suzanne for using inappropriate language (consequence). Suzanne's behavior is different under different environmental conditions. When the teacher is working one-to-one with Suzanne (antecedent trigger), Suzanne interacts appropriately and does her work (appropriate behavior). The teacher then praises Suzanne for working (consequence). In this example, from Suzanne's perspective similar consequences occur for both challenging and appropriate behaviors (i.e., interaction with the teacher). However, the antecedent triggers are different for appropriate behavior (attending to Suzanne) and challenging behavior (attending to peers and not attending to Suzanne). This information can be used to develop interventions to reduce challenging behavior. For example, the teacher might arrange to attend to Suzanne more frequently, thereby reducing the antecedent trigger for challenging behavior (no or infrequent attention) and, at the same time, increasing the trigger for appropriate behavior (frequent attention). The teacher also may stop providing a positive consequence following challenging behavior (i.e., reprimand) by ignoring Suzanne when she uses profanity and only interacting with her when she behaves appropriately.

Antecedent	Behavior	Consequence
Teacher attends to peers	Uses profanity	Reprimand
One-to-one instruction, frequent attention	Works on tasks	Praise

When we attempt to answer the question "Why does challenging behavior occur?" we must examine the current environment within which the behavior occurs and identify the variables that occur prior to the behavior and consequences that follow behavior. Intervention then must focus on altering these environmental variables so that they no longer trigger and support challenging behavior. Examination of variables in the current environment is often referred to as the ABC *assessment* or *three-term contingency*. Through this assessment we identify the Antecedents that occur prior to Behavior and the Consequences that follow behavior (Bijou, Peterson, & Ault, 1968; Kauffman, Mostert, Trent, & Hallahan, 1993; Kazdin, 2001; Sulzer-Azaroff & Mayer, 1991). This descriptive ABC assessment provides critical information about the conditions in which challenging and appropriate behaviors occur. However, in our experience, the ABC assessment alone does not provide sufficient information from which to develop effective intervention plans. The framework that comes from the second and third assumptions underlying functional assessment is critical to developing individualized, effective, and positive interventions.

ASSUMPTION 2: BEHAVIOR SERVES A FUNCTION

The second assumption builds on the first assumption. The first assumption—that challenging and appropriate behavior is supported by the current environment—directs us to describe the environmental conditions that are present prior to and following behavior. The second assumption—that behavior serves a function—directs us to identify *why* behavior occurs. We use the information obtained through the ABC descriptive assessment of the current environment to make a hypothesis about why the behavior occurs. Functional assessment assumes that challenging behavior occurs because it produces a desired outcome for the student. In other words, it produces a function (Carr, 1977; Carr, Levin, McConnachie, Carlson, Kemp, & Smith, 1994; Carr, Robinson, & Palumbo, 1990; Dunlap, Foster-Johnson, & Robbins, 1990; Repp & Horner, 1999). In answering the question "Why does challenging behavior occur?" we make a hypothesis about what the student obtains as a result of the antecedent, behavior, consequence sequences. In other words, we identify the function of the behavior.

Positive Reinforcement Function

We find it helpful to identify three basic functions of behavior (Box 3–1). Each of the three functions of behavior is discussed briefly here and in greater detail in subsequent chapters.

1. Positive reinforcement
2. Negative reinforcement
3. Sensory regulation/sensory stimulation

The first function, based on positive reinforcement, is that the student obtains something positive by engaging in the challenging behavior (Carr, Langdon, & Yarbrough, 1999; Iwata et al., 1982/1994; Repp & Karsh, 1990). This might include attention, control, materials, and so forth. In the example given earlier, Suzanne obtained attention from the teacher when she used profanity. The function of her behavior was positive reinforcement—she obtained teacher attention.

Antecedent	Behavior	Consequence	Function
Teacher attends to peers	Uses profanity	Reprimand	Positive reinforcement: obtains attention
One-to-one instruction, frequent attention	Works on tasks	Praise	Positive reinforcement: obtains attention

When we identify the function of behavior it is critical that we consider the student's perspective of, or response to, variables rather than our own perspectives. Suzanne's teacher thought that she was punishing Suzanne by reprimanding her. But for Suzanne the reprimand was positive, not punishing. From Suzanne's perspective the reprimand functioned as a form of teacher attention and for Suzanne, negative attention from the teacher was better than no attention from the teacher. Suzanne continued to swear when she was not receiving teacher attention because swearing immediately and consistently resulted in some form of teacher attention.

Negative Reinforcement Function

The second function, based on negative reinforcement, is that the student escapes or avoids something aversive by engaging in challenging behavior (Carr, Newsom, & Binkoff, 1980; Iwata et al., 1982/1994; Repp, Karsh, Munk, & Dahlquist, 1995). Students may avoid tasks, activities, places, people, materials, participation, and so forth. For example, Pat complains of a stomachache during physical education whenever the teacher announces that they are to run laps around the track. Pat then is allowed to go to the nurse's office to rest for the remainder of the period. Pat's behavior produces a desirable consequence (going to the nurse's office) and the function of her behavior is to avoid running laps. Pat's behavior will continue to occur every

Positive Reinforcement Function

time the class is to run laps because it is effective in achieving the avoid/escape function.

We must also consider the student's perspective when identifying the avoid/escape function. Often students engage in challenging behavior that results in being sent to time-out, the principal's office, or even suspension. These usually are considered punishment procedures. But if the student escapes or avoids an aversive task by going to the principal's office for example, then this consequence actually is desired and the behavior that results in being sent to the principal's office will continue (Nelson & Rutherford, 1983).

We also must consider the student's perspective of what is aversive. This can be difficult especially if the student is escaping from or avoiding a task that we have developed. For example, teachers of young children often spend much time and effort developing stimulating opening circle sessions. For most children, circle time is fun and exciting and they readily participate. But not Yolanda. She finds it difficult to understand the activity, answer group-directed questions, and sing along with her peers because she does not speak or understand English well. During circle Yolanda fidgets, screams, and hits peers until she is sent to time-out where she sits quietly and looks out

The teacher's perspective:
"I don't understand Brent.
This is going to be a great activity."

The student's perspective:
"Those frogs are disgusting.
Sitting in the Principal's office is a lot
better than cutting open a stupid frog."

Negative Reinforcement Function

the window. From Yolanda's perspective, circle was aversive and her behavior allowed her to escape circle.

Antecedent	Behavior	Consequence	Function
Circle in English (aversive activity)	Fidgets, hits, screams	Time-out	Negative Reinforcement: escape circle

Sensory Regulation/Sensory Stimulation Function

The third function is termed sensory regulation/sensory stimulation. Within this function the effects of behavior may be related to (1) sensory regulation, (2) sensory stimulation, or (3) specific biological or neurological outcomes. One unique aspect of the stimulation/sensory regulation function is that challenging behaviors are maintained by nonsocial outcomes (Shore & Iwata, 1999). The three categories of the sensory regulation/sensory stimulation function are described briefly in this chapter and in more detail in subsequent chapters. Our view of the sensory regulation/sensory stimulation function is somewhat broader than that of some educators and researchers who often refer to this function primarily as automatic reinforcement (Iwata, Pace, Dorsey, et al., 1994; Iwata, Vollmer, & Zarcone, 1990; Repp et al., 1995).

Sensory Regulation

This category, sometimes referred to as homeostasis or arousal modulation, is based on the optimal stimulation theory described by Zentall and Zentall (1983). Optimal stimulation theory postulates that the level of stimulation that is most appropriate (or optimal) for each individual is biologically determined and that the amount of stimulation that is most appropriate varies across individuals ranging from high to low levels of stimulation. It further states that individuals will seek to maintain stimulation at their optimal level (Berkson & Tupa, 2000; Guess & Carr, 1991; Repp, 1999; Repp & Karsh, 1990; Repp, Karsh, Deitz, & Singh, 1992; Repp et al., 1995).

Stimulation may occur within each of the sensory systems: tactile (touch), vestibular (sense of movement, body in space, and gravity), visual (vision), auditory (hearing), gustatory (taste), olfactory (smell), and proprioceptive (sensation in muscles, tendons, and joints). When the level of sensory stimulation is too low, students will engage in behavior that increases stimulation. When the level of stimulation is too high, students will engage in behavior that decreases sensory stimulation (Repp & Karsh, 1992). For example, Rodney was able to sit quietly during the first 10 minutes of lecture. After 10 minutes, however, he began to tap his pencil and kick the leg of his desk. These behaviors increased stimulation (i.e., they provided movement and auditory and tactile stimulation) in an environment that for him was not sufficiently stimulating. For Rodney, there was a mismatch between the type and amount of stimulation provided during lecture and his optimal level of stimulation.

Antecedent	Behavior	Consequence	Function
Long lecture, limited movement	Tap pencil, kick desk	Movement, noise	Increased stimulation

Students who fit the sensory regulation category of this function also may experience difficulty when transitioning between highly stimulating activities or environments and passive activities or environments. This is because they are not able to modulate their level of stimulation across different environmental conditions (Fouse & Wheeler, 1997; Guess & Carr, 1991). When the level of stimulation is high and students are overaroused, some students may find it difficult to transition to more passive activities. Or when the level of stimulation is low and students are underaroused, some students will find it difficult to transition to or begin highly stimulating activities. For instance, Inez was not able to alter her behavior to match the level of stimulation required by the task or activity. Inez did not transition well from highly stimulating activities to quiet, passive activities such as reading. When reading class followed recess (a very stimulating activity), Inez often left her seat and talked to peers or her teachers. As a result, she was reprimanded, did not complete her reading assignments, and received after-school detention. Inez was able to stay in her seat and remain on task, however, if reading class followed less stimulating tasks such as art or lecture. When this happened she remained on task and completed her reading assignments. Inez's behavior in reading was influenced by the level of stimulation in previous activities. When the stimulation level was high, she was not able to transition to quiet, passive activities. When the stimulation level was low to moderate, she easily made the transition to quiet, passive activities.

Antecedent	Behavior	Consequence	Function
Recess	Runs, talks, participates	Interaction, movement	Sensory Regulation/ Sensory Stimulation: high stimulation
Reading follows recess	Talks to peers, out of seat	Interaction, movement, detention	Sensory Regulation/ Sensory Stimulation: maintain high stimulation
Art or lecture	On-task, listens, takes notes	Praise, completes task	Sensory Regulation/ Sensory Stimulation: low–moderate stimulation
Reading follows art or lecture	Reads book, in seat, quiet	Praise, completes assignment	Sensory Regulation/ Sensory Stimulation: low–moderate stimulation

Sensory Stimulation

Challenging behavior within this category is thought to occur because it generates sensory/perceptual stimulation that is automatically reinforcing (Shore & Iwata, 1999). In other words, the behavior itself produces a positive outcome. Sensory stimulation may occur within the visual, tactile, auditory, gustatory, and vestibular systems. For example, eye gouging may stimulate the retina and result in visual stimulation for students who are blind or visually impaired (Berkson & Tupa, 2000; Mace & Mauk, 1999). Or hand mouthing may produce tactile and gustatory stimulation for a student with sensory integration problems.

Neurological Outcomes

This category most often refers to the most severe forms of self-injurious and self-stimulatory behavior. The neurological theory postulates that some challenging behavior is related to neurodevelopmental dysfunction or biochemical imbalances (Lewis, Baumeister, & Mailman, 1987; Mace & Mauk, 1999; Shore & Iwata, 1999). For example, researchers have proposed that some individuals may engage in self-injurious behavior because it produces endogenous opiates or endorphins, which are reinforcing and become addictive (Carr et al., 1999). They also have speculated that severe self-injurious behavior and excessive forms of stereotypy may be related to neurochemical imbalances such as the production of dopamine or they may be associated with obsessive–compulsive disorder (Mace & Mauk, 1999). Interventions for individuals whose behavior stems from neurological dysfunction typically involve medication in addition to behavior management strategies.

Before moving to the third assumption of functional assessment, we should point out that not all forms of challenging behavior that might be characterized as self-injurious, self-stimulating (e.g., running or shouting in the classroom), or stereotypical on the basis of their topography are related to the sensory regulation/sensory stimulation function (Carr, 1977; Iwata et al., 1982/1994; McEvoy & Reichle, 2000). Indeed, behaviors such as head banging, rocking, and running may occur because they produce a different function. For instance, they may produce a desired outcome such as parental attention (i.e., the positive reinforcement function). Or they result in escape or avoidance of an aversive task such as taking a test (i.e., negative reinforcement) (Iwata, Pace, Dorsey, et al., 1994; Pace, Iwata, Cowdery, Andree, & McIntyre, 1993; Zarcone, Iwata, Smith, Mazaleski, & Lerman, 1994). Functional assessment will help educators determine whether the function of behavior is positive reinforcement, negative reinforcement, or sensory regulation/sensory stimulation.

In summary, when we identify why challenging behavior occurs we should first identify the triggers and supports for the behavior in the current environment. Second, we should use that information to identify the function of the behavior: (1) The student obtains something positive (positive reinforcement), (2) the student escapes or avoids something aversive (negative reinforcement), or (3) the level of sensory stimulation is increased or decreased (sensory regulation/sensory stimulation). This information then will guide the development of interventions to address that behavior. This leads to the third assumption underlying functional assessment.

ASSUMPTION 3: CHALLENGING BEHAVIOR CAN BE CHANGED USING POSITIVE INTERVENTION STRATEGIES THAT ADDRESS THE FUNCTION OF BEHAVIOR

If we know the antecedent triggers and consequences that are related to the challenging behavior and the function of the challenging behavior, then we can design positive interventions that allow the student to achieve the same function by using appropriate behavior, rather than challenging behavior (Carr et al., 1990; Donnellan & LaVigna, 1990; McEvoy & Reichle, 2000; Repp, 1999).

There is little need to use punishment-based interventions within the functional assessment and intervention model (Chandler, Dahlquist, Repp, & Feltz, 1999; Repp, 1999). Punishment teaches a student what not to do; it does not teach a student what to do instead of challenging behavior. When we use punishment procedures we often see an immediate decrease in challenging behavior. However, the results often are short term. This is because our punishment strategies have not addressed the function of challenging behavior and, in failing to do so, they have left a void (Carr, 1977; Mace, 1994). When this occurs another form of behavior will fill the void and will achieve the same function as the original challenging behavior. More often than not the replacement behavior will be another challenging behavior. For instance, Miguel, who was very difficult to understand, frequently yelled at his peers when they ignored his initiations. A response cost procedure was added to his token economy so that he lost points when he yelled at peers. After 2 days, the frequency of yelling decreased to near zero. However, within 1 week of initiation of the response cost procedure, Miguel began to hit peers when they ignored his initiations. Although Miguel had learned not to yell at his peers, he had not learned an appropriate way to recruit peer attention.

Intervention strategies must address the function of the challenging behavior. In doing this, we change the current supports for challenging behavior and provide environmental supports for appropriate behaviors that will achieve the same function (Carr, Robinson & Palumbo, 1990; Carr, 1994; Luiselli, 1990; Mace, 1994). For Miguel who hits his peers, rather than punish his behavior, we might teach him to tap peers on the shoulder and then use picture cues to communicate with his peers. This would allow him to recruit peer attention, but to do so using an appropriate behavior. Thus Miguel achieves the same function, but he does so using an appropriate replacement behavior. For Yolanda who did not speak English and who escaped circle when she fidgeted, screamed, and hit peers, intervention should teach a more appropriate way for Yolanda to indicate that she wished to leave circle such as saying "Termino." The question to ask when designing interventions for each of the functions is "What should the student do instead? What is an appropriate replacement behavior?"

In some cases the goal of intervention may be to change the function. This often occurs when the function of challenging behavior is to escape or avoid activities and tasks. Escape is not always an appropriate function of behavior especially in school settings. Escape from school-based activities often reduces opportunities to learn academic skills and to engage in appropriate social behavior. When escape or avoidance is not appropriate, we must change the function so that students obtain something positive by participating in activities. For example, Yolanda's teacher indicated that escape from circle was not appropriate. It was important for Yolanda to sit in circle and to participate in the activity.

When we seek to change the function of challenging behavior we must evaluate why the task or activity is aversive for the student. Intervention should alter the aversive aspects of the activity and increase positive outcomes for participation. Yolanda found circle aversive because she could not understand the activity, answer group questions, or sing with her peers. An intervention to immediately reduce the aversive aspects of the circle activity would be to repeat key words in Spanish, ask Yolanda individual questions in Spanish, and build movement into group singing so that Yolanda was able to participate (even though she did not sing). The teacher also might teach Yolanda some of the group songs in English and teach other students some songs in Spanish and use both types of songs during circle. Intervention also should provide praise for Yolanda when she participates and remains in circle without screaming and hitting peers.

Antecedent	Behavior	Consequence	Function
Circle in English (aversive activity)	Fidgets, hits, screams	Time-out	Negative Reinforcement: escape circle
Intervention to teach appropriate replacement behavior that achieves the same function:			
Circle in English (aversive activity)	Request to leave circle	Allowed to leave circle	Negative Reinforcement: escape circle
Intervention to change the function from escape (negative reinforcement) to obtains something positive (positive reinforcement):			
Circle in Spanish plus movement	Participates, remains in circle	Praise, interacts with peers	Positive Reinforcement: obtains praise, fun, peer interaction

ASSUMPTION 4: FUNCTIONAL ASSESSMENT
SHOULD BE A TEAM-BASED PROCESS

The final assumption related to functional assessment is that functional assessment is most effective when it is a team-based process. Functional assessment will be most effective if all individuals who will work with a student who engages in challenging behavior understand the assumptions underlying functional assessment and the reasons for implementing selected interventions. This leads to a shared understanding of the variables that support behavior and common language and approach to use when addressing challenging behavior (Kazdin, 2001). It also increases consistency among team members in responding to challenging behavior and implementing interventions (Chandler et al., 1999; Katsiyannis & Maag, 1998).

Educators need to understand that adoption of the functional assessment and intervention model to address challenging behavior does not negate the philosophies or practices of other professions (e.g., counseling, social work, occupational therapy). For example, a counseling member of a team may believe that play therapy is needed to help a student deal with emotions related to a previous trauma. This is not incompatible with functional assessment. One form of intervention (functional assessment) addresses the variables supporting behavior in the current environment in which it occurs, and the other form of intervention (play therapy) addresses the impact of previous experiences on behavior and emotions (Kazdin, 2001). In our experience both types of interventions can be implemented without arguing about which philosophical viewpoint is correct—and both types of interventions can be effective.

In another example, an occupational therapist who works with a student who has sensory integrative disorder and engages in stereotypical behavior may have a brain-based perspective about why this student seeks increased sensory input. He may believe that sensory integration therapy is critical to address this student's problems. The adoption of sensory integration therapy is not incompatible with conducting functional assessment to identify the environmental variables related to challenging behavior in the classroom. Again, in our experience there is no need to debate which approach is correct. The occupational therapist would provide sensory integration therapy to the student. At the same time, the functional assessment team would identify appropriate behaviors that would provide the student with sensory stimulation in the classroom. In this case the occupational therapist, as a member of the team, would be extremely helpful in identifying developmentally appropriate replacement behaviors that would achieve the same type and level of sensory stimulation for the student and could provide suggestions for incorporating sensory-based activities into the curriculum.

In our opinion and practice, the responsibility for addressing challenging behavior should not be assigned to one individual. It should not be the responsibility of only the school psychologist, behavior analyst, or classroom teacher. Although functional assessment can be conducted and intervention strategies implemented by individual staff members, we recommend that it be conducted by an interdisciplinary team. Contributions from multiple professionals can greatly increase the skills and knowledge of the team as a whole. All individuals who work with a student have unique areas of professional expertise and focus as well as knowledge of the student. The team-based process incorporates the expertise of individual team members in order to change the current supports for challenging behavior and to promote the development of appropriate replacement behavior. It also promotes consistency among individuals who interact with the student in applying intervention strategies that withdraw the support for challenging behavior and that teach and support appropriate replacement behavior.

THE GOALS OF FUNCTIONAL ASSESSMENT

When the authors of this text are brought into classrooms it usually is to address existing problem behaviors. Often teachers are at the end of their rope because a student's behavior is well established and may be escalating. When this occurs our job is to remediate the student's challenging behavior and to replace that behavior with more appropriate behavior. This obviously is an important goal of functional assessment. We remediate challenging behavior by first identifying the antecedent variables that trigger challenging and appropriate behavior and the consequences that follow. We then alter these in order to withdraw support for challenging behavior and provide support for appropriate replacement behavior that will achieve the same function.

An equally, and some would argue more important goal of functional assessment is to anticipate and prevent the development and occurrence of challenging behavior (McGee, 1988; Munk & Karsh, 1999; Repp, 1999; Repp et al., 1994). If we are able to prevent challenging behavior from developing or from occurring once it is part of a student's repertoire, we will not need to remediate. The functional assessment and intervention model can be used to predict environmental conditions that will lead to challenging behavior. These then can be altered before challenging behavior occurs (Carr et al., 1994; McGee & Daly, 1999; Nielsen, Olive, Donovan, & McEvoy, 1998). This can be done for individual students and for the class as a whole (Chandler et al., 1999).

Often educators can anticipate when and where challenging behavior will occur. For example, teachers indicate that challenging behavior usually increases prior to and following holidays, school breaks (e.g., spring break), and recess, and during disliked and very difficult activities. For individual students increases in challenging behavior may occur during specific tasks (e.g., writing, reading), types of activities (e.g., group or individual work), or during specific times of the day (e.g., after lunch or when they must go home).

One very predictable event that leads to increased challenging behaviors at a class-wide level is the transition between activities. This is often referred to as "downtime." Students may run, shout, throw materials, fight, swear, and so on, during transition. When we examine transitions in the classroom, we note that they often are unstructured, with little supervision and instruction, and they involve relatively long periods of waiting (Lawry, Danko, & Strain, 2000; Strain & Hemmeter, 1997). There are few antecedent triggers or consequences for appropriate behavior because teachers are helping other students or are preparing for the next activity. When challenging behavior does occur teachers often use reactive measures such as reprimanding students or taking away privileges or points.

Rather than reacting to challenging behavior during transition, our goal should be to prevent challenging behavior from occurring during transition. To do this, we need to alter our transition practices. For example, we might provide structure by establishing rules and signals for appropriate transition behavior. Or we might employ transition-based teaching by providing opportunities for students to demonstrate or practice skills such as naming letters, counting items, and so on. (Wolery, Doyle, Gast, Ault, & Lichtenberg, 1991). We might assign students to specific jobs in order to reduce unstructured time during transition, or we might have students transition at different times (e.g., line up in pairs versus as a whole group). We also might have materials ready for the subsequent activity in order to reduce the amount of time involved in transition. These changes to the transition routine will prevent the occurrence of challenging behavior, thereby preventing the need to remediate established challenging behavior.

Prevention involves anticipating the development or occurrence of challenging behavior and manipulating the antecedents that will trigger challenging behavior and providing antecedents to trigger appropriate behavior. Remediation, the second goal of functional assessment, involves developing strategies to address challenging behavior after it is well established. This also involves manipulating antecedents related to appropriate and challenging behavior and changing the consequences that currently support challenging behavior so that they now support appropriate replacement behaviors.

SUMMARY

When teams employ the functional assessment and intervention model to address challenging behavior, they should understand and adopt the assumptions and goals that are essential to this model. Functional assessment is built on four assumptions concerning the development and maintenance of appropriate and challenging behavior. These assumptions are that behavior is supported by the current environment, behavior serves a function, challenging behavior can be changed with positive interventions that address the function of behavior, and functional assessment should be a team-based endeavor. These assumptions direct the focus of assessment and intervention. They lead to an assessment and intervention model that focuses on the settings in which challenging behavior currently occurs and a model that identifies and addresses the function of behavior.

The two goals of functional assessment also are fundamental to understanding and addressing challenging behavior. The first goal of functional assessment should be to anticipate and prevent challenging behavior by arranging environments that support appropriate behavior. We do recognize, however, that not all challenging behavior can be anticipated and prevented. When this occurs, the goal of functional assessment is to remediate challenging behavior through positive strategies. We do this by removing support for challenging behavior and (1) providing support for appropriate replacement behavior that achieves the same function or (2) changing the function from escape and avoidance (negative reinforcement) to obtain something positive (positive reinforcement).

Part Two

Conducting a Functional Assessment

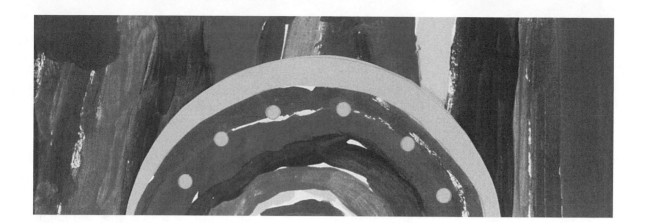

CHAPTER 4

Assessing the Current Environment

The first step in conducting functional assessment is to define the challenging behavior and identify the current supports for challenging behavior. This typically involves (1) obtaining a referral for functional assessment or behavioral support; (2) interviewing educators, parents or caregivers, and other individuals who have knowledge of the student and who have observed the challenging behavior; (3) interviewing the student who engages in the challenging behavior; and (4) collecting environmental data via direct observation. In the first section of this chapter, we discuss strategies for obtaining referrals and interviewing students and other individuals. In the last section we discuss how to obtain information through direct observation of the student and the environment.

COLLECTING INFORMATION THROUGH REFERRAL AND INTERVIEW

At a minimum, referral for behavioral support or functional assessment should provide demographic information about the student and program. For example, a referral may include the age of the student, the grade in which the student is enrolled, the type of services received (i.e., special education services), and the types of classrooms the student attends (i.e., regular education or self-contained classroom or a combination of classrooms). The referral also should identify the name of the school the child attends, the student's teacher, and the reason for referral. In addition to this type of basic information, referrals also should describe the student's challenging behavior in some detail and strategies that have been employed in the past. This helps the behavior specialist or other consultant (1) identify who should participate in interviews and (2) develop questions concerning behavior and intervention strategies that should be explored during an interview. A completed student referral form that is adapted from one used in the second author's program is provided in Box 4–1.

One of the first tasks in identifying current supports for challenging behavior is to interview individuals who have observed the student's challenging behavior or who are familiar with the student. This may include teachers, paraprofessionals, therapists, counselors or social workers and other educational staff, administrators, bus drivers and other school staff, and family members. One purpose of functional assessment interviews is to help define the challenging behavior so that all individuals are able to agree on instances and noninstances of the challenging behavior. As in all behavioral procedures, definitions of challenging behavior must be objective and describe observable behavior (Malott, Malott, & Trojan, 1999; Skinner, 1953, 1974; Sulzer-Azaroff & Mayer, 1991). For example, Mr. Lirta referred Chastity to the instructional strategies team because her behavior was "disrespectful." During the interview the team asked Mr. Lirta to describe what Chastity did that was disrespectful. He said that she turned her back to him during lecture, swore at him when he asked her to face the front of the room, and refused to take a turn writing on the blackboard. Further conversation with Mr. Lirta indicated that Chastity refused to take a turn at the blackboard by shouting, "Leave me alone" or "I don't have to and you can't make me." The interview also indicated that during lecture Chastity physically turned her chair so that it was facing the back wall of the room and that she swore at Mr. Lirta by "giving him the finger." This observable and objective information allowed all members of the team to identify the behaviors that Mr. Lirta termed disrespectful. Detailed information such as this will increase consistency among team members in conducting subsequent observations and applying intervention strategies.

In addition to defining behavior, interviews with school staff and family members will help the team identify environmental variables and other circumstances that may be associated with challenging behavior (Alberto & Troutman, 1999; Kazdin, 2001). Through interviews the team seeks to answer several questions about challenging behavior. These questions are listed in Table 4–1.

In addition to identifying factors that are associated with challenging behavior, we should identify during the interview factors that are *never* associated with challenging behavior (e.g., the behavior never occurs during cooperative group activities). We also should identify any appropriate behavior on the part of the student and the environmental factors that are associated with that appropriate behavior. Finally, we should identify student strengths, skills, and other previously unidentified needs (Dunlap & Kern, 1993; Schrader & Gaylord-Ross, 1990).

BOX 4–1
Sample student referral form

Student Name: Mickey Hacker   Age: 9   Grade: 3

Student's current program placement: regular education

Does the student receive special education services? Yes

If yes, what type of services does he or she receive?

Speech and language therapy, math resource room

Parents'/Guardians' Names: Joleen and Hector Hacker

Has the parent/guardian been made aware of this referral? Yes

District: 206   School: Ben Franklin
Teacher: Mrs. Corley   Phone: 964-5271   Fax: 964-5369

Name of contact person who will be primarily responsible for facilitating the referral and supporting the plan: Mrs. Corley

Additional team members who will be included in collaboration:
Name: Justin Granger   Role: Special Educator
Name: Linda Holmes   Role: Speech Pathologist

Please list concerns regarding the student's performance:

1. *Noncompliant behavior: The following behaviors are generally directed at an adult or authority figure: refuses to do ordinary, everyday work; does not listen to instruction—eyes down, draws, reads, daydreams; refuses to try cursive writing and math tasks; attempts to bargain to get out of task.*
2. *Leaves the classroom, aggressive when brought back to classroom.*

Briefly describe recent strategies attempted for the concerns listed above and the student's responses to the intervention strategies.

1. Strategy:
   Redirect Mickey's attention by using "disapproving teacher look," restating directions, pointing, turning page, standing or sitting next to him (several times each day).
1. Student Response:
   Startles—may get fidgety—arms and legs suddenly move; hits or slaps head; growls; scowls; covers work with arms and body; scratches at paper with fingernails; scribbles on work; crumples or rips paper; huffs and puffs.
2. Strategy:
   Prompt and guide student back to the classroom.
2. Student Response:
   Resistance, anger, tantrum, refusal, aggression.

TABLE 4–1
Questions to be asked during a functional assessment interview

1. What is the topography of the behavior?
2. When does the behavior typically occur or occur most often (e.g., specific time of day or day of the week)?
3. Where does the behavior typically occur or occur most often (e.g., gym, classroom, hallway, and lunchroom)?
4. What type of tasks or activities typically are present when the behavior occurs (e.g., math, reading, small group, lecture, individual work)?
5. What is the nature of the tasks or activities that are present when the behavior occurs (e.g., task duration, preferred or nonpreferred, difficult or easy, novel or familiar, boring or stimulating)?
6. What types of materials typically are present when the behavior occurs (e.g., fine motor or manipulatives, art products, computer, limited materials)?
7. Who usually is present in the environment when the behavior occurs and what are they doing (e.g., special educator, regular educator, therapist, teaching assistant, and specific peers)?
8. What variables typically precede the behavior and what consequences typically follow the behavior (e.g., instructions, questions, assignments, assistance, reprimand, and praise)?
9. What other contextual variables usually are related to behavior (e.g., physiological factors, noise levels, activity structure)?

For instance, the interview with Mr. Lirta revealed that Chastity turned her back, swore, and refused to write on the board primarily during math and spelling activities. It further indicated that she only did this when math and spelling activities involved lecture, individual work, board work, and small group activities. She did not engage in challenging behavior during science, history, and art activities or during nonacademic activities such as lunch and recess. She also did not engage in challenging behavior when she worked individually with the special educator on math and spelling tasks. In these situations Chastity was on task and completed her work. Information such as this—about variables that consistently are associated with challenging and appropriate behavior—will guide the team as it begins to identify potential antecedent triggers for consequences that support challenging behavior and appropriate behavior and to hypothesize the function of challenging behavior (Carr, Langdon, & Yarbrough, 1999; Reichle et al., 1996).

Teams may also wish to interview the student who exhibits challenging behavior when appropriate (Kern & Dunlap, 1999; Reed, Thomas, Sprague, & Horner, 1997). The student interview is designed to solicit the student's perspectives regarding the variables that are related to his or her challenging behavior. During a student interview, the student might be asked to describe his or her challenging behavior, to identify when and where it occurs, to identify contextual variables related to behavior such as illness or fatigue, and to identify the consequences that follow challenging behavior. For example, Chastity told the team that she hated math and spelling. When asked why she didn't like these subjects she said they were hard and that she wasn't going to make a fool of herself by writing on the board or working with her peers and doing the wrong thing. She said that she liked working with the special education teacher on spelling and math because he helped her get the right answers.

The information obtained through interviews with Mr. Lirta and Chastity indicated that Chastity engaged in challenging behavior during math and spelling tasks that involved peer observation of her work (antecedents). When she refused to participate, peers were not able to observe her work (consequences). The team hypothesized that the function of her challenging behavior might be to avoid performing poorly in front of her peers (negative reinforcement). This information was confirmed through subsequent observation.

Antecedents	Behavior	Consequence
Difficult subjects (math/spelling) with peer observation of her work (e.g., group work, board work)	Refuse to participate, profanity, shouting, turn chair to wall	Peers do not see her work, reprimand, left alone
Difficult subjects (math/spelling) 1:1 with teacher	On task	Completes work, assistance, praise
Easy subjects with peer observation of her work or nonacademic activities	On task, participates, interacts with peers	Completes work, peer interaction

The interview process may be highly structured and standardized or it may be based on informal conversations (Carr et al., 1999; Nielsen, Olive, Donovan, & McEvoy, 1998). Two of the most commonly employed standardized formats for interviewing an adult are (1) the Motivation Assessment Scale (Durand & Crimmins, 1988) and (2) the Functional Analysis Interview (O'Neill, Horner, Albin, Sprague, Storey, & Newton, 1997). The Motivation Assessment Scale (MAS) is a 16-item questionnaire that addresses the potential functions of behavior. The questions lead to descriptions of the conditions under which challenging behavior occurs, and the function of challenging behavior is inferred based on the information provided (Halle & Spradlin, 1993). The MAS is a quick assessment and it is easy to use (Nielsen et al., 1998). As a result, it is commonly employed as part of functional assessment. However, the MAS has been criticized by several researchers because of problems related to reliability calculations and outcomes (e.g., Crawford, Brockel, Schauss, & Miltenberger, 1992; Iwata, Vollmer, & Zarcone, 1990; Repp & Munk, 1999; Singh et al., 1993; Zarcone, Rodgers, Iwata, Rourke, & Dorsey, 1991). As a result, information obtained from this scale should be verified through observation.

The Functional Analysis Interview Form (O'Neill et al., 1997) is an extensive interview protocol that explores (1) the topography, frequency, duration, and intensity of challenging behaviors; (2) environmental conditions related to be-havior; (3) contextual variables that may be related to challenging behavior such as the student's history and biological or physiological status; (4) func-tional alternative behaviors and communication skills exhibited by the stu-dent; and (5) potential reinforcers and interventions. This interview leads to hy-potheses regarding the function of behavior based on the reports of individuals who are interviewed. The hypotheses then are verified or refuted during sub-sequent observations using the Functional Analysis Observation Form. Although the O'Neill et al. interview and observation forms yield useful infor-mation, some investigators find the duration required to obtain information prohibitive or they find that the information does not adequately reflect their population. As a result, they have developed their own forms and processes (McMahon, Lambros, & Sylva, 1998; Vaugn, Hales, Bush, & Fox, 1998). For ex-ample, McMahon and her colleagues (1998) developed a modified version of the Functional Analysis Interview Form to use in assessing children with chronic illness who displayed challenging behavior.

O'Neill and his colleagues (1997) also have developed a standardized stu-dent interview form and protocol (Reed et al., 1997). This interview is de-signed to solicit the student's perspectives regarding his or her behavior and the variables that are related to his or her challenging behavior. Another stu-dent interview was developed by Kern, Dunlap, Clarke, & Childs (1994). During this interview students provide information about their challenging behavior, variables that affect their behavior, and preferred activities and re-inforcers. They also provide information about liked and disliked activities and variables affecting each type of activity. Box 4–2 presents an adaptation of the Kern et al. (1994) interview for use with young children. The second author of this text uses this form when interviewing young children who ex-hibit challenging behaviors.

You may find it helpful to create an interview format and protocol for adults that are feasible and useful for your agency. For example, the second author of this text divides the interview process into two parts. During the first part she identifies the challenging behavior that the teacher or other re-ferring educators would like to change, the strategies that they have em-ployed to change the behavior, and the times of day that observations should be conducted. She then observes the student in the natural environment. This is followed by a more extensive interview with educational staff and an examination of the student's educational file. You also may find it helpful to develop a student interview that reflects the age and/or abilities of the stu-dents for whom you will conduct functional assessment. Regardless of the format employed, the information obtained from the interview should assist in identifying the potential supports for and the function of challenging be-havior, and serve as a guide for subsequent observations. The interviews de-scribed in this text and the nine questions presented earlier in Table 4–1 pro-vide resources that will help you develop your own interview forms and procedures.

BOX 4–2
Student-assisted
functional assessment
interview

1. Student _____

2. Date _____

3. My Day Today Was:

Wow   Good   OK   Try Again

4. Today I Was Feeling:

Happy   Sad   Quiet   Noisy   Busy   Tired   Mad

5. _____ was too long for me.

6. _____ was too hard for me.

7. _____ was fun for me.

8. _____ was easy for me.

I like when my teacher helps me.   YES   NO

I like when my friends help me.   YES   NO

My favorite part of school is _____.

My wish for school is _____ .

© 2002 Dahlquist and Chandler.

The interview process is a helpful first step in identifying the supports for challenging behavior. However, there are several threats to the validity and reliability of interviews that preclude developing interventions based solely on information obtained from interviews. For example, much of the information obtained from interviews is subjective, based on the experience, prior observations, and impressions of the individuals interviewed (Kazdin, 1980; Mace, Lalli, & Lalli, 1991). The individuals interviewed also may provide information based on an insufficient sample of behavior (e.g., the interviewee has only observed the behavior two times or has only observed the behavior during one time of the day). Or they may report infrequent but disruptive or dangerous behaviors as frequently occurring due to the saliency of these behaviors (Kazdin, 2001). For example, when the first author worked at a state hospital for individuals with disabilities, she found that residential staff frequently reported high occurrences of challenging behavior among residents to the psychiatrist who adjusted medication. Yet, data indicated that challenging behavior actually occurred very infrequently. In reporting challenging behavior to the psychiatrist, the staff were responding more to the severity of behavior than to the actual frequency of occurrence.

Interviewees also may not be able to identify the critical variables that are related to challenging behavior, or they may identify the wrong variables. In addition, information obtained from interviews may be based on a limited sample of individuals (e.g., only the student's teacher), and there may be poor reliability across individuals who are interviewed or between interview and subsequent observation (Mace, 1994; Repp & Munk, 1999; Zarcone et al., 1991).

Few guidelines exist to indicate how many individuals should be interviewed, who should be interviewed, and how often an individual should have observed the student's behavior and across how many settings, and so on, prior to providing information. It is generally agreed, however, that interviews alone do not provide sufficient information from which to identify the function of behavior and to develop function-based interventions. Interviews must be followed by observations within the environment in which the challenging behavior occurs (Carr et al., 1999; Iwata, 1994; Kazdin, 2001; O'Neill et al., 1990; Repp, 1999; Shore & Iwata, 1999).

COLLECTING INFORMATION THROUGH DIRECT OBSERVATION

Direct observation is the second part of identifying environmental and contextual variables that support challenging behavior. Through observations in the natural environment (i.e., the environment in which the behavior occurs), we identify variables that occur prior to challenging or appropriate behavior and those that follow challenging or appropriate behavior. As mentioned in Chapter 3, this descriptive observation is referred to as the ABC or Antecedent–Behavior–Consequence assessment (Bijou, Peterson, & Ault, 1968; Sulzer-Azaroff & Mayer, 1991). For each occurrence of behavior we record the behavior and the events that occur prior to or along with the behavior (antecedent conditions) and the events that follow the behavior (consequences) (Kauffman, Mostert, Trent, & Hallahan, 1993).

Table 4–2 provides a sample of a simple ABC recording form for Joe, who was referred to the team because of his noncompliant and disruptive behavior. This observation form indicates that Joe's challenging behavior occurs during history when he is given instructions or tasks to complete (antecedents). When Joe is noncompliant during history, he initially receives additional instructions and reprimands, but eventually the teacher leaves him alone or sends him to time-out (consequences). Joe's challenging be-

TABLE 4–2
Sample ABC recording form for Joe

Student: Joe Atwood
Observer: Gavin Beck

Date: 11/11–11/12

Setting: Regular Classroom, Playground, History, Science, Recess

Antecedents	Behavior	Consequence
Instruction to read history book	Throws textbook, talks to peer	Teacher tells him to pick up book
Instruction to begin history worksheet	Turns his worksheet over	Teacher shakes her head; walks away
Teacher asks if he needs help on worksheet	Tears worksheet	Sent to time-out
Teacher instruction to line up for recess	Lines up	Class moves to recess
Recess, free choice of activities	Plays soccer	Peer interaction
Teacher instruction to work on science project and to raise hand when done	Works on project, raises his hand	Teacher praises Joe's behavior and completed work

havior does not occur during group projects, science, and other activities that involve teacher instructions such as music, art, and recess. During those activities Joe is compliant and participates throughout the activity. Joe's noncompliant and disruptive challenging behavior occurs during history because it results in escape from a disliked task (the negative reinforcement function).

In addition to recording antecedents behavior, and consequences, it also is helpful to note student strengths, to identify reinforcers for the student, and to indicate other concerns that are related to the student. For example, we might note that Joe interacts well with peers and likes to work in cooperative groups. We might identify as concerns that not only is history a disliked subject, but that reading also is a difficult task for Joe and that often he "zones out" during activities that involve reading (even though "zoning out" is not a problem identified by the team). This information will assist in developing interventions to address Joe's challenging behavior.

When we collect data using the ABC approach we identify the variables that precede, co-occur, and follow each instance of behavior concurrently (Kazdin, 2001). However, to assist in understanding each of these variables, we discuss each separately. We also introduce and discuss a third type of variable that should be identified during observation and interview: setting events.

Antecedents

Antecedents are those environmental events that occur prior to or are concurrent with challenging and appropriate behavior. We often describe antecedents as environmental events that trigger or guide behavior. Other investigators have described antecedents as variables that set the occasion for behavior, or that set the stage for behavior (Rhode, Jenson, & Reavis, 1992; Sulzer-Azaroff & Mayer, 1991). Antecedents affect the probability of the occurrence of behavior as well as the rate, duration, and intensity of behavior (Dunlap, Kern-Dunlap, Clarke, & Robbins, 1991; Repp, 1999; Repp & Karsh, 1990). Antecedents can be vocal, gestural, pictorial, written, or physical. For example, teachers may provide picture cues or outlines that identify the steps for completing a task or they may provide a sample of a completed math problem at the beginning of a homework assignment. Or a teacher may point out to a student that she only has three more problems to complete on her worksheet or tell a student the first letter of the word she is trying to spell.

Antecedents often operate as signals that a particular consequence is available following behavior or as discriminative stimuli (Wacker & Reichle, 1993). Although antecedents do not always explicitly specify the consequences that are available following behavior, they achieve their discriminative signaling power through repeated pairing with reinforcing and punishing consequences in the ABC sequence (Michael, 1982; Sulzer-Azaroff & Mayer, 1991). For instance, a teacher may tell students after recess "I want you to quickly go to your seats and quiet down." Although she has not indicated what consequence will follow this behavior, students respond because in the past this behavior has been followed by watching a movie.

In another example, a strategy often used by parents and educators of young children is to count to three before placing a child in time-out. After repeated pairings of being placed in time-out after the parent counts to three, the words *one*, *two*, and *three* function as antecedent stimuli which signal that continued behavior will be followed by time-out.

Table 4–3 provides a list of antecedent stimuli that commonly occur in school settings. You may wish to add to this list as you begin to observe behavior in school settings and conduct functional assessments. You may notice that some of the items on this list occur after a behavior has occurred (e.g., success). By definition, these should be identified as consequences. However, often the consequences of behavior become antecedents for the next behavior, resulting in a cycle of antecedents, behavior, and consequences. For example, Mr. Ricoland tells Gay to complete her graphic organizer regarding the differences between the North and the South during the Civil War. Gay says "No." Mr. Ricoland then tells her again to do her graphic organizer. Gay shouts "Leave me alone." Mr. Ricoland then tells Gay that she has to do her work or she will fail the unit. Gay screams "No" and throws her paper on the floor. This type of cyclical interaction continues until eventually Mr. Ricoland leaves Gay alone or sends her to the back of the room. In this example, the consequence of giving another instruction also becomes the

TABLE 4–3
Common antecedents that occur prior to or are concurrent with appropriate and challenging behavior

Instructions	Questions
Safety signals	Presignals
Picture cues	Rules
Lack of attention	Peer or adult attention
Difficult activity	Easy, preferred activity
Boring activity	Fun, stimulating activity
Note taking forms	Physical models
"If this . . . then" statements	Outlines
Opportunities to respond	No opportunities to respond
Behavior models	Warnings
Errors	Success
Choice	Gestures
Teasing	Requests
Disliked materials or tasks	Preferred materials or tasks
Assistance	Prompts

© 2002 Chandler and Dahlquist.

antecedent for the next behavior. Thus, the ABC sequence looks like this: A B C/A B C/A B C/A B C/A B and so on.

Antecedent stimuli such as those listed in Table 4–3 can trigger appropriate behavior or they can trigger challenging behavior. Interviews and direct observation will identify how these stimuli currently affect the behavior of individual students and groups of students and provide clues concerning how they may be altered so that they prevent challenging behavior and guide appropriate behavior (Kazdin, 2001).

Consequences

Consequences are the events that follow behavior. Positive consequences strengthen or maintain behavior. They increase the probability that behavior will continue to occur in the future. Punishing or aversive consequences weaken behavior and decrease the probability that behavior will continue to occur in the future (Epstein & Skinner, 1982; Schloss & Smith, 1998; Skinner, 1953, 1974; Zirpoli & Melloy, 2001). Table 4–4 provides a list of consequences that commonly occur in school or home settings.

When we identify consequences during ABC observations it is important to be objective and describe the consequences that are observed. A common mistake when collecting observational data is to identify the hypothesized function rather than to describe the consequence. For example, observers often write as a consequence that the student obtained teacher attention rather than stating the teacher talked to or reprimanded the student. Teacher attention does not describe what was observed, rather it describes the function of the ABC sequence. Although the teacher does attend to the student when delivering a reprimand, that reprimand may be stimulating to the student or it may delay the onset of an activity. In other words,

TABLE 4–4
Common consequences
that follow appropriate
and challenging behavior

Praise	Reprimand
Peer laughter	Time-out
Control of activity	Stickers
Loss of tokens, points	Points, tokens
High five	Redirection
Feedback	Assistance
Hug, pat on back	Criticism
Sent to principal	Detention
Teacher assistance	Suspension
Happy face	Grades
Free time	Points
Reduced homework	Awards
Signaled or unsignaled ignoring	
Peer or adult rejection	
Change of activity, peers, and materials	
Increase or decrease in stimulation (e.g., movement, auditory, tactile)	
Withholding a previously delivered reinforcer (extinction)	

© 2002 Chandler and Dahlquist.

the consequence of teacher reprimand may function to increase stimulation or to escape an activity. If the observer simply writes teacher attention for each consequence, the team may attribute challenging behavior to "obtains teacher attention" (i.e., positive reinforcement) and may not consider the sensory regulation/sensory stimulation or escape/avoidance functions. The purpose of the observation phase of functional assessment is to provide *descriptive* information of variables that are related to behavior. At this point we are not making definitive statements or hypotheses about the function of behavior (although we may begin to formulate hypotheses). The purpose of the next phase, the function identification phase, is to *analyze* descriptive data and make hypotheses about the function of behavior based on multiple examples of Antecedent–Behavior–Consequence sequences.

Consequences can be observable environmental events such as teacher praise or tokens. Consequences also can be unobservable events or private events that occur within the individual such as a change in stimulation or automatic reinforcement. In school-based settings we typically do not have physical measures such as EEGs and heart monitors to document changes in stimulation following behavior. Changes in sensory input often are inferred based on the topography of the student's behavior.

Although unobservable consequences are harder to discriminate, both types of consequences are important to identify when conducting functional assessment. This is especially critical if the sensory regulation/sensory stimulation function is suspected. For example, when Raul runs in the classroom we should note observable consequences such as the teacher tells him to sit, as well as potential unobserved consequences, such as increased movement. Further observation will document consistencies across consequences that will help the team develop a hypothesis concerning the function of behavior. Identification of the consequences that currently support challenging behavior also will help identify how they may be changed so that they no longer support challenging behavior and, instead, support appropriate behavior. For instance, if the teacher only rarely tells Raul to sit down, we might hypothesize that teacher reaction is not the consequence supporting his behavior. In this case the increased movement from the behavior itself is the supporting consequence.

Setting Events

In addition to identifying and recording antecedents and consequences, we also should consider setting events and their influence on behavior. Setting events are situational or contextual factors that influence how a student responds to antecedents and consequences (Carr, Levin, McConnachie, Carlson, Kemp, & Smith, 1994; Carr, Reeve, & Magito-McLaughlin, 1996; Munk & Repp, 1994b; O'Reilly, 1997; Repp, 1994; Repp & Karsh, 1990; Wahler & Fox, 1981). Setting events may change the stimulus–response or antecedent–behavior relationship or they may alter the positive or negative properties of consequences. For example, on most days, Tuck enjoys a pat on the back when he has completed his work. However, Tuck went to the beach this weekend and he has a sunburn (setting event). Now, the pat on the back (consequence) is no longer reinforcing and he responds negatively when the teacher pats him on the back. Likewise, if his girlfriend says "Give me a hug" (something he usually likes to do), he may refuse to comply with this antecedent request and actually walk away from her when she tries to hug him. Tuck would not respond this way to antecedent requests or consequences if he did not have a sunburn. This setting event has influenced how he responds to typical antecedents and consequences.

Setting events may be divided into three categories: physiological/biological, physical/environmental, and social/situational variables. Table 4–5 provides examples of common setting events that may affect school-age students. Setting events may be relatively continuous variables (e.g., lighting in the classroom or the student's parents going through a divorce) or they may be infrequent, short-term events (e.g., falling down while entering the classroom, sleep deprivation, or illness) (O'Reilly, 1997).

Setting events may precede and accompany current behavior (e.g., noise level or time of day) or they may be temporally distant from the current behavior (e.g., fight with parents the previous day) (Kennedy & Itkonen, 1993). When setting events are temporally distant from the challenging behavior they may impact behavior by generating an emotional or physiological "state" that is present in the current setting (Halle & Spradlin, 1993). For example, Pam often fought with her mother before leaving for school. On the days that she fought with her mother, Pam entered school very upset and angry. On those days she typically refused to participate in classroom activities and often displayed aggression against peers.

Physiological/Biological	Physical/Environmental
Illness, allergy	Noise
Fatigue	Lighting
Hunger	Size of an area, crowding
Medication	High or low activity level
Pain	Visual distractions
Over- or under-stimulated	Unfamiliar setting
Time of day	Seating arrangements
Physical activity	Sequence of activities
Sleep deprivation	Activity level

Social/Situational	
School breaks, holidays	Family-related factors
Activity structure	Chaotic or "bad" morning
Negative peer interaction or fighting	Home-related factors
Being late for class or an activity	Classroom transitions
Change in routine or daily activities	Activity transitions
Negative student/teacher or adult interaction	
Presence or absence of particular individuals	

© 2002 Chandler & Dahlquist.

Many setting events are not observable, such as hunger, or they do not occur within the classroom setting, such as a poor parent/child relationship or other home and family-related factors. Often interviews with the student or members of the student's family are critical to the identification of nonobservable setting events. Table 4–6 provides a sample checklist of setting events that parents might identify during an interview. This checklist also might be sent home by the school at the end of each day and returned by the parent the next morning.

When setting events are present and operative the student responds one way to antecedents and consequences. When setting events are absent or not operative the student responds differently to antecedents and consequences (Van Camp, Lerman, Kelley, Roane, Contrucci, & Vorndran, 2000). Two examples will illustrate this point. First, when Woody is ill (setting event) he refuses (behavior) to follow instructions (antecedents) during physical education. When Woody is not ill he readily follows instructions during physical education. Carr and his colleagues (1994) suggest that setting events alone do not trigger behavior, but when they are combined with antecedents they may lead to challenging behavior because they make mildly negative events more aversive. For example, Carr, Newsom, and Binkoff (1980) reported that variability in escape-related challenging behavior was correlated with the presence and absence of setting events such as illness or classroom parties. In our experience setting events also may make neutral or even normally positive events aversive (Repp & Munk,

TABLE 4–6
Sample checklist of setting events that may be completed by families

---

Sleep: ___ broken ___ slept through night ___ restless
Comments:

Wake up time: ___ 4:30 ___ 5:00 ___ 5:30 ___ 6:00
             ___ 6:30 ___ 7:00 ___ 7:30 ___ 8:00
Comments:

Breakfast:___ none ___ some ___ average ___ large
Comments:

Mood: ___ fussy ___ tantrums ___ active ___ mad
      ___ fights ___ quiet ___ sad ___ happy ___ other
Comments:

Health:___ poor ___ average ___ good ___ seizure
Comments:

Bowel movement:___ yes___ no
Comments:

Interactions with family members: ___ poor ___ fighting ___ good
Comments:

Behavior: ___ good ___ sometimes good, sometimes not good
       ___ was in trouble or punished
Comments:

Are there other family-related issues that we should know about?

© 2002 Dahlquist and Chandler.

1999). For Woody, illness alters how he typically responds to the antecedent stimulus (instructions during PE) because the behavior being requested is aversive when this setting event is present.

In a second example, when Candy is overstimulated (setting event) she may respond negatively to enthusiastic and intense praise that provides additional stimulation (consequence). For instance, at the end of PE the teacher asks Candy to put the balls in the bin. After Candy does this, the teacher slaps Candy on the shoulder and loudly says "Great work Candy, give me a high five." Candy responds aggressively to the teacher. When Candy is not overstimulated, however, she often seeks and then responds appropriately to enthusiastic and intense praise. In this example the setting event alters the reinforcing value of the consequence (loud and physical praise)(Horner, Vaugn, Day, & Ard, 1996; Michael, 1982). We may find that eventually Candy will refuse to assist in cleanup at the end of PE because the consequence associated with following instructions (not the behavior being requested) is aversive when this setting event (being overstimulated) is present.

Candy also may engage in challenging behavior when instructions are delivered (antecedents) if the instructions—like the consequences—are enthusiastic and intense. Thus, a final way that setting events may influence behavior is that they make antecedent environmental stimuli aversive. Think about when this may happen to you. When you are exhausted you may yell at your children or your husband, wife, or roommate when he or she asks you a question or for assistance. Or when you are frustrated you may react to normal levels of sound by kicking or throwing your radio. In these examples when the setting event is present you behave so as to terminate ongoing aversive environmental stimuli or antecedent events.

We do not need to identify setting events for each Antecedent–Behavior–Consequence sequence. In most cases when behavior is consistent across antecedent and consequence conditions (whether behavior is challenging or appropriate) we do not need to look for setting events. For example, if Julio consistently engages in challenging behavior during math, we should change the antecedents that precede his challenging behavior. For instance, if math is very difficult we might do the first three problems with Julio before asking him to work independently. Or we might add antecedent prompts to look at the calculation signs (i.e., division, multiplication, addition, subtraction) or to keep working. In addition to altering or adding antecedent events, we also should examine and modify the consequences that follow appropriate and challenging behavior during math. For instance, we may increase positive consequences that follow appropriate behavior (e.g., we may frequently praise on-task or assistance-seeking behavior) and stop attending to challenging behavior.

If modifications of antecedent and consequence conditions do not change Julio's behavior, then we should look for setting events. For instance, we may find that recess occurs prior to math and that Julio's peers tease him each day during recess. This setting event changes how Julio responds to the next activity, math.

Two other types of situations should cause us to look for setting events. The first occurs when behavior is inconsistent across consistent antecedent conditions. For example, if Devlin engages in challenging behavior during geography on some days, but not on others, then we should look for setting events that are operative on the days when he engages in challenging behavior. It might be that when he engages in challenging behavior during geography, he had a difficult worksheet to complete during the previous period.

This concept also applies when students exhibit infrequent challenging behavior across consistent antecedent and consequence conditions. Devlin may only occasionally display challenging behavior during geography (e.g., three times a term). We might find that on those infrequent occasions, he completed a very difficult, long test during the previous period.

The second type of situation that indicates we should look for setting events is when challenging behavior occurs across a variety of antecedent and consequence conditions. This type of situation can occur frequently or infrequently and often is predictable. For example, we may find that Karrie consistently has "a bad day" every Thursday. Every Thursday, Karrie is tired, cranky, and often noncompliant across all periods and activities throughout the day. No problems are noted on the other days of the week. Interviews with Karrie and her family indicate that Karrie volunteers at a homeless shelter with her church every Wednesday evening. Visits to the homeless shelter are setting events that influence Karrie's behavior on Thursday.

In contrast, Salome's challenging behavior is not as easily predictable as Karrie's behavior. On some days she has a great day at school, and on other days, she is noncompliant and often cries when she is reprimanded. Interviews with Salome indicated that on the days she is noncompliant and cries easily, her brother who lives in a foster home has visited the night before or is scheduled to visit that evening. These visits are setting events that influence her behavior in school.

Considerable confusion and disagreement exist in the fields of applied behavior analysis and special education concerning the definitions and identification of antecedent events and setting events (and establishing operations, which are not discussed in this book). Investigators define these terms differently and provide different and contrasting examples of variables that are identified as setting events or as antecedents. Many investigators, including the authors, simply combine the two concepts (e.g., Repp, 1999) and discuss the context that occurs prior to or that co-occurs with behavior. We have separated the two concepts in this chapter to underscore the importance of identifying variables that are temporally related to behavior (antecedents and consequences) and to look beyond the immediate ABC sequence for variables that impact behavior under antecedent and consequence conditions (Wacker & Reichle, 1993). Some of the examples that we provide in this book combine setting events and antecedents and describe them as the context that occurs prior to or that co-occurs with behavior. Other examples identify setting events and antecedents separately.

In summary, during observations in the natural environment we should identify three categories of variables that influence behavior: (1) the antecedent variables that precede behavior or that co-occur with behavior, (2) the consequences that follow behavior, and (3) setting events that influence how the student responds to antecedents and consequences.

These are the variables that support challenging behavior and appropriate behavior.

Our experience indicates that although it is not commonly included as part of functional assessment observations, it is as important to observe sequences of appropriate behavior as it is to observe sequences of challenging behavior. We find that the environmental conditions that support challenging behavior are different from those that support appropriate behavior (Sulzer-Azaroff & Mayer, 1991). Information obtained from observations of appropriate behavior sequences will identify antecedents and consequences that may be incorporated into interventions to reduce challenging behavior and to increase appropriate replacement behaviors.

For instance, Russell looked out the window, doodled on his paper, and sharpened his pencil when given an assignment in Mr. Harrich's class. He did not do this when given an assignment in Ms. Ryland's class. In fact, in Ms. Ryland's class, Russell stayed on task and completed all assignments. Observation in both classes showed that Mr. Harrich usually gave multistep instructions to the entire class (e.g., everyone take out your workbooks, turn to Chapter 15, find the second worksheet, and do the first 10 problems). Ms. Ryland broke her instructions into smaller steps and she waited until the class had completed one instruction before giving another instruction. The antecedents (i.e., type of instruction) in these two situations were different. Identification of the antecedents that supported appropriate behavior led to interventions to alter Russell's behavior in Mr. Harrich's class. Mr. Harrich continued to provide multistep instructions to the entire class, but he also then provided smaller step instructional prompts to Russell.

To be most accurate in obtaining information about the supports for behavior, direct observation data should be obtained for each occurrence of behavior (i.e., anecdotal and event recording). However, many educators and other team members are not able to record this type of information *each* time the behavior occurs. The team could consider several observation alternatives if anecdotal/event recording is not feasible. First, the team may record observations only during those times of the day when the behavior is most likely to occur (e.g., during morning circle and at cleanup). Second, it might collect short, frequent samples of behavior across the day (e.g., time sampling at the end of 15-minute blocks). Third, team members might observe behavior for a relatively extended period each day but select different situations to observe each day (e.g., observe for 1 hour each day across different class periods). We also have worked with teams who have videotaped occurrences of behavior for later viewing and recording.

Another option, developed by Touchette, MacDonald, and Langer (1985), is to conduct a scatterplot analysis by collecting data on challenging behavior and environmental variables within 30-minute intervals across a 24-hour period. This information then can be used to identify when challenging behavior occurs throughout the day and the global environmental conditions that are correlated with challenging behavior such as time of day and type of activity (Lennox & Miltenberger, 1989). Although the scatterplot can provide useful information, Kahng et al. (1998) provide a discussion of pros and cons of relying solely on scatterplot analysis during the observation phase of assessment. They suggest that scatterplot analysis should not be the only form of data collection because it does not describe specific antecedents and consequences for individual behaviors. Scatterplot observations should be combined with direct ABC assessment.

No uniform rules exist for determining how much data must be collected or the conditions that must be sampled when collecting data. The duration of the observation phase may range from half-a-day to several weeks. Investigators generally recommend sampling behavior across a variety of situations and across several days or weeks. We also recommend sampling both challenging and appropriate behavior. Repp (1999) suggested that data collection may be terminated when conditional probabilities do not change over a few sessions.[1] In our experience this suggestion may be generalized to observations that are not based on conditional probabilities. In other words, initial data collection can be terminated when consistencies have been observed in setting events and antecedents (contextual variables) and/or consequences related to challenging behavior and appropriate behavior *and* the team is able to identify the relationship between setting events, antecedents, consequences, and behavior.

For example, the team working with Eric examined the data sheets at the end of the first week of observation.(See Table 4–7 for a summary ABC recording sheet.) They identified consistent antecedents, setting events, and consequences that were related to both challenging and appropriate behavior. They noted that Eric never brought his book to class or completed assigned homework when the subject was history (antecedent/setting event context). They also noted that Eric always brought his books to class and completed homework when the subjects were math and science. From the consequence side of the ABC recordings, they noted that when Eric was not prepared for history he was not allowed to participate in the history lesson: Eric's teacher either ignored Eric, told him he could not participate, or sent Eric to detention for the duration of the history period.

At this point the team stopped collecting pre-intervention data. Analysis of observational data allowed the team to formulate if–then statements

---

[1] Some investigators identify correlations or trends in data by conducting lag sequential analyses and developing conditional probabilities based on direct observation data (Repp, Felce, & Barton, 1988). This requires that data be collected sequentially in time using well-defined codes and data collection procedures. Unfortunately, this type of data collection and analysis is not always possible within school-based settings, without the assistance of research staff and computer-based observation equipment. For information on sequential lag analyses and conditional probabilities the reader is referred to chapters by Repp (1999) and Shores, Wehby, and Jack (1999). When this type of data collection and analysis is not possible, teams should at a minimum identify consistencies across direct observation data in the setting events, antecedents, and consequences that are related to challenging and appropriate behavior.

TABLE 4–7
Sample ABC *recording sheet for Eric*

Student: Eric Sewell   **Date:** 5/10–5/11   **Setting:** Regular Classroom,
Observer: Ivana Valdez   History, Math,
                                                                                              Science

Antecedents and Setting Events	Behavior	Consequence
History, group work	Not prepared	Reprimand, left alone
Math, group work	On task, prepared	Works with group
History, worksheets	Off task, homework incomplete	Ignored
History, group work	Not prepared	Told could not work with group
Science, lab	On task, prepared works with group	Praise
Science, worksheets	On task, homework complete	Praise
History, lecture	Off task	Ignored
History, turn in work	Homework incomplete	Given detention
Math, turn in work	Homework complete	Praise
Science, lab	On task, prepared	Allowed to work with group

regarding the contingencies or relationships between setting events, antecedents, behavior, and consequences (Sulzer-Azaroff & Mayer, 1991). When consistencies such as these are noted the team is ready to move to the next step in functional assessment—identification of the function of behavior.

SUMMARY

Observation and interviews are two tools that will help the team identify the supports for challenging behavior. Interviews should be conducted with those individuals who know the student well and who have observed both challenging and appropriate behavior (e.g., teachers, parents, and the student who engages in challenging behavior). During the interview phase, information also may be obtained by reviewing student records to identify strategies that have been previously employed, medical information, duration of challenging behavior, diagnosis, student strengths and needs, and so forth.

Observation should focus on the natural environments in which challenging behavior and appropriate behavior occur (e.g., home, classroom, gym). Observation should identify antecedents that occur prior to or that co-occur with challenging and appropriate behavior and consequences that follow behavior. Observation also should identify setting events that influence how a student responds to antecedents and consequences as well as student strengths and needs. The existence of setting events should be evaluated when (1) modification of antecedents and consequences does not alter challenging behavior, (2) challenging behavior is inconsistent across consistent antecedent and/or consequence conditions, and (3) challenging behavior occurs across a variety of antecedent and consequence conditions.

The information obtained from records reviews, interviews, and observations in the natural environment will pinpoint consistencies in setting events, antecedents, and consequences that are associated with challenging behavior. This information also will reveal consistencies in setting events, antecedents, and consequences that are related to appropriate behavior. The differences in the environmental situations that support challenging and appropriate behavior will help the team conduct the next step in functional assessment—identifying the function of behavior.

CHAPTER **5**

Identifying the Function of Challenging and Appropriate Behaviors

Students engage in challenging behavior because it produces a function. The second step in functional assessment is to identify which function is maintaining the student's challenging behavior. For example, Iwata and his colleagues (1982/1994) reported in a seminal study on functional assessment that they were able to identify three distinct functions of self-injurious behavior across subjects: automatic reinforcement, escape, and social disapproval (social attention) (see also Iwata, Pace, Dorsey et al., 1994).

We first identify the function of behavior by examining data obtained from direct observations and interview. When we are able to identify consistencies in setting events, antecedents, and/or consequences we generate statements about the variables that reliably trigger behavior and those that follow behavior. From this we formulate a hypothesis about the function of behavior (Carr, 1994; Carr, Robinson, & Palumbo, 1990; Kazdin, 2001; Repp, Karsh, Munk, & Dahlquist, 1995). This then guides the selection of intervention strategies. Intervention plans that are based on hypothesized functions that have been derived from an ABC assessment are more effective than intervention plans that are not based on hypothesized functions or that are based on other forms of assessment (Repp, Felce, & Barton, 1988).

	Student: Gloria Garcia	**Date:** 1/18–1/22	**Setting:** Regular Classroom,
TABLE 5–1 *Sample* **ABC** *recording sheet for* **Gloria**	**Observer:** Kerry Arient		Resource Room Library, Reading, Math, Science, Art

Antecedents and Setting Events	Behavior	Consequence
Independent reading	Talks to peers	Reprimand
Independent math quiz	Calls to teacher	Redirection
Group science project	On task, cooperative	Peer interaction
Library reading	Out of seat	Redirection
Class discussion	Answers question	Praise, feedback
Independent worksheets	Talks to peers	Loss of points
Small group work	On task	Peer interaction
1:1 work with teacher	On task	Teacher interaction
Independent reading	Off task	Reminder of task
Independent art project	Talks to peers	Redirection
Group discussion	Asks questions, answers questions	Answers questions, praise
Start homework	Calls to teacher	Teacher answers questions
Independent science project	Talks to peers, off task	Loss of points

An example of a completed ABC assessment form is presented in Table 5–1. This ABC recording form shows that Gloria's challenging behavior occurs repeatedly during independent seatwork and that when she engages in challenging behavior she usually receives some form of interaction from the teacher (e.g., redirection, reprimand, loss of points). We also note that Gloria does not engage in challenging behavior during small group activities or when the teacher is working individually with her. From this information we might conclude that the function of Gloria's behavior is positive reinforcement, that is, that she obtains teacher attention.

Table 5–2 provides a sample Antecedent–Behavior–Consequence recording form that can be used to collect observational data concerning challenging and appropriate behavior and the environmental and contextual variables related to behavior. This is followed by a set of questions and instructions to assist the team in identifying the function of behavior and developing positive intervention plans.

We find it helpful to consider three categories of functions when making hypotheses concerning challenging behavior. As mentioned in an earlier chapter, these three functions are positive reinforcement, negative reinforcement, and sensory regulation/sensory stimulation (Carr, 1977, 1994;

TABLE 5–2
Sample naturalistic function assessment observation form

Student _____ Setting _____

Observer _____

Date/Time	Setting Events	Antecedents	Behavior	Consequences

Identify the Function and Develop Interventions

1. Define the challenging behavior.

2. Are there consistent antecedents and setting events that precede or co-occur with challenging behavior?

3. Are there consistent consequences that follow challenging behavior?

4. Are there consistent antecedents and setting events that precede or co-occur with appropriate behavior?

5. Are there consistent consequences that follow appropriate behavior?

6. Identify the function of challenging behavior. Provide a rationale for the function you selected and why you eliminated the other functions.

7. Identify student strengths.

8. Identify reinforcers for the student.

9. Describe appropriate replacement behavior that will achieve the same function (i.e., what should the student do instead of challenging behavior?).

10. Describe a positive intervention plan to support appropriate replacement behavior and to withdraw support for challenging behavior.
    - Describe how antecedents and setting events will be changed and how consequences will be changed.
    - Describe when and where the intervention will be implemented and which staff will implement the program.
    - Describe how data will be collected to evaluate progress.

© 2002 Chandler and Dahlquist.

BOX 5–1
Schema of the functional assessment process

Setting Events	Antecedents
Physiological/biological	Activity/task variables
Physical/environmental	Staff/peers behavior
Social/situational	Structure/pace

Appropriate and Challenging Behavior

Sharing	On task	Running	Hitting	Peer interaction
Biting	Daydreaming	Asking questions		Spitting
Refusals	Rocking	Swearing	Yelling	Off task

Consequences

Feedback	Reprimand	Peers laugh	Increased movement
Praise	Hug	Tokens	Detention	Free time
Physical guidance	Assistance	Ignoring	

Function of Behavior

Positive Reinforcement	Negative Reinforcement	Sensory Regulation/ Sensory Stimulation

Obtain Something Positive	Escape/Avoid Something Aversive	Change Level of Stimulation
Attention, control, edibles, materials, task	Activity or task, location, materials, attention	Increase/decrease movement, tactile, visual, auditory, olfactory, gustatory

© 2002 Chandler and Dahlquist.

Chandler, Dahlquist, Repp, & Feltz, 1999; Iwata et al., 1982/1994; Repp, 1999; Repp et al., 1995). Box 5–1 provides a schema that illustrates the functional assessment process, starting with the context that occurs prior to behavior or that co-occurs with behavior and the consequences that follow behavior. From this information the function of behavior is hypothesized.

OBTAINS SOMETHING POSITIVE (POSITIVE REINFORCEMENT)

When the function of behavior is positive reinforcement, the student obtains something positive by engaging in certain behavior. In positive reinforcement an event or variable that is desired or positive for the student is added to the

Jennifer is impressed that throwing her book gets so much teacher attention.

Positive Reinforcement Function

situation following the student's behavior. Social attention from peers and access to desired tangible objects are two of the most common forms of reinforcement within the positive reinforcement function (Derby et al., 1992; Hanley, Piazza, & Fisher, 1997; Iwata, Pace, Dorsey, et al., 1994). Other forms of positive reinforcement might include control of an activity, access to preferred peers, preferred seating arrangements or locations, opportunities to respond, favored tasks or activities, access to food or drink, stickers, points, and tokens (Carr & McDowell, 1980; Derby et al., 1992; Iwata et al., 1982/1994).

Positive reinforcement increases the behavior that results in obtaining something positive. If *appropriate* behavior results in something positive, then that behavior will continue to occur within the same setting event, antecedent, and consequence conditions. If *challenging* behavior results in obtaining something positive, then that behavior will continue to occur within the same setting event, antecedent, and consequence conditions. Unfortunately, for many students challenging behavior is more effective at producing a positive outcome than appropriate behavior. It often is easier for students to obtain teacher attention by shouting or tantrumming than it is by sitting quietly and working on a task. Students learn to do the behaviors that produce positive outcomes.

As mentioned in previous chapters, we need to remember to consider the student's perspective of what constitutes a positive outcome. This is especially true when the function of behavior is to obtain attention or interaction. Many students do not discriminate between negative and positive attention. Disapproving comments from peers and positive comments from peers are both reinforcing for some students. Likewise, for many students reprimands and praise from adults both function as positive outcomes. When a student continues to display behavior that results in forms of attention or interaction that are aversive for most individuals (e.g., reprimand, teasing), we should consider the possibility that they actually are functioning as positive outcomes for that student and that the function of the student's behavior is positive reinforcement.

AVOIDS/ESCAPES SOMETHING AVERSIVE (NEGATIVE REINFORCEMENT)

When the function of behavior is negative reinforcement, students engage in behavior that results in escape or avoidance of an aversive event or stimulus. In negative reinforcement an event or stimulus is removed or terminated (escape) or not presented (avoidance) following the student's behavior. Students may avoid or escape tasks, activities, interaction with or attention from adults or peers, locations, seating arrangements, materials, participation, food or drink, loss of points or tokens, and poor grades (Carr & Durand, 1985; Carr & Newsom, 1985; Munk & Repp, 1994a, 1994b; Pace, Ivancic, & Jefferson, 1994). Just like positive reinforcement, negative reinforcement increases the behavior that results in escape or avoidance (Skinner, 1974). Both challenging behaviors and appropriate behaviors that allow the student to escape or avoid something aversive will continue to occur within the same setting event, antecedent, and consequence conditions. Students will engage in the types of behaviors (appropriate or challenging) that are most effective in producing escape or avoidance.

We also must consider the student's perspective when identifying antecedent and consequent events or stimuli as aversive. For example, many students escape from activities and tasks by engaging in behavior that results in time-out or suspension. Although time-out is considered a punishment procedure, it is not functioning as a punishing consequence if the antecedent task that the student escapes is more aversive to the student than time-out. The student will continue to engage in challenging behavior when given aversive tasks because time-out results in escape from the task (Nelson & Rutherford, 1983).

Time-out is just one example of a consequence that we often assume will be aversive or punishing, but that for many students is actually a desired outcome because it results in escape or avoidance of an aversive activity or task. Consider another example. We have worked with several students who are frequently involved in negative teacher/student interactions that escalate in intensity across time and episodes. For example, Wilbur often used profanity in class. When he did this Ms. Bryan, his teacher, told Wilbur to stop swearing. Wilbur would swear again and Ms. Bryan would remind him that swearing was not allowed in her classroom. Wilbur would swear again and tell Ms. Bryan that he could do what he wanted. Wilbur and Ms. Bryan would continue to argue until both were shouting. Their argument usually ended with the school bell signaling a change in periods (Wilbur moved to the next class). For many students this interaction would be aversive and punishing. For Wilbur, however, it was not. He initiated an argumentative interaction each time the class was instructed to complete a study guide. Wilbur had learned that he could argue with the teacher instead of completing his study guide. Negative interactions with the teacher resulted in escape from an aversive activity.

When the function of behavior is negative reinforcement observation of Antecedent–Behavior–Consequence sequences will indicate consistent aversive events such as a difficult activity, failure in a task, and negative peer interaction. The consequences that follow behavior will temporarily delay or terminate those aversive conditions. For example, a difficult activity or instructions may be withdrawn, the student may be removed from a disliked activity (e.g., the student is sent to time-out), teasing peers may walk away, or assistance may make a confusing task understandable. Thus, negative reinforcement strengthens behavior because the behavior effectively terminates an ongoing or probable aversive antecedent condition.

SENSORY REGULATION/SENSORY STIMULATION

In our model, when the function of behavior is sensory regulation/sensory stimulation, students obtain an increase or decrease in sensory stimulation (Repp & Karsh, 1990). Within this function behavior serves to either maintain (regulate) sensory input at an optimal level or to produce sensory input that is automatically reinforcing (Ellingson et al., 2000; Iwata et al., 1982/1994; Repp, 1999; Shore & Iwata, 1999). Many students employ appropriate behaviors that increase or decrease stimulation such as shaking a leg, doodling, or moving to a quiet area in the classroom. Unfortunately, the behaviors that some students employ in response to sensory input or to produce or reduce sensory stimulation are identified as challenging. For example, students may run to increase gross motor movement, hit themselves and touch others inappropriately in order to increase tactile stimulation, or they may talk out and hum to increase auditory stimulation during quiet activities. They also may shout and scream in order to shut out (decrease) classroom noise, refuse to participate in highly stimulating activities, or cover their eyes and ears in order to reduce auditory and visual stimulation.

Students engage in behavior to change the level of stimulation when there is a mismatch between the level and type of sensory stimulation available in the environment and the level and type of stimulation needed or required by the student (Berkson & Tupa, 2000; Chandler et al., 1999; Guess & Carr, 1991; Munk & Karsh, 1999; Repp, 1999). A mismatch may occur for a variety of reasons. Some students may have a biological need for higher levels of sensory stimulation than do other students. Their optimal level of stimulation is not met within a typical classroom environment. This often occurs for students who have attention deficit hyperactivity disorder. They may need greater levels of fine and gross motor movement or increased levels of auditory and tactile stimulation than other students (Friend & Bursuck, 1999). Other students, such as those with chronic fatigue syndrome, autism, and sensory integrative disorder, may require lower levels of stimulation and will engage in behavior to decrease sensory stimuli or they may have difficulty transitioning to high-level activities (Colby Trott, Laurel, & Windeck, 1993).

Some students who fit the sensory regulation/sensory stimulation function may do so because they experience difficulties in regulating levels of arousal. For example, during free play Randy, who was diagnosed with ADHD, selected only very active play activities such as the jungle gym, rocking boat, large blocks, and sociodramatic play. He seldom selected passive activities such as art and puzzles. As free play progressed, Randy's level of arousal increased. By the end of free play Randy was overstimulated. As a result, he was not able to follow instructions to cleanup; instead he shouted to peers and ran and hopped throughout the classroom. Randy was not able to calm down or relax for the next activity (reading books) because he was not able to regulate his level of stimulation once he became overstimulated.

The sensory regulation/sensory stimulation function also includes students who may exhibit atypical reactions to typical levels and types of sensory stimulation. This may occur for students who have sensory integrative disorders and do not process or interpret sensory stimulation correctly. They may respond aggressively to or recoil from touch, noise, or movement. For instance, Michael refused to walk on uneven or soft surfaces such as playgrounds with tanbark, sand, grass, or rock floors. He also insisted on walking close to walls and trailing his hand along the walls as he walked. He tantrummed and became very aggressive if his teachers or parents tried to force him to walk on uneven or soft surfaces or to walk in the middle of the classroom or hallway.

Finally, students with sensory integration difficulties and students with sensory deficits (e.g., students who are blind or hearing impaired) also may display challenging behavior in response to the levels of sensory stimuli available in school settings (e.g., light, noise, touch). For example, students who are blind or hearing impaired may respond negatively to normal levels or types of lighting or sound within a classroom or they may engage in behavior to produce sensory stimulation such as eye gouging, vocalizing, or head swinging (Berkson & Tupa, 2000; Favell, McGimsey, & Schell, 1982; Iwata et al., 1982/1994; Rincover & Devaney, 1982).

The sensory regulation/sensory stimulation function is not only a disability-based function. Students without disabilities also may have varying levels of tolerance for stimulation and need for sensory stimulation. Think about people you know or students in your programs. Do you work with students or have friends or family members who seem to have more energy than everyone else or who need very little sleep? Do you know anyone who never seems to sit still? Is he or she always moving—shaking a leg, tapping fingers, twirling hair or mustache, and so forth? These individuals need more stimulation than most, and they usually find relatively appropriate ways to increase their level of stimulation.

In school settings students who fit the sensory regulation/sensory stimulation categories of this function usually are referred for functional assessment more often than students who fit the neurological outcomes category (see Chapter 3). When challenging behavior is a function of neurochemical imbalances and neurodevelopmental dysfunction, physicians often prescribe medication in order to regulate behavior. The instructional strategies team also may develop interventions if needed to increase appropriate behavior. However, for these students, a comprehensive functional assessment itself *may* not be necessary. In many of these cases, the identification of the function of behavior is not needed because the student's challenging behavior is decreased via medication. The goal of intervention for these students is not to decrease challenging behavior by replacing it with appropriate behavior that achieves the same function. Rather, the goal of intervention is to teach appropriate behaviors. This can be done without conducting functional assessment. As a result, we will not focus on the neurological category of the sensory regulation/sensory stimulation function. Readers who are interested in the neurological outcomes category of the sensory regulation/sensory stimulation function are referred to Lewis, Baumeister, and Mailman (1987) and Mace and Mauk (1999).

IDENTIFYING AND VERIFYING THE FUNCTION OF BEHAVIOR

The three functions of behavior that are examined in our functional assessment model are positive reinforcement, negative reinforcement, and sensory regulation/sensory stimulation. When we identify the function of behavior we should do so on the basis of Antecedent–Behavior–Consequence sequences. A common mistake made by many teams is that they identify the function of behavior based on the topography of the student's behavior (Berkson & Tupa, 2000; McEvoy & Reichle, 2000; McMahon, Lambros, & Sylva, 1998). For instance a team may assume that the function of behavior for a student who yells "I hate this" and throws materials is to escape an activity or that the function for a student who runs in the classroom or hits herself is increased sensory stimulation. Yet each of these behaviors could function to obtain attention from teachers or peers. The key to identifying the function is to look at the relationship between behavior and the setting events, antecedents, and consequences that are related to it. For example, if the student who yells "I hate this" and throws materials only does this when the teacher is at his desk grading papers and the consequence for the behavior consistently is that the teacher stops grading papers and reprimands the student for his challenging behavior, then we would hypothesize that the function was positive reinforcement. If however, the student consistently displayed the challenging behavior when he was asked to do a particular activity such as write an essay and the consequence was being sent to the principal's office, then we would assume that the function was negative reinforcement.

Educators often ask if one behavior can be controlled by two functions. The answer to this question is yes and no. A student may engage in the same behavior (e.g., out of seat) that achieves different functions (e.g., sensory regulation/sensory stimulation and negative reinforcement) (Carr, Levin, McConnachie, Carlson, Kemp, & Smith, 1994; Day, Horner, & O'Neill, 1994; Horner, 1994; Iwata, Pace, et al., 1990; Romanczyk, 1997). However, when this occurs, the situations in which the behavior typically occurs are different (Derby et al., 2000). For example, Celeste often screams and throws materials when she is given an astronomy worksheet to complete. This behavior results in cessation of demands. The function of her behavior in these conditions is negative reinforcement—she escapes astronomy worksheets. However, Celeste also screams and throws materials when she is not allowed to be the leader of her group. This usually results in the rest of her group allowing her to be the leader. The function of her behavior in these conditions is positive reinforcement—she obtains control of the group. In most cases, when the same behavior achieves two functions, the functions will not be occurring simultaneously and the conditions that result in the challenging behavior will be different across the two functions. Interventions to address a challenging behavior that serves two distinct functions should address each function. For example, Derby, et al. (1994) found that an intervention to reduce challenging behavior that produced escape did not affect the same challenging behavior when that behavior produced access to preferred objects. Separate interventions were needed for each function.

In addition to an individual student, such as Celeste, employing the same behavior to achieve two different functions, different students may employ the same behavior to achieve different functions. For example, fighting may result in negative reinforcement for one student (e.g., the disliked student leaves), but it results in positive reinforcement (e.g., obtains peer attention or control of a situation) for a different student. This illustrates the importance of not basing intervention on the topography of the challenging behavior, but rather to base intervention on the function of the behavior for each student and situation. The interventions to address the different functions will be different even though the topography of the challenging behavior is the same for both students (Carr et al., 1994; Derby et al., 2000).

Students also may use multiple forms of behavior to achieve the same function (Horner, 1994; Iwata, Vollmer, & Zarcone, 1990). For example, hitting, spitting, and kicking each may result in negative reinforcement (e.g., escapes working with disliked peers). These behaviors may be thought of as a response class, as a group of behaviors that result in a desired function (Carr, 1988; Johnson & Pennypacker, 1980; Parrish, Cataldo, Kolko, Neef, & Egel, 1986; Sprague & Horner, 1999). Intervention may be directed to all challenging behaviors within the response class (Sprague & Horner, 1992).

In some circumstances, a secondary function is achieved as well as a primary function (Golonka, Wacker, Berg, Derby, Harding, & Peck, 2000; Mace, Shapiro,

& Mace, 1998). For example, when Willy is asked to perform nonpreferred, difficult tasks he responds by destroying task materials. When he does this, the teacher tells him that he has lost the points for that activity and leaves him alone to do an activity of his choice. The primary function of Willy's behavior is negative reinforcement. He escapes nonpreferred, difficult tasks. However, Willy also receives positive reinforcement by being allowed to select a preferred activity following his challenging behavior. For Willy, two functions are operating; however, negative reinforcement is the primary function with positive reinforcement serving a secondary and noncritical function. We know this because when Willy is left alone with no option to do alternative activity, he sits quietly in his seat. He does not actively seek a preferred activity. Thus while positive reinforcement is a secondary function, it is not the critical function supporting Willy's challenging behavior. For many students, when a behavior seems to be a result of more than one function, you should strive to identify the primary function and to then address that function during intervention.

However, for some students it may be important to address both functions. Golonka and his colleagues (2000) reported that students' escape-maintained challenging behavior was greater if they escaped disliked activities and obtained access to preferred activities than it was when they escaped disliked activities alone (i.e., they did not have access to preferred activities—they escaped to an alone condition). For these individuals, the addition of choice of preferred activities during escape increased the probability of escape-maintained behavior. Thus both functions (positive and negative reinforcement) were important in supporting challenging behavior. Similar results also were reported by Keeney, Fisher, Adelinis, and Wilder (2000). These authors found high levels of challenging behavior in conditions in which challenging behavior resulted in escape plus access to music. Lower levels of challenging behavior occurred when escape only was allowed. These studies indicate that even though there may be a primary function, the secondary function may also support challenging behavior. For some students, the primary and secondary functions of behavior may be addressed during intervention.

We find it helpful when we identify the function of behavior to provide a rationale for selecting the function that is selected and to describe why the two remaining functions were not selected. For instance, if the team selected the sensory regulation/sensory stimulation function, team members should be able to identify why they selected that particular function and why they believe the function is not positive reinforcement or negative reinforcement. This is not always an easy task but it is very important because the interventions will be different for different functions. Three examples of identifying the function and ruling out alternative functions will illustrate this point. The first two examples are based on the first author's experiences as a behavior analyst in state institutions.

Gina was a 35-year-old woman who had been a resident of a state hospital since age 5. The staff referred her case to the first author, the staff behavior analyst, citing that she frequently cut her wrists and arms. Observations supported the staff's concerns. Gina did cut her wrists and arms frequently, ranging from a low frequency of one to three times per week to a high of several times per day. Observation further indicated that every time she cut herself Gina calmly walked to the office and showed her cuts to the staff. The team (the behavior analyst and the staff) hypothesized that the function of Gina's self-abuse was positive reinforcement: She obtained staff attention as a result of her self-abuse. We hypothesized the positive reinforcement function because Gina cut herself when staff were attending to other residents or when staff were by themselves in the break room (antecedents). When Gina showed her wound to the staff, they scolded her and bandaged her cut (consequences). Further, Gina did not cut herself during antecedent conditions in which she was receiving ongoing staff attention.

We knew that the function of Gina's behavior was not sensory stimulation because Gina cut herself in a variety of sensory circumstances including active and stimulating tasks and passive tasks. A specific level of stimulation in the environment was not correlated with her behavior. In fact, the only consistent antecedent was no attention from staff or staff attention directed to other residents. In addition, we hypothesized that if the self-injurious behavior itself was automatically or self-reinforcing, then Gina would not consistently seek out staff immediately after cutting herself.

The team decided that the function of Gina's behavior was not negative reinforcement because she did not escape specific activities, tasks, peers, and so on, when she cut herself. Gina cut herself during leisure time, mealtime, outdoor recreation activities, school activities, and self-care activities. The residents who were present when she cut herself also varied as did the materials available and the locations. The only consistent antecedent was lack of staff attention and staff attention directed to other residents. Gina's behavior produced staff attention and was maintained by positive reinforcement.

Intervention for Gina's behavior was based on the positive reinforcement function. The team arranged for Gina to receive more frequent antecedent attention from staff through instruction, social and other interaction when she was not cutting herself. We also altered the consequence when she did cut herself. The staff continued to provide first aid but they did not scold Gina and did not talk to her while bandaging her cut.

Antecedents and Setting Events	Behavior	Consequence	Function
No attention	Cuts self	Staff provide first-aid, reprimand	Positive Reinforcement: obtains staff attention
Instruction, frequent social interaction	Participates	Praise	Positive Reinforcement: obtains staff attention

Sam will serve as another example of ruling out alternative functions. Sam often mouthed his hand. The team and his parents were concerned about this behavior because he had large blisters on his hands that often became infected. Further, we (the preschool teacher, staff, and parents) could not put medication on his hand because he essentially ate the medication when he put his hand in his mouth. We hypothesized that the function of hand mouthing was increased sensory stimulation. We selected the sensory regulation/sensory stimulation function because observations indicated that Sam only engaged in this behavior when he did not have a fine motor task to do. He did not mouth his hand if he had a fine motor task to do such as putting pegs in a board or squeezing a koosh ball. The function of his behavior was to increase tactile stimulation.

We hypothesized that the function of Sam's behavior was not positive reinforcement because he did not gain access to adults, peers, materials, activities, or so on, as a result of his behavior. His behavior remained the same when he was alone and when teachers attended to him by providing reprimands. There were no consistent consequences for his behavior other than tactile stimulation. Sam's behavior was not mediated by social reinforcement. We also decided that the function was not negative reinforcement because Sam did not escape identifiable aversive antecedent events. The only consistent antecedent was lack of a fine motor task. Hand mouthing resulted in increased sensory stimulation in an insufficiently stimulating environment.

Interventions to address his behavior were based on the sensory regulation/sensory stimulation function. We arranged for Sam to have consistent access to fine motor tasks and taught him a variety of hand movement activities that could be conducted in the absence of tasks such as rapidly tapping his fingers. We also provided him with a small koosh ball that could be easily carried across activities.

Antecedents and Setting Events	Behavior	Consequence	Function
No task	Mouth hand	Tactile stimulation	Sensory Regulation/ Sensory Stimulation: increase stimulation
Fine motor tasks, hand movements, koosh ball	Does task	Tactile stimulation	Sensory Regulation/ Sensory Stimulation: increase stimulation

Finally, when Jack was called on to read aloud in class he refused by saying "No" or shaking his head no. If his teacher, Ms. Hanaike, continued to request that he read aloud he threw his book at a peer. When he did this Ms. Hanaike told Jack that he had lost his opportunity to take a turn reading and moved onto the next student. At this point Jack sat quietly in his seat. The team hypothesized that the function of Jack's behavior was negative reinforcement because when he threw his book after being instructed to read in class (antecedent), he lost the opportunity to read in class and the teacher stopped telling him to read (consequence). His behavior terminated requests to read aloud in class (antecedent).

The team decided that Jack's behavior was not a function of positive reinforcement because if he had been seeking teacher or peer attention or other positive outcomes such as access to materials or locations, he would have continued to misbehave when the teacher moved on to another student. Once the aversive antecedent was removed, his challenging behavior ceased. His behavior also was not a function of sensory regulation/sensory stimulation because he only engaged in this behavior during reading when he was requested to read aloud. If Jack had needed an increase in sensory stimulation he would not have sat quietly after the reading requests were terminated. We also knew that he did not need a reduction in stimulation because he readily participated in very active tasks throughout the school day.

Interventions to address Jack's behavior were based on the negative reinforcement function. Prior to developing intervention strategies the team identified what was aversive about reading aloud from Jack's perspective. Through interviews and observations of Jack reading aloud to his teacher, the team learned that Jack was a very poor reader. He read very slowly and often mispronounced words. In the past when he had read aloud in class his peers had laughed and called him stupid. Intervention consisted of informing Jack the night before what passage he would be asked to read aloud and only asking him to read a short passage. Jack was able to practice his passage with his parents or teacher prior to reading in class. In addition, the teacher praised Jack for participating in class.

Antecedents and Setting Events	Behavior	Consequence	Function
Asked to read aloud	Refusal, throws book	Loses turn, ask another student to read	Negative Reinforcement: escapes reading
Short passage given night before, asked to read aloud	Reads aloud	Praise	Positive Reinforcement: obtains praise and success in reading

Interview, observation, and analysis of the Setting Event–Antecedent–Behavior–Consequence sequences guides the development of hypotheses regarding the function of challenging and appropriate behavior. However, we must point out that analysis of observational data does not actually verify the function of behavior. Verification can only be conducted by manipulating setting events, antecedents, and/or consequences and noting subsequent changes in behavior (Bijou, Peterson, & Ault, 1968; Lennox & Miltenberger, 1989; Mace, 1994). For example, we may withhold the consequence for a behavior, alter the antecedents, or introduce new antecedents and examine the change in behavior during these manipulations. Interviews and direct observations in the natural environment (e.g., classrooms) have been termed functional assessment, naturalistic functional assessment, and structural analysis (Peck, Sasso, & Stambaugh, 1998; Repp 1999). Experimental manipulation of variables to verify a hypothesis is termed functional analysis (Horner, 1994; Kazdin, 2001).[1]

Sometimes you will be able to conduct brief functional analyses in school settings prior to implementing intervention (Kazdin, 2001). For example, we might ask the teacher to stop attending to challenging behavior and to identify whether this altered consequence results in an increase or decrease in challenging behavior. Or we might ask the teacher to give each step in multistep instructions individually and identify whether this altered antecedent strategy changes behavior. At other times, however, it may not be possible or desirable to conduct functional analysis within school settings. For instance, it may be important to move to intervention as soon as possible, the classroom teacher may not allow the team to manipulate variables prior to intervention, or the manipulation of variables and the subsequent change in behavior may pose risks to the student or others in the environment.

The need to conduct functional analysis versus functional assessment and the utility and feasibility of conducting functional analysis in school-based setting is debated in the fields of special education and behavior analysis. Dunlap and Kern (1993) suggest that under most conditions within natural settings, good functional assessment is sufficient. They recommend conducting functional analysis if the team is not able to identify the function from observations, is unsure of the function of challenging behavior, or if it is necessary to firmly establish the function as might be required in research studies or legal proceedings.

---

[1] We are referring to functional analysis as the manipulation of variables within the natural setting. This does not include analogue functional assessment and subsequent analysis in which each function is briefly tested in a clinical or experimental environment (i.e., not the natural environment). Analogue functional analysis is not included in our model because observations are not conducted in the natural settings in which the challenging behavior occurs. As a result, investigators may not examine or consider variables in the natural environment that may control appropriate and challenging behavior, such as peers, teacher reactions, and so on (Kazdin, 2001; Repp et al., 1995). For this reason, the results of analogue functional analysis may not generalize outside the analogue setting (i.e., to the natural environment) (Carr, 1994; Halle & Spradlin, 1993; Mace, 1994). Nonetheless, many investigators conduct functional analysis using analogue assessment because it is a relatively quick method of assessment and it provides useful information when observations in the natural environment are not possible. (To learn more about analogue analysis see Iwata et al., 1982/1994; Iwata, Vollmer, et al., 1990; Repp & Munk, 1999; Sasso, et al., 1992; Shores, Wehby, & Jack, 1999; Wacker, Steege, Northrup, Reimers, et al., 1990; Wacker, Steege, Northrup, Sasso, et al., 1990.)

Our experience has been that when feasible (and this is determined by the team) functional analysis should be conducted in the classroom or other natural environments. This is especially true if the team needs to rule out competing hypotheses (e.g., the team is not sure if the function is escape or sensory regulation/sensory stimulation) or needs to provide information to be used in due process or court proceedings. However, if it is not feasible to conduct functional analysis, then functional assessment certainly is appropriate. We have found that sometimes observation across a variety of situations and observation of appropriate behavior as well as challenging behavior will provide the same type of information that would have been obtained if a functional analysis had been conducted. For example, two teams receive a referral for Xavier who often is out of his seat, runs in the classroom, shouts, and talks to peers at inappropriate times. Team 1 conducts functional analysis by manipulating levels of sensory stimulation (high versus low stimulation) in the environment and examining the corresponding change in behavior during each type of condition. Alternatively, team 2 conducts functional assessment by examining behavior under naturally occurring levels of sensory stimulation in the classroom and noting the different types of behavior that occur during each type of condition. Both teams identified a correlation between challenging behavior and highly stimulating activities and both teams developed interventions to reduce sensory stimulation for the student.

Regardless of the process employed to identify the function of behavior, if intervention does not quickly produce some change in behavior, then the team may have identified the wrong function and should return to the observation phase of functional assessment. The ultimate test of the validity or success of functional assessment is the effectiveness of the interventions derived from that assessment (Carr, 1994; Kazdin, 2001; Mace, 1994).

SUMMARY

The second step in functional assessment is to identify the function of challenging behavior and appropriate behavior. The three functions of behavior that should be considered are positive reinforcement, negative reinforcement, and sensory regulation/sensory stimulation. In positive reinforcement the student obtains something that he or she desires or prefers. In this function a positive event or variable is added to the situation following either challenging or appropriate behavior. In negative reinforcement the student escapes or avoids something that is aversive for the student. In this function an aversive or nonpreferred variable is removed or terminated following either challenging or appropriate behavior. In the sensory regulation/sensory stimulation function the student's behavior alters the amount and type of stimulation in the environment or it produces sensory feedback that is automatically reinforcing. In this function, sensory stimulation either increases or decreases as a result of the student's appropriate or challenging behavior.

Identification of the function of behavior follows examination of data obtained through observation, interview, and records review. Verification of the function of behavior can only be conducted through functional analysis: the experimental manipulation of antecedents and consequences. If functional analysis is not feasible, teams should conduct a comparative assessment of different naturally occurring conditions within the classroom or other natural settings. The comparative assessment will identify differences between setting events, antecedents, and consequences that trigger and support challenging behavior and those that trigger and support appropriate behaviors. This type of comparative assessment will lend support to the hypothesized function or it may cause the team to change their hypothesis regarding the function of challenging behavior. In addition to comparative assessment, the team can further support their hypothesis by describing why the particular function was selected and why the remaining functions were not selected.

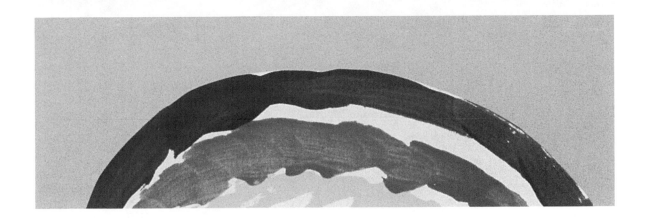

Part Three

Selecting and Implementing Function-Based Interventions

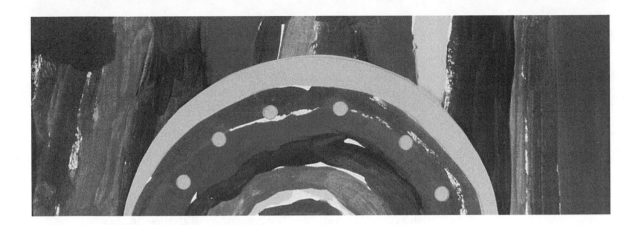

CHAPTER

Selecting Setting Event, Antecedent, and Consequence Strategies and Appropriate Replacement Behaviors

After identifying the function of behavior, the team is ready to develop intervention strategies. The team must consider each component of the ABC sequence (setting events, antecedents, behavior, and consequences) when developing an intervention plan. The team should decide if each component in the behavior sequence will be addressed as part of the intervention plan and, if so, how each component will be arranged.

For example, Vinnie grabs snack and lunch food from other students when his food is gone. Students usually do not protest when he does this because protests lead to aggression from Vinnie. The function of Vinnie's behavior is positive reinforcement; he obtains food. The team could develop an intervention plan that addresses only the setting events or antecedent variables that occur before Vinnie grabs food. For instance, they may provide Vinnie with extra food so that he does not run out of food and does not need to take food from peers. Alternatively, they may develop an intervention plan that addresses only the consequence side of the sequence. They may praise Vinnie and give him food if he asks for more food and put Vinnie in time-out when he takes food from peers. Finally, the team may develop a comprehensive intervention that addresses each component of the behavior sequence (Horner, 1994). In a comprehensive plan they may provide Vinnie with food prior to lunch or snack so that he is not as hungry as he typically is (setting event). Then, they may prompt Vinnie to ask for food when his food is gone (antecedent) and they might give him extra food after he requests more food (consequence). Each of these intervention strategies, if used individually, may reduce Vinnie's challenging behavior. However, we might expect the comprehensive plan to be most effective because it addresses each component in the behavior sequence (Horner, 1994). The comprehensive intervention plan supports appropriate replacement behavior by altering consequences for appropriate behavior. The comprehensive plan also addresses the prevention of challenging behavior by manipulating antecedents and setting events.

Even though comprehensive intervention plans may be most effective, it may not always be feasible to address each component of the behavior sequence. The intervention plans that teams develop should be based on staff resources, the time and effort involved in addressing each component, and the goals for the student. Strategies to alter or introduce setting events, antecedent events, and consequences are presented in the following sections.

SETTING EVENT AND ANTECEDENT-BASED INTERVENTION STRATEGIES

The goal of setting event and antecedent-based strategies is to prevent challenging behavior from occurring (or developing) by altering or withdrawing variables that currently trigger challenging behavior and by introducing variables that will trigger or set the stage for appropriate behavior (Carr, Reeve, & Magito-McLaughlin, 1996; Kennedy & Itkonen, 1993; Polloway & Patton, 1993; Rhode, Jenson, & Reavis, 1992). Intervention plans may address setting events and antecedents that are currently operating in the environment (i.e., those that are identified during interviews and observations) or they may introduce new setting events and antecedents to the environment.

Antecedents may be introduced as part of the intervention plan as indicated by the following examples. For instance, written rules may be posted on the classroom wall or on the student's desk. Outlines may be provided for difficult or new tasks. Social stories may be reviewed prior to activities in which challenging behavior typically occurs (Gray, 1994; Gray & Garland, 1993). Finally, students may be informed of the positive consequences that are available following completion of a task (antecedent) (e.g., "After you have finished your worksheet, you may move to the reading table and look at comic books or magazines").

Setting events also may be introduced as part of the intervention plan. For example, breakfast may be provided at school, quiet corners that provide low levels of calming sensory stimuli may be developed in the classroom, and small group activities may be introduced and alternated with large group activities, lecture, and independent work.

Existing setting events and antecedents may be altered and withdrawn (e.g., Horner, Day, Sprague, O'Brien, & Heathfield, 1991; Kennedy, 1994; Pace, Iwata, Cowdery, Andree, & McIntyre, 1993). For example, in an earlier chapter we learned about Russell, who had auditory processing problems and found it difficult to follow multistep instructions (antecedent). For Russell, antecedent instructions were altered by breaking them into small instructional steps. Instructions also might have been altered by using a different stimulus mode (e.g., written versus oral). In another example, teasing by Alex (antecedent), which preceded Becky's aggressive behavior, stopped when Alex was seated in a new location (away from Becky). In this example the antecedent trigger for Becky's aggression was withdrawn. Some examples of altering or withdrawing existing setting events include reducing the noise level in the classroom, removing distracting stimuli, alternating active and passive activities, and working with a student's family to ensure that the student gets sufficient sleep and a nutritious breakfast.

Some setting events, such as divorce, illness, and medication effects, cannot be altered. When we cannot alter setting events we may be able to instead reduce the negative impact of setting events on the student's behavior. We may do this by (1) changing our interactions with the student, (2) altering our expectations for the student, or (3) altering other variables in the school environment (Horner, Vaugn, Day, & Ard, 1996). For example, for a student who responds negatively to changes in classroom schedules and routines, we may provide frequent reminders and picture cues that there will be a change in the school schedule (setting event) such as a field trip. In another example, we may talk briefly with the student who visited her terminally ill mother in the hospital (setting event) if we see that she is upset when she enters the classroom, or we may allow the student to talk with a social worker about her visitation experience before expecting her to participate in classroom activities and routines. These examples do not change the presence of setting events, nor the fact that the setting events are operating. But they do neutralize or reduce the negative impact of the setting events on the student's behavior.

CONSEQUENCE-BASED INTERVENTION STRATEGIES

The goal of consequence-based intervention strategies is to provide support for appropriate behavior and to withdraw or alter current supports for challenging behavior. Interventions that address the consequence side of the ABC sequence may do so by altering or withdrawing consequences that are operating in the current environment or by introducing new consequences. This can be done by these means:

1. Alter the intensity, duration, frequency, or mode of consequences currently provided in the setting. For example, we may stop using high fives with a student who does not like to be touched and instead verbally praise

the student's appropriate behavior. Or we may whisper praise to a student who is easily overstimulated.

2. Withhold current desired consequences that support challenging behavior (a procedure identified as extinction). For instance, we stop attending to a student who shouts questions and answers in class. Or we no longer remove an aversive activity after the student rips his paper.

3. Introduce new consequences that will support appropriate behavior. For example, we develop a contract with a student in which he receives 15 minutes of free time for each day that he turns in his homework on time. Or we praise a student each time she initiates with peers.

4. Apply the consequences that currently support challenging behavior to different behaviors (i.e., consequences now follow appropriate replacement behaviors). For example, in addition to not attending to the student who shouts questions and answers in class, we attend to that student only when he raises his hand to ask or answer a question. Or instead of removing an aversive activity after a student rips his paper, we briefly remove an aversive activity after the student has completed two problems and requests a break.

Generally, consequence-based interventions within our functional assessment model consist of positive consequences that support appropriate replacement behavior, thus avoiding many of the side effects and negative outcomes that are related to punishment and focusing our attention on increasing appropriate behavior, rather than decreasing challenging behavior as the goal of intervention. Punishment has several potential disadvantages that are well documented in the behavior analysis literature (e.g., Bandura, 1965; Donnellan & LaVigna, 1990; Risley, 1968; Rose, 1983; Skinner, 1953, 1974; Sobsey, 1990; Sulzer-Azaroff & Mayer, 1977, 1991; Walker & Shea, 1999; Wood & Braaten, 1983). These disadvantages include the following:

1. Punishment teaches a student what not to do; it does not teach a student what to do instead of the challenging behavior. In other words, punishment focuses only on decreasing or terminating challenging behavior. Punishment alone does not address appropriate replacement behavior.

2. The results of punishment may be short term. Challenging behavior often reoccurs when punishment contingencies are withdrawn or have not been experienced for a period of time.

3. The results of punishment may be situation specific. Students may learn not to do the challenging behavior in one setting or in the presence of one individual, but the challenging behavior continues to occur in other settings and with other individuals.

4. Another form of challenging behavior may replace the current challenging behavior. If supports for appropriate behavior are not part of the intervention, then the student may substitute another challenging

behavior in place of the original challenging behavior. This new challenging behavior also then may be punished and so the student engages in a different challenging behavior and so on, continuing the cycle of punishment.

5. Punishment may result in aggression against the individuals who deliver the punishment or others.

6. Punishment may result in a general suppression of appropriate behavior and challenging behavior. Students may stop engaging in challenging behavior, but they also may stop participating in classroom activities and interacting with peers and adults.

7. The student may avoid the individual who delivers the punishment (e.g., parents, teachers, therapists).

8. Punishment can reduce self-esteem. Students who receive frequent punishment often also have poor self-esteem as measured in interviews and self-assessments (Sulzer-Azaroff & Mayer, 1991).

9. The student who is punished and other students may imitate the behavior of the punisher and apply punishment procedures to others. For example, a child who is spanked may hit peers, a student who loses tokens may take tokens from peers, or a student who is ridiculed by the teacher may ridicule other students.

10. Punishment may result in physical harm to the student.

11. Punishment may be overused and employed as the first (and continuing) reaction to challenging behavior (Skiba & Peterson, 2000). Educators may rely on punishment procedures and not attempt to change behavior using positive strategies.

If punishment strategies are included in the intervention plan (e.g., extinction, time-out, loss of privileges or points) they *must* be accompanied by positive strategies that support appropriate behavior. Punishment procedures also must conform to the guidelines established by federal and state legislation and local school system discipline plans (Wood & Braaten, 1983). For instance, if we stop reprimanding and commenting on Warren's tardiness (extinction of attention), we also must begin to attend to Warren when he is on time. Likewise if we remove tokens or points when Warren is late, we also must award points or tokens when Warren is punctual. While both of these examples deliver punishment contingent on Warren's tardy behavior, they also teach Warren that appropriate behavior results in positive outcomes (he either obtains teacher attention or tokens). Punishment alone would not necessarily do this. Several studies have shown that punishment combined with positive reinforcement is more effective than punishment alone (Golonka, Wacker, Berg, Derby, Harding, & Peck, 2000; Keeney, Fisher, Adelinis, & Wilder, 2000; Mazaleski, Iwata, Vollmer, Zarcone, & Smith, 1993; Zarcone, Iwata, Hughes, & Vollmer, 1993; Zarcone, Iwata, Vollmer, Jagtiani, Smith, & Mazaleski, 1993).

In summary, intervention plans should address, when appropriate, setting events, antecedents, and consequences that currently support challenging behavior and that will support appropriate replacement behavior. Setting events, antecedents, and consequences can be altered, introduced, or withdrawn. Intervention also can focus on changing educator interactions with the student and expectations for the student when setting events cannot be altered or withdrawn. As a general rule, consequence-based interventions should not include restrictive or severe punishment procedures when possible. If punishment procedures are employed, it is critical that they be paired with positive reinforcement strategies and that punishment procedures be faded as quickly as possible.

SELECTING INTERVENTION STRATEGIES AND APPROPRIATE REPLACEMENT BEHAVIORS

No universal rules have been determined to indicate how setting events, antecedents, and consequences should be altered and arranged during intervention. However, several recommendations do exist for selecting intervention strategies that will increase the probability of success in addressing challenging and appropriate behavior. These recommendations also will promote the generalization and maintenance of behavior. Generalization refers to the occurrence of behavior across new and different situations including generalization across persons, materials, activities and tasks, instructions, and settings. Maintenance refers to the continuation of behavior across time (Baer, Wolfe, & Risley, 1968; Carr, Levin, McConacchie, Carlson, Kemp, & Smith, 1994; Haring, 1988a, 1988b; Stokes & Baer, 1977; Sulzer-Azaroff & Mayer, 1991). The recommendations for selecting intervention strategies are identified in Table 6–1 and described in detail in the following paragraphs.

TABLE 6–1
Recommendations for selecting intervention strategies and appropriate replacement behaviors

Intervention Strategies

1. Intervention must address the function of challenging behavior.
2. Employ natural stimuli.
3. Intervention strategies must be feasible and acceptable.
4. Select normative intervention strategies.
5. Select strategies that can be applied class-wide.

Appropriate Replacement Behaviors

6. Select educational or functional replacement behaviors.
7. Select normative behaviors.
8. Select acceptable replacement behaviors.
9. Select efficient appropriate replacement behaviors.
10. Select appropriate behaviors that are incompatible with challenging behaviors.

1. Intervention Must Address the Function of Challenging Behavior

First and foremost, intervention strategies must be based on the function of challenging behavior. Intervention strategies often fail to change behavior because they are arbitrarily selected, with little understanding of why challenging behavior occurs. This results in a mismatch between intervention and the function of behavior (Iwata et al., 1982/1994; Mace, 1994). Interventions that are based on the function of behavior generally are more successful than those that are not based on the function of behavior (Kazdin, 2001; Repp & Karsh, 1994; Repp, Karsh, Munk, & Dahlquist, 1995).

Students engage in challenging behavior because it produces a function. Intervention to remediate challenging behavior must continue to provide the function, but the behavior that produces the function will be different. In other words, the replacement behavior must also produce the identified function (Dunlap, Foster-Johnson, & Robbins, 1990; Luiselli, 1990; McEvoy & Reichle, 2000; Repp & Karsh, 1990). If the student obtains something positive by exhibiting challenging behavior, then intervention must allow the student to obtain something positive by exhibiting appropriate behavior. Likewise, if the student escapes or avoids something aversive by engaging in challenging behavior, then intervention must allow the student to escape or avoid something aversive by engaging in appropriate behavior, or it must change the function from negative to positive reinforcement. Finally, if the student alters the level or type of sensory stimulation by engaging in challenging behavior, then intervention must allow the student to alter stimulation by engaging in appropriate behavior.

The need to consider the function of behavior was demonstrated by Meyer (1999). Meyer conducted functional assessment of off-task behavior for four students. For three students the function of off-task behavior was escape from difficult tasks. For the remaining student, the function of off-task behavior was positive reinforcement. This student engaged in off-task behavior when there were low levels of adult attention. During the first series of interventions, Meyer taught the students whose behavior was maintained by escape from difficult activities to request attention. She also taught the remaining student whose behavior was maintained by adult attention to request assistance. For each of these students the interventions did not address the function of their behavior and, as might be expected, little change was seen in their off-task behavior. Meyer then implemented interventions that considered the function of behavior for each student. As a result, the student whose behavior was a function of positive reinforcement (attention) was taught to request attention. The students whose behavior was maintained by escape, were taught to request assistance (thereby reducing the difficult aspects of the task). Only when the intervention addressed the function of challenging behavior were reduced levels of off-task behavior (and increased levels of on-task behavior) obtained.

Investigators often refer to this recommendation as matching the function of challenging behavior or developing functionally equivalent behaviors (e.g.,

Carr, 1988; Durand, Bertoli, & Weiner, 1993; Kern & Dunlap, 1999; Luiselli, 1990; Parrish & Roberts, 1993). Functional equivalence is the foundation of functional assessment interventions. Interventions must compete with existing conditions in producing the function if they are to be effective (Horner & Day, 1991; Kazdin, 2001; Mace, Lalli, & Lalli, 1991). Interventions must focus on what is important to the student (i.e., the function). Students do not necessarily care how the function is achieved—what is important to them is that the function *is* achieved. H*ow* the function is achieved (i.e., the form of behavior employed) is important to educators and family members who want the challenging behavior to decrease. When interventions match the function of challenging behavior, students learn new and appropriate methods to achieve important functions (Kazdin, 2001; Mace et al., 1991).

Functionally equivalent behaviors are more likely to generalize to new situations and be maintained across time as demonstrated by Durand and Carr (1992). These investigators evaluated the effects of two interventions. One intervention was designed to reduce challenging behavior by teaching a functionally equivalent behavior. The second intervention was designed to reduce behavior by applying a punishment technique (time-out). They reported that both interventions decreased challenging behavior, but only the functionally equivalent intervention resulted in long-term maintenance. As Carr and his colleagues (1994) have pointed out, before we can change behavior we must discover the purpose (function) of it. Only then are we in a position to teach new behaviors to achieve that same purpose (function). A discussion of changing the function from negative to positive reinforcement will be presented in the chapter on negative reinforcement interventions.

2. Employ Natural Stimuli

This recommendation refers to the selection of antecedent and consequence stimuli that will be part of the intervention plan. Natural stimuli are those stimuli that currently exist (are natural to that setting) or are likely to exist in school- or home-based settings in which behavior occurs (Repp & Karsh, 1990; Sulzer-Azaroff & Mayer, 1991). Students will be more likely to maintain appropriate behavior if it is triggered by natural antecedents and consequated by natural consequences (Billingsley, 1988; Liberty & Billingsley, 1988; White, 1988). For example, the natural consequence for asking for help is to receive help. A more artificial or less natural consequence (and one that may not be available in future settings) would be to receive points or a sticker after asking for help. A natural antecedent that might facilitate completing work on time may be a clock or a timer. A more artificial antecedent (and one that may not be available in multiple settings) would be frequent teacher cues informing the student how much time remained in the activity (e.g., "You have five minutes left, there are four minutes left," and so forth).

The stimuli that are considered natural or that are common to one setting (e.g., a token economy or edible reinforcers) may be considered artificial and inappropriate in another setting. As a result, the team must identify the antecedents and consequences that typically are employed or available in the settings in which intervention will be implemented. Natural stimuli will continue to be available after specific intervention strategies have terminated and so they should be incorporated in the intervention plan.

If artificial stimuli are introduced, they should be paired with natural stimuli. The terminal goal, when possible, should be to fade artificial stimuli so that behavior is supported by natural stimuli. For instance, the intervention plan to increase Haddie's on-task behavior consisted of frequent verbal prompts to "keep on working" and the delivery of one token for each 5 minutes of on-task behavior. Tokens also were paired with verbal praise. Tokens were not a natural (typical) consequence in Haddie's classroom but they were introduced because praise (the natural consequence in her classroom) initially was not a strong reinforcer for Haddie. Over time, however, praise gained strength as a positive reinforcer for Haddie by being paired with tokens. As Haddie's on-task behavior increased, verbal prompts were provided less frequently and tokens were faded by increasing the number of minutes Haddie had to remain on task prior to receiving a token. Praise continued to be delivered for on-task behavior. Eventually prompts and tokens were discontinued. At this point Haddie's on-task behavior was maintained by the natural consequence of praise.

3. Intervention Strategies Must Be Feasible and Acceptable

Interventions that are considered unfeasible or unacceptable by those who are expected to administer them may not be implemented or they may not be implemented correctly (Elliott, Witt, & Kratochwill, 1991; Johnson & Pugach, 1990; Odom, McConnell, & Chandler, 1994). Feasibility refers to intervention strategies that are practical and that can be implemented by educators within the classroom and other school-based settings. Horner (1994) refers to this as contextually appropriate interventions. He states that a contextually appropriate intervention "fits the skills, schedules, resources, and values of the people who must implement them" (p. 403). Intervention strategies are more likely to be considered feasible when they reflect program resources. These resources could include the following:

a. Schedules and daily activities and routines

b. Number of individuals available to administer intervention strategies

c. Amount of time and the effort required to administer intervention strategies

d. Amount of staff training and expertise required to administer intervention strategies

e. Safety of other students and staff (Sugai, Lewis-Palmer, & Hagan, 1998)

Acceptability refers to the perceived appropriateness, fairness, and reasonableness of intervention strategies (Elliott et al., 1991; Kazdin, 1981; O'Brien & Karsh, 1990; Wolf, 1978). Intervention plans should consider the philosophy and typical teaching practices of staff who will implement the strategies, school administrators, and the student and his or her family.

The recommendation to develop acceptable and feasible intervention plans does not mean that intervention strategies must be easy to implement, should require little staff time or effort, should require little staff training and/or expertise, or should be based only on practices that are typically employed in the school settings. It does mean, however, that interventions must be reasonable given the time and resources available in each setting.

The feasibility and acceptability of intervention strategies may vary across settings. For example, the intervention plan for Koshari's escape-motivated aggressive behavior involved (1) repeated instructions, (2) physical prompts, (3) extinction of aggressive behavior, and (4) praise of compliant behavior. Although this intervention eventually reduced Koshari's aggression and increased compliance, it did not do so immediately. In fact, Koshari's aggressive behavior initially increased in frequency and intensity as is common when extinction procedures are employed. As a result, this intervention plan required a second adult who could isolate or move students to another room when Koshari's aggression threatened their safety. (Koshari often threw furniture and materials at peers and staff.) This intervention would not be feasible if Koshari's classroom had contained only one teacher. However, it was considered feasible for her classroom because two staff members were available to implement the intervention plan.

The acceptability of the intervention for Koshari varied across individual team members (O'Brien & Karsh, 1990). Some members of the team felt that extinction was appropriate because it would teach Koshari that she could not escape an activity when she was aggressive. Other members felt that the (temporary) increase in aggression and potential danger to other students and adults was not acceptable and that other strategies might be equally effective at changing her behavior (e.g., redirection or physical prompts and praise). When conflicts such as this arise, the team should discuss each individual's concerns, the rationale for proposed strategies, and the pros and cons of potential intervention strategies. This may lead to the identification of resources that could be provided to make the intervention more feasible and acceptable, thus resulting in consensus in selecting intervention strategies. If consensus is not achieved, the team may need to adopt a short-term intervention plan that will be reviewed after a specified interim period and revised if needed. In Koshari's case, the team implemented the plan for 1 month and then reviewed progress. The consensus of the team was that progress had been made, and they continued to implement the intervention plan.

4. Select Normative Intervention Strategies

Setting event, antecedent, and consequence-based strategies should reflect the types of procedures that typically occur within the classroom or other school settings or that would be employed with other students. This recommendation is based on the principal of normalization (Wolfensburger, 1972), which indicates that settings, interventions, and experiences for students with disabilities (and in this case, students with challenging behavior) should be as close as possible to those that are provided for students without disabilities (or in this case to students who display consistent challenging behavior) (Haring, 1988a,b; White et al., 1988). Normative interventions often are more acceptable to staff, students, and families and may be easier to implement because they are familiar or are part of the ongoing classroom routines and practices. They also tend to draw less attention to a particular student.

We worked with a student, Fernando, who twirled his hair. This response was the first in a chain of behaviors that eventually led to shouting and running out of the classroom. The intervention strategy that had been recommended by a previous consultant was for Fernando to wear a knitted cap throughout the school day. This strategy was never implemented. The staff indicated that Fernando refused to wear the knitted cap (his peers and his father wore baseball caps). They also indicated that other students were not allowed to wear hats in the classroom and that this sent a mixed message to all the students. The staff felt that Fernando should not be allowed to do something that the other students were not allowed to do. The staff also felt that while it might be appropriate to wear a knitted cap during winter, it was not appropriate during other times of the year. From the staff and Fernando's perspectives, the knitted cap strategy was not a normative intervention.

Our observations indicated that Fernando usually twirled his hair and began his chain of challenging behaviors during unstructured activities. An alternative intervention was developed to direct Fernando to an activity when he twirled his hair and to eventually teach him to independently select activities during unstructured periods of time. This intervention was more normative than the knitted cap intervention because it did not draw particular attention to Fernando and it involved procedures that staff routinely implemented across students within the classroom.

Antecedent and Setting Events	Behavior	Consequence	Function
Unstructured activities	Twirls hair, shouts, runs from room	Stimulation	Sensory Regulation/ Sensory Stimulation: increase sensory stimulation
Structured activities for Fernando during unstructured sessions	Engaged in selected activities	Stimulation	Sensory Regulation/ Sensory Stimulation: increase sensory stimulation

5. Select Strategies That Can Be Applied Class-Wide

Although functional assessment is individualized for each student who exhibits challenging behavior, the interventions that are developed for one student may be appropriate for many or all students. It often is easier to apply setting event, antecedent, and consequence strategies to an entire class, rather than to an individual student. For example, we may employ unison or group responding to address one student's problems with waiting for a turn (Munk & Karsh, 1999). We may provide a sample problem on all math worksheets or break instructions into smaller steps for all students. In our own research we reported decreases in challenging behavior and increases in engagement and peer interaction for groups of students when interventions that were developed for one student were applied class-wide (Chandler, Dahlquist, Repp, & Feltz, 1999). These findings were replicated across self-contained classrooms for students with special education needs, inclusive or regular education classrooms, and classrooms for students at risk. We also found that appropriate student and staff behavior was maintained across time. Interventions that are applied class-wide may be more likely to be maintained by program staff because they become part of the daily routines and practices of the classroom.

In addition to selecting and arranging setting events, antecedents, and consequences as part of the intervention plan as discussed in the previous five recommendations, the team also must identify appropriate behaviors that will replace the challenging behavior yet achieve the same function. Several recommendations can guide the team in selecting appropriate replacement behaviors. These recommendations are listed in Table 6–1 and are described in detail in the following section.

6. Select Educational or Functional Replacement Behaviors

Appropriate replacement behaviors should be those that promote independence, expand the student's repertoire, and maximize participation in the student's home and least restrictive school and community environments (Billingsley, 1988; Dunlap et al., 1990; Ostrosky, Drasgow, & Halle, 1999). Functional or educational behaviors also are behaviors that are effective across multiple environments or that are prerequisites for more advanced skills (Carr et al., 1994; Durand & Carr, 1992; Munk & Karsh, 1999; Sulzer-Azaroff & Mayer, 1991). Chandler, Lubeck, and Fowler (1992) found in a retrospective review of published research that studies that identified educational or functional behaviors were more likely to obtain generalization and maintenance of those behaviors than studies that did not identify functional behaviors. They speculated that one reason for this is that functional behaviors are more likely to be supported by consequences in the natural environment and reinforced across a variety of settings.

When selecting appropriate alternative behaviors, the team may ask questions such as these: How does this replacement behavior help the student? Is this a useful skill for the student to learn? Will this behavior be effective in other classrooms or school settings? Will this behavior be effective at home? Will this behavior lead to the attainment of other skills?

7. Select Normative Behaviors

When selecting replacement behaviors the team should consider the student's chronological age, developmental level, and the behaviors that other students employ to achieve the same or similar functions. The team should select replacement behaviors that are as similar as possible to those that are employed by the student's peers and that would be appropriate given the student's chronological age. This is because normative and age-appropriate behaviors are more likely to be reinforced by multiple individuals and across multiple settings (Haring, 1988a,b).

For example, Repp and his colleagues (personal communication, 1992) worked with a 10-year-old student with mental retardation who required constant high levels of stimulation. When he did not have a task to complete or something to do, he ran in the classroom, climbed on furniture, disrupted ongoing lessons with other students, inappropriately touched other students and staff, disrobed, and hummed in a stereotypical manner. Intervention consisted of providing tasks for this student to complete throughout the entire school day. Even though this student's developmental level was below his chronological age, the team selected materials and adapted tasks that were appropriate for a 10-year-old student. For example, rather than complete a puzzle or string beads (tasks that are appropriate for preschool-aged children), the student completed tasks such as sorting objects by categories, cutting and pasting pictures from magazines, assisting with cleanup after lunch, and matching numbers and objects. The team found that if they did introduce activities that matched the student's developmental age—rather than age-appropriate activities—the student refused to complete these activities and instead engaged in challenging behavior.

It may not always be possible to select age-appropriate activities however. If a student is not able to perform behaviors that are age appropriate, then the team obviously should consider the student's developmental level and current skills. For example, if a student is not able to ask for assistance using a four-word sentence (e.g., "I need help, please") then the behavior may reflect the student's developmental language level. In this case, the replacement behavior may consist of a one-word sentence "Help" or the student may pat the teacher on the shoulder to request help. Although age-appropriate tasks usually are preferable, tasks and behaviors must be individualized for each student and must consider the ability and developmental level of each student.

8. Select Acceptable Replacement Behaviors

Replacement behaviors should be acceptable to (1) the student, (2) the student's family (and be within the family's cultural values and practices), (3) team members, and (4) the school and greater community. Behaviors that are unacceptable to the student are less likely to be employed or generalized and maintained after intervention has terminated. For example, Richard had a difficult time sitting still and attending. When he was required to sit and attend for more than 10 minutes, he tapped his pencil on his desk, kicked his seat, and ripped his paper. The team decided that Richard should raise his hand and tell the teacher that he needed a break when he wished to move. Richard refused to do this. He said that this would be embarrassing because it showed his peers that he was different and that he couldn't do what they were doing. So, an alternative set of behaviors was identified. Richard agreed to move his 3×5 point card to the corner of his desk when he needed a break (all students had point cards). When he did this, the teacher would give him a task to complete such as taking a note next door or putting a note in his backpack. Richard also was allowed to independently leave his seat once per session to sharpen his pencil, throw a paper in the trash can, or ask the teacher a question at her desk.

Replacement behaviors that are unacceptable to staff and/or family members or within the school and community are more likely to be punished or ignored. For instance, Lyla who was in second grade, often doodled, looked out the window, or slept when she was supposed to be working independently at her desk. Functional assessment indicated that Lyla most often did this when she did not understand the assigned task. The replacement behavior recommended by the team was for Lyla to briefly look at a peer's work or quietly ask a peer what they were supposed to do when she did not understand the task. This is a behavior that many teachers allow for students in younger grades. However, Mr. Sood, Lyla's teacher, said that this behavior was unacceptable. He said that the replacement behavior would disrupt Lyla's peers and that talking to a peer or looking at a peer's paper was considered cheating within his classroom. An alternative replacement behavior that was acceptable to Mr. Sood was selected. Lyla was taught to ask Mr. Sood for assistance when she did not understand the assignment.

The most obvious way to ensure that replacement behaviors are acceptable is to include critical individuals or stakeholders in intervention planning (Baer et al., 1968; Horner, 1994). This may include the student, the student's family, and staff who will implement the intervention.

9. Select Efficient Replacement Behaviors

If replacement behaviors are to be acquired and maintained, they must effectively compete with challenging behaviors in producing the desired function (Carr, 1988; Carr et al., 1994; Durand et al., 1993; McEvoy & Reichle, 2000; Reichle et al., 1996; Sprague & Horner, 1999). In addition to producing the same function, replacement behaviors will compete with challenging behavior when they

a. Require less time or effort to employ (e.g., it is easier to tell a peer no than it is to fight with a peer) (Horner & Day, 1991; Keeney et al., 2000)

b. Result in greater amounts or intensity of reinforcement (e.g., the student who is escape motivated receives a 10-minute break for compliance instead of 5-minutes of time-out for noncompliance)

c. Produce the function more frequently (e.g., teacher attention initially is delivered on a continuous schedule for appropriate behavior)

d. Result in more immediate reinforcement (e.g., the student receives a break from a task within 10 seconds of making the request).

Efficient replacement behaviors are more likely to be employed by the student as alternatives to challenging behavior than inefficient replacement behaviors, thus providing for a more rapid change in behavior.

10. Select Appropriate Behaviors That Are Incompatible with Challenging Behavior

The goal of remedial intervention in functional assessment is to decrease challenging behavior by increasing appropriate behavior that achieves the same function. One of the simplest ways to do this is to select replacement behaviors that are incompatible with the challenging behavior. In other words, the student cannot engage in both behaviors at the same time. For example, Whitney hits peers and takes their toys frequently. A logical intervention strategy might be to teach Whitney to ask for toys. This is a good first step. However, Whitney can ask for a toy and hit at the same time. An obvious problem with this is that Whitney may learn that the way to obtain toys is to ask and hit. An incompatible replacement behavior would teach Whitney to ask for a toy and hold out her hands to receive the toy. She cannot hit peers and hold out her hands simultaneously.

One strategy for selecting incompatible replacement behaviors is to select behaviors that are in the same response mode as the challenging behavior. For example, if the challenging behavior involves vocalizations, then the replacement behavior should involve vocalizations. Table 6–2 identifies

TABLE 6–2
Samples of challenging behaviors and appropriate behaviors that are incompatible with the challenging behaviors

Challenging Behavior	Incompatible Appropriate Behavior
Out of seat	In seat
Spitting	Telling a peer no
Sitting alone in the corner	Working in a small group
Hair twirling	Coloring or writing
Hand biting	Completing a puzzle
Wiggling in seat	Standing in the back of the room
Swearing	Requesting assistance
Hitting peer	Holding out hand to receive item
Stereotypical toy play	Appropriate toy play
Rocking	Walking
Screaming	Using words, singing
Running in the classroom	Doing Calisthenics
Off task	On task
Talking to peers	Reading a book

examples of challenging behaviors and appropriate replacement behaviors that are incompatible with the challenging behaviors.

It may not always be feasible or desirable, however, to select incompatible replacement behaviors. For example, Phil often screamed and swore when given a task to complete. The function of his behavior was escape or negative reinforcement. An incompatible behavior to screaming and swearing would be for Phil to tell the teacher he was not ready to do the task or that he did not want to do the task. However, the team decided that this was not an appropriate replacement behavior for Phil; they wanted Phil to complete assigned tasks, not say that he did not want to do those tasks. Therefore, an alternative replacement behavior selected for Phil was compliance with task instructions. This concept will be discussed in more detail in the next chapter.

SUMMARY

Teams must consider several variables when developing intervention plans. They must decide how setting events, antecedents, and consequences will be arranged. They must select appropriate behaviors that will compete with and eventually replace challenging behaviors and they must select intervention strategies that match the function of challenging behavior and that are likely to be implemented by staff. The more thought and consideration that is employed in the development phase, the more successful interventions will be.

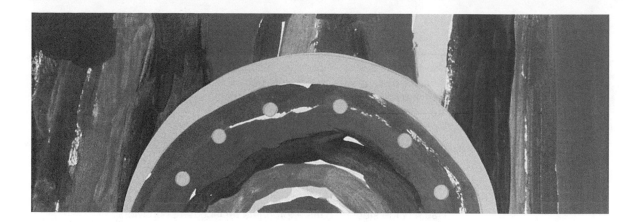

CHAPTER 7

Intervention Strategies Related to the Positive Reinforcement Function

Few resources identify specific intervention strategies that might be employed within each of the three functions of behavior. Yet, we have found it extremely helpful to begin with a basic set of common strategies that might be employed within each function. These initial lists of strategies assist teams in brainstorming and evaluating the pros and cons of various strategies. Teams then add to each list as they develop interventions for students in their programs. The next four chapters provide basic lists and examples of strategies that we, the teams that we have worked with, and our colleagues have employed within each function.[1] Our hope is that these lists and examples will assist you in understanding how the interventions match the different functions and that you, and the teams that you work with, will add your own intervention strategies to these lists. These lists are not meant to be comprehensive, rather, they should serve as a starting point for intervention planning.

---

[1] Many of the strategies presented in these chapters were described in the functional assessment workshops developed by these authors and their colleagues at the Educational Research and Services Center in DeKalb, Illinois. The Educational Research and Services Center received several federal grants to conduct functional assessment research in school-based settings. Many of the grants involved staff training regarding functional assessment. Many of the strategies that were included in our training workshops have been expanded in this text (e.g., Chandler, 1997, 1998; Chandler & Dahlquist, 1994, 1995, 1997, 1998; Dahlquist, Repp, Karsh, & Chandler, 1994; Repp, Karsh, Dahlquist, & Chandler, 1994).

TABLE 7-1
Intervention strategies
that are related to the
positive reinforcement
function

1. Use the reinforcer that the student currently obtains for challenging behavior to reinforce appropriate replacement behavior.
2. Stop providing, or prevent the delivery of, the reinforcer that the student currently obtains for challenging behavior.
3. Use differential reinforcement to increase appropriate behaviors.
4. Provide more reinforcement for appropriate behavior than the student currently receives for challenging behavior.
5. Provide positive reinforcement to peers who engage in the appropriate replacement behavior.
6. Identify appropriate behavior: Tell the student what to do versus what not to do.
7. Redirect the student to the appropriate replacement behavior.
8. Teach students appropriate methods to request reinforcement.
9. Provide presignals and safety signals.

© 2002 Chandler and Dahlquist.

When the function of challenging behavior is positive reinforcement, the student obtains something positive (from the student's perspective) by engaging in challenging behavior (Carr, Langdon, & Yarbrough, 1999; Repp, 1999; Repp & Karsh, 1990). In other words, an event or variable that functions as a positive reinforcer for the student is added to the situation as a result of the student's behavior. This might include adult or peer attention, preferred materials and activities, control of a situation, being the best or the winner in a situation, edible reinforcement, tokens, stickers, grades, and feedback (Carr & McDowell, 1980; Derby et al., 1992; Hanley, Piazza, & Fisher, 1997). The behaviors that result in obtaining something desirable or positive (i.e., a positive reinforcer) are strengthened or maintained (Skinner, 1953, 1974).

For challenging behavior that falls within the positive reinforcement function, your goal is to teach appropriate behavior that will replace the challenging behavior in producing positive reinforcement. Several intervention strategies commonly are employed by teams to address the positive reinforcement function. These strategies can be used individually or combined within a comprehensive intervention plan. These strategies are listed in Table 7–1 and explained in detail in the following section. Following the description of these strategies is a discussion of general tips for providing positive reinforcers.

POSITIVE REINFORCEMENT INTERVENTION STRATEGIES
1. Use the Reinforcer That the Student Currently Obtains for Challenging Behavior to Reinforce Appropriate Replacement Behavior

This strategy is based on the recommendation discussed earlier in Chapter 6 to match the function of challenging behavior or teach functionally equivalent behaviors (Carr, 1988; Dunlap, Foster-Johnson, &

Robbins, 1990; Durand, Bertoli, & Weiner, 1993; Kern & Dunlap, 1999; Luiselli, 1990; Repp & Karsh, 1990). Observation of the student in the natural environment will identify the reinforcer(s) that the student currently obtains as a result of challenging behavior. This reinforcer should be shifted during intervention so that it is delivered contingent on appropriate behavior and is no longer provided for challenging behavior. For example, if Raymond was able to sit next to his best friend (the positive reinforcer) by pushing other peers out of the way (challenging behavior), intervention would continue to allow Raymond to sit next to his friend (the positive reinforcer), but only when he politely asked peers to move (appropriate behavior). In this example Raymond continues to obtain the same reinforcer but that reinforcer is available only for an appropriate functionally equivalent behavior.

Antecedents and Setting Events	Behavior	Consequence	Function
Seat next to friend is taken by a peer	Pushes peer	Peer moves	Positive Reinforcement: obtains seat next to friend
Seat next to friend is taken by a peer	Asks peer to move	Peer moves	Positive Reinforcement: obtains seat next to friend

This strategy should only be used when the form of reinforcement that typically follows challenging behavior in the current setting is considered appropriate for the student and the current or future settings. In some cases, the team might decide that it is not appropriate to continue delivering the current form of reinforcement. For example, Ms. Webster reprimands Brin each time she talks out of turn. In this case, teacher reprimand is a positive reinforcer for Brin (it functions as a form of attention). It would not be logical, however, to use reprimand as a reinforcer for appropriate behavior. In this example, we would continue to provide attention as a reinforcer, but we would use a different form of attention (e.g., praise and receiving a turn when she raises her hand) to reinforce Brin's appropriate behavior.

Antecedents and Setting Events	Behavior	Consequence	Function
Waiting for a turn	Talks out	Reprimand	Positive Reinforcement: obtains attention
Waiting for a turn	Raises hand	Receives a turn, praise	Positive Reinforcement: obtains attention

2. Stop Providing, or Prevent the Delivery of, the Reinforcer That the Student Currently Obtains for Challenging Behavior

After we identify the positive reinforcer that the student currently obtains by engaging in challenging behavior, we should make sure that that reinforcer is no longer available for challenging behavior. We can do this by withholding previously identified reinforcers (e.g., attention) or by preventing access to previously identified reinforcers (e.g., materials, activities) (Iwata, Pace, Cowdery, & Miltenberger, 1994; Sulzer-Azaroff & Mayer, 1986, 1991). This strategy is referred to as extinction. For example, Annette's teacher knows that the reinforcer for running out of the classroom is being sent to the principal's office where Annette talks to the many adults and students who come in and out of the office. So Annette's teacher stops sending her to the principal's office when she runs out of the classroom. Annette eventually stops running out of the classroom because the previous reinforcer for this behavior is discontinued.

The extinction strategy should not be used in isolation. Rather, extinction should always be paired with strategies that provide reinforcement for appropriate behavior so that the student has opportunities to obtain positive reinforcement. For example, in addition to not sending Annette to the principal's office, her teacher should make sure that Annette has opportunities to obtain attention contingent on appropriate behavior such as staying in her seat. Remember that our goal in functional assessment is to teach appropriate behaviors that will achieve the same function as challenging behaviors. Extinction alone does not do this. It simply withholds reinforcement for challenging behavior. Extinction should be paired with reinforcement for appropriate behavior. Several studies have reported that interventions that include extinction of challenging behavior combined with positive reinforcement for appropriate behavior are more effective than positive reinforcement strategies alone (e.g., Mace & Belfiore, 1990; Mazaleski, Iwata, Vollmer, Zarcone, & Smith, 1993; Zarcone, Iwata, Hughes, & Vollmer, 1993).

For many individuals extinction is not an easy strategy to employ. Care must be taken to ensure that extinction is employed correctly and consistently if it is selected as a strategy. In addition to knowledge of how to implement the strategy, team members need to know what to expect during the initial stages of its implementation. When you use this strategy you should expect challenging behavior to increase before it begins to decrease (Goh & Iwata, 1994; Sulzer-Azaroff & Mayer, 1991). This is a common side effect of extinction. Students may engage in challenging behavior more frequently, for longer periods of time, and at increased intensity before they learn that reinforcement no longer follows challenging behavior.

For instance, Ricky seemed to always talk to his mother, Ellen, when she was on the telephone. He continued to talk to her until she responded to him (e.g., "Just a minute, Ricky," "I'm busy, Ricky," "I'll talk to you in a minute, Ricky," or "Please be quiet, Ricky"). This cycle of interaction continued throughout each telephone call. Ellen usually was forced to prematurely terminate her phone calls in order to attend to Ricky. Ricky had learned that he could obtain his mother's attention by interrupting her when she was talking to another individual on the phone.

Ellen decided to try extinction and positive reinforcement of appropriate behavior in order to decrease Ricky's interruptive behavior. So Ellen stopped attending to Ricky when he talked to her while she was on the phone. The first time that Ricky interrupted her, Ellen gave Ricky an antecedent prompt regarding his behavior. She told Ricky to wait quietly and that she would talk to him when she was off of the phone. Ellen then ignored subsequent requests for interaction. She did not repeat her instructions to wait quietly. As might be expected, at the beginning of this intervention Ricky pestered Ellen more frequently and he began to whine and cry when she did not respond to him. When this didn't work, he also pulled at his mother's clothes and he hit his mother. Eventually, however, Ricky stopped interrupting, crying, whining, and hitting and he waited quietly for Ellen to finish her telephone call. When she completed her call Ellen praised Ricky for waiting quietly and then interacted with him.

Antecedents and Setting Events	Behavior	Consequence	Function
Mother on phone, no attention	Talks, whines	Told to wait, reprimand	Positive Reinforcement: obtains mother's attention
Mother on phone, no attention, antecedent prompt	Initially talks, whines, hits mother; eventually waits quietly	Mother ignores behavior; praise and interaction	Positive Reinforcement: obtains mother's attention

We should point out that if you use extinction, you must carry through with the procedure (Sulzer-Azaroff & Mayer, 1986). Otherwise you may unwittingly reinforce more severe challenging behaviors. For instance, if Ellen had responded to Ricky when he was crying, whining, and hitting, she would have reinforced those behaviors. Ricky would have learned that talking is no longer successful in producing parent attention, but crying, whining, and hitting are successful; and he would have used these more disruptive behaviors each time his mother was on the phone. In order for extinction to successfully reduce challenging behavior, it must be applied consistently.

3. Use Differential Reinforcement to Increase Appropriate Behaviors

This suggestion combines two strategies: extinction of challenging behavior and reinforcement of specific types of appropriate replacement behavior

(Sulzer-Azaroff & Mayer, 1986). In differential reinforcement we identify the appropriate behavior that will replace the challenging behavior, and we provide reinforcement contingent on the occurrence of that replacement behavior. At the same time, we stop providing reinforcement for challenging behavior. Several types of differential reinforcement procedures are available. The different types vary in terms of the appropriate behaviors that are selected for reinforcement. Four types of differential reinforcement procedures are described next.

Differential *Reinforcement of* Incompatible *Behavior*

In the first type of differential reinforcement, the appropriate replacement behaviors that we reinforce are incompatible with the challenging behavior (differential reinforcement of incompatible behavior or DRI) (Deitz & Repp, 1983; Deitz, Repp, & Deitz, 1976). This type of differential reinforcement was described earlier in Chapter 6. In DRI, the appropriate behavior and challenging behavior cannot be displayed simultaneously. For example, a student cannot trade Pokemon cards with peers and read a book at the same time. Or a student cannot be in his seat and wander around the school grounds at the same time. The goal of DRI is to reinforce a behavior that is incompatible with the challenging behavior. As the incompatible behavior increases, a corresponding decrease in challenging behavior will occur because both behaviors cannot be displayed simultaneously.

Differential *Reinforcement of* Alternative *Behavior*

In the second type of differential reinforcement, the appropriate behavior that is reinforced may serve as an alternative to the challenging behavior (differential reinforcement of alternative behavior or DRA) (Carr & Durand, 1985; Polsgrove & Reith, 1983). For example, when the teacher tells students to line up for recess, Billy runs to the front of the line. He steps in front of peers and he threatens and pushes peers if they complain that he "cut in line." During intervention, Billy is reinforced for asking to be first in line to go to recess (the alternative behavior) by being allowed to be first in line. Billy no longer is reinforced when he runs to the front of the line and steps in front of peers, or when he threatens and pushes peers (previously reinforced behavior). In fact, when Billy does this, he is required to move to another less desirable space in the line. The goal of this form of differential reinforcement was to teach Billy an alternative appropriate behavior that would result in being first in line. This strategy also was combined with extinction (in this case, preventing access to the reinforcer that previously was contingent on challenging behavior) so that Billy received reinforcement for asking to be first in line and he did not receive reinforcement when he ran to the front of the line.

Antecedents and Setting Events	Behavior	Consequence	Function
Told to line up	Runs to recess, pushes, threatens peers	First in line front of line	Positive Reinforcement: obtains front-line position, first to go to recess
Told to line up for recess, told to ask to be first in line	Initially runs to front of line, threatens, pushes peers; eventually asks to be first in line	Moved to the end of the line; eventually allowed to be first in line	Positive Reinforcement: eventually obtains front-line position, first to go to recess

Differential Reinforcement of Other Behavior

The third type of differential reinforcement involves reinforcing any behavior other than the challenging behavior. In other words, we reinforce the nonoccurrence of challenging behavior (differential reinforcement of other behavior or DRO) (Cowdery, Iwata, & Pace, 1990; Deitz & Repp, 1983; Polsgrove & Reith, 1983; Repp & Deitz, 1974; Repp, Deitz, & Deitz, 1976). For example, Marinda receives a token at the end of each 10-minute period in which she does not throw her materials.

In DRO, the type of "other behavior" that the student employs is not specified. In this strategy, reinforcement is delivered as long as the specified challenging behavior is not exhibited. So in the example of Marinda, if she exhibits any behavior other than throwing materials, she receives reinforcement. Sometimes, however, reinforcing any behavior other than the identified challenging behavior can cause a problem. This is because the student may engage in other forms of challenging behavior during the DRO period. For instance, even though Marinda does not throw materials during the 10-minute period, if she rips her materials or hits peers during that period and then receives tokens we probably are inadvertently reinforcing other challenging behaviors.

If you use DRO it is important to not reinforce other challenging behaviors that might occur instead of the identified challenging behavior. If other challenging behaviors occur within the DRO time period, it is advisable to wait before delivering reinforcers until there is a brief period of time within which no challenging behavior has occurred. When possible, teams should select incompatible behavior (DRI) or alternative behavior (DRA) differential reinforcement procedures rather than DRO.

Differential Reinforcement of Low Rates of Behavior

The final differential reinforcement strategy is differential reinforcement of low rates of behavior (DRL) (Deitz & Repp, 1973, 1983). The purpose of this strategy is not to eliminate challenging behavior per se, but to have the challenging behavior occur less frequently. This strategy would be used when the student's behavior is challenging because of the frequency or high rate of occurrence. For example, behaviors such as interacting with peers, asking questions, or seeking assistance usually are considered appropriate behaviors. However, if they occur too frequently then they are identified as challenging behaviors. When this occurs our goal is to reduce the frequency or rate of behavior, rather than to eliminate the behavior entirely.

In DRL we provide reinforcement when the challenging behavior has not been emitted for a specific period of time or when it occurs at or below a pre-specified rate (sometimes referred to as differential reinforcement of diminishing rates). For instance, Zachary left his seat to ask his teacher, Mr. Snowden, for help an average of 10 times during a 20-minute individual seatwork period. Zachary's behavior of asking for help is not necessarily a challenging behavior. Mr. Snowden encourages his students to seek assistance when needed. It is the frequency of the behavior that makes it challenging because Zachary is not able to complete his work when he constantly is out of his seat. The goal of intervention then was to reduce the frequency of Zachary's behavior, not to eliminate the behavior. During intervention Zachary received 5 minutes of free time if he left his seat to ask for help no more than two times in a 20-minute period. This intervention reduced the frequency of asking for assistance and, as a result, Zachary finished his assigned work and received free time.

Antecedents and Setting Events	Behavior	Consequence	Function
Individual seatwork	Asks for help 10 times per period	Receives help, reprimand	Positive Reinforcement: obtains attention and help
Individual seatwork	Asks for help no more than two times per period	Receives help and free time	Positive Reinforcement: obtains help, attention, and free time

There also is a strategy identified as differential reinforcement of high rates of behavior (DRH) that might be employed. In this strategy, the focus is on the student employing higher rates of appropriate behavior that will serve as an alternative to challenging behavior. Like DRL, DRH focuses on behavior that the student already emits. The goal is to increase the frequency or rate of its occurrence. As appropriate behavior increases, a corresponding decrease in challenging behavior will be seen. The example of Tara and Mr. Albin illustrates how DRH can be used to increase the frequency of behavior.

This example, just like the previous example of Zachary, focuses on asking questions and requesting assistance. Mr. Albin who teaches Spanish gives the class their work assignments in Spanish. Sometimes Tara asks Mr. Albin questions about the assignment or for assistance as she is working on the assignment. Usually, however, when Tara does not understand the assignment, she simply sits quietly at her desk, not doing her work. Mr. Albin decided to use DRH to increase the frequency of Tara asking questions and asking for assistance. So he told Tara that he wanted her to ask questions when she did not understand the assignment. He told her that she could ask questions after he gave an assignment or that she could request help when she was working on an assignment. Mr. Albin then began asking students if they had questions after he gave assignments. When Tara and other students asked questions he praised them and provided appropriate clarification. He also praised Tara for asking for help when she was working on an assignment. As the frequency of Tara's question asking and assistance seeking behavior increased, a corresponding decrease was observed in her incomplete work assignments.

4. Provide More Reinforcement for Appropriate Behavior Than the Student Currently Receives for Challenging Behavior

In addition to identifying the type of reinforcer that the student obtains as a result of challenging behavior, you should identify how frequently reinforcers are delivered, how promptly reinforcers are delivered, and the amount and the intensity of reinforcement that the student receives when he or she engages in challenging behavior. In the previous chapter we indicated that appropriate behavior must compete with challenging behavior to produce the desired function (Mace, Lalli, & Lalli, 1991). In order for appropriate behavior to compete with challenging behavior, we need to arrange reinforcer delivery. There are several ways to do this. For example, the reinforcer for appropriate behavior may be delivered more frequently than the reinforcer for challenging behavior. The amount and intensity of the reinforcer may be greater for appropriate behavior than it is for challenging behavior. Less effort may be required to achieve the reinforcer for appropriate behavior than the effort required to achieve the reinforcer for challenging behavior. Or the reinforcer for appropriate behavior could be delivered more promptly than the reinforcer for challenging behavior (Dunlap & Kern, 1993; Horner & Day, 1991; Kern & Dunlap, 1999; Shore, Iwata, DeLeon, Kahng, & Smith, 1997; Zhou, Goff, & Iwata, 2000).

For instance, April frequently turned her homework in late even though points were deducted for late work. When she turned her work in, she provided the teacher with lengthy excuses (about 5 minutes in duration) about why her homework was late, thanked the teacher for accepting her homework, and promised to turn the next assignment in on time. The team hypothesized that extended one-to-one interaction with the teacher reinforced April's behavior of turning in homework late. So the team developed an intervention plan in which April was allowed to help the teacher post the daily schedule when she turned her homework in on time (this provided about 10 minutes of interaction). When April turned homework in late, the teacher accepted the work but did not listen to her explanation. After 1 week of intervention, April was turning homework in on time.

Antecedents and Setting Events	Behavior	Consequence	Function
Teacher collects homework	Turns in homework late, provides excuses	Teacher listens, reprimands	Positive Reinforcement: obtains teacher attention
Teacher collects homework	Turns in homework on time	Praise, assists teacher in posting daily schedule	Positive Reinforcement: obtains teacher attention

5. Provide Positive Reinforcement to Peers Who Engage in the Appropriate Replacement Behavior

This strategy allows a student with challenging behavior to observe peers as they obtain positive reinforcement by engaging in appropriate behavior. Often students will imitate the behavior of a model (i.e., peers). This is especially likely if the student observes his or her peers receiving reinforcement (Sulzer-Azaroff & Mayer, 1991; Walker, Colvin, & Ramsey, 1995). For example, when Jacob interrupts his teacher, Mr. Jack, Mr. Jack ignores Jacob and turns to Natalie and says, "Natalie, you are sitting quietly so it is your turn to write your problem on the board." Jacob imitates Natalie's quiet sitting behavior. He then receives a turn to write on the board. In another example, at the end of the spelling lesson Ms. Klein drew happy faces on each student's paper that contained at least 10 spelling words. John observed the other students receiving happy faces and completed his spelling worksheet the next time it was assigned. He also then received happy faces on his paper.

6. Identify Appropriate Behavior: Tell the Student What to Do versus What Not to Do

This strategy provides information about what the student should do. It does not leave the determination of what behavior will replace the challenging behavior to the student. Thus it prevents the potential problem of a new challenging behavior replacing the original challenging behavior. For example, instead of telling students to stop talking out of turn, we should tell students to raise their hand if they want a turn. Or instead of telling students to stop yelling, we might tell students to use their indoor voices or to talk quietly.

This strategy also avoids a continual focus on the challenging behavior. For many students, when we state "No _____" the word that they attend to is the challenging behavior that we have named. This word itself becomes an antecedent for further challenging behavior. For example if the teacher says, "No running in the classroom," the word *running* may actually trigger more running. The no running directive causes the student to attend to running behavior.

We often use an exercise in our workshops in which we ask the participants to picture the boy not hitting the girl. Or we ask them to picture the cat not pouncing on the mouse. Invariably, participants tell us that they picture the boy hitting the girl and that they see the cat pouncing on the mouse. This is what happens to many of our students when we say "No _____" or "Stop _____." As a result, we should identify the behavior that we want students to do (e.g., "walk in the classroom") and we should avoid identifying the behavior that we want students to stop doing (e.g., running in the classroom). This strategy, like extinction, should be paired with reinforcement for appropriate behavior. We should deliver reinforcement when students engage in the appropriate behavior that we have specified.

7. Redirect the Student to the Appropriate Replacement Behavior

This strategy also focuses on appropriate behaviors by redirecting the student to engage in those behaviors. When the student begins to engage in challenging behavior we should provide an antecedent prompt or instruction that identifies and redirects the student to engage in an alternative behavior. We then provide reinforcement when the student engages in the redirected behavior. For instance, when Wanda climbs on the tables, the teacher says "Wanda, I want you to pass out these papers." When Wanda begins to pass out the papers the teacher tells her, "You are doing a great job" and when she is done with this task, the teacher thanks her for helping. Notice in this example that the teacher does not acknowledge Wanda's challenging behavior of climbing on the tables. Rather, she identifies an alternative behavior. This is a very important idea to consider when the function of challenging behavior is attention. If the teacher were to reprimand Wanda, talk with Wanda about safety issues, or ask Wanda to state the classroom rules related to climbing on furniture, she would be attending to (and thus reinforcing) Wanda's challenging behavior. The result of this would be an increase in the behavior of climbing on the tables. The purpose of redirection is to direct students to appropriate replacement behaviors and to then provide reinforcement when students engage in those behaviors.

8. Teach Students Appropriate Methods to Request Reinforcement

Many investigators find it helpful to interpret challenging behavior as a form of communication (e.g., Carr & Durand, 1985; Carr, Levin, McConnachie, Carlson, Kemp, & Smith, 1994; Ostrosky, Drasgow, & Halle, 1999; Prizant &

Wetherby, 1987). For example, when Jimmy takes a toy from Frank, Jimmy's behavior indicates that he wants the toy. When Cindy pulls the teacher's hair, we may interpret that behavior as a request for teacher attention. When we interpret challenging behavior as a form of communication that produces positive reinforcement, our goal is to teach alternative appropriate strategies for requesting the desired consequence. This strategy is based on functional communication training or communication-based interventions (Carr & Durand, 1985; Carr et al., 1994; Dunlap & Kern, 1993; Durand & Carr, 1992; Durand et al., 1993; Wacker & Reichle, 1993). It focuses on teaching students alternative communication skills that produce the same function as challenging behavior. For example, we might teach Cindy to call the teacher's name or to tap her teacher on the shoulder rather than pulling the teacher's hair. We might teach Jimmy to ask for a toy using words or picture cues rather than taking toys from peers.

Antecedents and Setting Events	Behavior	Consequence	Function
Teacher working with other students or at her desk	Pulls teacher's hair	Reprimand	Positive Reinforcement: obtains teacher attention
Teacher working with other students or at her desk, antecedent prompt	Calls teacher or taps her shoulder	Teacher responds to Cindy, praises, ignores hair pulling	Positive Reinforcement: obtains teacher attention

The key to success in using this strategy is identifying appropriate replacement behaviors that communicate the same message as the challenging behavior and that also result in achieving the same form of reinforcement as the challenging behavior.

9. Provide Presignals and Safety Signals

This final suggestion introduces antecedents that will set the occasion for appropriate behavior. In this strategy, we provide antecedent prompts or instructions that indicate the appropriate behavior that students should exhibit or that identify the reinforcers that are available for exhibiting appropriate behavior (Dunlap & Kern, 1993; Mace, Shapiro, & Mace, 1998; Polloway & Patton, 1993; Rhode, Jenson, & Reavis, 1992). Antecedent prompts and instruction may be provided at the beginning of tasks or activities (presignals) and during tasks and activities (safety signals). Antecedent prompts or instructions include the following:

TABLE 7–2
General tips for delivering positive consequences to support appropriate replacement behavior

1. Provide reinforcers immediately and consistently following behavior.
2. Provide reinforcers contingent on appropriate behavior.
3. Vary reinforcers.
4. Individualize reinforcers.
5. Employ natural reinforcers.
6. Employ acceptable reinforcers.
7. Do not interrupt appropriate behavior when delivering reinforcers.
8. Provide effective social reinforcement.

A. *Vocal.* For example, before circle the teacher says "Raise your hand if you want a turn." During circle the teacher says "Everyone who sits in their chair gets a sticker when circle is over." At the end of an activity the teacher says "Remember to wait until I call on you before you line up at the door."

B. *Gestural.* For example, the teacher points to the garbage can before a student throws his paper out the open window.

C. *Modeled.* For example, the resource specialist demonstrates how to complete one problem for the student.

D. *Written.* For example, the teaching assistant places a note on the student's desk that says "Remember to stay in your seat." Or the student and teacher review the student's contract, which indicates that the student can skip the homework assignment if he correctly completes 20 problems during school.

E. *Pictorial.* For example, the teacher shows the child a picture of the child playing with his friends before free play. Or the instructional assistant and the student review a social story that shows the student waiting for a turn and then receiving a turn (Gray, 1994; Gray & Garland, 1993; Lazarus, 1998).

F. *Physical prompting.* For example, the teacher helps the child hang up his coat in his cubby and then praises this behavior. Note that in this example the teacher eventually will move from a physical prompt to a vocal prompt (e.g., "Hang up your coat").

In addition to employing one or more of the positive reinforcement function strategies that were discussed in the previous section, teams should carefully plan how reinforcers will be delivered in order to maximize the effectiveness of interventions. The next section discusses general tips for delivering positive consequences to support appropriate replacement behavior. These also are listed in Table 7–2.

TIPS FOR USING POSITIVE REINFORCEMENT
1. Provide Reinforcers Immediately and Consistently Following Behavior

The effects of positive reinforcement (i.e., an increase in or the maintenance of appropriate behavior) will be enhanced if reinforcers initially are delivered immediately following the emission of appropriate behavior and if reinforcers are delivered consistently across time (Malott, Malott, & Trojan, 2000; Sulzer-Azaroff & Mayer, 1986). The first goal of positive reinforcement strategies is to strengthen appropriate behavior so that it may replace challenging behavior in achieving the same function. To do this, reinforcers should be delivered *each* time the appropriate behavior occurs (a concept identified as continuous reinforcement) and immediately after the behavior occurs. The immediate and consistent delivery of reinforcers strengthens the bond between appropriate behavior and desirable consequences.

When the bond between appropriate behavior and positive consequences is strong and appropriate behavior is occurring at a satisfactory rate, reinforcer delivery should be changed from an immediate, consistent schedule to intermittent, delayed delivery schedules (Doyle, Gast, Wolery, Ault, & Farmer, 1990; Sulzer-Azaroff & Mayer, 1986; Walker & Shea, 1999). Intermittent delivery schedules provide reinforcers in a discontinuous or inconsistent fashion. In other words, some, but not all, instances of appropriate behavior are followed by a positive consequence (Rhode et al., 1992). Delayed schedules of reinforcement increase the amount of time or latency between appropriate behavior and reinforcer delivery (Fowler & Baer, 1981). Behaviors that are maintained by intermittent and delayed reinforcement are more likely to persevere in natural situations in which reinforcer delivery is not consistent and immediate (often referred to as resistant to extinction), and they are more likely to generalize across changing situations (Chandler, Lubeck, & Fowler, 1992; Dunlap, Koegel, Johnson, & O'Neill, 1987; Kazdin, 1982, 2001). The key to developing appropriate behaviors that are maintained by intermittent and delayed reinforcement is to initially strengthen the Antecedent–Behavior–Consequence bond by providing reinforcers immediately and consistently. Then the shift to intermittent schedules of reinforcement delivery should be made. Intermittent schedules of reinforcement will be further discussed in Chapter 11.

2. Provide Reinforcers Contingent on Appropriate Behavior

Positive reinforcers strengthen the behavior that they follow. Therefore, a reinforcer should be delivered only *after* the appropriate behavior has been emitted. If a reinforcer is delivered prior to the emission of the appropriate behavior, there is no guarantee that the appropriate behavior will occur or continue to occur (Malott et al., 2000). For example, Ms. Champs told students that if she let them watch a movie, they would need to complete their study guides (appropriate behavior) when the movie (potential reinforcer) ended. Ms. Champs was puzzled when her students did not complete their study guides. A more effective strategy would have been to provide the reinforcer only after the students had emitted the appropriate behavior. Ms. Champs should have required her students to complete their study guides and then reinforced that behavior by allowing them to watch the movie.

3. Vary Reinforcers

Students may become satiated (i.e., tired of) when a single type of consequence is employed as a positive reinforcer. When this happens, the consequence will cease to function as a positive reinforcer and the appropriate behavior that it follows may decrease (Rhode et al., 1992). For example, Teneshia likes to look at magazines, but she doesn't like to work on Spanish lessons and often does not complete her work during the Spanish work period. So Ms. Horst decides to use magazines as a reinforcer for appropriate behavior. She informs Teneshia that she can read magazines for 10 minutes if she stays on task and finishes her Spanish lesson on time. Initially, Teneshia stays on task and completes her lesson in a timely manner. After a few days, however, Teneshia stops working on her lesson and does not complete her Spanish lesson on time. When Ms. Horst reminds Teneshia that she can read magazines if she stays on task and completes her work, Teneshia says "I've read all those magazines, they are boring now." Teneshia was satiated by having the same reinforcer available each day. As a result, magazines lost their ability to positively reinforce her behavior.

One strategy to avoid satiation is to vary the types of reinforcers available to students (Alberto & Troutman, 1999). For example, Ms. Horst might allow Teneshia to choose from a variety of reinforcers including magazines, early recess, fewer homework problems, computer games, listening to music on her CD, and classroom tasks such as watering the plants or feeding the rabbit. Forms of reinforcers include the following:

A. Social praise, attention, or interaction (e.g., "Great paper you wrote," proximity, smiles, hand claps)
B. Physical contact (e.g., high five, handshake)
C. Tangible objects (e.g., stickers, happy faces, notes to parents)
D. Edible stimuli (e.g., popcorn, juice, crackers)
E. Access to activities (e.g., recess, computer games)
F. Access to sensory stimuli or sensory stimulation (e.g., access to music, movement)
G. Privileges and reduction of work (e.g., allowed to assist the teacher, serving as a peer mediator, fewer homework problems).

4. Individualize Reinforcers

When selecting reinforcers, we need to consider the student's perspectives of what stimuli are desirable, not our own. Students vary in their likes and dislikes and in terms of the stimuli that will function as reinforcers for their behavior. Not all stimuli will function as reinforcers for all students. Therefore, it is important to identify stimuli that will serve as reinforcing consequences for students and to individualize reinforcers across students (Romanczyk, 1997).

TABLE 7–3
Reinforcer sampling list

Indicate the types of activities or consequences that you prefer:

_____   Read magazines

_____   Work on class jigsaw puzzle

_____   Earn extra minutes of recess

_____   Listen to music on the earphones

_____   Use the computer

_____   Design the bulletin board

_____   Select from the mystery motivator box

_____   Be leader of my group

_____   Pass out materials

_____   Fewer homework problems

_____   Bonus points

_____   Check out videos/CDs

_____   Read comics

_____   Work on own art project

_____   _____

_____   _____

_____   _____

One way to do this is to conduct reinforcer-sampling procedures in which students provide information about preferred stimuli (Ayllon & Azrin, 1968; Mason & Egel, 1995; Northrup, George, Jones, Broussard, & Vollmer, 1996). For example, you might ask students to identify reinforcers. Or you might provide students with a menu or a list of potential reinforcers and ask them to select those that they prefer. Students also might prioritize items on a list of potential reinforcers.

Other strategies to identify reinforcers and to individualize reinforcer delivery are to observe students and identify the activities and objects that they spontaneously select during classroom activities, or, to provide a variety of reinforcer options so that students can select the stimuli that are reinforcing for them. For instance, when the students in Ms. Edwards' ninth-grade class exchanged tokens at the end of the day, 10 types of potential reinforcers were available. Ms. Edwards selected the 10 types of reinforcers after observing students in the classroom and asking students to prioritize reinforcers on a reinforcer-sampling list (see Table 7–3).

5. Employ Natural Reinforcers

This suggestion was discussed within the recommendation to employ natural stimuli in Chapter 6. Natural reinforcers are those consequences that typically exist in the current setting and that are not overly intrusive to deliver (Haring, 1988a,b; Liberty & Billingsley, 1988; Sulzer-Azaroff & Mayer, 1991; White et al., 1988). For example, praise, attention, points, stickers, and stars may be natural reinforcers in many classroom settings. Natural reinforcers also often are considered the logical consequences for behavior. For example, the natural, logical consequence for asking for a break is to receive a break. The logical, natural consequence for completing a worksheet may be a sense of accomplishment (intrinsic motivation) or the opportunity to engage in preferred activities. Teams should identify reinforcers that are natural to a setting and incorporate those stimuli into the intervention plan. If natural reinforcers do not function as reinforcing stimuli for a student, they should be paired with more artificial or extrinsic forms of reinforcement. Through repeated pairings, these neutral stimuli will gain strength as reinforcers and eventually they will function as positive reinforcers when presented alone (Alberto & Troutman, 1999; Sulzer-Azaroff & Mayer, 1986).

6. Employ Acceptable Reinforcers

The types of reinforcers employed should be acceptable to the educators who are expected to deliver them, the student, the student's family, and school administrators. For example, many families, administrators, and educators object to edible reinforcers such as pretzels, crackers, and candy. Many school districts now recommend that educators refrain from using physical forms of reinforcement such as hugs. Some students may find overt attention from educators or parents embarrassing and therefore unacceptable. Parents or educators may find reduced homework or extra privileges unacceptable forms of reinforcement.

Reinforcers that are unacceptable are less likely to be employed by educators and parents. Obviously for students, unacceptable reinforcers will not function as positively reinforcing stimuli and will not increase or maintain appropriate behavior. Therefore, prior to selecting reinforcers, it is advisable to talk with the student, educators, the student's family, and administrators.

7. Do Not Interrupt Appropriate Behavior When Delivering Reinforcers

Often, in an attempt to deliver immediate reinforcers, we deliver reinforcers as soon as we observe students engaging in appropriate behavior. This practice, however, often inadvertently terminates the appropriate behavior as students stop engaging in the behavior that has been reinforced and, instead, attend to the individual who is delivering the reinforcer. For instance, Semra who typically ignored peers, had an IEP goal to increase positive social interaction with peers. When Mr. Polse noticed Semra and Abigail working together on an art project, he walked over to the girls and praised them for working together. Both Semra and Abigail stopped talking to each other, stopped working on their joint project, and began to talk to Mr. Polse. After

Mr. Polse walked away from the girls, they did not return to their joint project. In fact, Semra followed Mr. Polse to his desk. While it is important for Mr. Polse to reinforce Semra's (and Abigail's) appropriate social behavior, a better strategy would have been to wait until there was a natural break in their interaction or until their interaction had ended. Or he might have used a less intrusive type of reinforcer such as a quick pat on the back or a "thumbs up" signal while the girls were interacting and then provided more overt praise at the end of their interaction.

8. Provide Effective Social Reinforcement

This tip includes several suggestions for delivering social reinforcers. First, social reinforcers such as vocal praise, attention, and smiles should be distinguishable from potentially punishing or neutral consequences such as reprimands, redirection, warnings, feedback, or disapproval. This is especially important for students who may not understand the specific words that are used to praise behavior (e.g., students with severe language disorders or hearing impairments or very young children). Social reinforcers may be distinguished by vocal tone, appropriate facial expressions, gestures, language, and so forth. Vocal praise should be sincere and heartfelt rather than monotonous or dull and routine. For instance, repeated monotone praise such as "Good job," "Good job," "Good job," "Good job" probably will not function as a strong reinforcer for most students. Facial expressions, gestures, and language should indicate that you are pleased or satisfied with the student's behavior (e.g., smile, wink, clap hands, affirmative head nod, and approval statements). The strength and effectiveness of social reinforcers may increase when multiple forms of reinforcers are combined. For example, you may smile at the student, clap your hands, and say, "Alright! You finished the puzzle."

Another recommendation for delivering social reinforcers is to provide specific praise by naming the appropriate behavior that the student has displayed. Specific praise calls attention to the student's behavior, which is what we hope will increase, rather than focusing on the student himself or herself. Specific praise also may serve as an antecedent cue for the appropriate behavior to continue. For example, in order to reduce Adam's challenging behavior of running in the hallway, Mr. Jeris reminds Adam to walk when the students enter the building. He then praises Adam by saying "Thank you, Adam, for walking in the hallway" when Adam is halfway through the hall. When Adam walks into the classroom Mr. Jeris tells him, "You did a great job of walking today" versus simply saying "Good job."

A final recommendation for delivering social reinforcers is to obtain student attention prior to delivering reinforcers. For example, you may be in proximity to the student before delivering praise or make eye contact with the student prior to employing smiles and gestures. This will ensure that the student attends to the reinforcing consequences that are delivered.

SUMMARY

When the function of challenging behavior is positive reinforcement, the goal of intervention is to teach and support appropriate behaviors that will achieve the same function as challenging behavior. Regardless of the strategy employed to meet this goal it is important that students have sufficient opportunities to practice appropriate replacement behaviors (Carr et al., 1994) and to obtain positive reinforcement for those behaviors. Many students will have a strong and lengthy history of obtaining something positive as a result of challenging behavior. Intervention must establish a new history for these students, one that breaks the bond between challenging behavior and positive reinforcement and one that establishes a new bond between appropriate behavior and positive reinforcement (Kazdin, 2001). The key to establishing this new history is frequent opportunities to practice appropriate replacement behaviors and consistency in obtaining reinforcement contingent on the occurrence of those behaviors.

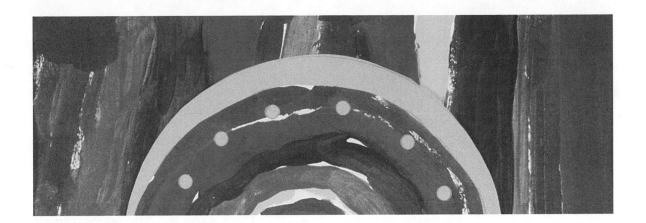

CHAPTER 8

Intervention Strategies Related to the Negative Reinforcement Function

Both the positive reinforcement and the negative reinforcement functions increase or strengthen behavior. In positive reinforcement, the student obtains something positive by engaging in challenging behavior. The behavior that results in obtaining something desirable or positive is strengthened or maintained. When the function of challenging behavior is negative reinforcement, the student avoids or escapes an aversive stimulus or event by engaging in challenging behavior (Carr, Newsom, & Binkoff, 1980; Iwata, Dorsey, Slifer, Bauman, & Richman, 1982/1994; Iwata, Pace, Dorsey et al., 1994; Repp, Karsh, Munk, & Dahlquist, 1995). In negative reinforcement, an aversive antecedent event or stimulus either is not presented or is removed from the situation following the student's behavior (remember that antecedents occur prior to or are concurrent with challenging behavior) (Sulzer-Azaroff & Mayer, 1986). Consequently, the behavior that allows the student to avoid or escape the aversive event is strengthened and will be more likely to occur the next time the aversive antecedent is present (Skinner, 1974). Students may avoid or escape tasks, activities, materials, people, settings, and so on, that are aversive to them (Carr & Durand, 1985; Carr & Newsom, 1985; Munk & Repp, 1994a, 1994b; Pace, Ivancic, & Jefferson, 1994).

Students may engage in very disruptive and/or dangerous behavior such as self-abuse, destroying property, tantrumming, arguing, and aggression, that results in escape and avoidance. Or they may engage in passive forms of noncompliance and nondisruptive behavior such as ignoring instructions, refusing to participate, negotiating, leaving an activity, or engaging in alternative activities (Walker & Sylwester, 1998). Regardless of the form of behavior, the function of challenging behavior in negative reinforcement is the same—avoidance of or escape from aversive antecedent events.

Antecedent events are not uniformly positive or aversive. A positive antecedent for one student may be an aversive antecedent for another. For example, when Ingrid is told to do a task that she has never done before, she readily begins the task because she likes new and challenging tasks. For Ingrid, the instructions and task are positive or neutral antecedents. Paul, however, dislikes anything new and when he is given a new task and told to begin the new task he refuses and continues to do a task that he has selected. If the teacher persists in telling him to do the new task, he tantrums until the task demand and the task is removed. For Paul, the task and instructions are aversive antecedents and he engages in behavior that initially results in not beginning the task (refusal) and that ultimately results in task and instruction removal (tantrum).

Antecedents and Setting Events	Behavior	Consequence	Function
Given a new task, told to begin new task	Refusal, tantrums	Stops giving instructions, removes task	Negative reinforcement: escapes instructions, avoids new task

It is important to identify each student's perspective regarding the positive or aversive nature of antecedent stimuli and to individualize interventions based on each student's response to antecedent events. However, through our experience in conducting functional assessment we have been able to identify some antecedents that are aversive for many students and that frequently lead to avoidance or escape motivated challenging behavior. These common antecedents include the following:

1. Tasks, materials, and activities that are difficult or associated with previous failure (Weeks & Gaylord-Ross, 1981)

2. Tasks, materials, and activities that are nonpreferred (i.e., the student would rather do something else)

3. Teacher-directed activities and tasks versus student-directed activities and tasks

4. Instructions to perform difficult, nonpreferred, or previously failed tasks and activities

5. Instructions to use difficult or nonpreferred materials

6. Unwanted attention from and interaction with adults, peers, and family members

7. Specific locations and seating arrangements
8. Requirements and instructions for participation

For behavior that falls within the negative reinforcement function, two major goals can be addressed through intervention. Before addressing either goal the team will need to decide if escape or avoidance is appropriate. The team will need to answer this question: Is it okay for the student to continue to avoid or escape the task, activity, materials, etc.? If the answer to this question is yes, then the goal of intervention will be to teach the student appropriate behaviors that will result in escape or avoidance. In other words, our goal is to teach appropriate replacement behaviors that will achieve the same function. Four intervention strategies can be used to address this goal. These are described in the following section and are listed in Table 8–1.

TEACH APPROPRIATE BEHAVIORS THAT RESULT IN ESCAPE OR AVOIDANCE

1. Teach Students Appropriate Methods to Indicate That They Do Not Want to Begin or Participate in an Activity, Use Materials, or Interact with Peers

This strategy allows students to avoid aversive events by communicating through appropriate behavior that they wish to avoid activities, peers, and materials (Ostrosky, Drasgow, & Halle, 1999). For example, Ruth previously avoided working at the computer by banging her head on her desk until the teacher walked away from her and stopped telling her to go to the computer. Now, instead of banging her head on her desk, Ruth avoids working at the computer by telling her teacher "No computer." When she does this, the teacher walks away and stops telling Ruth to go to the computer. Through intervention, Ruth has learned a more appropriate way to indicate that she does not want to work on the computer.

2. Teach Students Appropriate Methods to Request Alternative Activities, Tasks, Materials, People, or Locations

This strategy also allows students to avoid aversive events and to obtain alternative positive events. For example, Craig (who is nonverbal) used to scream when his teaching assistant began to review flashcards with him. Craig would do this until the teaching assistant stopped. Now after intervention, Craig points to the picture of a peer instead of screaming when the teaching assistant says that she will review his flashcards with him. When Craig does this, a peer tutor reviews flashcards with him, instead of the teaching assistant. This new form of communication (pointing versus screaming)

Teach Appropriate Behaviors That Result in Escape or Avoidance

1. Teach students appropriate methods to indicate that they do not want to begin or participate in activities or tasks, use materials, or interact with peers.
2. Teach students appropriate methods to request alternative activities, tasks, materials, people, or locations.
3. Teach students appropriate methods to request breaks from aversive tasks or activities.
4. Teach students appropriate methods to request an end to activities, interactions, or tasks.

Change the Task, Activity, Materials, or Peers

1. Reduce the difficulty: Make the instructions easier to understand, make the task or activity easier to do, or make the materials easier to use.
2. Reduce or change task demands or expectations or shorten the duration of the activity or task.
3. Provide choice of tasks, activities, materials, and peers.
4. Make the task, activity, or materials more interesting.

Arrange for Incremental and Continued Success in Performing the Task or Using the Materials

1. Provide assistance during the task or activity.
2. Provide positive corrective feedback during the task or activity.
3. Model task-related behavior and appropriate behavior.
4. Provide prompts and cues prior to the task or activity.
5. Reinforce partial task completion.
6. Reinforce participation and successive approximations toward the behavioral objective.
7. Teach the student appropriate ways to request assistance.
8. Use small cooperative groups or peer tutoring.

Intersperse Activities, Tasks, and Materials

1. Alternate tasks, activities, and materials.
2. Use behavioral momentum.
3. Use preferred activities and tasks to reinforce participation in nonpreferred activities and tasks.
4. Provide breaks during the activity or task.

Other General Strategies

1. Provide presignals and safety signals to increase self-control.
2. Ignore challenging behavior.
3. End the task or activity on a positive, successful note.

allows Craig to not only avoid working with the teaching assistant (aversive individual), it also allows him to work with a peer tutor (desired alternative individual).

Antecedents and Setting Events	Behavior	Consequence	Function
Told to work at computer	Head banging	Teacher walks away, stops giving instructions	Negative Reinforcement: escapes instructions, avoids the computer task
Told to work at computer	Tells teacher "No computer"	Teacher walks away, stops giving instructions	Negative Reinforcement: escapes instructions, avoids the computer task

3. Teach Students Appropriate Methods to Request Breaks from Aversive Tasks or Activities

This strategy allows students to temporarily escape ongoing aversive events such as tasks by requesting a break using an appropriate communicative behavior (Carr & Durand, 1985; Wacker, Steege, Northrup, Sasso, et al., 1990). For example, Uchie often threw his pencil across the room during writing practice sessions. When he did this he was instructed to get his pencil, sharpen the broken tip, and to get back to work (which he did). Now, instead of throwing his pencil across the room, Uchie requests a break from writing practice by signing "breaktime." When he signs breaktime Uchie is allowed to take a brief break. After his break, he returns to the writing task.

Antecedents and Setting Events	Behavior	Consequence	Function
Writing practice	Throws pencil	Told to get pencil, to sharpen it, and return to work	Negative Reinforcement: brief escape from writing task
Writing practice	Requests a break	Permission to take a break, praise for making request	Negative Reinforcement: brief escape from writing task

4. Teach Students Appropriate Methods to Request an End to Activities, Interactions, or Tasks

This strategy allows students to escape or terminate aversive events. For example, Melchor used to whine and cry during speech therapy until the speech and language pathologist gave up and allowed him to return to the classroom. Now, instead of crying and whining, Melchor has learned to say and sign "Done." When he does this, he is allowed to return to the classroom.

In each of the previous four strategies our goal is to teach appropriate functionally equivalent behavior that produces the same function as challenging behavior. The key to selecting appropriate alternative behavior is to first ask "What should the student do instead of the challenging behavior to communicate a desire to avoid or escape an aversive event?" and "What is an acceptable form of communication for this student?" In addition to asking what the student should do instead of the challenging behavior, we need to consider the communicative abilities of individual students when selecting an appropriate alternative behavior. The type of appropriate behavior that students will use to request escape from or avoidance of aversive events must reflect the abilities of each student. Some students may learn to request escape and avoidance using full sentences or incomplete sentences, while others may use gestures, head nods, picture cues, or sign language.

STRATEGIES TO CHANGE THE FUNCTION

As you read the four previous strategies for requesting escape or avoidance, you may have wondered if it was appropriate for the students to be able to avoid or terminate aversive activities. For example, you may have wondered if it was appropriate for Melchor to escape speech therapy or for Ruth to avoid working at the computer. In many cases, the answer to the question "Is it appropriate for the student to continue to escape or avoid the aversive antecedent event?" will be no. For example, it may be in Melchor's best interest to participate in speech therapy and it may be important for Ruth to learn to work at the computer because many of the projects in the next grade involve computer work. If the team decides that escape/avoidance is not appropriate, then the goal of intervention will be to change the function from negative reinforcement to positive reinforcement. Rather than escaping or avoiding aversive events, our goal is for students to obtain something positive by engaging in tasks and activities.

The strategies that are selected to change the function from negative to positive reinforcement will be determined by the team's analysis of why the activities, tasks, materials, peers, and so on, are aversive to the student (Horner, 1994). The team then must develop interventions to change the aversiveness of the antecedent events. For instance, Melchor did not want to go to speech because he enjoyed being in the classroom with his peers. Melchor did not find speech per se aversive, he found leaving the classroom and his peers aversive. An obvious intervention that might be employed for

Melchor is to provide speech therapy in the classroom. In doing this, the aversive event of leaving the classroom and peers is removed. In Ruth's case, she avoided using the computer because she found fine motor tasks difficult to do and she often made mistakes at the computer. Intervention for Ruth might involve reducing the amount of time Ruth was required to work at the computer, assisting her so that she experienced success at the computer, and interspersing easier activities such as gross motor and social activities with fine motor activities.

Several intervention strategies are available to help teams change the function from negative to positive reinforcement. These strategies are divided into four categories: (a) strategies that change the task, activity, peers, and materials; (b) strategies that arrange for student success; (c) strategies that intersperse activities, tasks, and materials; and (d) other general strategies. Each of these strategies can be used in isolation or combined with other strategies in a comprehensive intervention plan. The strategies are described in the following section and also are listed in Table 8–1.

CATEGORY ONE: CHANGE THE TASK, ACTIVITY, MATERIALS, AND PEERS

Students may escape or avoid tasks and activities (a) that are difficult to do, (b) that are disliked, (c) that seem overwhelming due to task demands, (d) that seem never ending due to task duration, (e) that are boring or uninteresting, or (f) that are selected and directed by the teacher. In addition to tasks and activities, students may escape or avoid materials that are difficult to use, not preferred, boring, or teacher selected. They also may avoid or escape peers who are not preferred, difficult or aversive to interact with, or who they perceive as boring or uninteresting. The goal of strategies in this category is to reduce the aversive nature of tasks, activities, and materials so that students are less likely to engage in escape or avoidance behavior and are more likely to use materials, engage in tasks, interact with peers, and participate in activities.

1. Reduce the Difficulty: Make the Instructions Easier to Understand, Make the Task or Activity Easier to Do, and Make the Materials Easier to Use

Many school-aged students avoid or escape activities and tasks that are difficult to do (Weeks & Gaylord-Ross, 1981). When this occurs we need to examine and alter those activities, tasks, and materials so that they are less difficult to do. For example, Scott has a problem getting started on his term paper. He can't even seem to write the first sentence. So he puts off (avoids) writing his paper until the night before it is due and, as a result, he doesn't complete his paper on time. This happens to Scott every time he is assigned a term paper. For Scott the task of writing a term paper is difficult, especially the initial stages of the task. To reduce the difficulty of starting the term paper, Mr. Santos now works briefly with Scott to help him develop an outline for his paper. He even helps Scott write the first paragraph of his paper. Scott then is able to complete the rest of his paper independently and he now turns his papers in on time.

Students also may refuse to use or stop using materials that are difficult to manipulate. For example, Renee, who has cerebral palsy, had a difficult time holding a regular sized spoon. If she dropped the spoon, which she did frequently, she ate her food with her fingers. Eventually she refused to use the spoon at all and only ate meals with her fingers. For Renee, using a spoon was too difficult. It caused her to eat very slowly and required too much fine motor effort. It was easier and faster for her to use her fingers during meals. However, eating with a spoon was a goal on Renee's Individualized Educational Plan and the team identified this goal as an important functional skill. As a result, escape was not an appropriate option. Therefore, the team changed the difficulty of spoon-feeding by placing a thick rubber cover over a regular sized spoon. Renee was able to hold the adapted spoon. She stopped using her fingers and began to use the spoon during meals. For students such as Renee and Scott, the task itself is not necessarily aversive. Rather, the difficulty of the task evokes challenging behavior (Dunlap & Kern, 1993).

Antecedents and Setting Events	Behavior	Consequence	Function
Mealtime, given spoon	Drops spoon, refuses to use spoon, eats with fingers	Able to eat faster, easier to use fingers	Negative Reinforcement: escapes from spoon-feeding
Mealtime, given adapted spoon	Eats with spoon	Able to eat faster	Positive Reinforcement: obtains food quickly and easily

Activities and tasks also may be difficult for students when they do not understand instructions concerning the task or activity (Dunlap, Kern-Dunlap, Clarke, & Robbins, 1991; Munk & Repp, 1994b). For example, students may avoid tasks that involve multistep, lengthy instructions or they may escape tasks for which few instructions are provided. They may avoid tasks when they do not understand the objective or final goal of the activity, or they do not know what materials are required to participate in the activity and to complete the task. When escape and avoidance behavior is related to poor instructions, consider strategies to alter instructions such as these:

A. Divide instructions into steps and provide a new step instruction only after the previous step has been completed.

B. Provide multimodal instructions (e.g., written and vocal instruction or pictorial and vocal instructions).

C. Simplify the language used in providing instructions (use words the student understands and speak at the student's linguistic level).

D. Include only relevant information in instructions.

E. Highlight relevant information in instructions.

F. Obtain student attention prior to providing instructions.

G. Check for student understanding after giving instructions, before beginning the task (Friend & Bursuck, 1999).

2. Reduce or Change Task Demands or Expectations or Shorten the Duration of the Activity or Task

Some students will avoid and escape tasks and activities that require extensive effort or time (Pace, Iwata, Cowdery, Andree, & McIntyre, 1993; Touchette, MacDonald, & Langer, 1985). For example, Gilbert refused to copy spelling words from the master list of 20 words. He would protest, "It's too many, I can't do this many, I can't do 20 words." For Gilbert, the task seemed overwhelming. When he protested, his teacher continued to give instructions to do the task and repeatedly threatened Gilbert with detention. This interaction continued until the end of the spelling lesson and Gilbert still hadn't copied a single word. The team decided to address his challenging behavior by slightly changing the task demands. They divided the task into four lists, each containing only five spelling words. The teacher gave Gilbert only one list at a time. When he finished copying the first list, he received praise and then the second list. With this task modification, the task did not seem overwhelming to Gilbert and he readily complied with the task until he had copied all 20 words.

Antecedents and Setting Events	Behavior	Consequence	Function
Spelling, instructions to copy spelling words	Protests	Repeated instructions, threatens detention	Negative Reinforcement: avoids spelling task
Spelling, instructed to copy spelling words, word list divided into small lists	Copies spelling words	Praise, task complete	Positive Reinforcement: obtains praise and good grade

In another example, Denise's mother told her to clean her room. It seemed like every time she did this Denise would whine and complain that it would take too long (it usually took over an hour to clean) and she didn't have time to clean her room. Denise usually complained until her mother said, "Okay, but you'll need to clean your room tomorrow" (which, of course, Denise never did). During intervention, Denise's mother broke the task into smaller steps and reduced the duration of the task each evening. Rather than telling Denise to clean her entire room at one time, her mother told Denise to clean her closet and desk for 30 minutes. The next night she told Denise to change her bed and vacuum for 30 minutes. She told Denise that if she cleaned for 30 minutes, then she could stop and watch her favorite TV show or talk with her friends on the phone. This intervention changed the function from avoidance to positive reinforcement by reducing the duration of the task and providing TV and phone calls as reinforcers for room cleaning behavior.

Note that not all examples of challenging behavior during lengthy tasks are a function of negative reinforcement. If students engage in challenging behavior related to the duration of a task because they are not able to sit or concentrate for a specified duration, then the function of their behavior is sensory regulation/sensory stimulation—not negative reinforcement. When we consider duration of tasks, negative reinforcement refers to escaping or avoiding events because the duration of the events is aversive. This applies to both Gilbert and Denise in the previous examples. Both of these students were able to complete the expected tasks. However, the duration of the tasks and the number of steps in the tasks were aversive for them. In sensory regulation/sensory stimulation there is a mismatch between expectations for the duration of behavior and the students' biological/neurological ability to meet those expectations.

3. Provide Choice of Tasks, Activities, Materials, and Peers

This strategy is directed to those students who refuse to begin tasks or participate in, teacher-directed activities. They also may refuse to use materials that are selected by the teacher or peers. These students often are reinforced by control; they seek to control situations. For these students, the activity or task that is selected by the teacher is not aversive, rather it is teacher selection and teacher direction itself that are aversive (Dunlap & Kern, 1993; Dyer, Dunlap, & Winterling, 1990; Munk & Karsh, 1999; Munk & Repp, 1994b; Reichle et al., 1996). This is because teacher selection and direction reduces the student's ability to control the situation. When these students engage in challenging behavior, teacher-directed activities and tasks usually are terminated either by being sent to time out or detention or by the removal of the task, instructions, or materials.

One way to address this problem is offer the student fixed choices. This allows the student to determine, within limits, the materials that he or she will use or the task and activity in which he or she will participate. For example, Dominic typically refused to complete his math worksheet. When his teacher, Mr. Lindeman, told Dominic to work he would argue until Mr. Lindeman either left him alone, telling him the worksheet would go home as homework, or sent him to the principal's office. Observation indicated that Dominic's behavior was not limited to math alone, his argumentative behavior occurred across each period and teacher. Dominic was negatively reinforced by escape from teacher-directed activities.

Intervention to address his behavior combined four strategies. First, Dominic's challenging behavior no longer resulted in escape (i.e., he was not sent to the principal's office and the teacher did not terminate task demands). Second, Mr. Lindeman and other teachers provided Dominic with limited choices so that the activities were both student directed and teacher directed. If Dominic refused to select a choice, the teachers selected for him. Third, the teachers used physical prompting to help Dominic complete tasks when needed. Finally, when Dominic complied with the task, he received positive reinforcement (even if the tasks were physically guided).

For instance, during math Mr. Lindeman asked Dominic if he wanted to solve the addition problems or the subtraction problems first. If Dominic selected addition, he was praised for making a choice. He also was praised and received one token for completing the addition problems. If Dominic argued that he wasn't going to do either type of problem, Mr. Lindeman told him to choose or he would choose for him. If Dominic continued to argue, Mr. Lindeman chose the addition problems. He then asked Dominic if he wanted to do the problems by himself or if he wanted Mr. Lindeman to provide assistance. Again, if Dominic argued, Mr. Lindeman chose for him—he assisted Dominic in completing the problems. Dominic then received a token for completing the problems. Eventually Dominic began to make choices and to follow through independently with his choices.

Choice may be offered along a number of dimensions including these:

A. *Materials.* For example, "Do you want to use a pen or a pencil?" or "Do you want to download pictures from the Internet or cut out pictures from magazines?"

B. *Amount of work.* For example, "Do you want to do one worksheet now and one later or do both now?" or "Should we read one story today or two?"

C. *Order of activities.* For example, "What should we do first, discuss the chapter or complete the graphic organizer?" or "Do you want to clean your room or do the dishes first?"

D. *Role in activities.* For example, "Do you want to be my helper today or sit with your friends?," "Do you want to be the recorder or reporter for your group?" or "Do you want to give your report at the beginning or end of the class?"

E. *Peer groupings.* For example, "Do you want to work with Sharisa or Gwen today?" or "You can join the red group or the green group."

F. *Location of work.* For example, "Should we do speech in my office or in the classroom today?" or "Do you want to work on your book report in the library or in the classroom?"

G. *Type of task.* For example, "Do you want to bounce on the ball or use the swing today in our therapy session?" or "Should we play baseball or practice the trampoline during gym today?"

H. *Type of reinforcer.* For example, "Do you want a popcorn party or extra recess?" or "Do you want to read comic books or play at the computer?"

The choices that are provided to students usually should be selected by the educator so that they address the goals of the activity or task. Choices also should be limited or fixed versus open ended. If you offer open-ended choices you run the risk that the student will select a choice that you are not prepared or able to fulfill. In the example of Dominic, if Mr. Lindeman had said during math, "What do you want to do?" Dominic might have replied, "I want to go home now" or "I don't want to do my worksheet." Obviously the choices selected by Dominic cannot be honored and do not meet the goal of completing math worksheets.

When you provide choices to students you must be prepared to follow through by selecting one of the choices for the student if the student does not independently select one of the choices (Carr, Levin, McConnachie, Carlson, Kemp, & Smith, 1994). For instance, Mr. Lindeman selected addition problems for Dominic when he refused to make a choice. Furthermore, you should be prepared to assist the students in complying with the choices that they make (or that you make for them). Eventually students will learn to select one of the choices and to follow through with the selected choice. After all, choice provides students with one form of control, and selecting a choice allows students to avoid the additional teacher direction that would follow if the teacher selected the activity and prompted the students' compliance. Finally, be sure to provide additional positive reinforcement for selecting a choice and following through with the chosen behavior. Dominic received praise and tokens in addition to the natural reinforcer of controlling the situation.

4. Make the Task, Activity, or Materials More Interesting

Many students escape or avoid tasks, activities, or materials that they perceive as boring or uninteresting (Dunlap & Kern, 1993; Ostrosky et al., 1999). Students may find tasks, activities, and materials boring that are not challenging or are too easy, that are tedious or dull, that are not developmentally or chronologically age appropriate, that are not relevant to the student's history, or that do not immediately impact the student's life or produce immediate reinforcers (Munk & Karsh, 1999).

When implementing this strategy it is important to identify for each student why the task, activity, and so on, is not interesting. The reasons will vary across students. For example, students who are gifted, who do not speak English well, or who are functioning below grade level may each find the daily lesson boring, but for different reasons. The gifted student may find the lesson boring because she has already mastered the content. The student who does not speak English may find the lesson boring because he does not understand the language used during lecture. The student who is functioning below grade level may find it boring because she is not able to understand the content of the lesson. Each of these students may engage in challenging behavior that leads to escape from the daily lesson.

The goal of this strategy is to alter tasks, activities, or materials so that they are more interesting for the student, thus reducing escape-motivated behavior. Students are more likely to participate when they are interested in the activities and materials (Ostrosky et al., 1999). For example, the gifted student might be paired with the student who is functioning below grade level and serve as a peer tutor for this student. Or the gifted student might be allowed to do an alternative activity or an enriched or advanced activity that is related to the content of the lesson (Friend & Bursuck, 1999). The student who does not speak or understand English well might receive readings and materials in his native language or use an interpreter during lecture. The student who is below grade level might have her lesson goals and materials adapted to meet her ability level.

Tasks and activities can be made more interesting by using visual aids, graphic organizers, hands-on materials, cooperative group activities, and variety in instructional delivery and student response mode. For instance, the instructional delivery may involve short periods of lecture, small group activities, reading, hands-on activities, and worksheets. Or students may respond during lecture by shouting answers in unison, writing answers, holding Yes/No answer cards, and raising their hands to be called on. Another strategy to increase student interest in tasks and activities is to make activities and tasks relevant to the students' experiences and to use preferred materials and reinforcers. For example, Mr. Banks assigns students to write a rap song about the Civil War versus writing a paper on this topic. Mrs. Silva has students divide a pizza into equal parts rather than a pie chart. Ms. Duncan provides examples on tests and worksheets that reflect favorite materials (e.g., Pokeman, McDonald's hamburgers, comic books), current local and national news items and controversial issues, and community events and values (e.g., basketball or football team events) that are relevant to her students. She also provides consequences that are immediately reinforcing for students such as being allowed to listen to preferred music, reduced homework, or time at the computer.

A final example will illustrate the importance of relevant activities. This example comes from a participant in one of our functional assessment workshops. Ms. Trainer asked her eighth-grade students to write a paper on what it felt like to be in love. The other students began to write their papers, but not Martina who was mildly retarded. She sat quietly at her desk throughout the period. At the end of the period, Martina turned in a paper that only contained her name. Martina told Ms. Trainer that she couldn't write her paper. Ms. Trainer told Martina that she would have to stay after school and they would talk about her paper then. After school Ms. Trainer told Martina that she was very disappointed in her. She said that she would give Martina until tomorrow morning to complete her paper. The next day Martina again turned in a piece of paper containing only her name. Ms. Trainer again indicated her disappointment and asked Martina why she refused to write her paper. Martina told Ms. Trainer that she wanted to write the paper, but she couldn't because she had never been in love, she'd never even had a boyfriend, and did not know what it was like to be in love. The topic of this paper was not immediately relevant to Martina, nor was it related to Martina's history and she did not have the creative or inferential skills needed to write this paper. So Ms. Trainer changed the topic of the paper so that it was relevant for Martina. The next day Martina turned in her paper titled "How It Feels to Have a Dog."

Antecedents and Setting Events	Behavior	Consequence	Function
Instructed to write a paper on an unfamiliar topic, assignment given as homework	Sat quietly at desk, did not do assignment	Stay after school, told to complete work at home, reprimand, questions	Negative Reinforcement: avoided writing difficult paper
Instructed to write a paper on an understandable topic	Completes assignment	Praise, good grade on assignment	Positive Reinforcement: completes assignment, obtains praise and good grade

CATEGORY TWO: ARRANGE FOR INCREMENTAL AND CONTINUED SUCCESS IN PERFORMING THE TASK OR USING THE MATERIALS

All too often, teachers come across students who refuse to begin or continue a task, to participate in an activity, or to use materials due to a previous history of failure. Students as young as preschool learn what they do well and what they do poorly. Unfortunately, many students, including preschool-aged children have learned that a very successful way to not fail is to escape or avoid those activities, tasks, and materials that are paired with failure. For example, Christopher was a 4-year-old boy attending an inclusive preschool for children with and without delays. Christopher had a cleft lip, gum, and palate and was very difficult to understand. At the beginning of the school year Christopher interacted with and talked to peers during all activities. Usually peers asked him to repeat what he had said and after he had repeated his words several times they told him they couldn't understand him and that he didn't "talk good." After the first month of preschool, Christopher refused to talk to or play with peers. Instead, he played in isolation and the other children ignored him. Christopher also refused to talk during speech lessons and circle activities that included peers. Christopher quickly learned to avoid failure in preschool by refusing to talk in peer-related activities.

A common saying is relevant to understanding these students: "If at first you don't succeed, try, try again. Then give up, there's no reason to be a darned fool." Students such as these receive little positive reinforcement for participation in difficult activities and tasks (Munk & Karsh, 1999; Sulzer-Azaroff & Mayer, 1986). These students often have poor self-esteem and at-

tribute poor grades and failed tasks to their own lack of skill (Friend & Bursuck, 1999). They often feel that there is nothing they can do to increase the frequency or level of success (Kalish, 1981; Zirpoli & Melloy, 2001). Such students have little motivation to attempt novel and/or difficult tasks or to continue when tasks become difficult. These students may refuse to begin worksheets, may not carry through with assigned tasks, and may not complete homework assignments. They also often refuse to answer or ask questions, refuse to perform in front of peers or to work in group activities, and do not begin or complete tests. The key to reversing this cycle of escape-motivated behavior is to provide the student with a new history in which he or she is successful at tasks and activities and in using materials. Success initially may be related to participation alone and later tied to skill level or proficiency. Students who are successful at any level are more likely to begin and continue difficult and novel tasks. Strategies to promote success are discussed in the following section and also are listed in Table 8–1.

1. Provide Assistance During the Task or Activity

Assistance can help the student perform the expected behaviors or complete the task correctly and thus result in success for the student. For example, Mrs. Bookman noticed that Felix had stopped working on his study guide questions. She went to his desk and asked to see what question he was on. Felix told her number 5, but said he didn't understand the question and couldn't answer it. Mrs. Bookman reworded the question using words with which Felix was familiar. He then understood the question and continued to answer the study questions. In another example, Ashi was putting together the animal shapes puzzle. She put the rabbit, dog, and cat pieces into their spaces but was having a hard time with the bird piece. Before she gave up and threw the bird piece and the whole puzzle on the floor (which she did often), Mr. Norman sat down with her and told her to turn the bird to the side. Ashi tried this and still was not able to fit the bird in its space. So Mr. Norman helped her turn the bird so that it fit in the puzzle space.

2. Provide Positive Corrective Feedback During the Task or Activity

Positive corrective feedback provides information to the student about how to do the task versus what the student is doing or has done wrong (Munk & Repp, 1994b; Polloway & Patton, 1993). Positive corrective feedback not only informs the student what to do or how to do the task, it also prevents the student from practicing mistakes (Lenz, Ellis, & Scanlon, 1996; Miltenberger, 1997; Sulzer-Azaroff & Mayer, 1986). For example, Mr. Chan tells Julia to reverse the *ie* in *receive* (Julia wrote *recieve*) and wrote the rule on the top of her paper (*i before e except after c*). Mr. Chan does not tell Julia that she made a mistake or spelled the word wrong. Instead he tells her what to do so that she will be successful. After she changes the spelling, Mr. Chan tells her, "Good job, you spelled it right."

It is important when providing feedback not to emphasize the student's mistakes, especially at the beginning of intervention. Remember that these students have a strong history of failure and identifying mistakes may add to this history and result in challenging, escape-motivated behavior (Polloway & Patton, 1993). Feedback should be used to teach a student how to do a task correctly, rather than to indicate that the student has made mistakes. In addition, feedback should be paired with positive reinforcement for appropriate behavior or those aspects of the task that are correct (Sulzer-Azaroff & Mayer, 1991).

3. Model Task-Related Behavior and Appropriate Behavior

One way to increase student success is to model the behavior for the student. The student then can imitate the modeled behavior (Lenz et al., 1996). For instance, Ms. Rogers knows that Lendra has difficulty with algebra and often doesn't begin algebra worksheets when they are assigned. So today, Ms. Rogers passed out the worksheets and then as other students were working, she walked to Lendra's desk and said, "Let me do the first problem, then we will do one together, and then you can do the rest of the problems." She showed Lendra how to do the first problem and then together they completed the second problem. Lendra then finished the rest of the problems independently. This strategy not only provided an *in vivo* model of performing the task and solving the problem, it also provided a permanent model of a completed problem that Lendra could refer to as she completed the remaining problems.

4. Provide Prompts and Cues Prior to the Task or Activity

Antecedent prompts and cues that are provided prior to an activity or task or before a student uses materials help the student begin and complete the task successfully. Antecedent prompts and cues may be vocal, gestural, modeled, physical, written, pictorial, and so on. You may remember that this strategy also was identified within the positive reinforcement function. In positive reinforcement the purpose of antecedent prompts and cues is to inform students of behavior that will result in positive reinforcement. In contrast, the purpose of antecedent prompts and cues in negative reinforcement is to promote success (Kennedy & Itkonen, 1993; Rhode, Jenson, & Reavis, 1992; Sulzer-Azaroff & Mayer, 1986, 1991).

For instance, to promote success and decrease refusals and off-task behavior, Ms. Samuels reminds Chiami to look at the math sign (i.e., addition, +; subtraction, −; division, /; and multiplication ×) before she does each problem. For another student, David, Ms. Samuels color codes the math signs on his worksheet so that addition problems are blue, subtraction problems are red, division problems are green, and multiplication problems are orange.

Antecedents and Setting Events	Behavior	Consequence	Function
Math class, instructions to complete worksheet	Refusals, off task	Engages in alternative task, reprimand	Negative Reinforcement: avoids math worksheet
Math class, instructions to complete worksheet, color code signs on sheet or reminders to look at signs	On task	Complete task	Positive Reinforcement: obtains success in task, praise, good grade

5. Reinforce Partial Task Completion

Reinforce a student when he or she has completed part of the task instead of waiting until the entire task is done. This provides for more immediate and frequent positive reinforcement within a task or activity. It also provides opportunities to monitor a student's behavior and provide corrective feedback if needed. For example, Mr. Hersey reinforced Kurt at the beginning of the science activity for getting his materials for the fossil dig (excavating chocolate drops baked in cookies). After Kurt found his first chocolate drop, Mr. Hersey gave Kurt a high five and encouraged him to find more fossils. This strategy also may be combined with reducing task demands and task difficulty by presenting small components of a task separately and then reinforcing completion of each partial step.

6. Reinforce Participation and Successive Approximations Toward the Behavioral Objective

This strategy is similar to reinforcing partial task completion in that we are providing positive reinforcement during the task or activity, rather than only at the end of a task. However, the focus of positive reinforcement in this strategy is to increase participation and small steps or approximations of the desired behavior or expected skill level (Malott, Malott, & Trojan, 2000; Sulzer-Azaroff & Mayer, 1991; Zirpoli & Melloy, 2001). This strategy, also known as shaping, should be used with students who do not have the skills to complete all steps in a task or to complete tasks at appropriate or expected levels. This strategy initially reduces expectations in terms of accuracy or skill and instead focuses on reinforcing students for participating in an activity, doing part of the activity, or for small improvements in skill or behavior (Anderson, Taras, & Cannon, 1996; Sulzer-Azaroff & Mayer, 1986). It allows a student to experience success even though the student is not able to do the task at appropriate or expected skill levels. This strategy obviously should be combined with skill training so that the student eventually is able to perform tasks accurately and use materials appropriately. As the student's skill increases, the focus of positive reinforcement may shift to improvements in skill as well as participation.

For instance, 6-year-old Liz has expressive language problems. Her vocabulary is very limited and the words that she does use are very difficult to understand. When she is asked to repeat words, she refuses by screaming "No." She then withdraws and will not participate in subsequent activities. Liz does this behavior at home and at school. Currently, Liz's parents and the educators at school ask her to repeat words that they do not understand and they require her to use understandable words prior to providing desired objects such as dessert or preferred materials. These strategies have only increased Liz's refusals and nonparticipation. The team decided to use shaping with Liz by reinforcing participation at Liz's current level and reinforcing small improvements in Liz's communicative behavior. First, they stopped asking Liz to repeat words. If they did not understand the words Liz used, they praised Liz for talking and asked her to show what she wanted. They then provided a model of saying the word for the desired object and gave the object to Liz. The next step involved asking Liz to imitate the model prior to providing the desired object. During this phase, praise and receiving the object was contingent on making sounds, not on the correct pronunciation of the sound or word. This phase was conducted during one activity per day and included preferred items. Next, praise and obtaining the desired object was contingent on pronouncing only the first sound in the word correctly. As Liz's communication skills increased (through these procedures and speech therapy), so did the criteria for positive reinforcement.

Other examples of shaping successive approximations of the terminal behavior include (a) praising students for answering questions even though the answer was not correct (then using positive corrective feedback to teach the correct answer); (b) providing stickers or tokens for sitting quietly during a singing activity (participation will be addressed after the student is able to sit quietly during the activity); (c) praising a student for bringing his textbook to class, even though he did not bring a pencil or his notebook; and (d) allowing a student who has worked for 5 minutes during a 20-minute activity to take a break. In each of these examples, as the student is able to perform the first step, expectations for behavior will be slowly increased.

7. Teach the Student Appropriate Ways to Request Assistance

This is a strategy that teaches the student a skill that he or she can initiate in order to increase success. Many students do not participate in activities, refuse to use materials, or refuse to begin or continue working on academic tasks when they do not know what to do. They may not understand (a) task-related instructions, (b) what materials are necessary to do a task, (c) how to use materials, (d) how to begin a task, (e) what the next step is in a task, (f) how to do the next step in a task, or (g) how to problem solve when confronted with uncertainty. This strategy should be used with those students who do not seek the assistance that would provide them with the information required to begin or complete an activity or task.

The form of assistance-seeking behavior that students use will vary depending on the developmental level of the student, grade level, and expectations in the classroom. Students may seek assistance by raising a hand, moving to the teacher's desk, calling the teacher's name, asking a peer, looking at a peer's work, using sign language or picture cards, or using other forms of signaling such as placing a card in the corner of the desk.

For example, each student in the class receives a turn using the computer and encyclopedias to research answers for a concept map on the topic of Ecuador. When it is Marilyn's turn at the computer, she turns the computer on, writes her name on her study guide, and types *Ecaudor*. The computer indicates that the site Ecaudor could not be found. Marilyn, who is not familiar with computers and uncomfortable using them, doesn't know what to do so she puts her pencil down, gets her nail file from her purse, and begins to file her nails. Even though Marilyn is the only student not working, Ms. Ling tells all the students that if they are having trouble locating Ecuador on the computer or in their books, they should raise their hand and that she will come to consult with them. When Marilyn raises her hand, Ms. Ling helps her problem solve why the site was not found and helps her find the correct site. She also tells Marilyn that if she has any more problems, she can raise her hand to ask for help.

In another example, Mrs. Johnson tells her second-grade class that they will be decorating Valentine boxes today during art. She gives the students the following instructions, "First, you need to get a box to decorate, red paper, scissors, and a bottle of glue. Then, you should cut the red paper and glue it to your box. After you have papered your box, you can get materials to decorate your box. We have felt pens, sequins, hearts, pipe cleaners, glitter, and Valentine pictures. Then you should decorate your box. When you are done decorating your Valentine box, you need to write your name on your box and put it in your cubby." Malcolm leaves his seat with the rest of the students, but he does not go to the art area and he does not get a box, red paper, scissors, or glue. Instead he wanders around the classroom for a few minutes and then he begins to play with the materials in the science station. Mrs. Johnson quietly asks Malcolm if he knows what he is supposed to be doing. He says, "I forget." She then reminds him that he can ask his friends what they are doing or he can ask her if he forgets. She encourages Malcolm to ask Ronnie what he is doing. When he does this, Ronnie tells him to get a box, paper, scissors, and glue. Malcolm then works next to Ronnie and successfully completes the task.

8. Use Small Cooperative Groups or Peer Tutoring

This strategy can increase student success in a number of ways. It permits students to observe models of behavior that they can imitate. It allows students to seek assistance from peers. It permits students to perform parts of an activity or task, rather than the entire task, and it also allows students to help each other master a skill or complete a task (Soodak & Podell, 1993). For instance, Jody had difficulty with written expression and often did not complete homework or classroom assignments that required a written product. Her geography teacher decided that although writing was an important skill, he was most interested in Jody learning geography. So during projects that required a written product, Jody worked with a small group of students (all students were assigned to small groups). Tasks within the groups were divided among students. Tasks might include obtain Internet and other resource materials, read and explain material to members of the group, obtain or draw pictures to illustrate the topic, develop concept maps, and write and edit the group paper. Jody participated in her group by drawing pictures for the paper and obtaining, reading, and describing resource materials. And, she received a good grade on her geography project.

Note that this strategy would not be appropriate if the goal of the activity was to improve or practice writing skills or to work independently. If writing or independent work were the focus of the activity, then different strategies would be employed to increase success such as shortening the task, providing assistance during the task, and shaping approximations of appropriate behavior. Since the goal of the geography activity was to increase knowledge of geography, it was appropriate to have Jody work with a group.

Antecedents and Setting Events	Behavior	Consequence	Function
Writing task	Refusals, incomplete work	Reprimand, failed grade	Negative Reinforcement: avoids writing tasks
Geography, written task, assigned to small group	Participates	Interaction with peers, complete task	Positive Reinforcement: obtains success in task, peer interaction

Several references discuss how to develop and implement cooperative group activities and peer tutoring programs (Friend & Bursuck, 1999; Greenwood et al., 1987; Johnson & Johnson, 1981; Kaplan, 1996; Polloway & Patton, 1993).

CATEGORY THREE: INTERSPERSE ACTIVITIES, TASKS, AND MATERIALS

The strategies in this group reduce challenging behavior by interspersing tasks, materials, and activities that are reinforcing with those that are aversive (those from which the student escapes). These strategies ensure that there are reinforcing tasks, activities, and materials present in the environment that may offset the aversive nature of tasks, activities, and materials.

1. Alternate Tasks, Activities, and Materials

Students may be more likely to begin and complete aversive tasks and activities if those events have been preceded or will be followed by events that are not aversive, than they would if several aversive events were presented consecutively (Blair, Umbreit, & Bos, 1999; Horner, Day, Sprague, O'Brien, & Heathfield, 1991; Winterling, Dunlap, & O'Neill, 1987). Alternations may occur between easy–difficult activities, tasks, or materials; successful–unsuccessful tasks and activities; and preferred–nonpreferred tasks, activities, and materials. For example, Gene is an excellent student in subjects that involve reading and language skills. Gene readily participates in reading, composition, spelling, and foreign language lessons. These subjects are easy for Gene and he experiences a great deal of success (e.g., good grades, few mistakes, and teacher praise) in these subjects. As a result, they are preferred classes. Gene is diagnosed with a learning disability in math and he does not do well in the subjects that require math skills such as math, science, and shop. He finds these subjects very difficult, and he seldom experiences success. Instead, he makes frequent mistakes, receives negative corrective feedback regarding his math skills, and usually receives poor grades in these subjects. As a result, these subjects are nonpreferred and Gene often avoids these classes.

TABLE 8–2
Gene's daily schedule

Previous Schedule	Revised Schedule
Reading (+)	Composition (+)
Spelling (+)	Math (−)
Composition (+)	Foreign Language (+)
Foreign Language (+)	Science (−)
Lunch	Lunch
Shop (−)	Spelling (+)
Science (−)	Shop (−)
Math (−)	Reading (+)

Note: (+) indicates activities that are easy and preferred by Gene and at which he experiences success; (−) indicates activities that are difficult and nonpreferred by Gene and at which he is unsuccessful.

Gene's previous schedule is presented in Table 8–2. The easy, successful, preferred subjects all were scheduled during the first half of the school day. The difficult, nonpreferred subjects all were scheduled following lunch. Gene often did not attend his afternoon classes; he usually skipped these classes 2 or 3 days per week. To address Gene's nonattendance, his schedule was revised. The revised schedule (also presented in Table 8–2) alternated difficult, nonpreferred activities with activities that were preferred, easy, and successful so that each type of activity occurred throughout the day. It also arranged for the day to begin and end with a preferred, successful activity. This schedule increased Gene's afternoon class attendance and participation in difficult activities. Note that in this example, the team also included strategies to make the difficult nonpreferred activities less aversive and to increase success such as providing prompts and cues prior to and during the task, reducing task demands, shortening the task, and reinforcing participation.

2. Use Behavioral Momentum

This strategy involves requesting several behaviors for which there is a high probability of student compliance or correct responding before requesting a behavior for which there is a low probability of compliance or correct responding (Carr et al., 1994; Davis, Brady, Williams, & Hamilton, 1992; Mace & Belfiore, 1990; Munk & Karsh, 1999; Singer, Singer, & Horner, 1987; Wehby & Hollohan, 2000). This strategy is most often used with students who are noncompliant, that is students who refuse to begin activities or tasks. This strategy allows students to experience success and other forms of positive reinforcement prior to responding to requests regarding nonpreferred, often unsuccessful tasks. This increases the probability that students will display the low probability behavior because of the positive momentum established in the previous request–response–positive reinforcement sequences.

For example, Rose disliked getting ready for bed (e.g., putting on her pajamas, washing her face, and brushing her teeth). She often delayed getting ready for bed by saying "Just a minute," "After this show," and "Wait until the commercial" when her father said, "Go upstairs and put on your pajamas." Rose's father decided to try behavioral momentum in order to reduce her avoidance behavior. This is the sequence of requests that he used:

Father: "Rose, get your book and show me what you made today in school."

Rose: (She gets her book from another room.) "Here it is, this is our house in the springtime when the flowers grow."

Father: "That is really a great picture! Tell me about this page."

Rose: "This is the firehouse we went to yesterday. Here's the fire truck and the fire dog."

Father: "What did the siren sound like?"

Rose: (Screams like the siren.)

Father: "That's loud. I hope you make some more pictures tomorrow. Go put your book in your backpack so you can take it back to school tomorrow."

Rose: (Places the book in her backpack.)

Father: "Okay now, Rose, go upstairs and put on your pajamas."

Rose: (Puts on her pajamas.)

Rose had complied with four requests and received positive reinforcement for complying with those requests before her father requested a nonpreferred, low probability behavior. Generally, three to five tasks that are easy to complete and of short duration should be requested and reinforced prior to presentation of the low probability task (Davis et al., 1992).

In another example, before requesting that her class quietly get their language books and turn to page 10, Ms. Brennan tells her class (a) to stand up, (b) to shake their hands, and to (c) give the person next to them a high five. Only after the students have complied with the first three requests does she tell them to quietly get their language books and turn to page 10.

3. Use Preferred Activities or Tasks to Reinforce Participation in Nonpreferred Activities and Tasks

This strategy is known as the Premack principle, Grandma's rule, or the "If this, then that" rule (Homme, deBaca, Devine, Steinhorst, & Rickert, 1976; Premack, 1959; Rhode et al., 1992; Sulzer-Azaroff & Mayer, 1986). This strategy requires the team to first identify activities that are preferred or that serve as positive reinforcers for students. This can be done by asking students to identify or select preferred activities or observing students during free-choice periods and identifying activities that they most frequently select. Access to preferred activities or materials then is contingent on student participation in nonpreferred activities (Horner et al., 1991; Mace & Belfiore, 1990). In other words, preferred activities are used to reinforce participation in nonpreferred or aversive activities.

For instance, Mrs. Kahn told the entire class: "As soon as you all put away the art materials and wash the tables (the nonpreferred activity) we will go outside for recess (the preferred activity)." In another example, Mr. Koogan allowed Billy to read comics in the back of the room after he finished his test. In both of these examples, student access to preferred activities was contingent on participation in less preferred or nonpreferred activities. In these examples, Mrs. Kahn informed students of the preferred activity that would follow completion of the nonpreferred activity; Mr. Koogan, however, did not. He simply presented the preferred activity after Billy had completed the test.

When students are informed of the reinforcer (preferred activity) that is available contingent on appropriate behavior, this strategy combines antecedent cues plus positive consequences. If students are not informed that a positive consequence is contingent on their behavior, then the strategy is solely a consequence-based strategy. It is not always necessary to include both components (antecedents and consequences) of the strategy. After all, consequences alone do affect behavior. However, it stands to reason that students will be more likely to exhibit appropriate behavior if they are informed of the positive consequences that will follow their behavior. Adding the antecedent cue or presignal brings an element of prevention to the intervention versus waiting for behavior to occur and then reacting to behavior by providing consequences. The presignal informs students of the appropriate behavior that is expected and of the desired consequence that will follow if the behavior is displayed.

4. Provide Breaks During the Activity or Task

This is similar to the alternating tasks strategy in that a preferred activity or task is alternated with a nonpreferred or aversive activity. However, in this strategy the student receives a break during an ongoing task and must return to the task or activity following the break. In addition, the break often is unstructured and the student chooses the behavior that he or she will do during the break. For instance, Reggie was learning how to work in a grocery store (how to bag groceries, stock shelves, etc.). However, he did not like the grocery store tasks that he was asked to complete. He often stopped working to talk to other individuals in the area or to look at the products that he was to bag or stock. To increase on-task behavior, Reggie received a 3-minute break at the end of each 10-minute work session, provided he had worked appropriately during the 10-minute session. At the end of his break Reggie returned to his job and worked on the assigned task for another 10 minutes.

Antecedents and Setting Events	Behavior	Consequence	Function
Grocery store training	Off task	Peer interaction, engage in alternative task	Negative Reinforcement: escape task
Grocery store training	On task	Break	Negative Reinforcement: brief escape from task

In another example, Roger received a 5-minute break after he had answered 10 study guide questions. During break he could leave his seat to work on the class jigsaw puzzle at the back of the room or do a task of his choice at his desk. At the end of the 5-minute break Roger returned to his desk and completed the next 10 questions. In both of these examples, Roger and Reggie were allowed to take breaks from the nonpreferred activities provided they worked appropriately during the specified work period. They then returned to and completed the activity.

CATEGORY FOUR: OTHER GENERAL STRATEGIES

These general strategies focus on increasing student tolerance and willingness to participate when presented with materials, tasks, and activities that are aversive by promoting self control. They also are designed to teach students that challenging behavior will no longer produce the negative reinforcement function. Rather, escape and avoidance are possible only when appropriate behavior is displayed.

1. Provide Presignals and Safety Signals to Increase Self-Control

Presignals are antecedent cues that are provided before the start of an activity. Safety signals are cues that are provided during an activity or task. Presignals and safety signals provide information concerning task or activity parameters (Mace, Shapiro, & Mace, 1998; Tustin, 1995). For example, presignals may identify the number of steps or problems the student is expected to complete and safety signals may identify the number of steps or problems remaining in a task. Presignals also might identify the expected total duration of an activity or task. Safety signals might identify the amount of time remaining in a task or activity. Finally, presignals and safety signals may inform the student that an ongoing activity is about to end and that a new activity will begin.

For example, Ed was always late to the next activity because he hadn't completed the previous task. He had not completed the previous activity because he didn't distribute his time well. When the teacher told students to clean up and get ready for the next activity, Ed spent several minutes completing his task and then several more minutes cleaning up. Ms. Harris, Ed's teacher, decided to use presignals and safety signals to help Ed distribute his time better throughout the activity so that he could complete the task in a timely fashion and begin the next activity on time. During art, Ms. Harris reminded Ed that in 15 minutes art would end and astronomy class would begin. She told Ed to quickly finish his art project. Five minutes before the end of art, Ms. Harris told Ed to begin cleaning up. At the beginning of the astronomy period Ms. Harris told the class that they had 20 minutes to work on their astronomy projects. Twice during the project work session Ms. Harris walked by Ed's desk and gave him a card on which she had written "ten minutes left" and then "five minutes left." This combination of presignals and safety signals helped Ed anticipate and plan for the end of art and the start of astronomy. During astronomy they also informed Ed how long he was expected to work on his astronomy task and the amount of time remaining in the astronomy period.

The purpose of presignals and safety signals in this strategy is to provide information that may increase self-control or self-management during aversive activities, thus enabling the student to begin and complete activities (Koegel, Koegel, & Parks, 1995; Reichle et al., 1996). Other strategies to teach and promote self-control are self-instruction, self-monitoring, self-reinforcement (Friend & Bursuck, 1999; Mastropieri & Scruggs, 2000; Smith, Polloway, Patton, & Dowdy, 1998), correspondence training (Guevremont, Osnes, & Stokes, 1986), behavioral relaxation (Poppin, 1988), and cognitive behavior modification strategies (Sulzer-Azaroff & Mayer, 1991).

2. Ignore Challenging Behavior

Many students escape and avoid activities and tasks by engaging in extended negative interactions with educators. For example, calling on Seth to read aloud in class was the first step in an extended argument between Seth and Mr. York. Their argument might consist of the following interactions:

Mr. York: "Seth, please read the first paragraph."

Seth: "I ain't reading in class."

Mr. York: "Seth, I asked you to read the first paragraph."

Seth: "It's a stupid book."

Mr. York: "I don't care what you think about the book. I want you to read the paragraph."

Seth: "Who do you think you are, my mother? I don't have to do what you say."

Mr. York: "I am your teacher and this is my classroom. When you are in my classroom, you do what I say."

Seth: "It ain't gonna happen, no matter how much you beg."

Mr. York: "I am not begging. If you don't read, you will fail this lesson."

Seth: "Who cares? This is a (*profanity*) book."

Mr. York: "Don't swear in my classroom."

Seth: "This is a (*profanity*) book and you are a (*profanity*)."

Mr. York: "I will not tolerate swearing in my classroom. Apologize right now."

Seth: "Get you, (*profanity, profanity*)."

This type of interaction sometimes continued until the end of the period or until Seth was sent out of the room. The function of the interaction for Seth was to avoid reading in class. For students like Seth, it is important to remember this: Do not be drawn into escalating and extended arguments and negative interactions (Walker, Colvin, & Ramsey, 1995; Walker & Walker, 1991). Also do not repeatedly threaten a student, provide lengthy reprimands when a student engages in challenging behavior, or try to persuade a student to perform the behavior or participate in an activity. Do not fall into the coercion trap (Rhode et al., 1992). Rather, ignore the student's challenging behavior and employ other strategies previously discussed in order to change the function of the student's behavior from negative reinforcement to positive reinforcement.

3. End the Task or Activity on a Positive, Successful Note

This final strategy addresses the issue of termination of an activity or task. If the goal of intervention is to have the student participate in activities and tasks and to use materials, then it is important that the student not be allowed to escape an activity as a result of challenging behavior. The goal of this strategy is to end the task contingent on appropriate behavior. The student must learn that he or she is no longer able to escape when he or she displays challenging behavior. In other words, challenging behavior no longer works; it does not produce the desired escape function. If the student engages in challenging behavior during the activity or task, wait until the student is not displaying challenging behavior before ending the task or assist the student in doing the task and then reinforce the student for task-related behavior.

For instance, Geraldine often hit herself when asked to practice writing her name. In the past, this behavior resulted in her teacher, Mr. Dunbar, leaving her alone. Geraldine's self-abuse was so alarming to Mr. Dunbar that he stopped asking her to practice writing her name. Note that there are two cases of negative reinforcement in this example: Mr. Dunbar escaped Geraldine's self-abusive behavior by not interacting with her. His walking away terminated her self-abuse. Geraldine avoided writing her name by engaging in self-abuse. Her self-abuse terminated Mr. Dunbar's instruction.

During intervention Mr. Dunbar told Geraldine to practice writing her name as he had done prior to intervention. Now, however, when Geraldine hit herself, Mr. Dunbar did not leave or withdraw the task. Instead, he ignored her self-abuse and provided physical guidance to help Geraldine write her name (even though she hit herself at the same time). He then told Geraldine, "Good job, you wrote your name. Now you are done," and ended the task. Eventually Geraldine wrote her name independently when told to do so.

Antecedents and Setting Events	Behavior	Consequence	Function
Instructed to write her name	Self-abuse	Withdrawal of instructions	Negative Reinforcement: escape instructions, avoid writing name
Instructed to write her name, physical guidance	Some self-abuse, writes name	Ignore self-abuse, told she did a good job	Positive Reinforcement: obtains praise and success in the task

Consider another example of 4-year-old Sissy who screamed and cried during teacher-directed activities and tasks until she was left alone and task demands were withdrawn. The team developed a multicomponent intervention that involved the following:

A. Provide presignals concerning the start of the activity and the number of steps Sissy needed to complete during the activity (e.g., put away five toys or do three puzzles).

B. Provide safety signals concerning the number of steps remaining in the activity (e.g., you have three more toys to put away).

C. Provide physical assistance during the activity.

D. Reduce task demands (initially she was required to do less than other students).

E. Alternate teacher-directed and child-directed tasks.

F. Praise Sissy for doing the required task (even when physical prompting was employed).

Intervention also included the strategy to end the activity on a positive note. The task ended only when Sissy had completed the task and was not crying and screaming. For Sissy, there was only a short window of opportunity within which she stopped crying and screaming, especially at the beginning of intervention. After assisting Sissy in completing the task, her teacher waited until Sissy took a breath between screams before ending the activity. At that point, the teacher told Sissy that she had put her toys away or she had finished her puzzle and was quiet so she was done with the activity. Eventually Sissy learned that she could not escape teacher-directed activities by screaming and crying. She also learned that she must engage in appropriate task-related behavior before the activity was terminated. Finally, teacher-directed activities became less aversive for Sissy because they were paired with positive reinforcement.

Many of the strategies to address the negative reinforcement function, including the previous two strategies, incorporate the strategy of extinction of escape-maintained behavior. Challenging behavior is not allowed to produce escape from task demands, activities, etc. (escape is the previous reinforcer that now is withheld) (Iwata, Pace, Kalsher, Cowdery, & Cataldo, 1990; Shore, Iwata, Lerman, & Shirley, 1994). Extinction of escape-maintained behavior combined with other positive and negative reinforcement strategies is a critical factor in determining the effectiveness of interventions in which the goal is to change the function from negative to positive reinforcement (Mazaleski, Iwata, Vollmer, Zarcone, & Smith, 1993; Zarcone, Iwata, Hughes, & Vollmer, 1993; Zarcone, Iwata, Vollmer, Jagtiani, Smith, & Mazaleski, 1993; Zarcone, Iwata, Smith, Mazaleski, & Lerman, 1994).

SUMMARY

Too many of our students engage in challenging behavior that functions to produce negative reinforcement. Students may avoid or escape activities that they do not know how to do, that have been paired with previous failure (i.e., learned helplessness), or that they do not want to do (i.e., the task is disliked, not relevant, uninteresting, nonpreferred, or overwhelming). The strategies to address the negative reinforcement function are designed to teach students appropriate behaviors that result in escape or avoidance and/or to change the function from negative to positive reinforcement by reducing the aversive nature of antecedent stimuli and events, promoting success, and providing positive reinforcement for appropriate behavior.

Intervention may focus on teaching appropriate ways to communicate a desire to escape and avoid aversive events when escape and avoidance are deemed appropriate. If escape and avoidance are not deemed appropriate, intervention will focus on changing the function from negative to positive reinforcement. Often, when the goal is to change the function from negative to positive reinforcement, we must begin intervention by allowing the student to escape. However, escape must be contingent on appropriate, not challenging behavior. At the same time, intervention should focus on increasing student success and changing the nature of activities and tasks and the delivery of antecedent instructions and tasks. Then, as students gain skills and experience success, the criterion for escape is increased (e.g., they must participate for longer durations, do a greater number of tasks). For example, Jeff disliked shop, a subject that he found difficult and in which he performed poorly. He often escaped shop by carelessly manipulating the shop tools and arguing with the instructor. When he did this he was sent to detention. Intervention to change Jeff's behavior initially allowed Jeff to escape shop if he spent 5 minutes in shop correctly manipulating the shop tools and not arguing with the instructor. At the same time, Jeff was paired with a peer-buddy and together they worked on shop projects. Slowly the amount of time that Jeff was required to spend in shop before he was allowed to escape was increased. By the end of 1 month, Jeff was spending the entire period in shop and was working appropriately on shop projects.

We recommend that teams combine several negative reinforcement strategies in addressing escape and avoidance behavior (Iwata, Pace, Cowdery et al., 1994). In the example above, we (a) initially shortened the duration of the task, (b) made the task more interesting and easier by pairing Jeff with another student, (c) allowed Jeff to escape by engaging in appropriate behavior, and (d) praised appropriate replacement behaviors (i.e., safe, on-task behaviors). In addition to combining several strategies within an intervention plan, we encourage teams to consider why each student engages in escape and avoidance-motivated behavior (i.e., the team identifies the aversive nature or aspects of antecedent events from the student's perspective). Intervention strategies should be individualized to reduce the aversive nature of antecedent events. In addition, positive consequences (from the student's perspective) should be included in each intervention plan in order to teach and strengthen appropriate replacement behavior.

Antecedents and Setting Events	Behavior	Consequence	Function
Shop	Careless with tools, argues with instructor	Detention	Negative Reinforcement: escape shop
Shop, paired with peer, amount of time on task increased over time	Careful, on task	Break, praise	Positive Reinforcement: escape shop initially, eventually stays in shop entire class, success in completing task, peer interaction and assistance

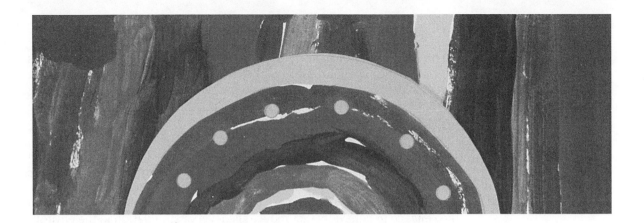

CHAPTER 9

General Intervention Strategies Related to the Sensory Regulation/Sensory Stimulation Function

When the function of challenging behavior is sensory regulation/sensory stimulation, the students' challenging behavior produces sensory input or it functions to regulate (i.e., increase or decrease) the level and type of sensory stimulation within the environment (Carr, Langdon, & Yarbrough, 1999; Repp, 1999; Zentall & Zentall, 1983). Stimulation may occur within each of the sensory systems. These systems include visual (vision), auditory (hearing), tactile (touch), olfactory (smell), gustatory (taste), vestibular (sense of movement in body and space), and proprioceptive (sensation in muscles, tendons, and joints). The amount of stimulation and sensory input that students desire and are able to tolerate will vary across individuals. Likewise, the ability to process sensory input will vary across students (Colby Trott, Laurel, & Windeck, 1993).

There are several types of students whose challenging behavior is a function of sensory regulation/sensory stimulation. For some students who fit the sensory regulation/sensory stimulation function, there is a mismatch between the type and level of stimulation required or needed by the student and the type and level of stimulation currently available to the student

(Berkson & Tupa, 2000). For these students, challenging behavior functions to change the type and level of stimulation in the environment so that it matches the student's needs (Berkson & Tupa, 2000; Guess & Carr, 1991; Repp, 1999; Shore & Iwata, 1999). Through both challenging and appropriate behavior, students obtain and maintain an optimal level of stimulation (Repp & Karsh, 1990; Repp, Karsh, Dietz, & Singh, 1992; Repp, Karsh, Munk, & Dahlquist, 1995). Some students may require greater levels of stimulation than are available in the environment and they engage in behaviors that produce high levels of stimulation (Goh et al., 1995; Repp & Karsh, 1992). Alternatively, some students may need low levels of sensory stimulation and they engage in behaviors that reduce the level of stimulation in the environment (Colby Trott et al., 1993; Guess & Carr, 1991).

Some students may require a specific form (e.g., movement) or multiple forms (e.g., movement and touch) of sensory input or they may need frequent variety in the types of sensory input that they experience. Other students may be unable to tolerate various forms of sensory input (Chicago Public Schools, 1998, Walker, Colvin, & Ramsey, 1995), or they may engage in challenging behavior when they are not able to correctly interpret sensory input. This often occurs for students with sensory processing problems or sensory integration disorders (Haldy & Haack, 1995; Reisman & Scott, 1991). These students may experience difficulty in registering, organizing, interpreting, and responding to sensory input. As a result, these students may be hypersensitive to sensory stimulation and respond disproportionately to normal levels of sensory input. Or they may be hyposensitive to sensory stimulation and seek increased—and often excessive—levels of sensory input (Colby Trott et al., 1993; Snider, 1991). Readers interested in additional information on sensory integration may examine the following resources: Ayres (1972, 1979), Bissel, Fisher, Owens, and Polsyn (1988), Colby Trott et al. (1993), Fink (1990), Fisher, Murray, and Bundy (1991), Haldy and Haack (1995), and Wilbarger and Wilbarger (1991).

The sensory regulation/sensory stimulation function also includes students who are not able to regulate their levels of arousal or excitement (Fouse & Wheeler, 1997; Guess & Carr, 1991). For example, some students easily become overstimulated or overaroused in highly stimulating activities and tasks. Once they are overstimulated, they are not able to reduce their level of arousal and active behavior during passive, less stimulating activities such as individual worksheets or reading (Colby Trott et al., 1993; Haldy & Haack, 1995). All too often these students are referred to as hyperactive, noncompliant, and as poor listeners when in fact the problem is one of sensory regulation. Other students may have difficulty becoming aroused or maintaining adequate levels of arousal. They are not able to increase their level of arousal and active behavior during active or passive tasks. These students unfortunately often are identified by educators as lazy or unmotivated when, again, the problem is related to sensory regulation.

Several goals can be addressed when the function of challenging behavior is sensory regulation/sensory stimulation:

TABLE 9–1
General intervention strategies related to the sensory regulation/ sensory stimulation function

1. Alternate active, highly stimulating tasks with passive, less stimulating tasks.
2. Provide multisensory stimuli and individualize types of sensory stimuli.
3. Redirect the student to an appropriate activity that provides required levels or forms of stimulation.
4. Provide presignals and safety signals.
5. Teach the student to request a change in stimulation or a break from stimulation.
6. Teach appropriate behaviors that result in desired levels and types of sensory stimulation.
7. Teach self-control and tolerance.
8. Increase your tolerance for the types of stimulation that students require.

© 2002 Chandler and Dahlquist.

A. To provide an environment that increases or decreases sensory input or that offers a variety of sensory stimuli in order to match the level and type of stimulation needed by the student (Haldy & Haack, 1995).

B. To assist students in regulating their level of stimulation so that they do not become over- or understimulated.

C. To teach students appropriate ways to indicate that they need a change in stimulation or that they do not like a particular form or level of sensory input.

D. To teach students appropriate behaviors that will produce the type and levels of desired stimulation.

E. To increase, within limits, students' ability to function in environments that do not provide optimal levels and types of stimulation.

Teams commonly use several intervention strategies to address challenging behavior within the sensory regulation/sensory stimulation function. These strategies are listed in Table 9–1 and are discussed in the following section.

We begin with general strategies related to the sensory regulation/sensory stimulation function. We discuss strategies that are designed to address students whose behavior functions to produce increases in sensory stimulation and those whose behavior functions to decrease sensory stimulation in the next chapter.

GENERAL SENSORY REGULATION/SENSORY STIMULATION STRATEGIES

1. Alternate Active, Highly Stimulating Tasks with Passive, Less Stimulating Tasks

This strategy is designed to prevent students from becoming overaroused or understimulated by modulating the level of stimulation within the environment (Chicago Public Schools, 1998; Munk & Karsh, 1999; Walker et al., 1995).

For example, we learned earlier about Randy, who selected only very stimulating activities during free play. He typically was overstimulated by the end of free play and was not able to reduce his level of arousal during subsequent passive activities. As a result, he was frequently "in trouble" during passive activities. Randy's teachers frequently told Randy to come to the reading area, to be quiet, to sit nicely, to wait for his turn, and to keep his hands to himself. They also reprimanded Randy for not complying with their requests, and when this did not decrease his challenging behavior, they sometimes sent Randy to the time-out chair or to another area of the room until he was "ready to calm down." As you might expect, these strategies had little effect on Randy's behavior. Rather than continue to address Randy's behavior *after* he was overstimulated, the staff decided to take a proactive approach and prevent overstimulation by maintaining a balanced level of stimulation during free play. So they alternated active and passive free-play activities for Randy. Together, the team developed a list of highly stimulating activities and a list of less stimulating or passive activities. Randy was allowed to select the first free-play activity from the highly stimulating list. He then selected an activity from the list of low stimulation activities and so forth. The alternation of active, stimulating tasks and passive tasks changed Randy's arousal level. Randy was no longer overstimulated at the end of free play and he was able to participate appropriately in the subsequent reading activity.

Antecedents and Setting Events	Behavior	Consequence	Function
Stimulating free-play activities, overstimulated	Does not come to reading, noisy, out of seat, touched peers	Instructions, reprimand, time-out	Sensory Regulation/ Sensory Stimulation: maintain high level of stimulation
Alternating stimulation level of free-play activities	Comes to reading, quiet, sits nicely	Praise, allowed to participate	Sensory Regulation/ Sensory Stimulation: maintain appropriate level of stimulation

In addition to alternating activities and tasks, you can imbed brief calming exercises within highly stimulating activities. For example, when the class gets too loud and excited during group work, Ms. Stauch has all students take a quiet break by putting their heads down on their desks for 30 seconds or she asks each student to write a brief summary of the progress their group has made. This calms students and they are able to return to group work with less noise and arousal.

You also may imbed brief stimulating exercises within lengthy passive tasks. For instance, during our workshops we provide some form of active task approximately every hour. For example, we may ask participants to work in small groups or to stand and engage in role-play activities. We also often throw a small bean bag to individuals who ask or answer questions. These strategies provide a stimulating break from sitting and listening to lecture and discussion and it enables participants to stay alert throughout the 6-hour workshop.

2. Provide Multisensory Stimuli and Individualize Types of Sensory Stimuli

Some students respond more readily to some types of sensory input than they do to other types of sensory input and they are better able to learn when preferred/required types of sensory input are present (Reisman & Scott, 1991). These students may be off task or inattentive when preferred/required types of sensory input are not present or they may engage in challenging behavior that produces the preferred forms of sensory input. One goal of this strategy is to increase the on-task and attending behavior of students by providing and/or allowing multisensory input during classroom activities, materials, and lessons. For example, Ms. Winston provides graphic organizers during lecture so that her students have visual as well as auditory sensory input. She does this because she knows that some of her students learn best with visual input, some learn best with auditory input, and some learn best with multiple types of sensory input. Mr. Whalen provides three-dimensional examples of fossils for his students to touch during a geography lesson. By doing this, Mr. Whalen allows students who learn best by touching or exploring access to tactile stimulation. In these examples, Mr. Whalen and Ms. Winston applied the intervention strategies class-wide rather than using them for individual students. While the graphic organizers and three-dimensional examples were beneficial to the individual students who required those forms of sensory input, they also probably increased interest in the activities for other students in the class, thus improving on task behavior across all students.

Although multisensory and varied input can be provided for groups of students as illustrated in the previous examples, it can be individualized to meet the needs of particular students. For example, Mr. Secor gives Deanna a copy of the overhead transparencies that he uses in lecture and he asks Ruth to give Deanna a copy of her lecture notes because Deanna does not learn well when she must listen and take notes at the same time. This is because Deanna has problems with written expression and she is not able to do two different tasks (writing and listening) simultaneously. When she does attempt to take lecture notes, she misses most of the lecture and is identified as displaying off task challenging behavior. Mr. Secor does not use this strategy for all students in his class because the other students are able to take notes and listen simultaneously and Mr. Secor considers this an important skill for other students to use. This strategy is used with Deanna to maximize her ability to learn. Her learning decreases when she attempts to listen and take notes simultaneously. Her learning is maximized when she is allowed to listen only, and she is no longer identified as engaging in challenging behavior.

A second goal of the strategy to provide individualized and multisensory stimuli is to teach students to obtain preferred types of sensory input in appropriate ways. For example, Barry has a great need for tactile stimulation. He often touches his peers and their personal belongings. Barry's peers do not like this behavior and have begun to yell at Barry and to hit him when he touches them or their belongings. They also generally avoid interacting with Barry throughout the school day. Rather than telling Barry to stop, punishing his behavior, or removing him from the group (strategies that have been unsuccessful in the past), the team decided to teach Barry to obtain tactile stimulation in appropriate ways. Barry's parents bought a small koosh ball, Silly Putty, and other small manipulatives. The team then taught Barry to use these items to gain tactile input instead of touching his friends and their belongings.

Antecedents and Setting Events	Behavior	Consequence	Function
Amount of time without tactile stimulation	Touches peers and their belongings	Tactile sensory input peers yell, hit, and avoid Barry	Sensory Regulation/ Sensory Stimulation: increase tactile stimulation
Amount of time without tactile stimulation	Squeeze koosh ball, touches small manipulatives	Tactile sensory input	Sensory Regulation/ Sensory Stimulation: increase tactile stimulation

3. Redirect the Student to an Appropriate Activity That Provides Required Levels or Forms of Stimulation

Many students obtain stimulation or regulate sensory input by engaging in behavior that others (e.g., parents, peers, or educators) identify as challenging behavior (Berkson & Tupa, 2000; Kennedy & Souza, 1995). Remember, however, that from the students' perspectives, they are engaging in behaviors that effectively produce the sensory regulation/sensory stimulation function. Several studies have shown that when stimulating activities are available, self-stimulatory behavior decreases as appropriate engagement increases. In addition, engagement increases further when individuals are directed to and/or assisted in using available materials (Chandler, Frich, Hein, & Burke, 1979; Dunst, McWilliam, & Holbert, 1986; Favell, McGimsey, & Schell, 1982; Horner, 1980; Koegel, Koegel, Frea, & Smith, 1995; Montes & Risley, 1975).

This strategy reduces challenging behavior by directing students to engage in appropriate activities that provide the same or similar levels or types of sensory input as the student had received by engaging in challenging behavior. For instance, TJ often practiced karate punches and kicks during transitions or other unstructured times. He often hit items and other individuals who were near him when he did this. His teachers decided to redirect his karate punches and kicks to more appropriate behaviors. When TJ performed his first karate punch or kick, his teachers directed him to do a variety of alternative tasks such as erase the chalkboard, pass out materials, obtain materials from the teacher's desk, or take a note to the teacher next door. This allowed TJ to continue to obtain gross motor stimulation, yet he did so by engaging in appropriate behaviors and activities. Eventually, the team *prevented* TJ's challenging behavior by directing TJ to appropriate gross motor tasks before he initiated his karate kicks and punches.

4. Provide Presignals and Safety Signals

You may recall that this strategy was identified and discussed within both the positive reinforcement and negative reinforcement functions. When it is used in positive reinforcement, the purpose is to identify appropriate behavior that students should exhibit or to identify the reinforcers that are contingent on appropriate behavior. In negative reinforcement, the purpose of antecedent presignals and safety signals is to promote success in difficult and aversive activities, and to facilitate self-management and self-control. When this strategy is used within the sensory regulation/sensory stimulation function the purpose is to provide students with information about the nature of specific tasks or activities and appropriate behavior to employ in response to specific types of sensory input or levels of stimulation (Flannery & Horner, 1994; Mace, Shapiro, & Mace, 1998; Tustin, 1995).

For instance, Ms. Gasparato knows that Leo dislikes noisy, crowded activities and does not transition well from quiet, isolated activities to activities that are noisy and in which he might be touched by others, such as recess, assembly, or gym. Often he runs out of the classroom or stands in an isolated corner of the room. To help Leo make the transition to noisy, crowded activities, Ms. Gasparato developed a written schedule of daily activities for Leo. She reviewed the schedule with Leo at the beginning of each day and reminded Leo that the class would be moving to a noisy, crowded activity in "x" number of minutes. During noisy, crowded activities Ms. Gasparato provided safety signals to inform Leo how much time remained in the activity (e.g., "Ten more minutes and then we return to the classroom"). She also used presignals and safety signals to identify appropriate behavior that Leo might employ in the aversive sensory environments (e.g., "Remember you can go stand in the back of the assembly hall if it gets too noisy," "Remember to ask your friends to move if they are standing too close to you," or "Let me know when you need to go back to the classroom").

This combination of presignals and safety signals helped Leo anticipate and plan for changes in sensory input during highly stimulating activities. They informed Leo that there would be a change in activity and provided information about the sensory nature of the new activity, when the new activity would occur, how long it would last, and appropriate behavior alternatives to employ during the activity.

Note that many students, like Leo, will require antecedent cues that identify appropriate behaviors that they can employ in environments that do not match their sensory needs. Simply informing students that there will be a change in stimulation or that there are "x" number of minutes remaining in an activity may not enable students to tolerate those sensory situations or teach students what to do when they need an increase or decrease in sensory stimulation. For example, although Leo was able to anticipate changes in sensory input and then was able to transition to crowded, noisy activities, he continued to need safety signals during activities to identify what he should do when the activities were difficult to tolerate. These safety signals allowed Leo to achieve the same function (i.e., reduce sensory input) through appropriate behavior, rather than by running from the room or standing in the corner.

Antecedents and Setting Events	Behavior	Consequence	Function
Transition to and participation in noisy, crowded activities	Runs from classroom or stands in corner	Reduced noise and touch	Sensory Regulation/ Sensory Stimulation: decrease auditory and tactile stimulation
Presignals and safety signals regarding activity and appropriate behavior	Transition to activity, asks peers to move, moves to back of room, requests return to classroom	Reduced noise and touch, praise for appropriate behavior	Sensory Regulation/ Sensory Stimulation: decrease auditory and tactile stimulation

5. Teach the Student to Request a Change in Stimulation or a Break from Stimulation

Many students recognize that (a) they need a change in sensory stimulation (e.g., "I can't sit any longer, I need to move"), (b) they are not able to tolerate certain types of sensory input (e.g., "I don't like it when people touch me"), or (c) they need particular forms of sensory input or output ("I won't remember what I read unless I can read it aloud") (Reisman & Scott, 1991). This strategy allows students to indicate their needs and to request specific types and levels of sensory input and changes in types and levels of stimulation before they engage in challenging behavior. This can be an especially useful strategy for students with sensory integration problems (problems in registering, organizing, interpreting, and responding to sensory input) (Haldy & Haack, 1995). Several examples will illustrate this strategy. Hilda signed that she needed a calming or quiet break during very stimulating activities. Theo held up his break card to request a movement break during seatwork activities. Lawrence asked to stand at the back of the line in order to avoid touch from other students. Adrianne completed oral quizzes because of problems processing visual stimuli (i.e., written quizzes). Bradley received copies of lecture notes because he experienced problems processing auditory stimuli. Finally, Chet completed multiple-choice tests because of problems with written expression (i.e., essay tests).

This strategy is built on the premise that parents and educators are willing and able to respect the student's need for a different type of sensory input or a change in stimulation and that they will respond positively to the student's request. This can cause problems, however, if students learn that they can request breaks or changes in stimulation in order to avoid or escape an aversive activity. When this happens, the function of their request is negative reinforcement, not sensory regulation/sensory stimulation. If you intend to use this strategy, it may be helpful to carefully monitor the student's behavior prior to initiation of this strategy. For example, identify the types of sensory inputs that are related to challenging behavior, how long the student can tolerate deficient or overstimulating sensory environments, and so forth.

Consider the example of Theo who requested movement breaks during seat-work activities. During baseline observations the team noted that Theo was able to sit quietly and work at his desk for approximately 10 minutes. After 10 minutes he often stood at his desk, wandered around the classroom, or talked to peers. When he was instructed to return to his work, he complied and worked for about another 10 minutes. Then the cycle was repeated. The team also noted that when Theo participated in small group activities or large group discussion he was able to stay on task for the entire activity. During intervention the team taught Theo to request breaks during individual seatwork activities by raising his break card. When he raised his break card his teacher nodded her head yes and Theo was allowed to walk to the back of the room and stretch for a few minutes. He then walked back to his desk and continued working.

Antecedents and Setting Events	Behavior	Consequence	Function
Ten minutes into a passive in-seat activity	Stands at desk, wanders in room, talks	Gross motor movement	Sensory Regulation/ Sensory Stimulation: increase motor to peers stimulation
Ten minutes into a passive in-seat activity, break card	Holds up break card, walks to back of room, stretches	Gross motor movement	Sensory Regulation/ Sensory Stimulation: increase motor stimulation

Theo quickly learned to use his break card to request breaks during individual seatwork and he did so approximately every 10 minutes. However, he began to request breaks during PE, a subject that he did not like. He also began to request breaks quite frequently (e.g., every 2 minutes) during individual reading activities, which also was a subject that he did not like and during reading tests. Thus, Theo not only learned to request breaks in appropriate situations based on the sensory regulation function, he also generalized that behavior as a strategy to escape aversive activities (the negative reinforcement function). As a result, the team informed Theo that he could only use his break card during individual seatwork activities and that he could only use his card once every 10 minutes. Note, that this incorporates the differential reinforcement of low rates strategy discussed in Chapter 7.

6. Teach Appropriate Behaviors That Result in Desired Levels and Types of Sensory Stimulation

This strategy is based on the assumption that intervention strategies must address the function of behavior. Students who need an increase in stimulation or who require a decrease in sensory input will achieve that function one way or another (Ellingson et al., 2000; Zhou, Goff, & Iwata, 2000). This strategy focuses on the type of behavior that students use to achieve the sensory regulation/sensory stimulation function. The goal of this strategy is to teach or promote appropriate replacement behaviors that will allow students to achieve the type and level of sensory stimulation that they require (Berkson & Tupa, 2000; Ellingson et al., 2000; Zhou et al., 2000).

For example, Joyce often twirled and pulled out her hair, picked at her nails and cuticles, and pulled at threads on her clothes. Her mother complained that she had ruined several of her outfits, that she was getting a bald spot on her head, and that her nails were raw and bleeding. The team noted that Joyce typically engaged in these behaviors during passive activities such as watching TV or reading when she was at home or during lecture at school. They hypothesized that she received tactile stimulation from these behaviors. They further hypothesized that the tactile stimulation functioned to increase Joyce's level of arousal during passive activities. The team decided to replace Joyce's challenging behaviors with more appropriate behaviors that would also provide tactile stimulation. So they gave her a small artist's pad and colored pencils and encouraged her to draw during TV and lectures. They also taught her to hold and manipulate objects such as paper clips, pencils, and rulers. They praised Joyce for using these new objects. Note that this incorporates the differential reinforcement of alternative behaviors discussed in Chapter 7.

Antecedents and Setting Events	Behavior	Consequence	Function
Passive activities	Twirls and pulls hair, picks nails and cuticles, pulls threads on clothes	Finger movement, reprimand	Sensory Regulation/ Sensory Stimulation: increase in tactile stimulation and arousal
Passive activities, provided with manipulative objects, prompts	Draws, manipulates objects	Finger movement, praise	Sensory Regulation/ Sensory Stimulation: increase in tactile stimulation and arousal

In general, interventions to teach appropriate behaviors that will result in sensory stimulation should match the type of sensory stimulation obtained through challenging behavior. For example, if a student's behavior functions to produce movement, then intervention should focus on increasing appropriate replacement behaviors that also produce movement. If a student receives oral stimulation, then intervention should focus on appropriate ways to produce oral stimulation and so forth. Occupational and physical therapists and speech pathologists often can provide guidance in identifying appropriate replacement behaviors that achieve the same sensory stimulus function. Table 9–2 provides a list of appropriate replacement behaviors that will result in increased or decreased levels of sensory stimulation. This list should serve as a starting point in identifying alternative appropriate behaviors that students may employ in order to regulate stimulation.

Another strategy to teach appropriate replacement behaviors that will increase or decrease stimulation is to teach students how to use materials and/or toys. Sometimes when students do not know how to use materials or materials are not developmentally or age appropriate they will increase stimulation by using materials inappropriately or using them in a stereotypical manner (e.g., repetitive banging, mouthing materials, or throwing materials) (Bailey & Wolery, 1992; Chandler et al., 1979). One way to reduce these types of inappropriate self-stimulating behaviors is to teach students alternative methods for using toys and materials (i.e., how to use materials and toys appropriately) (Brockman, Morgan, & Harmon, 1988). This will provide students with appropriate methods of producing stimulation that may compete with and thus reduce stereotypical behaviors that produce stimulation.

For example, Alvaro, an 8-year-old boy with severe cognitive delays, attended a self-contained classroom. His favorite and most frequent behavior was to sit on the floor, rock from side to side, tap his fingers against his chin, and hum quietly. When his teachers or parents gave him materials or toys he followed a predictable sequence of behavior. First, he smelled the object that he received. Second, he tasted the toy. Finally, he held the object in front of his face and tapped it as he returned to rocking and humming. Alvaro had very few appropriate toy play skills. He did not know what to do with toys other than to incorporate them as part of his typical stereotypical, self-stimulatory behavior.

The goal of intervention was to teach Alvaro to use six toys appropriately. The team selected six responsive toys that were easy to manipulate. Responsive toys are toys that react in response to behavior such as a music box, See and Say, or a pop-up box or they are toys that are multisensory such as tactile books with scented stickers (Bailey & Wolery, 1992). The team used vocal prompts, modeling, and physical guidance to teach Alvaro how to use the six toys that were selected. Appropriate toy play behavior was followed by social praise and hand claps, as well as the natural consequence produced by the toy. They found that following intervention, Alvaro used the six toys appropriately. He no longer used the six toys in a

TABLE 9–2
Appropriate replacement behaviors that students may employ to increase or decrease sensory stimulation

Sensory Increase

Stand at desk or while doing work	Exercise
Take short walks	Shake legs, hands, etc.
Finger movements, finger plays	Rub clothes
Drink ice water from sports bottle	Suck sour candy
View kaleidoscope, view finders	Drink with a straw
Draw, write during passive activities	Twirl hair
Frequent changes in position	Blow bubbles
Manipulate Silly Putty or clay	Squeeze hand weight
Quietly pat leg, arms, face, or desk	Use computer, calculator

Sit on vestibular cushion, vibrating cushion
Sit with feet and buttocks on seat of chair
Hold and manipulate preferred toys or materials
Use sand or bean table and materials in a sensory center
Chew gum or a crunchy food such as carrot sticks or pretzels
Request a change in the form of sensory input or an increase in the level
  of sensory stimulation
Manipulate small items such as koosh balls, pens, paper clips, beads,
  silicone ball, Nerf ball, jewelry
Initiate short tasks such as sharpening pencil, getting a drink
Complete assigned tasks such as taking a note to teach next door and
  assisting the teacher in preparing for a lesson, erasing the chalkboard

Sensory Decrease

Slow, rhythmical rocking	Self massage
Wear headphones to block noise	Suck sweet candy
Relaxation exercises	Deep breathing
Move to quiet area	Work in study carrel

Complete short passive tasks during stimulating activities
Lay head on desk for short period of time
Turn body or desk away from peers and other auditory and visual stimuli
Request a change in the form of sensory input or a decrease in the level
  of sensory stimulation
Listen to soft, rhythmical music

Note: These strategies are adapted from our experience conducting functional assessment and from the following references:
Colby Trott et al. (1993), Fouse and Wheeler (1997), Haldy and Haack (1995), and Snider (1991).
© 2002 Chandler and Dahlquist.

stereotypical manner. The team also found that although Alvaro continued to hum during toy play, his body-rocking behavior decreased. This intervention allowed Alvaro to continue to receive sensory stimulation, but he did so through appropriate play behavior rather than through stereotypical self-stimulation. This intervention also added additional positive consequences (social praise and hand claps) that were presented when Alvaro engaged in appropriate toy play.

Antecedents and Setting Events	Behavior	Consequence	Function
Provided with toys	Body-rocking, humming, smells, tastes, and taps toys	Gross and fine motor movement, oral input	Sensory Regulation/ Sensory Stimulation: increase in motor and oral stimulation
Provided with toys, prompts for appropriate toy play	Humming, appropriate toy play	Fine motor movement, oral input, praise, and hand claps	Sensory Regulation/ Sensory Stimulation: increase in motor and oral stimulation

7. Teach Self-Control and Tolerance

For some students it may be possible to increase their ability to tolerate sensory input and behave appropriately in environments that do not meet their sensory needs (Reichle et al., 1996). For example, during the last 30 minutes of the day, students in Mr. Alvarez's class worked on their homework assignments. Like many students with attention deficit, hyperactivity disorder, Hank found it difficult to attend to his homework assignment for more than 5, or sometimes 10, consecutive minutes. Instead, during this time he often drew pictures at his desk, looked out the window, or talked to himself, Mr. Alvarez, or his peers. Most of Hank's peers ignored him or told him to stop talking when he initiated to them. A few, however, talked with Hank, which resulted in both Hank and his peers being off task during the homework period. Mr. Alvarez eventually moved Hank's desk to the back corner of the room so that he could not easily talk to peers. Mr. Alvarez also constantly reprimanded Hank for being off task and for talking to peers, to himself, or to Mr. Alvarez.

Mr. Alvarez developed an intervention system to increase the amount of time that Hank was on task during homework sessions. He placed a timer on Hank's desk to indicate the amount of time left in the session. Mr. Alvarez provided vocal prompts to remind Hank to keep working when Hank was off task, and peers reminded Hank to keep working when he talked to them. Mr. Alvarez also taught Hank to mark his on-task checklist at the end of each 3-minute session in which he was on task. In addition, he frequently praised Hank's on-task behavior and provided a token at the end of each 3-minute period in which Hank was on task. This intervention eventually increased Hank's on-task behavior to 15 consecutive minutes.

Antecedents and Setting Events	Behavior	Consequence	Function
Homework tasks, instructions to work individually	Talks to peers, self, and teacher, looks out of window, draws in book	Interaction with peers, reprimand, visual, tactile, and auditory stimulation	Sensory Regulation/ Sensory Stimulation: increased variety in stimulation
Homework task, instructions to work individually, timer, on-task checklist, prompts	On task, marks on-task checklist	Tokens, praise, visual, tactile, and auditory stimulation	Sensory Regulation/ Sensory Stimulation: increased variety in stimulation

You can use several approaches to increase students' tolerance and self-control, including these:

1. Social stories that describe specific situations and appropriate behavior to employ in those situations (Gray, 1994; Gray & Garland, 1993)

2. Picture cues

3. Timers

4. Daily schedules

5. Work outlines and checklists

6. Problem-solving instruction

7. Self-monitoring and self-reinforcement training (Koegel, Koegel, & Parks, 1995; Lloyd, Landrum, & Hallahan, 1991; Sugai & Rowe, 1984; Sulzer-Azaroff & Mayer, 1986; Walker et al., 1995)

8. Behavior or task checklists

9. Correspondence training (Guevremont, Osnes, & Stokes, 1986)

10. Alternative behavior training

Many of these approaches will involve preview and discussion, rehearsal or role-play, review, and reinforcement. They also should include presignals and safety signals to act as antecedent cues for behavior. These approaches help students anticipate what will happen, when it will happen, and how to handle adverse sensory situations.

When your goal is to increase student's tolerance and self-control, it is important that your goal for the student's behavior is reasonable given the student's need for stimulation and responses to sensory input. It may not be possible to greatly alter the student's need for stimulation or tolerance for various types and levels of stimulation. For example, it may never be possible for Hank to remain on task for the 30-minute homework period. However, it was possible to increase his on-task behavior from 5 to 15 minutes. For many students a more appropriate strategy than teaching tolerance will be to teach appropriate ways to produce or decrease sensory stimulation and appropriate ways to respond to sensory input. Or it may be desirable to combine two strategies: Teach tolerance and self-control as possible and also teach appropriate behaviors that will achieve the same function. For Hank, in addition to the intervention previously described, we might also teach him to request breaks during the homework sessions and appropriate behaviors to employ during his breaks.

8. Increase Your Tolerance for the Types of Stimulation That Students Require

This is not a strategy to change student behavior, rather it is a suggestion that as educators and parents we recognize and respect the student's need for an increase or decrease in stimulation or for specific types of stimulation. Consistently working against the sensory needs of the student will inevitably lead to challenging behaviors (Fouse & Wheeler, 1997). For many students whose challenging behavior fits the sensory regulation/sensory stimulation function, the basic demands of a school environment such as sitting still, staying on task, listening and attending, waiting quietly, interacting appropriately with others, and following instructions are extremely difficult to do (Colby Trott et al., 1993; Reisman & Scott, 1991). Rather than trying to force, request, entice, or punish students into changing their behavior, it would be better to anticipate student reactions and student needs and work within the limitations of the student's sensory system (Williams & Shellenberger, 1996).

Several examples will illustrate this point. Telling a student who needs to move to "sit still" typically will not result in the student sitting still. It would be better to allow the student to move quietly throughout an activity or to take brief movement breaks. Punishing a student with a short attention span for not attending or for being off task will not increase the student's attention span or on-task behavior. However, if we recognize that the student has a short attention span we might shorten the duration of the task or break the task into small steps. Or we might provide a study carrel to reduce distractions that contribute to the student's poor attending and off-task behavior. Forcing a student with tactile defensiveness to use finger paints will not decrease that student's defensiveness and will increase challenging behaviors. It would be better to acknowledge the student's tactile defensiveness and let the student wear plastic gloves, for example, when using finger paints or to allow the student to use alternative art materials. Warning a student who craves tactile stimulation to keep her hands in her lap probably will not decrease inappropriate touching. It would be more appropriate to let the student hold and manipulate an object that provides tactile stimulation such as a koosh ball or Silly Putty® and to build tactile stimulation into some daily activities. Finally, informing a student who needs low levels of stimulation that she will receive stickers or tokens if she behaves appropriately in a highly stimulating environment will not increase the student's ability to do so. Instead, the student should be allowed to move to an area of the classroom that provides reduced levels of stimulation when the levels of stimulation are too great.

In each of these examples, the educator initially expects the student to do what other students are required (and able) to do (i.e., to behave like the other students). The educator also expects the student to voluntarily modify his or her behavior on request, to tolerate all types of sensory input, and to adjust to environments with varying levels and types of stimulation. Yet, if the function of challenging behavior is sensory regulation/sensory stimulation, these often are unreasonable expectations that are impossible for students to meet. We would be much more successful when working with these students if we recognize, respect, and work within their sensory stimulation and regulation needs.

SUMMARY

The general sensory regulation/sensory stimulation intervention strategies that were discussed in this chapter may be used for all students whose behavior functions to regulate the level or type of sensory input and stimulation. They also may be used with students whose behavior functions to produce sensory stimulation, students who are hypersensitive or hyposensitive to specific forms of sensory input, and students who have problems regulating levels of stimulation when they are overstimulated or underaroused.

Before developing and implementing intervention strategies teams should identify why or how the student's challenging behavior fits within the sensory regulation/sensory stimulation function. For example, is the student hypersensitive to tactile stimulation? Does the student require increased levels of sensory stimulation? Does the student become overstimulated easily? Analysis of why the student's behavior fits within the sensory regulation/sensory stimulation function will guide the development of intervention strategies.

The strategies that are selected for intervention should directly address the reasons for challenging behavior (i.e., specific problems related to sensory regulation/sensory stimulation). For example, if a student becomes easily overstimulated, then we should alternate active, highly stimulating activities with passive, less stimulating tasks. If a student is hypersensitive to tactile stimulation, then intervention should reduce tactile stimulation in activities and in providing some forms of reinforcement. For example, the student may do an art project on the computer instead of using finger paints. The student's teacher would use stickers, grades, or points as reinforcing stimuli instead of high fives or pats on the back.

We recommend that teams combine several strategies in order to develop comprehensive intervention plans to address students' behavior. The general strategies also may be combined with strategies that specifically address the need for increased stimulation and those that address the need for decreased stimulation. These strategies are described in the next chapter.

10

Specific Intervention Strategies Related to the Increase and Decrease Sensory Regulation/Sensory Stimulation Functions

This chapter provides specific intervention strategies that match each category of the sensory regulation/sensory stimulation function. We begin with strategies that can be used for students whose behavior is maintained by the increase sensory regulation/sensory stimulation category, followed by strategies that can be used with students whose behavior is maintained by the decrease sensory regulation/sensory stimulation category of this function.

STRATEGIES THAT MATCH THE INCREASE SENSORY REGULATION/SENSORY STIMULATION FUNCTION

Students within the increase sensory regulation/sensory stimulation category increase their level of sensory input and stimulation by engaging in challenging behavior (Carr, Langdon, & Yarbrough, 1999; Goh et al., 1995; Repp, 1999; Repp & Karsh, 1992; Zentall & Zentall, 1983). They may seek out highly stimulating activities or excessive forms of stimulation (i.e., students who are hyposensitive to sensory input), or they may become easily overaroused (Snider, 1991). Once they are overaroused, they may not be able to reduce their state of arousal in a sufficient amount of time or to an acceptable level (Colby Trott, Laurel, & Windeck, 1993; Guess & Carr, 1991; Haldy & Haack, 1995; Snider, 1991). Students who fit the increase sensory regulation/sensory stimulation function may exhibit challenging behavior during unstructured periods, activity transitions, and when moving from one environment to another (e.g., from the playground to the classroom). These students often are described as being off task, disruptive, hyperactive, inattentive, impulsive, unorganized, noncompliant, and as having short attention spans (Reisman & Scott, 1991).

Several strategies can be used to provide increased sensory environments for these students and to teach students to use appropriate behaviors to produce sensory stimulation. These strategies, which are listed in Table 10–1 and described in the following section, may be combined with the general sensory regulation/sensory stimulation strategies discussed in the previous chapter.

For some kids, free choice time is too free.

TABLE 10–1
Strategies that match the increase sensory regulation/sensory stimulation function

1. Provide stimulating activities and materials during and between activities and tasks.
2. Develop effective and efficient transitions.
3. Reduce waiting.
4. Add movement to activities and movement breaks.
5. Increase the pace of instruction and interaction.
6. Provide variety in instruction, materials, and student response.
7. Use stimulating social reinforcement.
8. Conduct calming activities at the end of stimulating activities.

© 2002 Chandler and Dahlquist.

1. Provide Stimulating Activities and Materials During and Between Activities and Tasks

Students are more likely to be engaged and to remain on task when stimulating materials, tasks, and activities are available (Chicago Public Schools, 1998; Favell, McGimsey, & Schell, 1982; Horner, 1980; Walker, Colvin, & Ramsey, 1995; Wodrich, 1994). Environments that do not provide stimulating activities and materials are correlated with increases in challenging behavior such as self-stimulation, self-abuse, and off-task, or aggressive behavior (Dunst, McWilliam, & Holbert, 1986; Montes & Risley, 1975). This finding is especially prevalent during unstructured periods such as the transition between activities or classes, free time, recess, and when students are required to sit for long periods of time (e.g., during assembly). When students who need high levels of stimulation have free time or do not have activities to do or materials to use, they may engage in challenging behavior that increases stimulation (Chandler, Frich, Hein, & Burke, 1979; Repp, 1999; Repp, Karsh, Deitz, & Singh, 1992). They may run, shout, throw materials, fight, seek stimulating attention, or engage in stereotypical behavior.

For instance, 11-year-old Seneca had a long ride to and from school each day. She was the first student on the bus in the morning and the last student off the bus in the afternoon. During bus rides, Seneca often left her seat, ran up and down the aisle, hit peers who were seated next to her, or hit the window. Her behavior had become so dangerous to herself and others that the bus driver had banned her from the bus.

The team hypothesized that Seneca engaged in these behaviors because she did not have something appropriate to do during the long bus rides. Seneca did not exhibit similar challenging behavior during school or at home; these behaviors only occurred during bus rides. So, the team decided to increase stimulation for Seneca by providing stimulating activities that she could do on the bus. Seneca's parents bought her a portable CD player with headphones that she could use on the bus. In addition, at the end of each school day Seneca selected a favorite activity or materials to use on the bus such as a comic book, Beanie Baby,™ or Pokémon™ cards. The team also employed a home–bus–school note program in which the bus driver indicated whether Seneca had displayed appropriate or challenging behavior on the bus (Jenson, Rhode, & Reavis,

1994). Seneca received praise from school staff, her family, and the bus driver when she behaved appropriately on the bus. This intervention decreased the frequency of Seneca's challenging behavior.

Antecedents and Setting Events	Behavior	Consequence	Function
Long bus ride with no task, low level of stimulation	Runs up and down aisle, hits peers, hits window	Reprimand, instructions to behave, gross motor and tactile sensory input	Sensory Regulation/ Sensory Stimulation: increased movement tactile stimulation
Long bus ride with selected activities and materials, medium level of stimulation	Stays in seat, uses materials, listens to CDs	Tactile and auditory sensory input, home– bus–school note program with praise	Sensory Regulation/ Sensory Stimulation: increased auditory and tactile stimulation

Table 10–2 provides a list of strategies to increase stimulation and arousal in educational settings. This list should serve as a starting point in identifying intervention strategies that will increase stimulation during and between activities and tasks and that will promote the use of stimulating materials.

Several variables should be considered when selecting and arranging activities and materials that provide increased levels of stimulation and that maintain appropriate levels of arousal. Novel materials and activities and tasks that present a slight challenge often are more stimulating to students than are familiar materials and easy activities (McGee & Daly, 1999). It is a good idea to rotate materials throughout the school year. For example, Mr. Lundy changes the materials in the science center every 2 weeks and Ms. Shipp changes the materials and props in the dramatic play center weekly. Mrs. Johnson changes the comic books and magazines in the free reading corner every 2 weeks. This maintains the novelty effect of materials and provides variety within activities. Multisensory materials, three-dimensional materials, materials that students can manipulate, preferred materials, and responsive materials also increase stimulation and engagement (Bailey & Wolery, 1992). Peer-mediation or peer-tutoring and cooperative group activities often are more stimulating than individual-work activities. Peer and cooperative learning groups provide increased opportunities for interaction and active participation (e.g., turn-taking) and can result in increased engagement and positive academic outcomes (Greenwood, 1991; Greenwood et al., 1987; Jenkins & Jenkins, 1981; Johnson & Johnson, 1981).

TABLE 10–2

Strategies to increase stimulation and maintain arousal during and between activities and for providing stimulating materials

---

Provide active breaks during passive activities.

Lead students in brief exercises prior to beginning tasks.

Teach appropriate and multiple uses of materials and toys.

Use group or unison responding during lessons.

Use frequent active responding during lessons.

Use multisensory activities and materials.

Use bright lighting.

Allow students to complete graphic organizers during lecture.

Ask the student to provide assistance at the beginning and end of activities. For example, the student may pass out papers, collect tests, erase the chalkboard, or clean up materials.

Assign short movement tasks during an activity such as taking a note next door or moving to the teacher's desk to show work.

Use cooperative learning groups.

Assign students to work in pairs as peer tutors.

Have students work problems on the blackboard.

Have students obtain materials for activities and clean up materials at the end of activities.

Provide small manipulatives.

Provide responsive toys and materials.

Task variation and materials variation.

Conduct arousal or jump start activities at the beginning of tasks and during tasks.

Provide a sensory table and holding activities for students to use at the end of activities, during transitions, and during activities as a brief stimulating break.

Allow students to chew gum, suck sour candy, chew crunchy foods.

Allows students to sip ice water from sports bottles or straws.

Use stimulating forms of positive reinforcers.

Provide scented markers, stickers, etc.

Lead students in stretching.

Add movement to passive activities.

Allow students to change position frequently or to stand during activities.

Open windows or use fans to increase air flow.

Note: These strategies are adapted from our experience conducting functional assessment and from the following references: Colby Trott et al. (1993), Fouse and Wheeler (1997), Haldy and Haack (1995), Reisman and Scott (1991), and Snider (1991).

© 2002 Chandler and Dahlquist.

A final variable to consider in developing stimulating activities is the duration of activities and tasks. Students may become bored when they are required to do any one task for an extended period of time (even if the task initially was stimulating). When this occurs, the recommended strategy is to change tasks frequently (Dunlap & Kern, 1993). Task variation is accomplished by presenting consecutive tasks for short periods of time, rather than presenting one task for an extended duration (Munk & Karsh, 1999). The duration of tasks will need to be individualized across students, based on baseline observations of the amount of time each student is able to remain on task.

Stimulating materials and activities should be readily available during unstructured periods or free time (Dunst et al., 1986; Montes & Risley, 1975). For example, Ms. Colton provided activities such as group jigsaw puzzles, preferred reading materials, and computer games for students to use who completed their tests or worksheets before other students. This strategy greatly reduced the disruptive behaviors often observed among students who completed assignments early (e.g., talking to peers, rustling papers, fidgeting). Materials and tasks such as those provided by Ms. Colton should be within reach of students (i.e., not locked away or out of the classroom) so that students may independently initiate activities. Students who do not independently select activities may be directed to appropriate activities using antecedent cues and redirection.

2. Develop Effective and Efficient Transitions

As mentioned earlier, transitions frequently are correlated with challenging behavior. This is because transitions often are unstructured, lengthy, and chaotic, with little focused direction and stimulation (Strain & Hemmeter, 1997). These characteristics of transition are illustrated in the example of Ms. Mangurten's classroom. Ms. Mangurten tells students to clean up their art projects and to get ready to go to the lunchroom. Some students begin to put materials away; however, others continue to work on their uncompleted projects. Other students do not clean up; instead, they wander about the classroom. For instance, Jocelyn follows instructions and begins to return the supplies at her table to the art closet. Peggy yells at Jocelyn for taking the art supplies. Jocelyn in turn complains to Ms. Mangurten that Peggy yelled at her and that Peggy won't clean up. Peggy then pushes Jocelyn who falls into Harry. Harry hits Jocelyn who then begins to scream. Meanwhile, Kenny and a few friends leave the classroom and run to the lunchroom. Manny turns on the record player and begins to sing and dance to the music. Several peers join him. Ms. Mangurten gets angry and tells the students to stop what they are doing and to line up. The students then move to the lunchroom. At this point Ms. Mangurten returns to her classroom, turns off the record player, and cleans up the remaining art materials.

To reduce challenging behavior associated with transitions, we must develop more effective and efficient transitions (Bailey & Wolery, 1992; Lawry, Danko, & Strain, 2000). Effective and efficient transitions are as short as possible so that the periods of low stimulation are minimal. They also are structured (as much as possible) so that students know what transition-related behaviors are expected and have options to increase stimulation during transition. In Ms. Mangurten's class, this can be done in these ways:

A. Give clear instructions for transition behavior. For example, "Put your supplies back on the art shelf and then line up at the door."

B. Provide students who need high levels of stimulation with a specific task or job to do during transition. For example, "Kenny, I would like you to wash the tables."

C. Facilitate an end to the ongoing activity and signal impending transitions (Haldy & Haack, 1995). For example, "In ten minutes we will clean up so you need to finish your project now."

D. Provide appropriate activities for students to do as they wait for the end of transition (e.g., students may draw or write on the class mural, assist other students, or work on crossword puzzles or graphic organizers that may be completed for extra points).

E. Decrease the number of large group transitions (McGee & Daly, 1999). For example, Ms. Mangurten staggers transition across small groups in order to reduce waiting for students and the chaotic nature of her class transitions. Students in Group A use the restroom while students in Group B get materials for the next activity. Then students in Group B use the restroom while students in Group A get materials for the next activity.

Antecedents and Setting Events	Behavior	Consequence	Function
Instruction to clean up and get ready for lunch (unclear instructions, no activities)	Fighting, compliance, noncompliance, leave class, run to lunchroom, wandering, screaming, yelling	Reprimand, instructions, interaction, movement, move to lunch	Sensory Regulation/ Sensory Stimulation: increase sensory stimulation
Presignals to end activity, clear instructions, transition tasks available, assign specific tasks, staggered groups and tasks	Compliance with instructions, on task	Able to end activity, movement, other forms of sensory input, move to lunch	Sensory Regulation/ Sensory Stimulation: increase sensory stimulation

3. Reduce Waiting

Situations in which students must wait frequently lead to challenging behavior. Examples in which students often wait include the following:

A. *Waiting for materials.* For example, waiting for art supplies, books, worksheets, toys, tests, or snack.

B. *Waiting in line*. For example, standing in line prior to, or at the end of, recess or to obtain lunch; waiting in line to wash hands or get a drink and even waiting for a turn to stand in line (e.g., if names are called alphabetically) and then standing in line.

C. *Waiting for a turn to participate during an activity*. For example, waiting to answer or ask questions or to state an opinion; waiting for a turn to write on the board, to read aloud, or take a turn in a game.

D. *Waiting for assistance*. For example, waiting to receive assistance when using the computer, to obtain feedback on a worksheet problem, or to receive individual instructions.

E. *Waiting for a turn to use materials*. For example, waiting for the drums, glue, computer, blocks, or encyclopedia.

F. *Waiting during transition*. For example, waiting between the end of one activity and the start of another or between the end of one class period and the start of another.

For many students, waiting is very unstimulating; it is tedious. Many students fill the stimulation void by engaging in behavior that produces stimulation such as talking to peers, fidgeting, leaving the area, shouting answers out of turn, and acting aggressively. If we are able to reduce waiting, we will reduce the challenging behavior that typically occurs during these periods (Lawry et al., 2000; Rhode, Jenson, & Reavis, 1992; Strain & Hemmeter, 1997). In the example of transition in Ms. Mangurten's classroom, Kenny had to wait and he had nothing to do while he was waiting. As a result, he and several of his friends ran out of the classroom and to the lunchroom. Instead of making Kenny wait, Ms. Mangurten could have assigned him a specific task that would last throughout the transition period such as washing the tables or she could have had activities available for Kenny to do while he was waiting.

When implementing this strategy the team will need to decide whether waiting will be reduced for one student or for the entire class. In some cases, it is easy to make changes on a class-wide basis. In other cases, however, class-wide changes may not be feasible and strategies are instead applied to the student or the few students who experience problems with waiting. Here are some strategies to reduce waiting for individual students or class-wide:

A. Have students obtain materials needed for a task rather than asking them to sit while an adult obtains materials (e.g., each student obtains materials needed to dissect a frog). Alternatively, have one student assist in passing out materials.

B. Have students put materials away and involve students in the clean-up process at the end of activities (e.g., the student erases the board versus the teacher). Alternatively, have a few students assist in clean-up.

C. Have students line up as a whole group or small groups rather than calling individual names (e.g., everyone who has tennis shoes on could line up at one time).

D. Use transition-based teaching strategies (e.g., ask students to recite the alphabet or to practice flashcards with a partner when they are standing in line) (Wolery, Doyle, Gast, Ault, & Lichtenberg, 1991).

E. Ask students as a group to answer questions rather than individual students (e.g., everyone tell me what the answer is) (Munk & Karsh, 1999).

F. Give a student more frequent turns to answer questions or to participate.

G. Provide individual materials (e.g., each student or pair of students has a bottle of glue). Note, however, that this strategy may decrease social interaction among students. Limited materials increase social interaction as students share the materials, but it also can lead to aggression and other challenging behaviors as students are required to wait (Chandler, Fowler, & Lubeck, 1992).

H. When students must wait, give them something to do or provide a form of sensory stimulation while they are waiting (e.g., read comic books or magazines, draw at their desks, work on a jigsaw puzzle at the back of the classroom, or play music preferred by students).

4. Add Movement to Activities and Movement Breaks

Students who need high levels of stimulation find it very difficult to sit quietly for extended periods of time, especially during passive or low stimulation activities. (Note that the amount of time students are able to sit quietly will vary across students.) These students often increase stimulation by engaging in inappropriate (to the school setting) gross or fine motor behaviors such as frequently leaving their seats to wander or run or to perform unnecessary tasks such as throwing trash in the garbage can or using the restroom. They also may rock, stand, or constantly shift with their bodies half in and half out of their seats. They may touch others, kick their desks, or tap their fingers, pencils, calculators, and other materials on their desks. They also may engage in other forms of sensory stimulation (e.g., vocal and auditory stimulation) when they are not allowed to move for extended periods of time.

　　The keys to reducing these forms of challenging behavior are (a) to reduce the duration of passive activities, (b) to provide movement breaks during passive activities when needed or on a set schedule, and (c) to include movement as a part of passive activities (Colby Trott et al., 1993). For example, during morning circle, Ms. Janzten has her students hold hands and sway as they sing the "hello" song. She also has each student walk to the felt board to point to the day of the week (as well as say the name of the weekday) rather than answering from their seats. Mr. Ginocchio provides a movement break by having students stand, touch their toes, and give each other high fives in the middle of his lecture. He also has teams of students work math problems at the blackboard. Hong, who has more difficulty sitting than other students in the class, is allowed to stand at his desk or to take short walks in the hallway.

　　Finally, one teacher we know adds movement to her lesson on shapes by having students play the game "musical chairs" or in this case, "musical shapes." In her lesson students stand on shapes when the music stops, rather than sitting on chairs. Students name the shapes as they are put on the floor and then as a group they identify the shapes on which they are standing. (Multiple students can stand on a shape—in this way no student is excluded as happens in musical chairs.) At the end of the lesson all students crowd onto one shape (Lewandowski, personal communication, 1996). This musical shapes lesson reduced the off-task and inattentive behavior that students previously displayed when the teacher taught shapes during small group, in-seat activities. It also incorporated the concept of affection or friendship activities by having students interact with each other during the lesson (McEvoy et al., 1988; Twardosz, Nordquist, Simon, & Botkin, 1983).

Antecedents and Setting Events	Behavior	Consequence	Function
Lesson on shapes, instructions, passive activity	Fidgeting, out of seat, inattentive	Reprimand, instructions, movement	Sensory Regulation/ Sensory Stimulation: increased movement
Lesson on shapes, instructions, active activity	Walk around shapes, shout answers	Praise, movement	Sensory Regulation/ Sensory Stimulation: increased movement, auditory and tactile stimulation

Each of the previous examples provides an opportunity for students to gain motor stimulation through appropriate behaviors. Movement not only increases stimulation for some students, it also may increase arousal and ability to attend. The frequency of movement activities or breaks and the duration of those activities and breaks will be determined by each team and should match the needs of the student(s). In general, the effects of movement breaks last approximately 30 minutes, although there will be variability across students (Colby Trott et al., 1993). In addition, the types of movement that students perform should be acceptable to the classroom staff and parents. Table 10–2 in the previous section provided ideas for appropriate ways to obtain movement stimulation in and between classroom activities, tasks, and routines. This may be a starting point in developing alternative replacement behaviors that fit the needs of individual students.

5. Increase the Pace of Instruction and Interaction

This strategy increases or maintains stimulation by increasing the pace of instruction (i.e., teacher presentation and student response) and task and materials presentation. Fast-paced instruction reduces challenging behavior and increases student engagement because it provides increased opportunities for individual students and groups of students to respond and it decreases the amount of waiting that students often do in slower paced instruction (Munk & Karsh, 1999; Munk & Repp, 1994b; Repp & Karsh, 1992). Strategies to increase the pace of instruction include these: (a) ask frequent questions, (b) provide prompts if students are not able to answer questions (i.e., to reduce the latency between teacher presentation and student response), (c) increase the rate of task and materials presentation, and (d) decrease the amount of time (i.e., the intertrial interval) between instructional sequences.

Direct instruction provides a good example of effective fast-paced instruction. In direct instruction, educators begin instruction with a brief review of previous material and reteach material when necessary. During this review students frequently answer questions regarding previous material. The review is followed by presentation of new material. This includes teacher presentation, frequent active responding and practice by all students as well as individual students, and frequent feedback and reinforcement. New material is presented in small steps using a variety of stimulating teaching practices such as examples, illustrations, and demonstrations. Students then engage in individual practice, which again involves frequent feedback and reinforcement (Aber, Bachman, Campbell, & O'Malley, 1994; Carnine, 1976; Friend & Bursuck, 1999).

Obviously the pace of instruction and materials and task presentation should be individualized across students when providing one-to-one instruction. When applying this strategy to groups of students, educators should vary the pace of teacher presentation and student opportunity for active responding and evaluate the impact on the group. An appropriate pace will maximize opportunities for students to respond, result in correct responding, and decrease challenging behaviors.

6. Provide Variety in Instruction, Materials, and Student Response

Variety is another strategy used to increase stimulation during activities. Variety may occur in teacher-directed instruction, student-centered learning, cooperative group activities, and student responding.

Variety in teacher-directed instruction can be increased by adding visual stimuli to lecture and discussion. Visual stimuli include overhead transparencies, various types of graphic organizers (see Friend & Bursuck, 1999, for examples of graphic organizers), models, pictures, videotapes, and examples of objects. In addition to visual stimuli, the stimulation level of teacher-directed instruction can be enhanced by changing the mode of instruction frequently or by using a variety of instructional modes within a lesson. For example, you might intersperse active instructional modes (e.g., small group projects, modeling, solving problems at blackboard) with more passive instructional modes (e.g., lecture, individual worksheets). Different modes of instruction include lecture and discussion, teacher or student reading of textual material, small and large group activities, computer-assisted instruction, modeling and demonstration, authentic or performance based activities, case studies, peer mediation or peer tutoring, experimentation and discovery learning, and individual seatwork.

The level of stimulation provided during student-centered learning may be increased by using cooperative group activities and peer tutoring (Jenson et al., 1994) and by providing graphic organizers, models or actual examples of objects, pictures, manipulatives, and video- or audiotapes.

Variety in student responding and participation can be achieved by incorporating vocal, visual, motor, gestural, and written responses into teacher-directed and student-centered lessons. For example, students may respond in unison as a whole group as well as individually. They may hold up answer cards or write answers on a chalkboard (Rhode et al., 1992). Students might tell answers to questions to a neighbor or come to the front of the room to work problems on the board. Students also may participate by reading aloud (either standing or sitting at their seats), restating concepts, drawing pictures of concepts, presenting a play or engaging in role-play presentations, and by completing written worksheets, graphic organizers, and tests.

7. Use Stimulating Social Reinforcement

Students who need high levels of stimulation will respond more readily and appropriately to multisensory, stimulating reinforcement than they do to passive reinforcement. For these students you should deliver praise with much enthusiasm. For example, you might clap your hands and praise behavior in a loud voice or you may pat a student on the back. If you do use physical reinforcement with students, be sure that the type of physical reinforcement used is age appropriate and acceptable to the student and within the values of the community. For example, you might hug, tickle, or dance with a young child. For older students you might give a high five, shake a student's hand, or pat the student on the back. Sulzer-Azaroff and Mayer (1991, pp. 162–163) provide a list of potential social reinforcers that can be used with children and youth and adults.

You also can provide stimulating reinforcement by allowing access to activity reinforcers and presenting sensory stimuli. Examples of these forms of reinforcement include scratch and sniff stickers; bubbles; koosh balls and yo-yos or other types of manipulatives; music or computer games; assisting the teacher or running an errand; and extra recess. Novel materials and activities and variety in types of reinforcers (e.g., selecting items from a surprise box, choice of reinforcers as in a token economy, access to new materials) also increase the stimulating aspects of positive reinforcement.

As stated earlier in Chapter 7, artificial or contrived forms of positive reinforcement always should be paired with the natural consequences of behavior as well as with social reinforcement (Liberty & Billingsley, 1988; Sulzer-Azaroff & Mayer, 1986, 1991; White, 1988; White et al., 1988).

8. Conduct Calming Activities at the End of Stimulating Activities

This strategy will help decrease students' state of arousal or level of stimulation so that they are better able to transition to, and participate in, passive activities (Walker et al., 1995). For instance, Ms. Slater found that many of her first- and second-grade students had a difficult time "settling down" at the end of stimulating activities such as free play, recess, and cooperative group activities. She said that her students did not pay attention during the lessons that followed these highly stimulating activities. Instead, her students talked out of turn, looked at their materials, laughed, and squirmed in their seats.

The team suggested that Ms. Slater have her students perform motor-related songs as a calming activity before she introduced passive activities. For example, during the song "Alabama, Mississippi" (Gill, 1993) Ms. Slater and her students initially shook different parts of their bodies while singing loudly. Then with each successive verse, they decreased the volume and speed of body movement. By the end of the song Ms. Slater and her students were whispering the verse and moving their body parts very slowly. Only at this point did Ms. Slater introduce low-stimulation, passive activities such as reading or writing. This type of calming activity can be done with any motor-related songs such as "The Hokey-Pokey" and "If You're Happy and You Know It." Other examples of calming activities and/or stimuli include playing quiet, rhythmical music, soft singing, providing a backrub, wearing weighted vests or carrying heavy objects, low or indirect lighting, and slow rocking.

Another suggestion for introducing calming activities is to insert medium stimulation activities between highly stimulating and quiet activities to provide a gradual change in stimulation (Bailey & Wolery, 1992). For example, students may participate in a small group activity or peer tutoring after recess before being asked to work individually on study guides or worksheets.

Antecedents and Setting Events	Behavior	Consequence	Function
End of highly stimulating activity, start of passive activity	Talks out of turn, laughs, squirms, looks at materials, inattentive	Maintain stimulation (e.g., motor, visual, tactile vocal)	Sensory Regulation/ Sensory Stimulation: increased sensory stimulation
End of highly stimulating activity, introduce calming motor-song activity, start of passive activity	Participates in calming activity, quiet and attentive during passive activity	Maintain and then slowly decrease stimulation	Sensory Regulation/ Sensory Stimulation: regulates stimulation by (reducing stimulation following a stimulating activity)

In summary, the eight strategies just discussed can be used for students whose behavior functions to increase stimulation or sensory input and for students who have difficulties regulating or decreasing their level of arousal as they transition from highly stimulating activities to activities with low levels of stimulation. Strategy selection should be based on the needs of the student(s), acceptability to educators and parents, and the feasibility for implementation within classrooms and other educational settings.

STRATEGIES THAT MATCH THE DECREASE SENSORY REGULATION/SENSORY STIMULATION FUNCTION

Students within the sensory decrease regulation/sensory stimulation category reduce their level of sensory input and stimulation by engaging in challenging behavior (Colby Trott et al., 1993; Guess & Carr, 1991). They also may avoid specific forms of sensory input (e.g., students who are hypersensitive to sensory input) by engaging in challenging behavior (Colby Trott et al., 1993; Snider, 1991). These students may seek activities and environments that provide low levels of sensory stimulation and they may respond negatively in environments that are highly stimulating or that provide specific forms of sensory input. These students also may have difficulties becoming

TABLE 10–3
Strategies that match the decrease sensory regulation/sensory stimulation function

1. Develop areas that provide low levels of stimulation.
2. Decrease the level of sensory input and stimulation.
3. Structure the environment and provide predictable schedules.
4. Reduce the pace of instruction and interaction.
5. Use reinforcement that provides low levels of stimulation.
6. Conduct arousal or jump-start activities at the beginning of stimulating activities.

© 2002 Chandler and Dahlquist.

aroused or maintaining adequate levels of arousal (Fouse & Wheeler, 1997; Guess & Carr, 1991). Students within the sensory decrease regulation/sensory stimulation category may experience problems starting and completing activities, attending to tasks, interacting with peers, responding to novel or unexpected activities, and participating in stimulating environments. They often are described as being "slow," lazy, unmotivated, noncompliant, and nonsocial or withdrawn (Reisman & Scott, 1991).

Several strategies can be used to provide decreased sensory environments for students who fit this category of the function and to teach students appropriate behaviors that will decrease sensory stimulation and regulate sensory input. These strategies are described in detail in the following section and listed in Table 10–3.

1. Develop Areas That Provide Low Levels of Stimulation

This strategy allows students who need a temporary or continuous reduction in stimulation access to environments that provide low levels of stimulation. For example, many classrooms provide quiet centers that (a) are located away from noisy areas (to reduce auditory stimulation), (b) are defined by physical boundaries such as bookshelves (to reduce visual stimulation), and (c) are relatively small (so that only one or two students may use the center simultaneously). These centers often contain quiet, passive materials such as books or writing/coloring books. They also may include furniture for relaxation such as bean bag chairs or pillows or they may include individual desks.

Other strategies for creating areas with low levels of stimulation include providing study carrels or other forms of desk screens, designating one area on the playground for quiet, passive activities, setting up a tent in the classroom or home, and placing a rocking chair in a quiet corner of the classroom (Colby Trott et al., 1993).

Calming, low-stimulation areas should be available to students when they need a reduction in stimulation. These areas should not be considered time-out areas or used to punish students. They simply are areas that provide reduced levels of stimulation. Students may have the option of using these areas when needed, or educators or parents may direct students to these areas when the level of stimulation in the environment has a negative effect on their behavior. In addition, quiet, calming centers may be used by students during activities that require focused concentration such as tests or worksheets. These areas reduce external visual and auditory input, thus promoting concentration for students who are easily distracted.

For example, Ming found it difficult to tune out auditory and visual stimulation during activities. During individual activities such as tests or worksheets, she found herself focusing on the sounds made by peers as they wrote on their papers, shuffled their papers, turned pages in books, shook their legs, and so on. She often ordered peers to be quiet or hummed repeatedly to herself as a means of reducing other auditory stimulation.

Mr. Gross referred Ming for functional assessment because he and the other students found Ming's humming and ordering behavior very rude and disruptive. During her student interview, Ming indicated that she couldn't concentrate and was not able to do her work because the classroom was too noisy. She said that she ordered peers to be quiet because she got frustrated with how noisy they were (even though she knew they weren't being noisy on purpose). Ming also said that she sang to herself because then she couldn't hear the noise from her peers and thus was able to do her work. Observation verified Ming's analysis of her own behavior. Intervention to address Ming's behavior involved providing a study carrel in the back of the classroom. The study carrel was equipped with headphones and faced away from the rest of the students. Ming was allowed to use this study carrel whenever she needed a reduction in stimulation. With this intervention, Ming's ordering and self-humming behavior decreased.

Antecedents and Setting Events	Behavior	Consequence	Function
Individual activities such as tests, desk in middle of room	Orders peers to be quiet, hums aloud	Reduce auditory stimulation	Sensory Regulation/ Sensory Stimulation: decrease auditory stimulation
Individual activities, study carrel at back of room with headphones	Works on assigned task	Reduce visual and auditory stimulation	Sensory Regulation/ Sensory Stimulation: decrease auditory stimulation

2. Decrease the Level of Sensory Input and Stimulation

Not all students who are sensitive to sensory input or who seek to reduce sensory stimulation will need to use secluded low-stimulation centers. Many students will be able to function in typical classroom settings with adaptations to the classroom environment and classroom activities and tasks (Wodrich, 1994). Such adaptations can be achieved by alternating active, highly stimulating tasks and passive, low stimulating tasks; providing options during free play or leisure time for low stimulating activities and materials; and shortening the duration of highly stimulating activities. Stimulation can be reduced for individual students by providing alternative activities during highly stimulating activities such as allowing the student to read a book after participating for a brief period of time in recess or to listen to music with headphones during leisure time.

Strategic seating also can reduce sensory stimulation. For example, to reduce auditory and visual stimulation you might seat the student next to a calm, quiet peer, next to the wall, or at the front of the classroom. You may create an area within the classroom that has little or no visual stimuli (e.g., pictures, bulletin boards) and then seat the student in that area. You also may reduce auditory and visual input by seating the student away from the door, windows, high traffic areas, and noisy work areas (Chicago Public Schools, 1998; Haldy & Haack, 1995; Wodrich, 1994).

Auditory stimulation may be reduced by allowing the student to wear headphones or earplugs, or permitting the student to listen to quiet music during activities. Auditory stimulation also may be reduced by dividing students into dyads or small groups instead of employing large groups during activities. To reduce visual stimulation for some students, especially students with attention deficit hyperactivity disorder, therapists recommend providing soft nonfluorescent lighting (Colby Trott et al., 1993). Tactile stimulation may be reduced by placing the student at the end of a line, increasing the amount of space between student chairs or desks, employing nonphysical forms of reinforcement, and providing firm, direct and anticipated touch.

Strategies such as these reduce stimulation for those students who need decreased sensory input or who are hypersensitive to specific types of sensory input and they provide options for reduced stimulation when needed. This will allow many students to participate in classroom activities and routines and to interact with peers. Table 10–4 provides a list of strategies that can be used to decrease the level of sensory input and stimulation.

3. Structure the Environment and Provide Predictable Schedules

Some students who need decreased sensory stimulation experience problems during unstructured activities and when there are unexpected changes in activities, schedules, routines, people, and environments. These students often are not able to change their behavior to fit the demands of new or unexpected situations (Chicago Public Schools, 1998; Haldy & Haack, 1995; Koegel, Koegel, & Parks, 1995). This often occurs in students with sensory integration or processing disorders and other disabilities such as autism and attention deficit hyperactivity disorder (Colby Trott et al., 1993; Reisman & Scott, 1991; Wodrich, 1994). These students may display a variety of challenging behaviors during unstructured activities or when there are unexpected changes in

TABLE 10–4
Strategies to decrease sensory stimulation and to maintain a calm level of stimulation

Give one direction at a time.
Provide simple and specific instructions and cues.
Divide tasks into small steps.
Use one sensory channel at a time.
Provide a rocking chair for slow rocking.
Provide deep massage.
Seat student at the front of the classroom to reduce visual and auditory input.
Provide headphones, screens, study carrels.
Develop a quiet area in the classroom and other environments.
Provide low, indirect lighting.
Play soft, rhythmical music.
Reduce visual materials on walls.
Turn student's desk or position student away from peers and other forms of stimulation.
Provide passive breaks during stimulating activities.
Allow students to wear plastic gloves during tactile activities such as painting, use of clay, etc.
Conduct calming activities at the end of active tasks and prior to the start of new tasks.
Provide short, structured transitions.
Do not force students to engage in activities that require or involve forms of sensory input to which the student is hypersensitive. Provide alternative activities for these students.
Do not force students to engage in highly stimulating activities.
Place student at the end of a line.
Provide passive activity options during leisure time, recess, and free play.
Use passive forms of reinforcers.
Speak in a soft, calming voice.
Use firm, sustained, and expected touch.
Reduce lighting during quiet breaks and in the quiet area.
Use small groups during cooperative group activities.

Note: These strategies are adapted from our experience conducting functional assessment and from the following references: Colby Trott et al. (1993), Fouse and Wheeler (1997), Haldy and Haack (1995), Reisman and Scott (1991), and Snider (1991).
© 2002 Chandler and Dahlquist.

aspects of the daily schedule, activities and routines, or within the classroom environment. For example, they may tantrum, cry, refuse to participate, or become withdrawn, aggressive, or self-abusive.

These students often benefit from short, structured activity transitions and from consistent structure in the sequence of activities, daily routines, and daily schedules. For example, Kelvin reviews his written schedule, which describes the order of daily activities and tasks at the beginning of each day. He then carries his schedule with him throughout the day. This provides sufficient structure and predictability for Kelvin and reduces challenging behavior that previously was associated with unpredictable schedules and daily activities and routines. Max uses an adaptable schedule in which only one activity or class period is displayed at a time. When a class period ends, he turns the card for that activity over and then places the card for the next class period in the schedule.

When changes must be made in predictable activities, routines, and schedules, or in the physical aspects of the environment, you should prepare students in advance for those changes. Antecedent cues can inform students of upcoming changes and review with the students how to react when changes occur. Antecedent cues such as presignals and safety signals may be vocal, visual, gestural, or written. These cues help students anticipate change in the level and type of stimulation across activities and alterations to typical or expected daily schedules and routines. It also is helpful to prepare students as much as possible when other aspects of the environment change such as visits from volunteers, introduction of a new unit, a change in classroom materials and visual stimuli, seating changes, and furniture arrangement. Social stories also can be used as antecedent prompts to prepare students for changes in schedules and routines and how to react when changes do occur (Gray, 1994; Gray & Garland, 1993).

For example, Ms. Doyle changed the daily schedule so that reading occurred after recess rather than at the end of the day. On the first day that the schedule changed Alicia argued with Ms. Doyle about the change, insisting that she wait until the end of the day to read the book. Eventually Alicia became so upset and disruptive that she was sent to the principal's office and her mother was called to come pick her up. This type of interaction and behavior occurred every time there was a change in the schedule. Ms. Doyle decided that the next time there was a change in the daily routine, she would prepare Alicia ahead of time. She told Alicia about the next scheduled change as soon as it was planned (e.g., 1 week in advance). She also reminded Alicia about the upcoming change daily, and she informed Alicia's mother about the schedule change and asked her to remind Alicia daily. Ms. Doyle also gave Alicia a written schedule that illustrated the change and developed a social story with Alicia that indicated what Alicia should do if she was upset about the change. These strategies enabled Alicia to respond positively to schedule changes.

Antecedents and Setting Events	Behavior	Consequence	Function
Unexpected change in daily schedule	Argues, resists change, disruptive	Sent to principal, sent home	Sensory Regulation/ Sensory Stimulation: reduce unexpected changes to schedule, regulate stimulation
Informed of change in daily schedule, change and social story reviewed daily, change is anticipated	Participates	Praise	Sensory Regulation/ Sensory Stimulation: reduce unexpected changes to schedule, regulate stimulation

Strategies such as those employed with Alicia provide an external structure that often helps students anticipate and process sensory information, thereby enabling them to regulate their behavior to fit the demands of new situations (Haldy & Haack, 1995).

4. Reduce the Pace of Instruction and Interaction

This strategy is the opposite of the one recommended for students who fit the sensory increase category of this function. This strategy involves slowing the pace of the instruction and interaction (Munk & Karsh, 1999; Munk & Repp, 1994b). For example, increasing the intertrial interval (the amount of time between teacher initiation and student response) gives students time to process the question, decide on an answer, and then answer the question. Other methods to reduce the pace of instruction include asking questions less frequently, waiting until one task is complete before giving additional tasks and materials, breaking instructions into smaller steps, and providing parts of a task such as placing half of the problems on one worksheet and the other half on a separate worksheet, or using a visual screen to cover uncompleted parts of a page.

A final method for reducing the pace of instruction is to give students additional time. Students who have problems achieving and maintaining adequate levels of arousal may be slower to begin and complete activities. These students may take longer than other students to obtain materials, develop a plan for conducting activities, and carry out those plans. For these students additional time, combined with other strategies such as arousal techniques (see strategy 6), antecedent presignals, calming centers, and task outlines will allow them to begin and to complete tasks.

5. Use Reinforcement That Provides Low Levels of Stimulation

All students learn best when appropriate behavior is followed by positive reinforcement. However, the form of reinforcement employed must match the sensory needs of each student. Students who need low levels of stimulation or who respond negatively to specific forms of sensory input will respond more readily to reinforcers that provide low levels of stimulation than they will to highly stimulating forms of reinforcement. For these students, praise should be delivered in a quiet, albeit enthusiastic, voice. Passive forms of social reinforcement such as eye contact, smiles, and thumbs up and okay signals often work well with these students.

Written or textual forms of reinforcement such as happy faces, stars, or hand stamps, written grades or comments on papers, stickers, points, certificates, or positive notes to take home also provide low levels of stimulation. It also may be useful to provide choice of reinforcers or to offer access to passive activities and materials as reinforcers so that students can select reinforcers that match their sensory needs. Finally, some students who need decreased sensory stimulation may not respond well to physical touch such as pats on the back or high fives, especially if the touch is not expected. If you do use touch with students who are tactilely defensive (students who avoid or respond negatively to touch), your touch should be firm, not light, and the student should be expecting the touch (Haldy & Haack, 1995).

6. Conduct Arousal or Jump-Start Activities at the Beginning of Stimulating Activities

This strategy will help increase students' state of arousal or level of stimulation so that they are able to transition to and participate in activities. Many students will work better during stimulating (as well as passive) activities if their level of arousal in increased prior to initiation of the activity. This can be especially effective when stimulating activities follow passive activities such as bus rides, naps, reading, or individual seatwork. Activities that require movement are good arousal or jump-start activities. Arousing movement activities include jumping jacks, dancing, running, crossing arms in front of the body, rolling the head, shaking hands or legs, and stretching. Arousal also can be increased through group songs, finger plays, group shouts, and loud music.

For some students it also will be important to provide arousal activities during a task. For example, you might ask the student to take a note to the teacher next door or to come to your desk to show current work. This breaks the cycle of low stimulation. Arousal also can be increased during activities by allowing students to drink ice water, chew gum, or suck candy. Small manipulatives such as paper clips, Silly Putty, or koosh balls also may be used to maintain arousal during activities. Another technique to increase arousal is to provide reinforcement during the activity. Even passive levels of reinforcement, as described in the previous suggestion, can be arousing.

For example, Jackie often falls asleep in class or lays her head on her desk during academic assignments. When this happens Ms. Hacker, her teacher, tells her to wake up and get to work, reminds Jackie that she will get a failing grade if she doesn't complete her work, and sometimes she requires Jackie to stay after school to finish her work. These strategies have not been successful so Ms. Hacker referred Jackie to the instructional strategies team.

Through interview with Jackie the team learned that Jackie works in her parents' restaurant at night and that she usually does not go to bed until midnight. As a result she only sleeps an average of 5 hours per night. Conversations with the family indicate that reducing Jackie's restaurant workload is not an option at this time. So, the team decided to introduce arousal techniques prior to and during academic assignments in order to help Jackie remain awake and sufficiently aroused. During intervention

Ms. Hacker asked Jackie to pass out materials to other students at the beginning of the activity, assigned her to work with peers in small groups when possible, and allowed Jackie to have a plastic bottle of cold water on her desk and to suck lemon drops. Ms. Hacker also patted Jackie on the back during the activity as she praised Jackie for being on task. These strategies increased the amount of time that Jackie was able to work on a task and maintain her level of arousal during class work.

Arousal activities that are implemented prior to and during educational activities should reflect the sensory needs of the students. For example, if a student were hypersensitive to noise, you would not use an auditory-based arousal activity. Arousal activities may be applied to all students within a classroom or they may be applied to individual students. For instance, all students may benefit from stretching or other motor exercises prior to the start of an activity. Not all students, however, may need arousal activities during tasks. When this occurs, arousal activities may be implemented as necessary for individual students.

Antecedents and Setting Events	Behavior	Consequence	Function
Academic assignment	Sleeps, lays head on desk	Instructions, threat of poor grades, detention	Sensory Regulation/ Sensory Stimulation: low level of arousal, decreased stimulation
Academic assignment, arousal techniques	On task, completes work	Praise, pat on back, good grades	Sensory Regulation/ Sensory Stimulation: maintains/regulates level of arousal

In summary, the six strategies just discussed can be used for students whose behavior functions to decrease stimulation or sensory input and for students who have difficulty maintaining a sufficient level of arousal. As with all strategies, these should be based on the needs of the students, acceptability to students, educators, and parents, and the feasibility for implementation within school-based settings.

SUMMARY

When possible, you should consult with an occupational therapist before developing interventions for students whose challenging behavior is a function of sensory regulation/sensory stimulation. An occupational therapist may be able to suggest specific strategies to provide or reduce stimulation that reflect the student's sensory needs. Sometimes, these strategies may not be ones that are typically employed in classroom settings or readily identified by educators. For example, an occupational therapist may recommend that a student wear a weighted vest or ankle weights. Or the occupational therapist may recommend power walks, floor cushions, and specific oral stimulation, and fine motor or gross motor activities. If it is not possible to consult with an occupational therapist, closely monitor the student's behavior during intervention to evaluate the effects of sensory-based interventions on the student and the student's behavior.

In addition to consulting with an occupational therapist, it often is important to identify the type of sensory input and stimulation the student is receiving or reducing as a function of challenging behavior. For example, Rapp, Miltenberger, Galensky, Ellington, and Long (1999) reported a study in which a young woman pulled out her hair and manipulated the pulled hair between her fingers. Prior to developing intervention strategies to reduce this behavior they decided to determine what specific type of stimulation the young woman received from this behavior. Observation indicated that the act of hair pulling itself did not provide the critical sensory input. Rather, the child received digital-tactile (sensory-perceptual) stimulation produced by playing with the hair after it was pulled from her head. Experimental intervention focused on providing alternative sources of digital stimulation rather than focusing on the act of hair pulling even though the identified challenging behavior was hair pulling. When they provided her with alternative stimuli to twirl in her fingers (they provided alternate pieces of hair to manipulate) she stopped pulling out her hair.

For many students, such as the one described in the previous paragraph, intervention should match the type of sensory input as well as the amount of stimulation that the student obtains or reduces through challenging behavior. For example, if a student's behavior produces movement, then intervention should focus on movement. If a student's behavior produces decreases in auditory or visual sensory input, then intervention should achieve the same sensory function. Or if a student's behavior produces oral stimulation such as mouthing objects or a hand, it may be necessary to provide alternative means of obtaining oral stimulation such as chewing gum or sugarless hard candies.

Matching the type of sensory input, however, is not required for all students. The team will need to decide if the form of stimulation *or* the level of stimulation is the critical factor to address during intervention. For example, remember Seneca who ran up and down the bus aisle, hit peers, and hit the bus window during long bus rides. The intervention to address her challenging behaviors (she listened to music from a CD player and played with a Beanie Baby™ or other similar toys) continued to provide tactile or fine motor stimulation through activities and materials, but it did not provide gross motor stimulation during the bus ride. Instead, the intervention added auditory stimulation during the bus ride.

For Seneca, the type of stimulation was not as important as the amount of stimulation. Seneca simply needed something stimulating to do during long passive bus rides. The form of stimulation was not a critical factor in reducing her challenging behavior. When working with students whose challenging behavior is a function of the sensory regulation/sensory stimulation function, the team will need to decide if one or both of these variables (the type and amount of stimulation) should be addressed during intervention. This will guide the selection of intervention strategies.

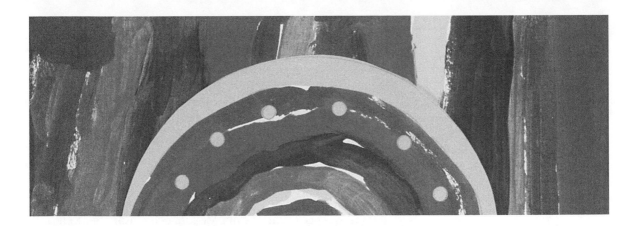

CHAPTER 11

Prevention Strategies and Strategies to Promote Generalization and Maintenance of Behavior

In addition to selecting and implementing intervention strategies within each of the functions, the team also must select and implement strategies to promote the generalization and maintenance of behavior. The team also should develop and implement strategies to prevent the development of challenging behavior and the occurrence of established challenging behavior. We begin this chapter by discussing the concepts of generalization and maintenance and then present strategies that can be used to promote generalization and maintenance. We then discuss strategies that are designed to prevent challenging behavior.

GENERALIZATION AND MAINTENANCE

A comprehensive intervention plan must include strategies that address the function of behavior as well as strategies to promote the generalization and maintenance of behavior. In their seminal article on generalization, Stokes and Baer (1977) defined generalization as "the occurrence of relevant behavior under different, nontraining conditions. . . without the scheduling of the same events in those conditions as had been scheduled in the training conditions" (p. 350). Three types of generalization can occur: stimulus generalization, response generalization, and generalization across time (Drabman, Hammer, & Rosenbaum, 1979).

Stimulus generalization is attained when behavior that is learned in one situation or set of circumstances occurs in new situations or when aspects of the current situation change (Haring, 1988a; Stokes & Osnes, 1988, 1989; Sulzer-Azaroff & Mayer, 1991). In other words, behavior continues to occur in the presence of new or different stimuli. Behavior may generalize (occur) across settings, people, materials, antecedent stimuli, materials, activities and tasks, and consequences (Carr, Levin, McConnachie, Carlson, Kemp, & Smith, 1994; Skinner, 1953). For example, Mr. Deutz implemented an intervention designed to increase the duration of Vera's in-seat behavior during lectures from 2 to 10 minutes in length. The intervention was successful. Vera now remains in her seat for 10 minutes during lecture. She also remains in her seat during individual seatwork and cooperative group activities (generalization across activities). Mr. Deutz also notices that Vera stays in her seat when there is a substitute teacher in class and when the class is working in the library or attending assembly (generalization across people and settings).

The second type of generalization, response generalization, occurs when the form or topography of appropriate behavior changes and extends to a variety of related behaviors (Carr, 1988; McMahon, Wacker, Sasso, & Melloy, 1994; Skinner, 1953; Stokes & Baer, 1977; Sulzer-Azaroff & Mayer, 1991). For example, Ahmed is taught to do finger plays at his desk in order to increase his tactile/digital stimulation during passive activities. He also begins to manipulate a paper clip, squeeze his rubber erasure, and rotate the cap on his pen even though these particular behaviors were not taught as part of the intervention.

The third type of generalization, typically referred to as maintenance, or generalization across time, is achieved when the student continues to emit appropriate behavior (and does not emit challenging behavior) over time, after intervention has ended (Favell & Reid, 1988; Skinner, 1953; Stokes & Baer, 1977; Stokes & Osnes, 1988). For example, a 6-month progress check indicates that Hughey continues to raise his hand and does not shout out answers to questions. Brittany's teacher notes that she continues to initiate to peers after the summer break. Vera continues to stay in her seat for 10 minutes throughout the school year and Ahmed continues to use finger games to increase tactile/digital stimulation during passive activities. In each of these examples, appropriate behavior continues to occur even though direct intervention has terminated.

In addressing generalization and maintenance, the functional assessment and intervention model should be thought of as a two-stage process. The focus of the first stage is acquisition, during which we implement interventions to reduce challenging behavior and to increase appropriate replacement behavior. The focus of the second stage is generalization and maintenance (Green, 1990; Haring, 1988b; Walker, 2000). This stage is based on the belief that the often used "train and hope" practice, in which we implement inter-

TABLE 11–1
Strategies to actively promote generalization and maintenance

1. Select and teach functional target behaviors.
2. Program common and natural stimuli and consequences.
3. Train loosely.
4. Provide sufficient exemplars.
5. Use indiscriminable and intermittent contingencies.
6. Teach mediation strategies.
7. Specify a fluency criterion.
8. Employ sequential modification.

Note: Additional information about these strategies can be obtained from the following references: Baer (1981), Carr et al. (1994), Chandler (1992), Chandler, Lubeck, et al. (1992), Haring (1987), Horner, Dunlap, and Koegel (1988), Kirby and Bickel (1988), Koegel and Rincover (1977), Stokes and Baer (1977), Stokes and Osnes (1986, 1988), and Sulzer-Azaroff and Mayer (1991).

vention strategies and then hope that generalization will automatically occur, usually does not result in generalization and maintenance (Stokes & Baer, 1977). Rather, generalization and maintenance must be actively promoted through specific strategies (Baer, 1981; Baer, Wolfe, & Risley, 1968; Chandler, Lubeck, & Fowler, 1992; Stokes & Baer, 1977; Stokes & Osnes, 1988, 1989, White et al., 1988). Table 11–1 provides a list of specific strategies that can be employed to promote generalization and maintenance. It also provides several references that provide additional information regarding generalization promotion strategies. Each of these strategies is briefly described in the following section.

STRATEGIES TO PROMOTE GENERALIZATION AND MAINTENANCE

1. Select and Teach Functional Target Behaviors

When selecting appropriate replacement skills and behaviors, it is important to consider the functional utility of potential skills and behaviors. Functional skills and behaviors were discussed in Chapter 6 as a strategy for selecting appropriate replacement behaviors. Functional behaviors are those skills and behaviors that can be expected to (a) promote independence, (b) be effective in multiple settings, (c) be reinforced by others in the natural environment and across environments, (d) be immediately useful to the student, and (e) maximize participation in least restrictive environments (Billingsley, 1988; Carr et al., 1994; Dunlap, Foster-Johnson, & Robbins, 1990; Haring, 1988a,b; McMahon, Lambros, & Sylva, 1998; Munk & Karsh, 1999; Sulzer-Azaroff & Mayer, 1991).

Functional skills are likely to generalize across situations and time because they lead to meaningful outcomes, they are valued by the natural community, and they result in positive consequences in new and multiple situations (Green, 1990; Sailor, Goetz, Anderson, Hunt, & Gee, 1988). An example of selecting functional target behaviors comes from the work of Tremblay, Strain, Hendrickson, and Shores (1980). These investigators conducted observations during freeplay in the natural environment in order to identify the social behaviors to which children most often responded. These functional skills then were used in subsequent studies to increase social interaction between children with and without social delays (e.g., Hendrickson, Strain, Tremblay, & Shores, 1982; Odom, Chandler, Ostrosky, McConnell, & Reaney, 1992; Odom et al., 1999; Odom, Hoyson, Jamieson, & Strain, 1985).

Carr and his colleagues (Carr, Robinson, & Palumbo, 1990) have focused on one specific type of functional skill: functional communication. They hypothesize that for many individuals with disabilities, especially those with poor communication skills, challenging behavior serves as a form of communication. For example, tantrumming may indicate a desire for attention; biting may indicate a desire to escape a difficult activity; and head banging may indicate a need for sensory stimulation.

Carr and his colleagues recommend teaching communicative skills as functional replacement behaviors. Functional communication skills allow students to communicate their needs and desires using alternative appropriate forms of communication rather than communicating their desires through challenging behavior (Mullen & Frea, 1996). For instance, Carr and Durand (1985) reported a decrease in disruptive behavior during difficult activities when they taught the child to say "I don't understand". This functional communication training allowed the student to achieve the same function as disruptive behavior. The numerous studies conducted by Carr and his colleagues provide overwhelming support for teaching functional communication skills as a strategy to promote acquisition as well as generalization and maintenance of appropriate behavior (e.g., Carr et al., 1994; Carr & Lindquist, 1987; Carr, Newsom, & Binkoff, 1980; Durand & Carr, 1987).

In a retrospective review of studies that assessed generalization, Chandler, Lubeck, et al., (1992) reported that the selection of functional communication skills and the selection of other functional skills were the most common strategies employed in studies that successfully produced generalization. When selecting appropriate replacement skills and behaviors, it is important to consider the functional utility of potential skills and behaviors.

2. Employ Common and Natural Stimuli and Consequences

This strategy also was discussed in Chapter 6 as a consideration in selecting stimuli and consequences for interventions. This strategy involves using materials, instructions, locations, and consequences that are familiar to the student and are a natural part of the environment(s) in which behavior is and will be expected to occur (Carr et al., 1994; Favell & Reid, 1988; Liberty & Billingsley, 1988; Mahur & Rutherford, 1991; Repp & Karsh, 1990; Stokes & Osnes, 1988).

Students are more likely to generalize appropriate behavior when it is triggered by familiar, natural antecedents and when it is consequated by familiar, natural consequences (White, 1988). The greater the similarity between intervention and nonintervention situations, the greater the probability of generalization and maintenance (Chandler, 1992; Sailor et al., 1988). For example, during intervention, the teacher prompted Frank to ask a peer for assistance and Frank received tokens when he did this. However, Frank will not always have an adult present to prompt assistance-seeking behavior and he will not always receive tokens for asking a peer for assistance. It is important to the generalization and maintenance of this goal to incorporate common, natural stimuli as part of the intervention. For instance, the natural antecedent in Frank's environment for requesting assistance is the presence of a problem, not a teacher telling the student to ask for assistance. Frank needs to learn to identify and respond to this natural antecedent. Likewise, the natural consequence for asking for assistance is receiving assistance, not a token. Therefore, support for asking for assistance will need to be shifted from tokens to receiving assistance. Natural antecedents and consequences such as these are more likely to exist across new settings and situations after specific interventions have ended.

In addition to providing common and natural stimuli and consequences it may be important to involve other individuals in generalization. This strategy often is referred to as recruiting natural communities of reinforcement (Stokes & Baer, 1977). For example, we may teach parents, bus drivers, and other educators in the school building to prompt and consequate appropriate behavior. This increases the probability that the student will have opportunities to engage in appropriate behavior and to receive reinforcement for appropriate behavior when staff who implemented the intervention are not present.

A final strategy that makes use of common, natural stimuli and consequences is to implement interventions in the natural environment in which the behavior is to be employed (Kazdin, 2001; Liberty & Billingsley, 1988; Sailor et al., 1988; White, 1988). There are numerous anecdotal stories of students learning a skill or behavior in one setting and only using the skill in that setting. For example, a student may learn to use two-word sentences in speech therapy that is conducted in the speech therapist's office. Yet, the student does not use two-word sentences in the classroom. If we expect the student to use two-word sentences in the classroom, then we often will need to teach in the classroom. In another example, the first author has toilet trained many students in school or center-based programs only to find that they are not toilet trained at home or in their residential placements. Training should occur in natural environments. In their retrospective review of generalization research, Chandler, Lubeck, et al., (1992) found that studies that provided training in natural environments were more successful at achieving generalization than those studies that provided training in experimental or non-natural environments. If you must train in a different environment (e.g., social skills training may be done by a special educator in the resource room), then it is important to provide practice of the new skill in the natural environment.

3. Train Loosely

This strategy involves systematically varying aspects of training or intervention so that the student does not respond to irrelevant aspects of the training situation (Albin & Horner, 1988; Rosenblatt, Bloom, & Koegel, 1995; Stokes & Baer, 1977). Variation may occur across people, materials, instructions and prompts, consequences, settings and locations, and time. The type or form of behavior displayed by the student also may vary (Stokes & Baer, 1977). The purpose of this strategy is to expose students to a variety of stimuli or situations that they may experience during or following intervention. Diversity is the key to this strategy. For example, if we wish to teach Greta to initiate to peers, then a variety of peers (not just one peer) should be involved in social skills training. We also should have Greta practice peer initiations in a variety of environments (e.g., on the playground, in class, in the hallway, and in the gym) and we should teach her several ways to initiate to peers. This will increase the probability that Greta will generalize peer initiation strategies when she is confronted with new peers and in different situations and settings.

4. Provide Sufficient Exemplars

When implementing this strategy we provide multiple examples of a concept or behavior. The number of examples required during intervention is determined by the student's behavior. A sufficient number of examples have been introduced when the student's behavior generalizes to novel examples (Stokes & Baer, 1977; Sulzer-Azaroff & Mayer, 1991).

For instance, Ms. Slater taught the students in her class to use conflict resolution strategies when there were problems between students. The first example she taught was how to apply the strategies to problems with physical aggression. But this one example was not sufficient for students to generalize the conflict resolution strategies to different peer problems such as verbal aggression, stealing personal property, inappropriate touching, and teasing. So, Ms. Slater introduced another example of peer conflict and guided students through the conflict resolution process. She then introduced and guided students through two more examples. At this point (after practice with four examples of peer conflict) the students were able to independently and fluently apply conflict resolution strategies to new (i.e., untrained) conflict examples. Only then did she terminate conflict resolution training. In addition to changing the type of conflict that student's addressed, Ms. Slater also changed the gender of students involved, the number of students involved in the conflict, and the location of the conflict. This provided students with a variety of examples of peer conflict and reflected the types of conflicts that students would likely encounter following training. In this example, Ms. Slater combined the strategies of train loosely and train sufficient exemplars—a combination of strategies that is often identified as general case programming (Alberto & Troutman, 1999; Day & Horner, 1986; Horner & Billingsley, 1988; Horner, McDonnell, & Bellamy, 1986; Horner, Sprague, & Wilcox, 1982; Sprague & Horner, 1984).

5. Use Indiscriminable and Intermittent Contingencies

When we implement interventions to address acquisition, we initially provide frequent and consistent antecedent prompts and consequences for appropriate behavior. This strategy is important for strengthening the bond between antecedents, appropriate behavior, and desired outcomes. However, the frequency and consistency of antecedent stimuli and consequences typically provided during the acquisition stage may, unfortunately, result in dependence on those antecedents and consequences (e.g., Anderson, Taras, & Cannon, 1996; Goldstein & Wickstrom, 1986; Odom et al., 1985). In other words, behavior does not occur without an antecedent prompt and does not continue to occur if consequences are terminated.

In addition, the frequency and consistency of antecedents and consequences applied during acquisition often is greater than will occur in the natural environment after intervention has ended (Liberty & Billingsley, 1988). In the natural environment, antecedents may not be continuously available (e.g., the teacher is working with a different group of students and is not available to prompt Frank to ask a peer for assistance or to prompt Julia to respond to peer initiations). In addition, not every occurrence of behavior will result in a positive or desired consequence. Rather, consequences may be delivered intermittently or they may be delayed.

The goal of this strategy then is to shift from the continuous and frequent application of antecedents and consequences to a schedule of intermittent and indiscriminable contingencies (Favell & Reid, 1988; Stokes & Baer, 1977). This will reduce students' dependence on, and the predictability of, antecedents and consequences. It also will approximate conditions that are likely to exist in the natural environment when training ends or in different situations during the course of intervention. Indiscriminable contingencies can be achieved by delivering antecedents and consequences intermittently, that is, they are not provided each time behavior occurs (consequences) or should occur (antecedents) (Rhode, Jenson, & Reavis, 1992): by delaying the delivery of antecedent prompts and/or reinforcement (e.g., Doyle, Gast, Wolery, Ault, & Farmer, 1990; Dunlap & Plienis, 1988; Dyer, Dunlap, & Winterling, 1990; Fowler & Baer, 1981; Kazdin, 1982); by increasing or varying the amount of behavior required before reinforcement is delivered (e.g., increase the number of responses or duration of behavior); and by fading antecedents and consequences (e.g., Anderson et al., 1996; Kennedy, 1994; Pace, Iwata, Cowdery, Andree, & McIntyre, 1993).

An example of using indiscriminable contingencies was provided by Odom and his colleagues who reduced students' dependence on antecedent prompts and consequences during social skills training by fading antecedents and consequences (Odom et al., 1992). Antecedent prompts were faded in two ways. First, we shifted from prompts that identified specific behavior for the students to employ (e.g., "Ask Suzy to share the blocks with you") to general, vague prompts (e.g., "Remember to play with your friend"). Second, we reduced the frequency of prompts across time from very frequent to intermittent prompts. We also faded reinforcement. Initially students received a happy face on a card for each episode of social interaction. Then, although we continued to provide happy faces, the students did not see the card until the end of the session. Finally, we stopped using happy face cards and told students to "Count their own happy faces in their head." These fading strategies successfully shifted control from continuous and predictable contingencies to intermittent and indiscriminable contingencies. At the end of the study, during a maintenance phase in which all adult-delivered antecedents and consequences were terminated, students continued to use social interaction strategies.

The key to success in this strategy is to first produce behavior that occurs in an adequate quantity (e.g., frequency, rate, duration) and is of an appropriate quality or fluency. Then slowly alter the delivery of antecedents and consequences so that they are occurring at intermittent and normalized levels (Dunlap & Kern, 1993).

6. Teach Mediation Strategies

The goal of this strategy is to teach students self-mediated or self-regulated strategies that they can employ in various settings and situations. Mediation strategies include correspondence training (Guevremont, Osnes, & Stokes, 1986); problem solving (Mastropieri & Scruggs, 2000; Slaby, Roedell, Arezzo, & Hendrix, 1995; Zirpoli & Melloy, 2001); self-recording, self-instruction, and self-reinforcement (Friend & Bursuck, 1999; Koegel, Koegel, & Parks, 1995; Lloyd, Landrum, & Hallahan, 1991; Sugai & Rowe, 1984); requesting reinforcement from others (Baer, 1981); conflict resolution (Walker, Colvin, & Ramsey, 1995); and behavioral relaxation (Poppin, 1988). Students who learn mediation techniques are able to implement those strategies in situations and settings that do not provide consistent and overt antecedents and consequences. For example, Dino was referred to the school psychologist by his English teacher because he often refused to take tests and emitted nervous tics in these situations. The school psychologist taught Dino to employ behavioral relaxation when he had to complete an English test. This greatly reduced his nervous tics and his refusals to complete his English tests. Dino was also able to use behavioral relaxation in other classes when he was asked to complete tests and quizzes. Thus, behavioral relaxation served as a strategy that Dino could employ to mediate his own behavior. Mediation strategies not only reduce dependence on external variables, they also provide self-delivered antecedents and supports for appropriate behavior.

7. Specify a Fluency Criterion

Some researchers have speculated that generalization fails to occur because behavior was not sufficiently learned during the acquisition phase of intervention (Baer, 1981; Chandler, 1992; Kazdin, 1975; Strain, 1981). This strategy addresses that problem by identifying how well a student must perform the behavior before fading and/or terminating intervention. Behavior that is performed consistently and fluently may be more likely to be emitted in other settings and to continue to be used after intervention has terminated.

Measures of fluency can focus on duration, frequency, rate, latency, quality, and appropriateness of behavior. For example, a student may be able to identify the rules for entering a peer group, but when opportunities arise to use those skills, the student does not use them or whispers his request. Clearly this is not fluent behavior. Although the student can identify the required behavior, he is not fluent at applying the skill in natural contexts. Fluency may be promoted by providing many opportunities to practice skills in multiple situations, providing useful feedback, and allowing frequent access to reinforcers. Haring (1987, 1988a,b) suggests that to ensure that fluency is addressed, teams add criteria for fluency to generalization goals on Individualized Educational Plans. After fluency is achieved, the shift to intermittent and natural contingencies may begin.

8. Employ Sequential Modification

This strategy involves implementing interventions in settings or situations in which generalization or maintenance has not occurred. For example, if the student engages in appropriate behavior in the setting in which intervention is implemented, but continues to use challenging behavior in other settings, then intervention should be employed in the other settings as well. For instance, we worked with a student named Alexandria who was self-abusive and aggressive in the classroom, at home, and in community-based settings such as church or the park district pool. We implemented an intervention in the classroom that involved attending to appropriate behavior, attending to the "victims" or targets of her aggressive behavior, and ignoring self-abusive behavior. Although Alexandria stopped engaging in self-abuse and aggression in the classroom, she continued to engage in these behaviors at home and in community settings. The social worker on the team then discussed the intervention strategies with the family and they implemented the interventions at home and then in community-based settings. Only at this point did Alexandria's challenging behavior decrease at home and in community-based settings.

Sequential modification technically is not a strategy to promote generalization because we actually implement the intervention in situations in which generalization has not occurred. However, it should be employed when generalization has not occurred because it ensures that behavior is employed in those additional settings. In addition, as intervention is employed in a second and third setting, generalization to additional settings may occur (Chandler, Lubeck, et al., 1992; Odom et al., 1985).

IMPLEMENTING STRATEGIES TO PROMOTE GENERALIZATION AND MAINTENANCE

Few guidelines are available to identify which specific generalization and maintenance strategies to employ, when to employ specific strategies, or how many strategies to employ at one time (Chandler, Lubeck, et al., 1992; Liberty, White, Billingsley, Haring, Lynch, et al., 1988; McMahon et al., 1994, 1998). Until such guidelines are provided, teams should consider the strategies presented in this chapter and employ those strategies that are (a) acceptable to the team, (b) feasible to employ within school (and home) settings, and (c) that address the individuals needs of each student.

Even though generalization and maintenance can be thought of as the second stage in functional assessment, many of the strategies to promote generalization and maintenance should be implemented during the acquisition phase (Baer, 1981; Chandler, 1991, 1992; Stokes & Osnes, 1988). Thus many generalization promotion strategies should be blended with teaching strategies and become part of the intervention plan at the beginning of treatment. For example, variety in terms of the educators (e.g., primary teacher, paraprofessional, resource room teacher) who provide antecedent stimuli or who consequate appropriate behavior should be included in the initial stages of intervention, rather than introduced at the end of intervention. Likewise, natural antecedents and consequences should be paired with "contrived" stimuli at the start of intervention, not at the end of intervention. Generalization and maintenance is an integral part of behavior change and should not be an afterthought of intervention (Chandler, Lubeck, et al., 1992; Green, 1990; Stokes & Osnes, 1988; Wolery & Gast, 1990).

Although the acquisition and generalization and maintenance phases of intervention are related, teams should expect that the duration of the generalization and maintenance phase will be greater than that for the acquisition phase (Walker, 2000). This is because it takes time to move from continuous schedules to intermittent schedules of reinforcement and indiscriminable contingencies and because students need adequate practice to develop fluent appropriate replacement behaviors. However, the duration and effort employed to promote generalization and maintenance will decrease as appropriate behavior increases and becomes part of the student's repertoire (Walker, 2000).

In summary, although the acquisition of appropriate replacement behavior is an important first step of functional assessment, it is not the only, or the fundamental, goal of functional assessment (Baer, Wolfe, & Risley, 1968, 1987). Carr and his colleagues (1994) identified the fundamental goal of functional assessment as a normalized lifestyle change: the generalization of appropriate behavior across stimuli, generalization across functional behaviors, and the maintenance of appropriate behavior across time. If we do not achieve generalization and maintenance of behavior, then there is little overall benefit to the student and we should not consider our intervention as successful or complete (Baer, 1982; Carr et al., 1994; Chandler, Lubeck, et al.,

1992; Guess, 1990; Liberty, White, Billingsley, & Haring, 1988; Schroeder, Oldenquist, & Rojahn, 1990; Kazdin, 1975). This is because students will not continue to employ appropriate behavior when circumstances change, intervention ends, or across time and they are likely to revert to previously successful challenging behavior in order to achieve desired functions. A comprehensive intervention plan must actively address all phases of behavior change: acquisition, fluency, generalization, and maintenance.

PREVENTION STRATEGIES

The two goals of functional assessment are to anticipate and prevent the development and/or occurrence of challenging behavior and to remediate established challenging behavior. Often, remediation is the first concern of educators and families. Challenging behavior can interfere with teaching and learning, cause harm to the student who engages in challenging behavior and to others, and disrupt or prevent the development of positive social relationships with peers and adults, and it may also require excessive time from educators and parents (Abrams & Segal, 1998; Carr, Taylor, & Robinson, 1991; Hains, Fowler, & Chandler, 1988; Kern, Childs, Dunlap, Clark, & Falk, 1994; Reynaud, 1999; Soodak & Podell, 1993). For these reasons, educators often focus on remediation as the primary goal of functional assessment and they design interventions to address challenging behavior when it occurs (i.e., eliminating consequences that support challenging behavior, providing consequences that support appropriate replacement behavior, and/or providing consequences that punish challenging behavior).

We argue, however, that much of our efforts as educators and parents should be aimed at prevention. It is more difficult to remediate established challenging behavior than it is to prevent it (Rhode et al., 1992). If we are able to prevent the development of challenging behavior or to stop challenging behavior from being displayed after it is part of a student's repertoire, we will not need to employ the often time-consuming and extra effort-requiring remediation strategies (McGee, 1988; Munk & Karsh, 1999; Repp, 1999; Repp, Karsh, Dahlquist, & Chandler, 1994).

The goal of prevention can be achieved by arranging the environment so that it triggers and supports appropriate behavior (Carr et al., 1994; Krantz & Risley, 1974; McGee & Daly, 1999; Nielsen, Olive, Donovan, & McEvoy, 1998; Repp, 1999). In doing this we manipulate antecedents and consequences that are associated with and that specifically trigger and support challenging behavior. We also introduce new consequences and antecedents that will trigger and support appropriate replacement behavior (Haring & Kennedy, 1990; Kennedy, 1994; Kennedy & Itkonen, 1993). For example, in the past, Mr. Carter regularly argued with Lewis when Lewis complained that he didn't want to do his worksheets. Now, Mr. Carter no longer argues with Lewis when he complains. Instead, Mr. Carter tells Lewis as he hands out the assignment that after Lewis completes the first 10 problems, he can have a break during which he does an activity of his choice. Mr. Carter also provides frequent feedback and reinforcement for appropriate worksheet-related behavior and assistance as necessary. Lewis now does the specified number of problems and then receives a break. This antecedent and consequence-based intervention successfully has prevented the start of an argument between Lewis and Mr. Carter.

Often, setting events also may be introduced, altered, or eliminated in order to evoke appropriate behavior (Horner, Day, Sprague, O'Brien, & Heathfield, 1991; Horner, Vaugn, Day, & Ard, 1996). For example, we may introduce a setting event such as providing a visual schedule for students in order to indicate the activities that will occur on a daily basis and those that may change from day to day. We may reduce auditory distractions as a setting event during a quiz by closing the door and allowing students who have completed the quiz to go to the library. Or we can eliminate a setting event by changing the seating arrangements for two students who distract each other or fight frequently.

When existing setting events cannot be altered or eliminated (e.g., divorce, illness), we may reduce the impact of setting events on behavior by altering the class or activity schedule, task demands, or our interactions with and expectations for students (see Chapter 6). For instance, we may reduce the impact of a setting event by talking with a student who is upset about a problem occurring at home before asking the student to begin his or her work.

When planning prevention strategies, it is helpful to think of two types of prevention. First, efforts may be aimed at preventing the development of challenging behavior. Second, efforts may be aimed at preventing established challenging behavior from occurring or from becoming entrenched in the student's repertoire (Carr et al., 1990; Kern & Dunlap, 1999; Nelson, Crabtree, Marchand-Martella, & Martella, 1998). The key to both types of prevention is to anticipate problems and structure the environment before challenging behavior has a chance to occur.

Earlier in this text we discussed the problems that often occur during activity transitions. Students may run, shout, tease, fight, throw materials, leave the classroom, and so on, during activity transitions (Lawry, Danko, & Strain, 2000; Strain & Hemmeter, 1997). In classrooms where students currently engage in challenging behavior during transitions, prevention may be achieved by changing the existing antecedent triggers for challenging behavior (e.g., loose structure and little supervision) and by introducing antecedents that will set the occasion for more appropriate behavior (e.g., presignals and safety signals concerning the beginning and end of transition, rules for transition behavior, and supervision). Interventions such as these increase the probability that students will no longer engage in challenging behavior during transitions and will, instead, engage in appropriate behavior.

Preventing the development of challenging behavior during transition can be achieved by anticipating the potential for challenging behavior and starting the school year with structured and supervised transitions (i.e., the school year begins with antecedents in place that set the occasion for ap-

BOX 11–1
Steps in preventing predictable challenging behavior

1. Identify when challenging behaviors most often occur or may be expected to occur.
2. Identify antecedents, setting events, and consequences related to challenging behavior.
3. Arrange antecedents, setting events, and consequences so that they no longer trigger and support challenging behavior.
4. Arrange antecedents, setting events, and consequences so that they set the occasion for and support appropriate behavior.

propriate behavior and provide positive consequences for appropriate transition behavior).

Many challenging behaviors and the situations in which they occur can be predicted. Planning and arranging the environment before these behaviors occur can prevent the development of challenging behavior and the continued occurrence of established challenging behavior (Dunlap et al., 1990; Dunlap & Fox, 1996; Repp, 1999). There are four steps that should be followed in preventing predictable challenging behavior. These are listed in Box 11–1. The first step in the planning process will be identifying when challenging behaviors most often occur or may be expected to occur. When this is done for established challenging behaviors it may be helpful to use a scatterplot (see Chapter 4) to identify the times of the day in which behavior most frequently occurs (Touchette, MacDonald, & Langer, 1985). Or you may be able to anticipate or predict when challenging behavior will occur based on previous experience with the student and challenging behavior (Strain & Hemmeter, 1997).

The next step in the prevention process is to identify antecedents, setting events, and consequences that are related to the challenging behavior. You may consider several categories of variables when doing this analysis. These categories are presented in Table 11–2. This table does not represent a comprehensive list of variables that should be considered. However, it may be useful in guiding observations and analysis of environments. For example, when we observe students and analyze the classroom or other environments, we consider the status and arrangement of these variables and we analyze if and how they affect current behavior. In fact, on one of our observation sheets, the categories are listed as options that may be checked during observation (in an abbreviated form, of course). We encourage your teams to add items to this list as you identify additional variables through observation and analysis.

The third and fourth steps in preventing predictable challenging behaviors are to arrange antecedents and consequences so that they no longer trigger and support challenging behavior; instead, they set the occasion for, and support, appropriate behavior. These four steps are illustrated in the following example. McGee and Daly (1999) reported a study in which they identified that peer-directed verbal and physical aggression occurred most frequently during free-play activities (prevention step 1). Free-play activities

TABLE 11–2
*Variables to consider
when conducting a
prevention analysis*

Activity or task: type (reading, writing, fine or gross motor, computer, leisure or free play, test, etc.), duration, specific subject (math, science, shop, etc.), difficulty level, preferred–nonpreferred, previous success, frequency of errors, order or sequence of activities and tasks

Seating arrangements: desk arrangement (rows, grouped in sets, etc.), location of desk, who sits next to whom, preferred seating, choice of seating

Student grouping: large groups, small groups, dyads, individual work, preferred–nonpreferred grouping, choice of partners or groups, familiar–unfamiliar peers

Peer interaction: positive, negative, verbal, physical, frequency, no interaction, previous experiences with peers

Materials: number and type, location and availability, sensory characteristics, developmental or academic level, manipulative–static, familiar–novel, shared or own set of materials, difficulty level, preferred–nonpreferred, choice given

Structure: teacher-directed, student-directed, supervision, choice and varying structure, posted and reviewed rules, change in routine, predictability of activities and routines

Activity level: active, passive, duration of active or passive tasks, opportunities for movement, variety in sensory input, variety in the order or sequence of activity level

Adults: number, proximity to students, eye contact, familiar–unfamiliar, preferred–nonpreferred, frequency of attention to students, type and frequency of response to appropriate behavior, type and frequency of response to challenging behavior, prompts (safety signals and presignals), type of reinforcers and punishers employed, student–adult ratio

Physical environment: location (classroom, lunchroom, playground, bathroom, hallway, library, etc.), noise level, crowding, confined space, lighting, visual input, temperature, familiar–unfamiliar, accessibility

Transition: structured, duration, signaled, transition tasks, buddy assignments, transition-based teaching

Instruction: whole-class lecture, large or small group discussion, cooperative groups, video- or audiotapes or movies, pacing, duration, unison responding, opportunities to respond, clear directions and requests, mode of instruction (visual, textual, auditory, etc.)

Physiological states: medication, illness, allergy, hunger, menses, fatigue, overstimulated, understimulated, pain, intoxicated, drug-induced states

Situational factors: problems or changes at home (e.g., divorce, homeless), mood or emotional state, depression, school breaks, parties, holidays, critical incidents (e.g., fight on the bus), time of day

Note: The information in this table reflects our own experience in conducting functional assessment and the following references: Chandler, Fowler, and Lubeck (1992), Jenson, Rhode, and Reavis (1994), McGee and Daly (1999), Munk and Karsh (1999), Munk and Repp (1994b). © 2002 Chandler and Dahlquist.

included familiar toys that were available on child-sized shelves. The authors indicated that many students became bored with the familiar toys and that some students did not know how to play with available toys (prevention step 2). To prevent continued instances of verbal and physical aggression, they developed an intervention strategy that reduced familiarity with toys by introducing a toy rotation plan (to maintain novelty among materials) and individualized hobby boxes that contained toys designed to address the unique needs of individual children (prevention steps 3 and 4). Hobby boxes were distributed to children when they were not otherwise engaged. These interventions prevented further occurrences of verbal and physical aggression and increased the frequency of appropriate and interactive play. This study illustrates the prevention process and the importance of examining the current environment and arranging it so that it triggers and supports appropriate behavior.

In developing and applying strategies to prevent the development and occurrence of challenging behavior, we must consider each component of the ABC sequence (setting events, antecedents, behavior, and consequences) (Horner, 1994). Challenging behavior can be prevented from developing or occurring by manipulating the setting events and antecedents that occur prior to or that co-occur with the challenging behavior. Setting events and antecedents may be arranged within each of the functions (positive reinforcement, negative reinforcement, and sensory regulation/sensory stimulation) (Munk & Karsh, 1999). In the positive reinforcement function, antecedents and/or setting events may be introduced or existing antecedents and setting events may be altered so that they will set the occasion for appropriate behavior to occur (Dunlap & Kern, 1993; Mace, Shapiro, & Mace, 1998). For example, at the beginning of an activity a teacher might tell all students to raise a hand when they know the answer. A therapist might tell her student to ask for the desired object before he opens her cupboard door. Or a teacher may provide opportunities throughout the day for students to interact with peers (thus enabling them to obtain attention from peers) in order to prevent peer interaction during inappropriate periods (e.g., telling jokes or talking during an individual reading period).

Antecedents also can be used to redirect students to engage in appropriate replacement behavior as they *begin* to display challenging behavior. For example, during the morning phonemic awareness activities, Serina often leaves her seat, wanders about the classroom, and plays with materials in the classroom. In the past, Serina's teacher, Mrs. Tull, has tried a variety of reactive consequence-based strategies including reprimanding her behavior, taking away privileges, having Serina state the rules for classroom conduct, having Serina apologize to the class for her disruptive behavior, and talking individually with Serina about her behavior. None of these strategies has worked. Mrs. Tull hypothesized that the function of Serina's out-of-seat behavior was positive reinforcement. Her observations indicated that Serina usually received some form of teacher and/or peer attention when she left her seat. Furthermore, Serina engaged in appropriate behavior when she worked in small groups with peers, one on one with the teacher, and on days when she was the helper during phonemic awareness activities. Serina primarily engaged in challenging behavior when the teacher was talking to the whole class and students were required to take turns answering questions.

Intervention to address Serina's challenging behavior focused on introducing antecedent strategies to trigger appropriate behavior. At the beginning of phonemic awareness activities, Mrs. Tull told the class, "Everyone who is in their seat during our activity gets a raffle ticket at the end" (Rhode et al., 1992). She also frequently asked Serina to answer questions or to assist in the activity. She also had students tell each other the answers to questions, thus providing Serina with peer as well as teacher attention. These antecedent strategies, combined with praise and raffle tickets that were provided contingent on appropriate behavior and extinction of challenging behavior, increased Serina's in-seat behavior and participation during morning phonemic awareness activities.

Antecedents and Setting Events	Behavior	Consequence	Function
Circle, teacher attention to whole group	Out-of-seat, wanders, plays with materials	Reprimand, apologize to class, talk with teacher, peer laughter	Positive Reinforcement: obtains attention
Circle, teacher attention to whole group and to Serina, safety signals, tell peer answers	In-seat, participates, assists teacher, talks to peers	Praise, 1:1 teacher interaction, raffle ticket, interaction with peers, ignore challenging behavior	Positive Reinforcement: obtains attention

When the function of challenging behavior is negative reinforcement, antecedents also can be arranged to set the occasion for appropriate behavior. For example, presignals or safety signals may provide information about the duration of an activity, the amount of time remaining in an activity, or the number and type of behaviors required or remaining before an activity ends (Kennedy & Itkonen, 1993; Rhode et al., 1992; Sulzer-Azaroff & Mayer, 1986, 1991). For instance, a paraprofessional may tell a student that after he completes eight problems, he can take a break. Or a teacher might inform students that there are 10 minutes left to complete the worksheet. Many of the middle schools and high schools in our area employ a school-wide antecedent strategy during class transitions in order to address the problem of students arriving to class late or remaining in the hallway after the end of transition. The goal of this strategy is to provide an antecedent cue that will signal the end of transition and the beginning of the next class session. These schools now play music over the loud speaker during transition. As long as the music is playing, students are allowed to interact and "hang out" in the hallways of the school. When there is 1 minute left in transition, the music stops. This antecedent cue promotes on-time behavior (thus preventing tardy behavior) by signaling that students are to go to their next class at this time. This school-wide strategy, combined with points for on-time behavior, has greatly increased on-time behavior and, thus, prevented tardy (i.e., challenging) behavior.

Antecedents and Setting Events	Behavior	Consequence	Function
End of transition	Remain in hallway, late arrival to class	Peer interaction, able to do own activity, detention	Negative Reinforcement: avoids going to class
End of transition, music signals during transition, music stops when 1 minute remains in transition	Goes to class, arrives on time	Points	Positive Reinforcement: obtains points for going to class

Antecedents and setting events also may be arranged to reduce the aversiveness of existing variables within the negative reinforcement function. Students often escape or avoid activities, tasks, and materials that are disliked, boring, teacher directed, overwhelming, of long duration, difficult to perform, or associated with previous failure. To reduce the aversive nature of a difficult task, a teacher may assist a student in completing part of the task. Or a teacher might show a student how to do the first problem on a homework assignment or provide a sample of a completed problem broken into critical performance steps. Eliminating aversive antecedent conditions or reducing the aversive nature of antecedent variables increases the probability that students will use materials, engage in tasks, and participate in activities rather than engaging in escape and avoidance-motivated behavior.

In the sensory regulation/sensory stimulation function, setting events and antecedents may be arranged to prevent overstimulation, understimulation, and negative reactions to sensory input. Prevention in this function can be achieved by providing the type and level of sensory input desired or needed by the student before challenging behavior occurs and providing variety in the level and type of sensory stimulation available to the student (Chicago Public Schools, 1998;

Favell, McGimsey, & Schell, 1982; Flannery & Horner, 1994; Horner, 1980; Reisman & Scott, 1991; Tustin, 1995; Walker et al., 1995; Wodrich, 1994).

For example, Eduardo is a student with autism enrolled in a regular education kindergarten/first-grade class. Eduardo loves morning circle, group reading activities, and independent seatwork, and he readily participates in these activities. Unfortunately, he does not readily participate in other activities. When students are told to select work centers or are placed in cooperative groups, Eduardo often tries to leave the classroom. If he is directed to an activity, he begins to flap his hand, bite his hand, and yell. When he does this, his teacher, Mr. Rattikin, typically tells him to stop and attempts to provide physical assistance in order to make Eduardo participate. This usually continues until the end of the task or until Mr. Rattikin gives up and allows Eduardo to move to an isolated area of the classroom.

The team hypothesized that Eduardo disliked activities that were noisy and often crowded. So Mr. Rattikin altered his classroom environment in order to prevent Eduardo's negative reaction to noisy, crowded centers and to increase participation during center time. Mr. Rattikin developed several center options that contained quiet and more passive activities and that could accommodate a small number of students at one time. He also allowed Eduardo to work independently at his desk on activities and with materials that typically were part of the noisier and crowded centers. Mr. Rattikin also provided Eduardo with a list of centers that would meet his sensory needs and prompted him to select one of those centers at the beginning of center time. These antecedent strategies decreased Eduardo's challenging behavior and increased appropriate participation behavior.

Antecedents and Setting Events	Behavior	Consequence	Function
Centers, crowded, increased noise, verbal and physical prompts	Leaves class, flaps hand, bites hand, yells	Additional verbal and physical prompts, left alone	Sensory Regulation/ Sensory Stimulation: decrease auditory input and crowding
Centers, option of quiet, passive, and uncrowded centers; verbal, physical, and visual prompts	Selects a center, participates	Praise	Sensory Regulation/ Sensory Stimulation: decrease auditory input and crowding

Table 11–3 presents a list of common antecedent strategies that can be employed to prevent challenging behavior. Many of these strategies involve manipulation of specific antecedent stimuli that are correlated with challenging behavior. Others are simply effective antecedent teaching practices that keep students engaged, thus preventing challenging behavior.

TABLE 11–3
Antecedent strategies that can be employed to prevent challenging behavior

1. Give appropriate and clear directions and requests (instructions should be short, simple, easy to understand, match the linguistic ability of the student, given when the student is attending, divided into steps, etc.).
2. Establish effective transitions or leisure times [e.g., have materials or activities available during leisure times, signal transition beginning and end, provide structure, reduce transition duration, use transition-based teaching (Wolery, Doyle, Gast, Ault, & Lichtenberg, 1991), assign buddies or partners during transition, assign tasks or jobs during transition].
3. Provide safety signals and presignals.
4. Prompt appropriate behavior.
5. Tell students what to do versus what not to do. Give initiating versus terminating requests (Walker & Sylwester, 1998) (e.g., "Tell me when you need a break" versus "Don't leave your seat").
6. Provide choice and student-directed activities.
7. Present instructions as mands, not as questions that imply choice (e.g., "Get your book and read Chapter 5" versus "Are you ready to read your science chapter?").
8. Post and review rules for appropriate behavior.
9. Institute behavioral contracting (Alberto & Troutman, 1999; Friend & Bursuck, 1999; Sulzer-Azaroff & Mayer, 1991).
10. Provide frequent attention, supervision, and proximity.
11. Provide assistance, arrange for success.
12. Change the activities, tasks, materials, and peers.
13. Interrupt challenging behavior and redirect.
14. Model appropriate behavior.
15. Reinforce peers who engage in appropriate behavior.
16. Attend to appropriate behavior—"Catch 'em being good" and "Good Behavior Game" (Barrish, Saunders, & Wolf, 1969).
17. Reduce waiting, provide opportunities to respond, employ unison responding.
18. Alternate active and passive tasks.
19. Provide variation in instructional style and materials.
20. Inform students that preferred activities will follow completion of less preferred activities (Homme, deBaca, Devine, Steinhorst, & Rickert, 1976; Premack, 1959).
21. Develop and review social stories (Gray, 1994; Gray & Garland, 1993).
22. Provide passive, low stimulation areas, activities, and materials.
23. Use behavioral contracts (e.g., Lassman, Jolivette, & Wehby, 1999).

Note: The information in this table reflects our own experience in conducting functional assessment and the following references: Cangelosi (1993), Chandler and Dahlquist (1999b), Chandler, Dahlquist, Repp, and Feltz (1999), Munk and Karsh (1999), Munk and Repp (1994b), Strain and Hemmeter (1997), and Walker (1998).
© 2002 Chandler and Dahlquist.

In addition to arranging antecedent stimuli and setting events to prevent challenging behavior, we must provide consequences that will support appropriate behavior when it occurs. For example, remember Serina who often left her seat, wandered about the classroom, and played with materials during the morning phonemic awareness activities. The consequences for her behavior typically consisted of reprimands, making her apologize to the class, talking to the teacher, and so forth. Although Mrs. Tull used these consequences in an attempt to reduce Serina's challenging behavior, these consequences actually supported Serina's challenging behavior by providing attention. As a result, the consequences were changed so that they supported appropriate, rather than challenging behavior. Mrs. Tull praised Serina and provided her with a raffle ticket when she participated during the activities. Mrs. Tull also ignored Serina's wandering, nonparticipatory behavior and she interacted with Serina only when she participated in the activities. These altered consequences, combined with antecedent strategies, increased Serina's appropriate behavior and at the same time prevented future occurrences of challenging behavior.

It is important to remember that consequences can strengthen, maintain, or weaken behavior (Skinner, 1953, 1974). As discussed in Chapter 4, positive or desired consequences (from the student's perspective) will strengthen or maintain behavior. Punishing or undesired consequences (from the student's perspective) will weaken or decrease the behavior that they follow. A list of consequences commonly employed in school settings and that may support both challenging and appropriate behavior was provided in Chapter 4.

The goal of prevention is to prevent the development of challenging behavior or the use of established challenging behavior. Therefore, it follows that the earlier prevention strategies are employed, the more effective they will be (Dunlap et al., 1990). For example, proactive prevention strategies within our school systems should begin when children enter preschool (McGee, 1988). This can prevent these young students from developing and practicing challenging behaviors such as aggression and noncompliance that will interfere with learning and development in preschool and that are likely to continue into and adversely affect learning and development in elementary school (Dunlap & Fox, 1996; Dunlap et al., 1990; McGee, 1988; McGee & Daly, 1999; Sprague & Walker, 2000).

The same concept applies to the school year. The earlier in the school year that prevention strategies are employed, the more successful prevention efforts will be. This is because prevention strategies and the appropriate behavior that they support will not need to compete with well-established challenging behaviors and the supports for those behaviors. For example, many educators recommend establishing a set of class-wide rules for behavior at the beginning of the school year (Cangelosi, 1993). A list of the rules should be posted in the classroom and they should be discussed frequently during the first weeks of the year. The rules then should be reviewed periodically throughout the year. Students also should be reinforced (e.g., with praise, points, tokens) for following established rules. For example, rules for cooperative group activities might include these:

1. Take turns.
2. Listen to each other's opinions and comments.

3. Do your assigned job.

4. Help your peers when asked.

5. Share materials.

6. Stay on task.

For more information on establishing class-wide rules and promoting rule following behavior see the following resources: Alberto and Troutman (1999), Kerr and Nelson (1998), Rhode et al. (1992), Sulzer-Azaroff and Mayer (1986, 1991), and Walker et al.(1995).

Establishing rules at the beginning of the school year and periodically reviewing those rules is much more effective at preventing challenging behavior than the often used strategy in which rules and consequences are established one at a time in reaction to individual instances of challenging behavior.

SUMMARY

Prevention is an important goal of functional assessment. Although initial efforts in functional assessment may focus on remediating established challenging behavior, the long-term goal should be to prevent the development of challenging behavior and to prevent established challenging behavior from occurring. The goal of preventing the development of challenging behavior can be achieved by arranging antecedents and setting events that will set the occasion for or trigger appropriate behavior. Desired or positive consequences then are provided following appropriate behavior in order to strengthen and maintain that behavior. The goal of preventing the occurrence or emission of established challenging behavior can be achieved by examining the current environment. Antecedents that currently set the occasion for challenging behavior, setting events that are associated with challenging behavior, and consequences that support challenging behavior must be altered or removed and replaced by setting events, antecedents, and consequences that will trigger and support appropriate behavior.

In addition to focusing on prevention, teams must address the generalization and maintenance of behavior. Generalization is achieved when behavior occurs across nonintervention situations and settings and across behaviors. Maintenance is achieved when behavior continues to occur after intervention strategies have been terminated (i.e., behavior continues to occur across time). For many students, generalization and maintenance is not an automatic or guaranteed outcome of intervention. Rather, for these students generalization and maintenance must be actively promoted by implementing specific strategies.

Generalization is not a new concept within the field of behavior analysis and special education (e.g., Skinner, 1953, 1974). In their seminal article on behavior analysis Baer et al. (1968) identified generalization as one of the primary goals of behavior analysis. Yet, the efforts to promote generalization and the success of achieving generalization and maintenance continue to lag behind that of acquisition (Baer et al., 1987; Chandler, Lubeck, et al., 1992; Haring, 1987). Stokes and Osnes (1988) refer to educators' ethical obligation to actively address generalization and maintenance. Generalization and maintenance must be included as part of a comprehensive intervention plan if we are to achieve our goal of long-term lifestyle change. Liberty and her colleagues (Liberty & Billingsley, 1988; Liberty et al., 1988a, 1988b) recommend that teams write goals that specifically address generalization and maintenance and that these goals be added to a student's Individualized Educational Plan (Haring, 1988a,b). They provide specific instructions for writing these goals and their research supports the effectiveness of these goals in focusing teacher efforts on promoting and obtaining generalization and maintenance.

Part Four

Functional Assessment Within School Settings

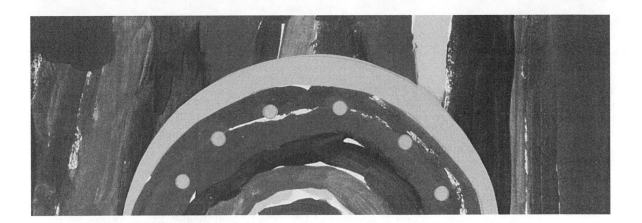

12

Guidelines for Program Implementation and Consultation

This chapter addresses program implementation and consultation. Let us begin by acknowledging that the functional assessment and intervention model presented in this textbook is not a simple, easy model to implement in school and home settings. It requires time, effort, and skill to conduct the observations of appropriate and challenging behavior and the current environment, interview critical individuals, and analyze why challenging behavior is occurring. It then takes additional time, effort, and skill to develop and implement strategies to reduce challenging behavior and to increase appropriate replacement behavior (Walker, 1998). In our experience, however, the amount of time and effort devoted to functional assessment generally is the same or less than the amount of time and effort educators currently employ in reacting to challenging behavior. And the interventions employed through the functional assessment model are much more cost effective than those employed in reaction to challenging behavior. As we continue to apply interventions and to provide support for appropriate behavior, the amount of time and effort required will decrease, although it may never disappear completely, because we should continue to monitor behavior and reinforce appropriate behavior (Walker, 1998). In addition to reduced time and effort, our experiences have taught us that skill in conducting functional assessment and selecting and implementing intervention strategies increases with practice.

Our own experience and research as well as the research of other investigators documents the effectiveness of the functional assessment and intervention model for addressing challenging behavior in school-based settings (Carr, Levin, McConnachie, Carlson, Kemp, & Smith, 1994; Chandler, Dahlquist, Repp, & Feltz, 1999; Drasgow, Halle, Ostrosky, & Harbors, 1996; Journal of Applied Behavior Analysis, 1994; Kern, Childs, Dunlap, Clarke, & Falk, 1994; Repp, 1999; Repp, Felce, & Barton, 1988). However, the success of functional assessment is not guaranteed. You should consider several guidelines as you implement the functional assessment and implementation model in school-based settings and when providing consultation to educators, staff, and families. These guidelines will increase the probability of success. We begin this chapter by discussing tips for conducting functional assessment and implementing interventions, followed by many of the most frequently asked questions or issues of resistance. We then end this chapter with a discussion of guidelines for teaching functional assessment and providing consultation.

GUIDELINES FOR CONDUCTING FUNCTIONAL ASSESSMENT AND IMPLEMENTING INTERVENTIONS

Tips and guidelines for conducting functional assessment and selecting and implementing function-based strategies have been provided throughout the book and many were specifically addressed in Chapters 5 and 6. The guidelines that we present in this chapter are ones that have not been previously discussed. These guidelines are listed in Table 12–1. The first guideline actually is not directly related to functional assessment; rather, this guideline addresses crisis situations in which unpredicted and severe, often dangerous, challenging behavior occurs.

1. Learn How to Respond During a Crisis

Many educators are willing to implement interventions based on functional assessment, but are not sure what to do in crisis situations. Often they resort to previously employed reactionary and often punishing consequences. The first rule of crisis management is this: You cannot teach in crisis. The immediate purpose of intervention during a crisis is to interrupt and stop the challenging behavior and to redirect the student to more appropriate behavior. Long-term intervention to reduce challenging behavior and increase appropriate replacement behavior should follow crisis situations and be based on an understanding of the function of the challenging behavior.

TABLE 12–1
Guidelines for conducting functional assessment and implementing interventions

1. Learn how to respond during a crisis.
2. Involve the family.
3. Be patient.
4. Expect increases in challenging behavior and periodic regressions of behavior.
5. View intervention as a dynamic and evolving process.
6. Apply intervention and prevention strategies class-wide.

Carr and his colleagues (1994) and Walker and his colleagues (1995) identify several steps to follow in crisis situations:

A. Ignore the challenging behavior when possible. It may be that the behavior will de-escalate without direct intervention from a staff member. This strategy can be used for minor challenging behavior that often results in more severe challenging behavior when it leads to teacher or peer attention.

B. Protect the student and other individuals from harm. This may involve going to and physically guarding the "victim" rather than interacting with the student who is engaged in challenging behavior, telling peers to move to different areas of the classroom, putting a pillow under a student's head to protect from damage due to head banging, removing dangerous objects, and so forth.

C. Momentarily restrain the student if needed. Restraint is used when the form and severity of behavior is likely to lead to injury to the student or other individuals. Restraint procedures should not be used without prior training. It is easy to harm yourself and the student if restraint is done incorrectly. Therefore, be sure to learn what types of restraint procedures are allowed within your school district or cooperative and attend in-service training on how to use restraint in crisis situations.

D. Remove peers and adults from the crisis situation. Sometimes it will be necessary for all students to leave the classroom until the crisis situation has passed. For example, in one classroom in which the second author worked, when Jerry began to throw garbage cans and to physically attack peers and teachers, the primary teacher told the other students and the teaching assistant to wait in the hallway or go to the gym. They returned to the classroom after the crisis and dangerous challenging behaviors had ended.

E. Introduce antecedent cues to evoke appropriate or calming behavior. Do not argue, threaten, scold, negotiate, or try to talk with the student about their behavior during crisis. These behaviors can escalate the crisis and do not identify appropriate replacement behavior. Instead, (1) using a calm voice, identify appropriate behavior, (2) use physical prompting to evoke appropriate behavior, and (3) when possible, redirect the student to appropriate behavior that is incompatible with (i.e., within the same response class) the challenging behavior. For example, if a student is screaming and swearing, have the student suck cold water with a straw. Or if a student is throwing garbage cans, have the student complete a fine motor or gross motor task such as writing his name or putting materials away.

If it is not possible to select an appropriate replacement behavior that is incompatible with the challenging behavior, then focus on helping the student complete a passive task such as completing a puzzle or doing one problem on a worksheet. The second author of this textbook also recommends using sabotage in addition to assisting the student in performing an appropriate behavior. Sabotage is a strategy often associated with incidental teaching in which the educator engages in an unexpected behavior or prevents an activity from occurring (e.g., Ostrosky & Kaiser, 1991). For example, a teacher may assist a student in writing his name, but spell the name wrong or use a ruler to write the student's name. Or she may put a child's coat on backwards or put the child's coat on herself. This type of sabotage often effectively interrupts challenging behavior as the student seeks to correct the teacher's mistakes.

F. Resume normal activities and routines. After the student has calmed and is no longer a threat to himself or herself and other individuals, return to the previous or scheduled classroom activities and routines. Walker and his colleagues (1995) recommend implementing individual work at this phase rather than group or interactive activities. The type of activity selected for this phase should be based on the needs of the student.

G. Provide debriefing. This final phase is a time to review with the student the triggers for the challenging crisis behavior and alternative behaviors that should have been employed. Students may practice alternative behaviors and participate in developing a plan for future crisis situations. The debriefing phase should occur only after the student is calm, has participated in a normal classroom activity or routine, and has displayed appropriate and calm behavior for at least a half hour.

Crisis situations are not opportunities to teach appropriate replacement behavior. Your goal in crisis situations is to interrupt and stop behavior and to ensure the safety of students and adults. Crisis situations should be examined, however, in order to identify antecedents and setting events that set the occasion for or triggered the crisis situation and to identify consequences that may have supported challenging behavior during a crisis. These should be altered when possible in order to prevent future crisis situations. In addition, a plan should be developed based on the function of challenging behavior so that all staff know how to respond during crisis situations.

2. Involve the Family

Although the majority of this textbook deals with challenging behavior within school settings, it is important to consider and involve the family when implementing interventions (Walker, 1998; Walker et al., 1995). Family members may be able to provide insight regarding antecedents and consequences that trigger and support challenging behavior and they may be able to pinpoint setting events that are not known or identified by educators (e.g., illness, divorce, visits with separated parent). They also may be able to identify intervention strategies that have been successful or that have failed in the past (Arndorfer, Miltenberger, Woster, Rortvedt, & Gaffaney, 1994; Boulware, Schwartz, & McBride, 1999).

Family members also may be involved as a component of the intervention plan. For example, they may sign a checklist indicating that a student worked on homework for a fixed period of time. Or, they may provide consequences (e.g., the student is allowed to rent a video) contingent on the display of appropriate behavior at school. Finally, family members may implement intervention strategies at home and in the community in order to promote behavior change in multiple settings, thereby facilitating generalization and maintenance (Schreibman, 1988). Remember Alexandria (who was discussed under the sequential modification generalization promotion strategy in Chapter 11) who engaged in self-abuse and aggression in school, home, and community-based settings? After intervention had decreased her challenging behavior and increased appropriate behavior in the classroom, her family implemented interventions at home and in community settings. This reduced aggression and self-abuse and increased appropriate play and communication at home and in community settings.

The point at which families should be involved in intervention and the type and amount of involvement should be discussed with families. The final decision concerning participation lies with the family and will vary across families depending on their available time, the amount of effort required, and their interest in addressing their child's behavior (Chandler, Fowler, & Lubeck, 1986; Chandler, Fowler, & Stahursky, 1995; Fowler, Chandler, Johnson, & Stella, 1988; Turnbull & Turnbull, 1997). Some families may want to understand the functional assessment process and will begin participation at the observation and analysis stage. Other families may want to understand the rationale for intervention prior to implementing interventions at home. Other families, like Alexandria's parents, may wish to implement interventions only after they have demonstrated successful behavior change in the classroom. And some families may simply wish to be informed about functional assessment and intervention plans (Johnson, Chandler, Kerns, & Fowler, 1986).

At a minimal level of participation, families should be informed that functional assessment will be conducted on their child's behavior and then they should be informed about what intervention strategies will be implemented at school. In some school districts or situations, parents may be required to provide consent for functional assessment and before intervention strategies are employed. When families are informed about the initiation of functional assessment, they should be provided with a list of options for participation and they should be allowed to add options to the list. Options for participation might include these:

A. Participate in an interview about my child.

B. Observe my child at school.

C. Observe my child at home.

D. Collect data concerning my child's behavior at home.

E. Attend a workshop on functional assessment (or other training options).

F. Attend team meetings regarding my child's behavior.

G. Be informed of intervention strategies that will be used in the classroom to address my child's behavior.

H. Be informed of progress and/or changes in my child's behavior.

I. Implement intervention strategies at home and in the community to address my child's behavior.

J. Teach other individuals (e.g., caregivers, home tutors) to implement intervention strategies at home and in the community.

Very little has been written about involving families in school-based functional assessment. However, several studies have documented the success of teaching families to apply functionally based intervention strategies within their homes in order to address the challenging behavior of their children (Boulware et al., 1999; Dunlap & Fox, 1996; Koegel, Koegel, Kellegrew, & Mullen, 1996; Timm, 1993; Wacker, Peck, Derby, Berg, & Harding, 1996). These studies demonstrate the benefits to children and families and the effectiveness of involving families in the functional assessment process.

3. Be Patient

Often educators expect and hope that behavior will change quickly (i.e., in a single session or day). Unfortunately, this seldom happens. Although you may see some change in behavior soon after intervention is implemented, it typically takes time for appropriate replacement behavior to increase to desired levels and for challenging behavior to decrease or terminate (Mace, 1994; Skinner, 1953; Sulzer-Azaroff & Mayer, 1991). Students need multiple opportunities to experience the new or altered contingencies in order to establish a new and stable pattern of behavior. Remember, some of these students have an extensive history of using challenging behavior. They may have employed challenging behavior for months or even years. They need time to establish a new history (Kazdin, 2001). As a result, we should not expect immediate, complete behavior change. It may take days, weeks, or in some cases months for challenging behavior to decrease and appropriate replacement behavior to increase to acceptable and desirable levels.

For example, the little girl Alexandria who engaged in self-abuse and aggression, had done so for 1.5 years before we conducted functional assessment. As we implemented intervention, her challenging behavior slowly decreased and appropriate replacement behavior (toy play and communication) slowly increased. After about 4 weeks of intervention, Alexandria engaged in toy play and verbal communication and she engaged self-abuse and aggression with equal frequency. As we continued to apply the intervention, Alexandria began to use appropriate behavior more frequently than challenging behavior. After 12 weeks of intervention, Alexandria consistently engaged in appropriate behavior and seldom engaged in challenging behavior. Three months of intervention may seem like a long period of time, however, remember that Alexandria's self-abuse and aggressive behavior had successfully produced positive reinforcement (adult attention) for the previous 1.5 years. Alexandria needed time and practice to learn (a) that these behaviors no longer resulted in attention and (b) that there were new behaviors that would produce attention.

In addition to hoping that behavior will change quickly, educators often hope that intervention will be easy to implement. Unfortunately, this is not always possible. For many students, it may be necessary to temporarily disrupt classroom routines or to have an "extra pair of hands" in the classroom in order to monitor behavior and implement the intervention. For those students we often recommend that the team or educator start small. They may choose one time of the day or one setting in which to implement interventions. This causes less overall disruption to classroom activities and routines. Then, as behavior changes, the intervention can be implemented in other settings or during other times of the day.

When deciding whether to implement intervention throughout the day or only during part of the day, it is important to consider how much time and effort currently is employed in response to challenging behavior. If you consistently are disrupting classroom activities and routines to address challenging behavior, then it may be desirable to implement intervention throughout the day. The intensity of intervention application and the correlated disruption of classroom activities and routines will decrease over time as appropriate behavior increases.

4. Expect Increases in Challenging Behavior and Periodic Regressions of Behavior

Although challenging behavior will decrease over time, for many students, you will observe an immediate increase in challenging behavior at the beginning of intervention. This is because their behavior is no longer producing the desired function and they may not know how to produce the desired function using appropriate replacement behaviors. Because challenging behavior produced the desired function in the past, they try harder to make that behavior work. In doing this students may increase the intensity, duration, or frequency of challenging behavior.

For example, Alexandria hit herself more often and for longer periods of time at the beginning of intervention (when we ignored her self-abuse and attended only to toy play and verbal forms of communication). It is tempting to assume that intervention has failed when initial increases in challenging behavior are seen. After all, the student's behavior is getting worse, not better. However, this initial increase actually may be a sign that you are on the right track; that you have correctly identified the function. For example, we knew that we had correctly identified teacher and parent attention as the function of Alexandria's self-abuse because she tried harder to obtain that attention when it was no longer delivered contingent on self-abuse. As reported earlier, Alexandria's abusive and aggressive behavior decreased as we continued to attend to toy play and verbal communication. Teams should expect, and be prepared to respond to, temporary increases in challenging behavior. Teams then should expect a gradual reduction in challenging behavior.

As teams, we also should expect and be prepared for periodic regression or spontaneous recovery in behavior (Skinner, 1953). Although challenging behavior will decrease and appropriate behavior will take its place in producing the desired function, the challenging behavior may not be entirely eliminated from the student's repertoire. As a result, it may be substituted for appropriate behavior if appropriate behaviors do not produce the desired function or when it is triggered by other unknown factors such as illness. Remember, old habits die hard. If the challenging behavior once again successfully produces the desired function, it may return to previous levels of intensity, duration, or frequency (Carr et al., 1994). When this happens it is very important to be consistent in applying the intervention strategies. For example, Janey, who had not used profanity in class for 4 months, once again started to swear in class when Ms. Barbera replaced Ms. Gains who left on pregnancy leave. Ms. Barbera was not familiar with previous intervention strategies and inadvertently reinforced Janey's profanity. As a result, her profanity quickly returned to previous levels. At this point, the team reinstated the previous intervention and taught Ms. Barbera to apply the intervention strategies. This quickly and successfully reduced the frequency of Janey's swearing. When spontaneous recovery occurs, it does not mean that the intervention has failed, it simply means that we need to be sure that intervention strategies are applied to both challenging and appropriate behavior and that they are applied consistently. If challenging behavior continues to occur even though intervention strategies are consistently applied, it may be that a new functional assessment is warranted.

5. View Intervention as a Dynamic and Evolving Process

As we discussed in the previous chapter, intervention does not end with the acquisition of appropriate replacement behavior. We also must promote fluency, generalization, and maintenance. In doing this, we continuously monitor behavior and intervention and we revise intervention strategies and goals as needed (Horner, 1994).

Monitoring and revision go hand in hand. First, we monitor behavior to identify if a behavior change has occurred and, if so, how much. For example, we may collect data on the frequency, rate, duration, latency (the amount of time between the presentation of an antecedent stimulus and behavior), and intensity of behavior. We also may discuss behavior change during staff meetings. Information about changes in behavior can be used to revise expectations or goals for behavior or to change the form of behavior. For example, Shaw often did not comply with teacher requests or if he did comply, the average latency of his compliance was 15 minutes after the request had been made. During intervention Shaw was allowed to select bingo numbers that might match his bingo card if he complied within 10 minutes of a request (Rhode, Jenson, & Reavis, 1992). After 2 weeks of intervention Shaw complied with teacher requests within 10 minutes of the request. At this point, the team revised their expectations for behavior. The new goal was for Shaw to respond appropriately to teacher requests within 5 minutes of the request.

We also monitor behavior in order to make decisions about generalization and maintenance promotion strategies. For example, information about behavior change can be used to determine (a) when to shift from contrived to more natural reinforcers, (b) when to fade antecedent prompts, (c) when to change from continuous to intermittent reinforcement, (d) when to introduce new examples (i.e., sufficient exemplars) or train in additional settings (i.e., sequential modification), and (e) when to involve families or other individuals in intervention, and so forth.

In addition to monitoring the student's behavior, we also should monitor the fidelity of intervention. In other words, we observe individuals applying the intervention strategies to ensure that they are implementing the strategies correctly and consistently. Information obtained from these observations may be used to retrain staff and revise intervention strategies. For example, Mr. Avion indicated that the intervention he was employing to reduce Amy's disruptive and out-of-seat behavior was not working. Observation indicated that Mr. Avion no longer spoke to Amy when she disrupted his lectures or left her seat. However, he did sigh, roll his eyes, and shake his head when she engaged in these behaviors. This small amount of behavior by Mr. Avion was sufficient to maintain Amy's challenging behavior (she obtained control and attention). Her behavior decreased after the intervention was revised so that Mr. Avion no longer responded when Amy engaged in challenging behavior.

Finally, we should continue to monitor behavior and the environment (sometimes for years or indefinitely) as circumstances and environments change and after formal intervention strategies have been terminated (Carr et al., 1990; Walker, 2000). This will indicate when there are occurrences of spontaneous recovery, the subsequent response to challenging behavior, and changes in antecedent stimuli, reinforcer preferences, and so forth. For example, functional assessment conducted when Leah was in preschool indicated that Leah easily became overstimulated during active activities such as free play, gross motor, and other outdoor activities. When Leah was overstimulated she was not able to participate appropriately in more passive activities such as book reading and circle and she was very disruptive during passive activities. The team implemented strategies to help Leah maintain an even level of stimulation throughout the day. These strategies were implemented throughout the preschool year. Unfortunately, they were not implemented when Leah transitioned to kindergarten. As might be expected, Leah frequently became overstimulated, which resulted in classroom disruption and interfered with Leah's learning during passive activities. As a result, Leah was referred for a case study evaluation. The team reviewed Leah's previous records, observed Leah in the classroom, and decided to implement the strategies that had been successfully employed in preschool. These strategies again helped Leah maintain an even level of stimulation and she had a very successful year in kindergarten. This example illustrates the importance of monitoring behavior across time.

6. Apply Intervention and Prevention Strategies Class-Wide

You may have noticed that many of the strategies derived from functional assessment conducted for individual students can be applied class-wide. We often find that it is easier to apply strategies to the entire class than it is to apply strategies to individual students. For instance, all children may be allowed to hold a bear during circle time even though the intervention was specifically designed to address one student's behavior. Or all students may receive a sample completed problem on a worksheet, study guides, or written and verbal instructions. We also have found that the interventions that may be developed for one student, in fact, are helpful for other students as well. For example, we reported significant decreases in challenging behavior and nonengagement and significant increases in active engagement and positive social interactions when strategies that were developed on the basis of individual functional assessments were applied to all students in the classroom (Chandler et al., 1999). These results were replicated across three classrooms for students at risk and eight self-contained classrooms for students with special education needs. Likewise, Munk and Karsh (1999) reported a 60% reduction in challenging behavior across students when specific preventative antecedent teaching strategies were applied class-wide (see also Repp & Karsh, 1990, 1992).

Several researchers and educators advocate the use of school-wide as well as class-wide policies and practices as a means of preventing challenging behavior. They also advocate universal or school-wide interventions to address mild and moderate levels and forms of challenging behavior when it does occur (Jenson, Rhode, & Reavis, 1994; McGee & Daly, 1999; Nelson, Roberts, Mathur, & Rutherford, 1998; Schmid, 1998; Sprague & Walker, 2000; Walker, 1998, 2000; Walker et al., 1995). Examples of recommended universal interventions include anger management, relaxation training, problem solving, conflict resolution, social skills training, arrangement of antecedent variables within the school and classroom environments (e.g., music during transition), and school-wide consequences for challenging behavior (Mehas, Boling, Sobieniak, Sprague, Burke, & Hagan, 1998; Poppin, 1988; Schmid, 1998; Skiba & Peterson, 2000; Sprague & Walker, 2000; Walker, 1998, 2000; Walker & Walker, 1991; Walker et al., 1995).

For example, Nelson and his colleagues (1998) described a multilevel school-wide system to prevent and remediate challenging behavior. The first component of their system involves arranging school environments and providing supervision in those environments in order to set the occasion for appropriate behavior. The first component also involves establishing clear and consistent rules and expectations for appropriate behavior and directly teaching students to follow stated rules.

The second component addresses challenging behavior when it occurs. The purpose of this component is to prevent challenging behavior from becoming entrenched in the students' repertoire. This component consists of three levels. First, teachers "catch disruptive behavior early" (p. 6) by prompting or redirecting a student to engage in appropriate replacement behavior. Second, if the student does not comply with antecedent prompts, the teacher directs the student to a classroom where the student spends time thinking about his or her challenging behavior. Before the student leaves the Think Time classroom, the student completes a debriefing form on which he or she essentially (a) identifies the challenging behavior, (b) indicates the function or intent of the challenging behavior, (c) indicates the success of the challenging behavior in achieving the desired function, and (d) identifies appropriate replacement behavior. This form is reviewed by the teacher in the Think Time classroom and then by the student's primary teacher. At this point, the student returns to the classroom and joins ongoing classroom activities. Finally, students who do not respond to school-wide prevention strategies are addressed at the third level of this component. This level provides individualized interventions to remediate challenging behavior such as functional assessment, behavior contracting, and "wraparound" services (Eber, Nelson, & Miles, 1977).

School-wide prevention practices such as these identify consistent rules and expectations for appropriate behavior, provide antecedent prompts and environmental arrangements that set the occasion for appropriate behavior, and teach skills that students may use in response to aversive situations (e.g., problem solving, anger management)(Dwyer, Osher, & Hoffman, 2000; Walker, 2000). When school-wide practices do not prevent challenging behavior, then functional assessment of individual student behavior should be implemented (Walker, 1998, 2000). Functional assessment thus becomes part of a multilevel approach to the prevention and remediation of challenging behavior (Dwyer et al., 2000).

The six guidelines described in this section will assist the team in conducting functional assessment and implementing interventions. They should be combined with other guidelines that have been provided throughout the text. The next section identifies potential staff and family objections to or concerns about functional assessment and behavioral interventions and describes strategies to address those objections or concerns.

FREQUENT OBJECTIONS TO INTERVENTION OR REASONS FOR RESISTANCE

As a consultant or member of a team that is conducting functional assessment and recommending intervention strategies, you are likely to encounter resistance. Resistance may come from other members of the functional assessment team as well as from staff who are expected to implement interventions and from family members. This section includes the six most frequent objections or concerns that we have encountered in

TABLE 12–2
Frequent objections to intervention or reasons for resistance

1. Students should be self-motivated.
2. I don't have time to do this.
3. It is not my job.
4. It is not fair to treat students differently.
5. It is not my fault.
6. It won't work or I tried that already and it didn't work.

Common reasons for resistance.

Students should be
self-motivated.

I don't have time to do this.

It is not my job.

It is not fair to treat one
student differently.

It is not my fault.

It won't work.
I tried that already
and it didn't work.

working with educators. These are listed in Table 12–2. In our opinion, some of the concerns are legitimate; some are not. However, the issue cannot be one of who is right and who is wrong. As a consultant and team member, your job is to address stated (and sometimes unstated) concerns in a positive manner and to persuade staff to collaborate in the functional assessment process. This section also provides the strategies that we have used to address educator objections and concerns.

1. Students Should Be Self-Motivated

Many educators feel that students should be intrinsically motivated to behave appropriately and to learn or, as described by Malott, Malott, & Trojan, (2000), they feel that student's ought to want to learn and behave appropriately. These individuals feel that students should not require external forms of reinforcement and that when we provide positive consequences, we are bribing students to do what they should already be doing. They also are fearful that students will not behave appropriately or learn unless there are external reinforcers (i.e., they will become dependent on external reinforcers) (Alberto & Troutman, 1999).

The response to this objection must be made on a practical level. Do not argue about free will and the "evils" of reinforcement or that fact that bribes technically come before behavior occurs (Malott et al., 2000). This is an argument that neither side can win and it will cause more division among team members.

When educators voice this concern to us, we agree that it would be great if students were self-motivated to behave appropriately and to learn without the use of contrived reinforcers. We indicate that this is our long-term goal if possible. We also point out though that, unfortunately, students are not always self-motivated and that they certainly are not self-motivated right now; and talking and reasoning with students about self-motivation is probably not going to change their behavior, especially when the environment currently supports their challenging behavior. We then agree that self-motivation is the ultimate goal of intervention and we discuss strategies to address self-motivation and to fade external reinforcers. For instance, we talk about pairing external reinforcers with natural reinforcers as a first step in teaching self-motivation. Then as students begin to respond to the natural reinforcers, the external forms of reinforcement or motivation may be faded and perhaps eliminated completely.

For those educators who resist using any forms of external reinforcement, we do talk about the fact that many behaviors are learned and maintained by external forms of positive reinforcement. For example, we may identify potential positive reinforcers such as paychecks, compliments, interaction with peers, good grades, praise, smiles, happy faces, high five or thumbs-up signs, a good evaluation, and preferred activities. Reinforcers such as these are a regular part of our lives and of the lives of our students. They are continuously present and affect behavior in the classroom. Thus, our goal should not be to eliminate reinforcement (self-motivated behavior after all is self-reinforced behavior). Rather our goal should be to use reinforcement to the benefit of the student to promote appropriate, functional behavior. A second goal should be to shift from contrived forms of external reinforcement (e.g., tokens and stickers) to natural forms of reinforcement (e.g., telling yourself you did a good job on the test or receiving a turn upon request) and to reinforcers that are normative components of educational settings (e.g., good grades and praise from parents or teachers).

2. I Don't Have Time to Do This

Educators who voice this objection want challenging behavior to be changed yesterday and they want behavior change to require little effort on their part. One way to address this objection is to talk with educators about the amount of time and effort they currently spend *reacting* to behavior. You can ask them to describe the amount of time and effort they currently employ. You also can present data from functional assessment observations. Often when teachers realize that they already are expending precious time and effort, they are willing to do so in a more proactive manner. It also is helpful to let educators know that the amount of time and effort that may be required in the initial phases of intervention will decrease over time and that eventually the time and effort required will be less than they currently employ.

As discussed in the previous section, you also may ask teachers to implement the interventions at one time of the day or in one class or activity, rather than throughout the day. This decreases the amount of time and effort that educators need to employ during intervention. Then, as behavior begins to improve in that smaller time period, the intervention may be expanded to other time periods.

3. It Is Not My Job

Classroom teachers and other school staff often feel that the behavior specialist or school psychologist should be changing the student's behavior. They believe that the teacher's job is to teach academic subjects and the school psychologist's job is to fix behavior. Unfortunately, behavior doesn't occur in a vacuum and it must be addressed in the environments in which it occurs and by those individuals who are in those environments. Thus, challenging behavior becomes part of everyone's job.

In the past, students who exhibited challenging behavior were transferred to self-contained classrooms for students with special education needs (Fuchs, Fuchs, & Bahr, 1990; McMahon & McNamarra, 2000). This is not the model typically used in schools today. Challenging behavior does not automatically result in a change in placement. In fact, it is the responsibility of the school to demonstrate that they have conducted functional assessment and implemented positive intervention strategies to address challenging behavior before a permanent change of placement can be made (Armstrong & Kauffman, 1999; Individuals with Disabilities Education Act, 1997; Katsiyannis & Maag, 1998). This is required whether a student is in an inclusion or self-contained classroom.

As we stated earlier in this text, challenging behavior is not the responsibility of one individual. It is the responsibility of every individual who interacts with the student. School psychologists, behavior analysts, or members of an instructional strategies team may conduct the assessment portion of functional assessment and intervention model in conjunction with the student's teacher(s). However, all individuals who work with the student (e.g., teachers, assistants, therapists) or who interact with the student (e.g., administrators, bus drivers, librarians) are responsible for applying appropriate intervention strategies.

4. It Is Not Fair to Treat Students Differently

Some educators feel that all students should be treated the same. They feel that it is not fair to have different expectations for students or to deliver different antecedents and consequences across students. This is a difficult issue. In response to this concern we sometimes talk with teachers about examples in their classrooms when students are not all treated the same. For example, are all students required to stay in the lunchroom until the last student has finished eating or to sit at their desks until the last student has completed a test? Are all students required to make identical art projects or to write identical stories? Or must all students need a study group in order for it to be scheduled? A discussion such as this can open the door to talking about individualization that currently occurs in the classroom and making the extension to individualization of behavior goals and interventions.

In addition, we also sometimes suggest applying antecedents and consequences to all students if feasible. For example, many students appreciate movement breaks during passive activities and function better when they are applied even though they may not "require" such breaks and are able to stay on task without them. All students may benefit from completing a graphic organizer or participating in a review of the daily schedule, even though these interventions were developed in response to one student's behavior.

Richard LaVoie (1985) discusses the concept of fairness by pointing out that fairness means that every student gets what he or she needs to learn. It does not mean that every student is treated the same. Some students need individualized interventions that address challenging behavior and trigger and support appropriate behavior in order to learn.

Teachers also sometimes wonder what they should tell students who want to know why one student gets something the other students do not get or why one student does not have to do what the other students are doing. In our experience students often have fewer objections to individualization than teachers. However, when students do ask questions we suggest answering honestly and at the child's level of understanding. McEwan and Damer (2000) suggest talking with all students about individual strengths and needs and then explaining that the intervention strategies that are applied to one student address the needs of a particular student. Then when they are asked about individual students, they can do what many teachers (of all ages of students) have told us that they do; they simply tell class or the student that the student in question needs x, y, or z and that the other students do not. These teachers also have reported that this type of explanation usually is sufficient.

5. It Is Not My Fault

Often educators believe that if they are asked to change their behavior or to alter their own teaching strategies and routines that they are at fault—they are bad teachers and have caused the challenging behavior. They also may feel threatened when an observer enters their classroom (Stephenson, Linfoot, & Martin, 2000). They believe that the purpose of observation is to identify what they are doing wrong. This is not what we want teachers to think and certainly is not the message of functional assessment. We suggest pointing out the great things that teachers are doing and telling teachers that what they are doing works for most of the students in the classroom, but that for this one student, something different is needed. It is helpful to keep the focus on behavior, the function of the behavior, and changes that can be made to support appropriate behavior for this student.

6. It Won't Work or I Tried That Already and It Didn't Work

When this happens we often find that the educators did indeed try an intervention, but they implemented that intervention infrequently or inconsistently or they implemented it for 1 or 2 days and then moved to a different intervention. This objection also occurs when behavior change is slow and staff may not notice small (albeit positive) changes in behavior. When this happens, let the educators explain what they did, how long they implemented the intervention, and how it worked. Then acknowledge their efforts and ask them to try it again. It is important to get them to agree to a specific timeline for implementing the intervention. During implementation, behavior change should be observed, intervention fidelity should be monitored, staff should receive feedback and reinforcement for their efforts, and the team should meet and discuss behavior change and revise the intervention as needed or set new implementation timelines.

You also may find this objection among veteran teachers who have been teaching for many years and have experienced every one of the latest trends and fads in education. These educators have a right to be skeptical! Again, it is important to provide a good, nontechnical rationale for why the challenging behavior is occurring, why the strategies have been selected, and why the interventions are expected to change behavior. It also is important to spend time in the classroom observing and implementing the intervention, providing feedback and reinforcement to the teacher, and revising strategies as needed. Demonstrating the effectiveness of functional assessment is the best answer to this objection.

This section identified several common objections or concerns related to functional assessment and the strategies that we have used to address those concerns and strategies that increase staff and parent willingness to participate in functional assessment and implement functional interventions in classroom and other settings. This leads to the final section of this chapter. The next section provides tips for providing consultation and for serving as a member of functional assessment teams.

TIPS FOR PROVIDING FUNCTIONAL ASSESSMENT CONSULTATION

Our role as behavior analysts is often to provide consultation to individual teachers or to educational teams. We have found that good collaboration and supervision skills are essential to success in consultation (Friend & Cook, 2000; Hundert & Hopkins, 1992). A skilled consultant will anticipate objections and address them before they become serious problems and will identify and employ consultation behaviors that lead to positive interactions and cooperation among team members. This final section provides our top 10 list of tips that we have found useful in providing consultation to individual educators and that we have used as members of functional assessment teams. These tips also are listed in Table 12–3. It is beyond the scope of this book to provide a thorough discussion on effective teaming and collaboration. For further information on consultation, collaboration, and effective teaming see the following references: Barbour and Barbour (1997), Friend and Cook (2000), Hoff (1992), Sugai and Tindal (1993) and Turnbull and Turnbull (1997).

1. Begin with One Teacher Who Is Willing to Participate and Spread the Word about Success

This is a helpful strategy when there is general resistance within a school building or district. There usually will be one teacher who is willing to try functional assessment either because he or she has heard about it in previous courses or workshops or because he or she is desperate for something that will work in the classroom. When this teacher achieves successful behavior change in the classroom, he or she will tell other educators about that change. This first teacher will become an advocate for you and the functional assessment and intervention model. Word of mouth or accounts of personal experience can be the best advertisement for your

TABLE 12–3
Tips for providing functional assessment consultation

1. Begin with one teacher who is willing to participate and spread the word about success.
2. Reduce jargon.
3. Emphasize that the functional assessment/intervention model is one of many tools.
4. Do not blame or criticize.
5. Acknowledge the expertise and skills of educators with whom you are consulting.
6. Demonstrate understanding of the variables that affect staff.
7. Anticipate and be prepared to respond to resistance issues.
8. Brainstorm with staff versus telling them what to do.
9. Directly administer and monitor intervention strategies.
10. Teach others how to do functional assessment.

© 2002 Chandler and Dahlquist.

services. As other educators observe or hear about success and teacher satisfaction, they also will invite you into their classrooms.

We also recommend that *you* inform others of success. Inform administrators of the success of intervention and point out the good job that educators have done in achieving their goals. Give presentations at staff meetings (with staff if they will participate) that demonstrate the success of functional assessment. Write short articles for school newsletters. This not only allows you to reinforce staff who have participated in functional assessment, it also serves as a form of advertisement and will entice other educators to try functional assessment.

2. Reduce Jargon

One of the interesting things we have found is that the philosophy underlying functional assessment and the practice of functional assessment is not objectionable to most educators. However, the language used to describe applied behavior analysis, functional assessment, and the underlying philosophy often is objectionable and leads to immediate resistance (Chandler, 2000; Guess, 1990; Malott et al., 2000). As Elliott, Witt, and Kratchowill (1991) point out, the evaluation and acceptance of interventions vary as a function of the name of the interventions and the language used to describe the intervention strategies. For example, educators have objected to terms such as behavior *management*, behavior *modification*, *treatment* plan, *manipulation* of variables, *controlling* variables, and *teaching* appropriate behavior. Terms such as these often cause negative, emotional reactions from educators who interpret these terms as meaning that our goal is to control students and to coerce behavior by reducing student choice or freedom (Malott, 1973; Sulzer-Azaroff & Mayer, 1991). This is unfortunate because functional assessment actually increases choice for students by promoting alternative behaviors that achieve functions that are desired by the student.

Some educators also believe that technical behavioral terms imply that the students are bad or have a condition that must be treated much as an illness is treated, or that the behavior the student employs is inherently bad or abnormal (Malott et al., 2000) (versus focusing on the environment that supports functional behavior). Some educators and family members also object to terms such as *challenging, inappropriate, deviant, atypical, aberrant*, and *maladaptive* behavior because they feel these terms imply that the student is doing something wrong, rather than focusing on the environmental supports for those behaviors. We agree that these terms can be misleading and often can imply that the student's behavior is bad, rather than pointing to the functionality of behavior within a particular setting. We continue to use the term *challenging behavior*, not only because it is a commonly used term, but also because we find it descriptive as discussed in Chapter 1. The student's behavior represents a challenge to learning and development. In other words, it interferes with or serves as a barrier to learning and development. Notice that

this perspective relates back to our original definition of challenging behavior—that it must be considered from the student's perspective. If the student's behavior interferes with learning and development, then it may be identified as challenging.

We find it useful when providing workshops on functional assessment and when working with staff to not use terms that cause negative emotional reactions or that may be misinterpreted. For example, we typically talk about *promoting* versus teaching behavior, *intervention* versus treatment plans, *changing* or *altering* variables and strategies to change the environment so that it supports appropriate behavior versus changing inappropriate behavior. In some cases, when we must use terms that may be misunderstood (such as challenging behavior), we try to explain what *we* mean by those terms.

We also have found that some individuals do not understand or cannot remember the definition of the technical terms of functional assessment and behavior analysis such as setting events, antecedents, positive reinforcement, negative reinforcement, extinction, differential reinforcement, homeostasis, and discriminative stimuli (terms we no longer use in preservice and in-service training). For instance, individuals often confuse the concepts of negative reinforcement and punishment. So, we either substitute nontechnical terms in place of the technical terms or we pair nontechnical terms with the technical terms (Malott et al., 2000). For example, we may refer to the negative reinforcement function as escape and avoidance as well as negative reinforcement. Likewise, we may refer to the positive reinforcement function as obtainment as well as positive reinforcement. We use the term *ignoring* instead of or in conjunction with the term *extinction*. We also use the terms *trigger* or *context* in conjunction with the terms *setting events* and *antecedent stimuli*. Although our preference may be for all individuals to use and understand the appropriate terms when describing behavior and functional assessment, if the use of nontechnical terms increases the likelihood that individuals will understand and implement our interventions, then it is a small price to pay (Malott, 1973).

3. Emphasize That the Functional Assessment/ Intervention Model Is One of Many Tools

This tip represents a hard learned lesson on the part of the authors (and many behavior analysts). In the past, we often found ourselves arguing with educators who had different (i.e., nonbehavioral) philosophies about behavior and who believed in different types of intervention models to address challenging behavior. The arguments often centered on which type of intervention model and associated philosophy was best or correct (e.g., play therapy or functional assessment or sensory integration therapy or functional assessment). The assumption made by many educators was that if they adopted the functional assessment model, then it meant that their own belief systems were wrong and that the models they espoused were useless. Arguments such as this are futile. Our job as consultants is not to convince educators that we are right and they are wrong. The students must remain the focus.

We now tell educators who have different beliefs and who are trained in other models of intervention (and philosophical approaches) that they should think of functional assessment as an additional model, not as a replacement model. We often use the analogy of a tool belt. Functional assessment is one more tool on their belt of interventions. We do not argue or give our personal opinions about their preferred intervention models unless of course they are ones that actually may harm the student or are illegal (for example, the first author was informed by one educator that they placed students in time-out in the janitor's closet for an hour at a time—this is something she discussed with the educator).

We suggest telling educators that functional assessment does not need to be the only intervention model employed. For example, a student might benefit from sensory integration therapy, counseling, time-out or response-cost interventions, or even medication as well as interventions derived from functional assessment. We have adopted this strategy because we have learned that we alienate important members of the team if we claim that functional assessment is the only model that should be employed (Chandler, 2000). We also have adopted this strategy because we do recognize, based on our experience in public schools, that other models of intervention can be effective at addressing challenging behavior and student problems.

4. Do Not Blame or Criticize

This strategy reflects one of the objections discussed in the previous section. Often the intervention strategies involve asking educators, therapists, staff, or parents to change their behavior or to adopt new behaviors or to change the environment or daily activities and routines. This can be threatening, especially if we present this intervention by first telling educators that what they are doing is bad or wrong. There is no need to blame, but there is a need to change the environment so that it supports appropriate behavior (Skinner, 1971). If educators feel that they are being blamed, you will lose their cooperation.

When discussing interventions, make it clear that this is not an issue of who is right or wrong, rather it is an issue of matching strategies to the needs of the student and of selecting strategies to change the environment in order to change behavior. This tip should be combined with the next tip in which we point out positive behaviors and teaching strategies that teachers are currently using in their classrooms.

5. Acknowledge the Expertise and Skills of Educators with Whom You Are Consulting

This strategy builds on the "how to win friends and influence people" philosophy espoused by Dale Carnegie (1994). He recommended first identifying strengths before discussing areas that should be changed. Before discussing intervention strategies, we should identify positive teaching practices and other strengths exhibited by teachers and point out that their strategies work with most of the students in class. Then we begin to discuss how these might be adapted to meet the needs of the student for whom they are not working. We also build on existing strengths as part of the intervention (e.g., "You are really good at praising students. If you could do it more often for Barry, I think it would really make a difference in his behavior"). When working with educators, it is important to maintain a balance between identifying strengths and working on changes that will be made during intervention.

6. Demonstrate Understanding of the Variables That Affect Staff

Interventions must be feasible and acceptable to those who are expected to implement them (Horner, 1994; Johnson & Pugach, 1990; Odom, Chandler, Ostrosky, McConnell, & Reaney, 1992). As consultants we must be aware of and respect variables that will influence intervention implementation such as time, staff–student ratio, daily routines and schedules, and materials. Information about these variables may be obtained from observations in the classroom during the assessment phase as well as from discussion with staff during intervention design. As discussed in Chapter 6, interventions that are not acceptable or feasible have a low probability of being implemented or they may be implemented inappropriately or inconsistently. We must work within the resources of the classroom (McMahon & McNamarra, 2000; O'Brien & Karsh, 1990; Stephenson et al., 2000).

7. Anticipate and Be Prepared to Respond to Resistance Issues

The previous section identified several common objections and concerns related to functional assessment and strategies to resolve those objections (there isn't enough time, it's not my job, issues of fairness, etc.). You should be able to prevent the development of some of these objections by good consultative practices such as those listed in this section and in other resources. However, you should expect that a number of concerns and objections will arise at some point in your consultation. As a result, you should plan how you will respond when they arise. It is much easier to respond with a planned reaction than it is to be caught off guard.

When you do respond, it is important to do so in a positive manner; do not become defensive. If you are defensive, staff will be defensive as well and their resistance will increase, leading to a perpetual tug of war. Remember, be positive, identify staff strengths, acknowledge their feelings, do not threaten, and do not argue, but do collaborate (in addition to specific strategies identified under specific concerns in the previous section).

8. Brainstorm with Staff versus Telling Them What to Do

Friend and Cook (2000) indicate that effective consultation requires active participation from all participants (i.e., the consultant and those who will implement the intervention). If educators are passive recipients of intervention plans, they are less likely to correctly and consistently implement those plans. When educators and parents are treated as unequal partners or, as stated by Elliott et al. (1991), if they are treated as "subordinate junior partners" (p. 121), they may resist consultation or they may become too dependent on the consultant. Plans that are based on input from those who are responsible for implementing them on a daily basis increase ownership of the plan. It is important to consider their information and observations as well as your own observations and analyses.

Another reason to brainstorm with staff is to improve their observation and analysis skills. One goal of consultation should be to improve educators' knowledge and skills as well as to change student behavior (Elliott et al., 1991; McMahon & McNamarra, 2000). The more staff are actively involved in the functional assessment process, the more independent they will become. For example, teachers that we have worked with who have previously participated in functional assessment for a student in their classroom often are able to hypothesize the function of a subsequent student's behavior before we begin formal observations. They also are more able and willing to identify and implement intervention strategies following the assessment phase of the model.

9. Directly Administer and Monitor Intervention Strategies

We suggest that consultants administer intervention strategies in classroom and other settings, monitor intervention during the initial stages, and work with the team to revise intervention strategies as necessary. The model of monitoring and consultation during intervention that we have used involves the following steps:

A. After reviewing functional assessment information and brainstorming with the team, provide a written and vocal description of the interventions that were selected by the team and a rationale for how the interventions selected address the function of behavior.

B. Model application of the interventions with the student in the classroom setting. This allows staff to see the application of intervention strategies, thus providing training through observation, and it facilitates interaction because you are able to talk with staff about the strategies. We find that staff not only benefit from observing implementation of the strategies, but they also benefit by seeing that even we (the experts) may have difficulty or need to revise strategies. When the first author was working with infants and families, her rule of thumb was "I won't ask parents to do anything that I can't do or am not willing to do." We think this is a good suggestion for consultants. We also find that it is much easier to judge the feasibility of applying intervention strategies in the classroom and to provide feedback and suggestions for revision if we have experienced the intervention firsthand.

C. Observe staff implementing the interventions. We recommend observing staff for two reasons. First, it is important to verify that staff are able to implement the intervention strategies correctly. When they are struggling with intervention strategies or applying them incorrectly, we have the opportunity to discuss their concerns and to provide corrective feedback (i.e., point out what they are doing well and what they can do to improve versus telling them what they are doing wrong). The second reason to observe staff is so that we can support them by providing positive reinforcement for their efforts.

D. Revise the intervention plan as needed. Revisions to the intervention plan may be made during team planning meetings or when observing in the classroom or directly working with the student in the classroom (Chandler et al., 1999). Revisions may be made when there are problems with the intervention (e.g., there is insufficient behavior change, the strategies are too difficult to implement, or the teaching assistant quit). Revisions also may be made as we change our goals for behavior or include strategies to promote fluency, generalization, and maintenance. Revisions should be discussed verbally and written so that all members of the team are informed of proposed changes (Bahr, Whitten, Dieker, Kocarek, & Manson, 1999).

E. Maintain routine contact after the initial intervention. Contact with individuals who are implementing the intervention strategies should be frequent initially (e.g., weekly face-to-face or telephone contact) and then faded to an as-needed basis. Staff should feel free to communicate with the consultant when needed even though formal consultation has ended (Barbour & Barbour, 1997). This increases the probability that you will be informed of and so can address potential problems, behavior regression, and so on, in a timely manner (Bahr et al., 1999). The model for fading contact with staff and then maintaining contact after consultation has terminated will depend on your caseload and resources. The ultimate goal of functional assessment consultation is for staff to independently implement intervention strategies. They should not become dependent on the consultant. However, the consultant should continue as a support when important questions or problems arise.

10. Teach Others How to Do Functional Assessment

We have consistently found that educators who have had initial training in functional assessment are better able to assist in the assessment phase of functional assessment and in selecting intervention strategies than educators with no prior training. This is because they have a basic understanding of the goals of functional assessment, the methods involved in assessment, the three functions of behavior, and the rationale for the interventions selected. They also are more likely to embrace the process of functional assessment because they have read about or seen demonstrations of its effectiveness during preservice or in-service training (Chandler, 2000). They also are more willing to apply time-consuming and effort-filled interventions and to promote the generalization and maintenance of behavior.

Preservice or in-service training may range from daily or multiple day sessions (e.g. Chandler et al., 1999; Vaugn, Hales, Bush, & Fox, 1998) to semester-long training as part of a university program (e.g., Iwata et al., 2000; McEvoy, Reichle, & Davis, 1995; McMahon & McNamarra, 2000; Northrup, Wacker, Berg, Kelly, Sasso, & Deradd, 1994; Semmel, Abernathy, & Butera, 1991; Stephenson et al., 2000). Training goals can focus on knowledge or awareness, attitude change, and skill acquisition and fluency (Friend & Cook, 2000). Clearly, shorter training sessions will focus on awareness and attitude change, while more intense and lengthy sessions will focus on skill development and fluency.

Our model in schools has been to provide 1- to 2-day workshops with the goal of increasing participants' awareness of and knowledge about functional assessment. We then work on the acquisition and refinement of functional assessment skills when we consult with educators in their settings and with their own students. During our workshops, we focus on the application (i.e., nontheoretical) side of functional assessment. We discuss the (a) assumptions and goals of functional assessment; (b) why challenging behavior occurs and the myths about why challenging behavior occurs; (c) the process of identifying setting events, antecedents, and consequences; (d) the functions of behavior; and (e) strategies related to the three functions of behavior. We demonstrate functional assessment through videotaped examples and supplement this with case studies. We also ask participants to practice various parts of functional assessment through small group activities.

Our primary goal during short training sessions is for participants to gain a basic understanding of the functional assessment approach and process (awareness level) and to "buy into" the functional assessment approach (attitude change). Informal follow-up feedback from participants indicates that some participants are able to conduct functional assessment in their classrooms at the conclusion of this type of workshop. Most participants are able to implement parts of the model and they think differently about challenging behavior and intervention strategies, and a few participants simply are ready to work with a functional assessment consultant.

We also provide semester-long preservice training in functional assessment at the university level. Extended training programs typically focus not only on the functional assessment process, but also on the theoretical and historical underpinnings of functional assessment. These courses also may teach functional analysis and analogue and naturalistic functional assessment procedures. Students usually read multiple articles and chapters on functional assessment and complete one or more functional assessment projects and write and report the success of those projects to classroom peers. We also find it helpful to discuss issues related to consultation and resistance in extended trainings. Many participants in our extended trainings (especially in-service trainings) are individuals who will serve as behavior specialists or functional assessment consultants. They often have questions about how to get other educators to implement interventions, how to teach functional assessment within their own school districts, and what to do when they encounter resistance to functional assessment. Issues such as these should not be overlooked in extensive training classes.

There is no right or wrong model for teaching functional assessment (Vaugn et al., 1998). The format and duration of training depends on the goals of training and the resources available to trainers, educators, and the school system. In our opinion, any level of training in functional assessment is better than none and functional assessment training should be a component of all preservice and in-service training programs for regular and special education teachers, behavior analysts, other educators (e.g., therapists, school psychologists, and counselors), and administrators (McMahon & McNamarra, 2000; Reichle et al., 1996).

SUMMARY

This chapter provided information to assist consultants and teams in implementing the functional assessment and intervention model. We began by acknowledging that functional assessment is not a simple and easy process. It takes time, collaboration, and effort to conduct the analysis and develop and implement interventions. However, we and others feel that the time and effort are well spent because functional assessment ultimately focuses our efforts on understanding and addressing appropriate behavior, rather than reacting to challenging behavior (e.g., Arndorfer & Miltenberger, 1993; Carr, Langdon, & Yarbrough, 1999; Davis, 1998; McGee & Daly, 1999; Reichle et al., 1996; Repp, 1999).

The first section of this chapter presented guidelines for intervention implementation and for working with families and responding to crisis situations. This was followed by a discussion of the most frequent objections or sources of resistance to functional assessment and recommendations for addressing these issues. The chapter ended with a section on tips for providing consultation to individual educators and for members of a functional assessment team. As you begin to work with other individuals or as a member of functional assessment teams or if you work as a functional assessment consultant, you should add tips and guidelines to these lists. Knowledge of how to do functional assessment and skill in conducting functional assessment and developing interventions will be useless unless teachers and other educators implement those interventions. Functional assessment knowledge and skill must be paired with good consultation and collaboration skills.

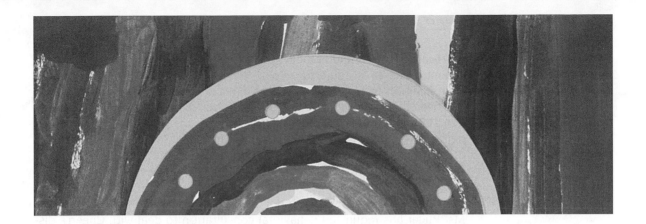

13

Problem-Solving Case Studies

This final chapter gives you, the reader, opportunities to practice some of the skills that were discussed in previous chapters. You will have the opportunity to (a) determine if a student's behavior should be identified as challenging behavior and if it should be changed using functional assessment, (b) determine the function of challenging behavior, (c) develop intervention plans based on the function of behavior, and (d) identify strategies to reduce resistance to functional assessment and consultant/educator collaboration.

CASE STUDIES SET ONE: IS THIS CHALLENGING BEHAVIOR? SHOULD THIS BEHAVIOR BE CHANGED?

Your job for these two case studies is to identify whether the student's behavior should be identified as challenging behavior and if the student's behavior should be changed using the functional assessment and intervention model described in this textbook. To make this decision you should review the discussion concerning the identification of behavior as challenging and the definition of challenging behavior. This information was presented in Chapter 1.

Cheeri

Cheeri is a fifth-grade student attending a classroom for gifted students in her school district. Cheeri really likes school. She gets along well with peers, generally complies with teacher instructions, and works hard on academic assignments and cooperative group activities. Cheeri's favorite subject is physical education and her least preferred subject is music. Cheeri gets excellent grades in all subjects.

In addition to being gifted, Cheeri has several disability diagnoses. She has been diagnosed with Tourette's syndrome, obsessive compulsive disorder, and attention deficit disorder. Cheeri takes medication for these disorders and receives private and in-school counseling. Cheeri is concerned that other students will reject or ridicule her if they become aware of her disabilities. As a result, she and her parents have requested privacy concerning her diagnoses.

There is one teacher, Ms. Ruder, in Cheeri's classroom and 25 students. Ms. Ruder has requested behavioral consultation to deal with Cheeri's disruptive behaviors. Ms. Ruder indicates that Cheeri displays the following challenging behaviors at various times throughout the day:

Taps the desk or paper with her pen or pencil.

Rubs her legs.

Rocks in her chair.

Manipulates Silly Putty into shapes.

Blurts out answers or questions without raising her hand.

Blows air from her mouth and clears her throat.

Takes apart her pens and other manipulatives.

Ms. Ruder worries about the effect of these behaviors on Cheeri's peers and about Cheeri's ability to attend to lessons and complete work when she is displaying behaviors such as these. She further feels that Cheeri should have more self-control and more respect for her peers and for Ms. Ruder. She wants these behaviors to stop.

The behavioral consultant observed Cheeri in her classroom and was able to observe several of the behaviors identified by her teacher. The consultant also observed several examples of appropriate behavior. The consultant also noted the contexts in which Cheeri's behavior occurred (antecedents and setting events) and potential consequences for those behaviors. These are described on the following ABC recording sheet:

Antecedents and Setting Events	Behavior	Consequence
Individual writing task (desks grouped in pods of five)	Writing, taps paper with pen five times after each answer, then moves to next question, frequently clears her throat	Most peers ignore her behavior, Andy tells her to be quiet, tactile and auditory stimulation
Andy tells her to be quiet	Says, "I'm sorry," sits quietly, stares ahead	Peer says, "It's okay, just be quiet"

Antecedents and Setting Events	Behavior	Consequence
Individual task, trying to be still and quiet	Grimaces, tells Andy, "I'm sorry, I can't" Taps her paper five times, rubs her legs five times, and blows air five times, then begins to work	Tactile, oral stimulation
Completes work	Talks with Andy while rocking in her chair	Peer interaction
Group project presentations, students seated on floor, she is seated at rear of group	Plays with Silly Putty, clears throat, grimaces, asks presenters questions, claps for presenters when they are finished	Tactile, oral stimulation, peers answer questions
Her turn to present	Joins group for presentation, presents her part of project, answers questions about project	Peer interaction, movement
Peers turn to present	Waits quietly, rocking while peers present their part of project	Movement
Return to seat, other groups present	Rubs legs and grunts five times, rubs face, picks up pen and takes it apart	Tactile, oral stimulation
Seated at desks, teacher-led answer game regarding states and capitals	Playing with koosh ball, calls out answers to questions, rocks in place, and blows air five times	Teacher acknowledged answers, earns points for team, tactile, movement, oral stimulation

Ms. Ruder is requesting that the behavioral consultant develop interventions to stop Cheeri's behavior. Based on the initial observations by the behavioral consultant, should Cheeri's behavior be considered as challenging behavior and, if so, should her behavior be changed through the functional assessment and intervention model described in this book? Why or why not?

Leonard

Leonard is a third-grade student enrolled in regular education class with 27 other students. There is one teacher and one teaching assistant in his class. Leonard really likes school and his teacher and the teaching assistant. His teacher describes Leonard as a polite and compliant student who responds well to positive feedback. However, he does not do well in school. In fact, he receives poor grades in most subjects. His favorite times of the day are physical education, lunch, and recess. His least favorite and least successful areas are writing and math.

Leonard's desk has been placed at the rear of the classroom because of his frequent fidgety and out-of-seat behavior. His teacher, Ms. Allison has recommended that Leonard be tested for ADHD and evaluated for special education services, but his parents have refused to consent to both of these recommendations. Ms. Allison made the recommendations for diagnostic testing and evaluation because Leonard rarely completes his work during the day, does not turn in homework assignments, often leaves his seat during work periods, and frequently walks away from adults when they are providing assistance with schoolwork.

Ms. Allison has requested special education/behavioral consultation in order to address Leonard's behavior. Her referral included a list of behaviors that she observed during a 20-minute observation period during which students received large group instructions followed by individual seatwork:

Alternates sitting on his feet and sitting on the end of the chair.

Alternates sitting at his desk and standing at his desk.

Rocks his chair, balances on his chair legs, climbs on his chair.

Repeatedly drops and picks up his pencil.

Rubs his limbs and whole body against his desk.

Taps his pencil, hits his books.

Bites his pencil, bites his fingers.

Repeatedly sharpens his pencil.

Repeatedly asks questions.

Leaves his seat and wanders in the classroom repeatedly.

Yawns loudly.

The special education consultant observed Leonard and recorded the following information concerning his behavior:

Antecedents and Setting Events	Behavior	Consequence
Individual seatwork, teacher at her desk with another student, assistant rotating among students providing help	Leaves seat, skips to back of room, plays with manipulatives	Teacher tells him to return to his seat and work, movement, tactile stimulation
Teacher tells him to return to his seat and work	Begins to return to his seat but stops to chat with peer	Peer stops working and talks with him

Antecedents and Setting Events	Behavior	Consequences
Teacher instruction to whole class	Standing at desk, walks to pencil sharpener, sharpens pencil	Teacher tells him to sit down, movement
Teacher tells him to sit	Continues to sharpen pencil	Teacher tells him to sit again
Teacher tells him to sit again	Returns to seat, sits on edge of chair, bites fingers	Teacher continues lecture, assistant moves to desk and takes fingers out of his mouth each time he bites them, tactile stimulation
Auditorium, waiting for school presentation	Kneeling on seat, rocking, chatting with peers, falls out of seat	Teacher tells him to sit in his chair, movement, peer interaction
Told to sit in his seat	Returns to seat, chats with peers, walks to aisle to pick up paper	Teacher tells him to sit in his seat, peer interaction, movement
Told to sit in seat, presentation begins	Returns to seat, bites fingers, bounces up and down in his seat	Peers tell him to sit down so they can see, assistant moves to sit next to him, repeats instructions to sit, tactile, movement stimulation
Presentation ends	Jumps out of seat, runs back to classroom, trips over peers	Teacher runs after him, reprimands him for running, peers push him off of their bodies and yell, movement
Working with teacher on worksheet	Walks away from desk	Told to return to desk and work, movement
Principal arrives, teacher leaves to talk to principal	Runs to plants and waters them	Told to do three problems and then he can help carry objects to principal's office
Told to do three problems, then can help carry objects to principal's office	Returns to desk, does three problems, runs to teacher, turns in worksheet (*Note:* Worksheet very messy, not complete, most problems done incorrectly)	Allowed to carry objects to principal's office, movement

Ms. Allison looked at the ABC recording sheet and said that it was typical of Leonard's behavior on most days. She said he behaved liked this in almost all daily activities and routines.

Ms. Allison is requesting that the special education consultant develop interventions to stop Leonard's behavior. Based on the initial observations by the special education consultant, should Leonard's behavior be considered as challenging behavior and, if so, should his behavior be changed through the functional assessment and intervention model described in this book? Why or why not?

CASE STUDIES SET TWO: WHAT IS THE FUNCTION OF THE STUDENT'S CHALLENGING BEHAVIOR?

Your job for the four case studies in Set Two is to identify the function of the student's challenging behavior. Each case study will provide a brief description of a student, the student's classroom setting, and an ABC recording form presenting the antecedents and setting events (context) related to behavior and the consequences that follow behavior. From this information, you should (a) identify the function of behavior, (b) provide a rationale for why you selected that function, and (c) discuss why you think the behavior is not one of the other functions.

Information to assist you in identifying the function was presented in Chapter 5. You may wish to review this chapter before completing these four case studies. In addition, as you examine the ABC recording forms provided for each case study, you should pay attention to occurrences of challenging and appropriate behavior, as well as the contexts (antecedents and setting events) and consequences related to each type of behavior. Note that the behavior in each of the four case studies fits a different function (positive reinforcement, negative reinforcement, sensory stimulation/ regulation increase, and sensory stimulation/regulation decrease).

Ani

Ani is a 15-year-old student enrolled in a regular education classroom. Her teacher, Mr. Barnes, uses an active learning approach that involves frequent cooperative group activities, choice in activities and assignments, individualized and adapted instruction and goals, self-evaluation, and feedback from peers and the teacher. In addition, Mr. Barnes's classroom has a small-enclosed area that he refers to as the private office. This area is quiet and contains writing materials, books, and headphones with quiet music. Students are allowed to use these offices for independent projects, reading, time alone, and so forth.

Ani is a very good student who does well in all subject areas. She especially enjoys working on the computer, reading, and creative writing. She turns in all homework assignments and does well on exams. Ani often tutors individual students in her class on assignments and she tutors students in younger grades after school. Her peers often consult with her when they are having problems with academic material.

Ani has one or two friends in her classroom, however, she seems to prefer interacting with adults and often seeks their company instead of interacting with her friends. For example, during recess she often talks to teachers instead of playing with peers. In the lunchroom she often eats alone or, if she is with peers, she always sits at the periphery of the group.

Although Ani is a good student, Mr. Barnes is very concerned about her behavior. Mr. Barnes feels that Ani uses the private office too much. He tells the instructional strategies coordinator that Ani spends most of the school day in the private office. For example, Mr. Barnes says that today it took a lot of coaxing to get Ani to leave the private office in order to join a group for a cooperative learning activity. When she did finally join a group, she sat at the edge of the group and only contributed to the group if someone asked her a question. After about 10 minutes in the group, Ani got up and returned to the private office.

Mr. Barnes indicates that recently, Ani has refused to leave the private office in order to join the class. He says that if he persists in asking her to join the class, or if he insists that she join a group activity, Ani says that she is sick and requests permission to go to the nurse.

The instructional strategies coordinator observed Ani across several days and recorded the following information about both appropriate and challenging behavior:

Antecedents and Setting Events	Behavior	Consequence
Recess, many students are playing soccer	Sits on bench, watches the game, talks to peer	Peer interaction
Teacher lecture and discussion	Takes notes, answers questions	Praise for correct answers
Cooperative groups that are loud, unstructured, with lots of movement	Moves to a private office	Teacher tells her to return to group
Told to return to group	Refuses	Told to return to group

Note: This interaction repeats several times until Ani complies and returns to her group.

Told to return to group	Returns to group, sits on periphery	Peer asks her a question
Peer asks her question	Answers question	Peer says, "I knew she would know"
Group continues for about 15 minutes	Returns to private office	Left alone
Students are reading passages of book aloud, teacher asks questions about the book	Reads aloud, answers questions	Praise for reading and correct answers

Antecedents and Setting Events	Behavior	Consequence
Partner reading and worksheet activity	Works with partner	Peer interaction, completes activity
Teacher led "Who Wants to Be a Millionaire"-type game (teacher asks questions, students shout answers, the first and loudest team to shout answers wins the points)	Ten minutes into game moves to private office, seems agitated	Left alone
Recess	Talks to teacher assistant about the story she is writing	Teacher interaction
Transition, students moving to lunch	Goes to private office until other students have left the classroom	Left alone
Mr. Barnes tells her it is time for lunch	Walks to lunchroom, sits at end of table with peers	Alone in the hall

What is the function of Ani's challenging behavior? In order to answer this question, you should use the information provided on the ABC recording form completed by the instructional strategies team coordinator and the information provided by Mr. Barnes. You also may wish to review Chapter 5. After you have identified the function of Ani's behavior provide a rationale for why you selected that function and why you think it is not one of the other functions.

Miles

Miles is a 7-year-old student with a diagnosis of failure to thrive. He has been in five foster homes and has been hospitalized for most of his young life. Miles recently was adopted by a loving family and is enrolled in a regular education second-grade classroom. There are 24 other students in this classroom, many of them with factors that place them at risk for school failure (factors identified by this school district include poverty, drug and excessive alcohol use by families, and English as a second language). There also are several students in the class with disability diagnoses who have Individualized Educational Plans and receive special education services. This classroom is co-taught by a regular and a special education teacher.

Miles loves to read and has excellent expressive and receptive language skills. He likes to interact with teachers and peers. His favorite time of the day is recess and free choice centers. He also likes paper-and-pencil activities. His least favorite and most difficult times of the day occur during teacher-directed activities.

Ms. Babcock, the regular education teacher, and Mr. Ong, the special education teacher, both are concerned with Miles's inappropriate and sometimes aggressive behavior. They indicate that he often is mean to other students and that he has been aggressive against peers and teachers. Ms. Babcock and Mr. Ong developed a list of behaviors that Miles exhibited during the past week:

Does not follow classroom instructions and rules.

Does not complete work on time.

Does not accept or follow redirection.

Takes materials from peers.

Makes fun of peers.

Hits peers and adults.

Off task.

To more fully understand Miles's challenging behavior, the teachers decide to conduct several functional assessment observations during a 2-week period. To do this, they decide that when Mr. Ong is collecting observational data, Ms. Babcock will teach the class. When Ms. Babcock collects observational data, Mr. Ong will teach the class. Below is a sample of the observations that Mr. Ong and Ms. Babcock collected.

Antecedents and Setting Events	Behavior	Consequence
Individual seatwork, teachers rotate among students	Leaves seat, walks to peer, takes his pencil	Peer protests
Peer demands pencil	Miles says no, returns to desk	Peer calls teacher
Teacher tells him to return pencil to peer	Screams "No!"	Teacher repeats instructions
Tells him to return pencil	Screams "No!"	Teacher repeats instructions
Note: This interaction repeats several times.		
Tells him to return pencil	Screams "No!"	Teacher gives peer a new pencil and moves to help another student
Teacher helping peer	Walks to first peer and returns pencil	Teacher says, "It's about time you did what I asked"
In the quiet room reading with teacher, teacher gives choices	Reads aloud, makes choices	Praise for correct reading

Antecedents and Setting Events	Behavior	Consequence
Peer enters in a wheel-chair, says hello to teacher, teacher says hello to peer	Calls peer a name	Teacher tells him to be nice
Teacher tells him to be nice	Calls peer a name again	Teacher tells him to apologize
Teacher tells him to apologize	Says he didn't mean it	Teacher tells him to be nicer next time and continues with reading lesson
Time to get ready to leave. Teacher asks Miles to put his coat on	Miles says no and continues to sort crayons in his pencil box	Teacher says Miles will have to sleep at school, then moves to help peers
Teacher helping peers	Runs to teacher, demands help with coat	Teacher tells him to say please
Teacher tells him to say please	Says please	Teacher helps him with his coat
Teacher asks for volunteer to help with bulletin board	Raises hand	Teacher selects him
One-to-one with teacher, teacher gives instructions about bulletin board	Follows instructions	Teacher interaction and praise
Teacher asks for volunteer to help with bulletin board	Raises hand	Teacher tells him he did it yesterday and calls on peer
Teacher calls on peer	Hits peer who was selected	Teacher tells him to apologize
Teacher tells him to apologize	Hits teacher	Teacher and peer walk away
Teacher working with peer	Walks to teacher, apologizes to peer and teacher	Both accept apology, allowed to assist in changing the bulletin board

What is the function of Miles's challenging behavior? To answer this question, you should use the information provided on the ABC recording form completed by Ms. Babcock and Mr. Ong and the information provided in the case study. You also may wish to review Chapter 5. After you have identified the function of Miles's behavior, provide a rationale for why you selected that function and why you think it is not one of the other functions.

Ruben

Ruben is a 3½-year-old child diagnosed with developmental delay. He exhibits moderate delays in cognitive, motor, and communication skills. Ruben's family speaks only Spanish at home, although he has an older brother who is learning English at school. Ruben is enrolled in a bilingual self-contained classroom for children with disabilities. His classroom contains nine other children who have moderate to severe disabilities. There is one primary teacher and one bilingual instructional assistant. Ruben has been enrolled in this program for 6 months. He did not receive early intervention services, so preschool is his first program experience.

Ruben is a happy child who likes to interact with the other children and with the teacher, Mr. Gilbert, and the bilingual assistant, Mr. Sanchez. Currently, Ruben primarily points to communicate although he does say "no" and "more." He does seem to have age-appropriate receptive language in Spanish however. He receives speech therapy three times per week and his teachers support communication goals in the classroom.

Both Mr. Gilbert and Mr. Sanchez are concerned about the disruptive behavior that Ruben exhibits in the classroom. He often throws toys and does not play with toys appropriately, does not follow directions, does not pay attention for a sufficient length of time during activities such as circle and reading, runs away from activities, and he sometimes bites adults when they attempt to help Ruben comply with instructions.

The school psychologist, Dr. Shipley, has been assigned to assist Mr. Gilbert and Mr. Sanchez in addressing Ruben's challenging behavior. Because Dr. Shipley has a very full caseload and is not completely fluent in Spanish, she asks Mr. Gilbert and Mr. Sanchez to collect data using the ABC recording form. Dr. Shipley also completes this form during her observations in the classroom. Samples of observations collected by Dr. Shipley, Mr. Gilbert, and Mr. Sanchez are provided below:

Antecedents and Setting Events	Behavior	Consequence
Teacher reading large book to class	Watches teacher read for a few minutes, then slides off cube chair, moves to teacher, pats teacher's leg, grabs book	Teacher looks at Ruben, shakes head no, tells him to return to his seat, movement
Pledge of allegiance	Stands and recites pledge with peers	Movement, auditory stimulation
Weather, calendar group time, his turn to answer a question	Walks to board and points to picture of the sun	Praise by teacher, movement

Antecedents and Setting Events	Behavior	Consequence
Weather, calendar group time, students take turns answering questions, Ruben's turn is over	Moves next to assistant, pats his leg	Assistant removes Ruben's hand and points to calendar
Assistant removes hand and points to calendar	Slaps assistant's hand hard	Assistant says no
Assistant says no	Continues to hit assistant	Assistance takes him to office to pick up mail
Takes to office to pick up mail	Holds assistant's hand, walks to office	Assistant talks to him, movement
Art, students doing individual projects	Leaves art table, moves to play with blocks	Left alone, movement
Free choice of centers	Joins peers at block area, knocks down blocks, moves to rocking boat, next selects music instruments, then Romper Stompers	Peer interaction, movement, auditory stimulation
Given a puzzle by the teacher	Bangs pieces together	Left alone
Teacher physically prompts putting puzzle piece in puzzle	Resists, throws puzzle and pieces	Physical assistance to pick up puzzle and pieces
Physical assistance to pick up puzzle and pieces	Picks up puzzle and pieces, pats teacher, runs away from teacher	Teacher reprimand, runs after him, movement
Marching band	Selects musical instrument, lines up for march, marches with peers	Movement, auditory stimulation
Nap time	Resists laying on mat, leaves mat, runs to centers, plays with toys	Physical prompting, allowed to select toy to play with at his mat
Allowed to select toy to use during nap time	Selects and plays with Slinky while laying on nap mat	Left alone
Snack, assigned to pass out cups and napkins	Passes out cups and napkins, sits in chair, talks to peers and teachers, eats snack, throws garbage in can, washes hands, selects center to play in until peers have finished snack	Peer and teacher interaction, gustatory, tactile, auditory, movement stimulation

What is the function of Ruben's challenging behavior? To answer this question, you should use the information provided on the ABC recording form completed by Dr. Shipley and Mr. Gilbert and Mr. Sanchez and the information provided in the case study. You also may wish to review Chapter 5. After you have identified the function of Ruben's behavior, provide a rationale for why you selected that function and why you think it is not one of the other functions.

ShariLynn

ShariLynn is a 13-year-old student enrolled in a regular education classroom. She receives daily special education services in the resource room and speech and language therapy in the speech pathologist's office 2 days per week. ShariLynn is diagnosed with a learning disability in reading and communication delays. Her regular education classroom contains 25 other students and one teacher.

ShariLynn generally enjoys school, especially her regular education classroom. She likes her teacher and has many friends. She really likes to participate in cooperative group activities. She readily participates in most activities and routines and gets good grades on assignments that do not involve reading skills. ShariLynn excels in sports and is a member of the school soccer team and recently qualified for membership on the track team.

ShariLynn also likes the teacher in the resource room and the speech and language pathologist. However, she does not like leaving regular education to go to her special education class. She is afraid that other students will make fun of her when she leaves and often she refuses to go to speech therapy and the resource room. The frequency of refusals and noncompliant behavior is increasing, and this behavior is expanding to other activities and routines within the regular classroom and other school settings. Together, the educators working with ShariLynn have made a referral for behavioral consultation. They are concerned about her increasing noncompliance in speech therapy, the resource room, and the regular education classroom.

Dr. Knofler, the behavior analyst for the school district, observed ShariLynn and recorded both challenging and appropriate behavior on the ABC recording form. Some of these observations are presented below:

Antecedents and Setting Events	Behavior	Consequence
Cooperative groups, working on science experiment	Works with group	Peer interaction
Told it was time to go to resource room	Says her group project is not finished, continues working	Prompted again to go to resource room

Antecedents and Setting Events	Behavior	Consequence
Prompted to go to resource room	Refuses, says she doesn't need any special help	Prompted again to go to resource room

Note: This interaction continues with escalation in prompting and arguing between the teacher and ShariLynn.

Antecedents and Setting Events	Behavior	Consequence
Threatened with detention if she doesn't go to the resource room	Goes to resource room (there are only 10 minutes left in the period)	Detention threat withdrawn, spends little time in resource room
Resource room teacher asks her to read short story	Says no, puts head down on the desk	Teacher says she will work with someone who wants to learn and works with peer
Given homework reading and study guide assignment	Throws study guide in trash on leaving school	No assignment to complete
Given math worksheet	Works at desk	Completes worksheet, allowed to play computer game
Students take turns reading parts of story, ShariLynn is called on to read	Says she left her book at home	Teacher calls on a different student
Regular class, given note that it is time to go to speech therapy	Tells teacher the speech pathologist told her not to come today	Teacher calls to verify
Teacher tells her she is supposed to go to speech therapy and not to lie to her again	Says she will go as soon as she finishes her project	Teacher gives her 5 minutes to finish her project
Ten minutes later, teacher tells her to go to speech therapy right now	Refuses	Teacher threatens with detention
Threat of detention	Still refuses	Teacher gives her detention and walks away
Students take turns reading parts of story, ShariLynn is called upon to read	Says she left her book at home	Teacher asks peer to share her book with ShariLynn
Teacher asks a peer to share her book with ShariLynn	Says she doesn't feel like reading	Instructed to read
Instructed to read	Refused	Sent to office for discipline

Antecedents and Setting Events	Behavior	Consequence
Sent to office for discipline	Stops at resource room, talks to teacher	Teacher asks where she is supposed to be
Teacher asks where she is supposed to be	Tells her in the office	Sends her onto the office
Sent onto the office	Stops at speech therapy office, talks to speech pathologist	Speech pathologist talks to her about missing speech yesterday

What is the function of ShariLynn's challenging behavior? To answer this question, you should use the information provided on the ABC recording form completed by Dr. Knofler and the information provided in the case study. You way wish to review Chapter 5 to identify the function of her behavior. After you have identified the function of ShariLynn's behavior, provide a rationale for why you selected that function and why you think it is not one of the other functions.

CASE STUDIES SET THREE: DEVELOPING INTERVENTIONS

Your job for these four case studies is to develop intervention plans based on the function of behavior. Each case study will provide a brief description of the student, the student's classroom setting, and an ABC recording form presenting the antecedents and setting events (context) related to the behavior and the consequences that follow it. For each case study, the function of challenging behavior also will be identified and a rationale provided for selecting that function.

After reading each case study, you will have the opportunity to develop a comprehensive intervention plan to decrease challenging behavior and increase appropriate behavior that will replace the challenging behavior.

In developing your intervention plans you should consider changing the antecedents and setting events as well as the consequences. It may help to reread Chapters 6 and 11 as you select antecedent, setting events, and consequence-based strategies. You also may wish to examine Chapters 7 through 10 as you develop interventions for each of the functions of behavior.

Roland

Roland is a 17-year-old student enrolled in a self-contained classroom for students with behavior disorders. There are eight students in this classroom and one teacher. There also are a number of instructional assistants who work in the classroom at various times throughout the day.

Roland is a very handsome, outgoing student. He is very interested in cars and motorcycles and enjoys talking about these subjects with peers and teachers. He has good expressive language skills and frequently attempts to engage peers and teachers in conversation. He has a good sense of humor and peers often seek his company, in and out of class.

Often, Roland's conversation with peers and adults includes inappropriate sexual or racial comments and comments related to using violence, drugs, or weapons. These comments typically cause laughter and continuing conversation between Roland and his peers. They also sometimes lead to arguments between Roland and adults or peers who object to such comments.

In addition to making inappropriate comments, Roland often objects to beginning tasks, preferring to do tasks that he chooses. He also may attempt to negotiate the amount of time or work that must be completed prior to ending a task and being allowed to work on a task of his choice. Roland also often directs profanity toward adults who are giving him instructions or tasks. However, once Roland does begin an assigned task he generally works well for an appropriate amount of time.

Roland's teacher, Ms. Schneider, seeks assistance from the teacher assistance team to deal with Roland's increasing use of profanity, loud arguing, threats, and aggressive posturing. She indicates that these behaviors generally are directed at adults, although he has, on occasion, directed them at peers. Ms. Schneider indicates that his challenging behavior has increased since students returned to school following Christmas break. The teacher assistance team coordinator observed Roland for 7 hours across 3 days. He observed the following sample sequences of both challenging and appropriate behavior:

Antecedents and Setting Events	Behavior	Consequence
Teacher asks for two volunteers to take books to the library	Roland volunteers	Roland and peer take books to the library
Individual worksheets	Protests about the number of problems, requests break after doing half of the problems	Teacher argues, instructs him to begin, eventually asks if he can have a five-minute break after doing half the problems
Teacher says he can have break after doing half the problems	Completes half the problems	Receives break, chooses break activity
Teacher lectures to whole class	Shouts questions to teacher	Teacher ignores questions
Teacher ignores questions	Shouts again, turns to peer and begins to talk about race cars	Peers talks with him, teacher tells both students to be quiet

Antecedents and Setting Events	Behavior	Consequence
Teacher tells Roland and peer to be quiet	Swears and makes inappropriate sexual comment about teacher	Peers laugh, teacher reprimands
Peers laugh, teacher reprimands	Continues to make inappropriate comments	Peers laugh, teacher instruction to stop
Teacher tells him to go to principal's office	Says, "Okay, I'll stop, what's the big deal? I was just kidding anyway," makes a face at peers seated close to him	Allowed to stay in class, peers laugh, lecture continues
Cooperative groups	Serves as group leader, on task	Peer interaction
Working individually with assistant	On task, answers questions, follows directions	Praise, interaction
Peer joins group	Makes inappropriate racial comment about peer	Peer protests, assistant demands he apologize
Assistant demands apology	Swears at peer and assistant, repeats comment	Assistant tells him to leave the area
Assistant tells him to leave the area	Leaves, joins teacher-led group	Assistant works with peer, teacher tells him he cannot join this group
Teacher tells him he cannot join this group	Returns to assistant and peer, says he didn't mean anything by his comment	Allowed to rejoin activity, peer and assistant interaction
Free-choice period	Works on building model car, shows model to teacher	Praise, interaction
Teacher suggests he include a picture of the model in his assessment portfolio	Refuses, says the car is just for him	Teacher tries to convince him to put model in portfolio

Note: This interaction continues for several minutes until the teacher leaves to talk to another student. Roland continues to work on his car model.

Roland exhibited several appropriate and challenging behaviors during the observations conducted in his classroom. For example, Roland volunteered to do tasks, served as leader of his cooperative group, was on task during a variety of activities, and worked well with teachers and adults. On the other hand, he made inappropriate comments about the teacher and peers, argued with the teacher and assistant, was noncompliant, used profanity, and shouted during activities.

The teacher assistance team coordinator identified the function of Roland's challenging behavior as positive reinforcement. Roland's behavior produces attention from teachers and from peers in situations in which he is not receiving attention. His behavior also produces control of a situation.

Examination of the ABC recording form indicates that the antecedent conditions that are in effect when Roland engages in appropriate behavior are situations in which he is working individually with a teacher or when he is directly in charge or control of an activity (such as leading a group, free choice). In contrast, conditions that precede his challenging behavior most often include situations in which he is expected to work alone (e.g., individual worksheets), teacher attention is not directed to him (e.g., it is directed to the whole group or to another peer), or he is not in control of and has little choice during the activity (e.g., being told what to do by the teacher).

On the other side of the behavior equation, the consequences for both appropriate and challenging behavior typically provide some form of attention from teachers and peers and they often lead to control of and choice in an activity. Note that, from Roland's perspective, the type of attention he receives is irrelevant. He is reinforced by both positive attention (e.g., praise) and negative attention (e.g., reprimand, arguments) from teachers or peers.

The function of Roland's challenging behavior is not negative reinforcement because Roland does not consistently escape particular activities or tasks and once he does begin a task about which he has been arguing, he completes the task. In fact, when he is dismissed from an activity or threatened with dismissal, he stops engaging in challenging behavior. If his behavior were a function of escape, he would be happy to leave an activity.

His challenging behavior also is not a function of the sensory stimulation/ regulation increase or decrease functions. We know this because there were no consistencies in the stimulation level of antecedent conditions and there were no consistent changes in the level of stimulation following challenging behavior. Roland engaged in challenging behavior during both high and low stimulation activities and the consequences of his behavior sometimes increased and sometimes decreased stimulation. The lack of consistent levels of stimulation that preceded challenging behavior and the fact that there were no consistent changes in the levels of stimulation following challenging behavior indicate that his behavior is not a function of sensory stimulation/regulation.

In designing an intervention plan to address Roland's behavior, you should match the function of his behavior. In other words, the intervention should, in part at least, allow Roland to achieve the same function as he currently achieves through challenging behavior. Your intervention plan also should address what will happen if/when challenging behavior does occur. Finally, in addition to addressing appropriate replacement behaviors and the supports for those behaviors, you also should think about how to change antecedent conditions so that you can prevent Roland from engaging in challenging behavior.

Matt

Matt is a 5-year-old student who attends a half-day regular education kindergarten program. This is his first school experience. There are 21 other students in his classroom, one teacher, and one teaching assistant who is assigned to the classroom because of other students who have IEPs. However, the assistant also works with Matt due to his challenging behavior.

Matt's teacher describes him as an alert student who tries to participate in all academic and social activities and routines. He likes peers and often tries to interact with them; however, his initiations are a bit rough and many peers are afraid of him and avoid interacting with him. Matt's favorite activities are dramatic play, art and writing activities, and activities that involve gross motor skills.

Matt exhibits several behaviors that concern his teacher, Mrs. Yellin-Clarke. She feels that these behaviors interfere with Matt's learning and progress and the learning and progress of other students in the classroom. For example, Matt often rocks wildly in his chair, puts materials and fingers in his mouth, seeks hugs from adults and peers, and constantly changes position or moves to different locations during activities. He also often will leave activities and begin a different, self-selected activity.

Mrs. Yellin-Clarke says that Matt also has trouble waiting in line or for his turn during activities. He often runs during transition instead of putting materials away and following transition routines. Finally, Mrs. Yellin-Clarke indicates that Matt does not follow whole-class instructions and often takes much individual attention from her or the assistant in order to begin an activity, continue working on an activity, and behaving appropriately during an activity. She feels that the amount of time Matt requires reduces the amount of time that she should be devoting to other students. Mrs. Yellin-Clarke believes that the behaviors she has described warrant placement in a self-contained special education classroom. She has referred Matt for special education evaluation. As part of the multidisciplinary case study evaluation, Dr. Calder conducts functional assessment of Matt's behavior.

The following information is a sample of Dr. Calder's observations using the ABC recording form:

Antecedents and Setting Events	Behavior	Consequence
Group acting out the *Three Little Pigs* story	Participates as the wolf	Group praise, movement
Second group acting out a story	Rocks in place, talks to teacher	Told to sit still and be quiet

Antecedents and Setting Events	Behavior	Consequence
Third group acting out a story	Leaves carpet area, begins to play with puzzles	Left alone
Open-center activity	Selects woodworking area, science center, then makes mailbox in literacy center	Left alone, tactile and movement stimulation
Teacher suggests Matt work in reading area or on the computer	Refuses to work in these centers	Left alone
Teacher reading story to whole class using large book, unison responding	Listens, rocks on floor, puts fingers in mouth, shouts answers with group	Movement, auditory oral, tactile stimulation
Recess, peers playing on the jungle gym	Runs to peers, jumps on top of Gretchen, hugs her	Gretchen cries, peers yell, teacher "rescues" Gretchen, tells Matt to play somewhere else
Told to play elsewhere	Runs to boys playing ball and joins game	Peer interaction, movement
Art activity	On task	Praise, completes project, hangs project on wall
Transition to next activity	Runs in classroom	Redirection, movement
Whole class given instructions regarding matching worksheet	Sits at desk, no pencil, raps fingers on desk	Teacher tells him to go get a pencil
Teacher tells him to go get a pencil	Skips to pencil box, gets pencil, skips back to desk	Teacher tells him to begin working
Teacher tells him to begin working	Rocks in chair, taps pencil on paper	Teacher shows how to do a problem, stays with him as he completes the worksheet
Recess	Plays on climbing equipment, runs, swings, plays ball	Movement, tactile stimulation
Following recess, one-to-one activity with assistant	Rocks, shakes head side to side, tries to leave area	Repeated instructions, reprimand
Repeated instructions	Refuses, leaves area, plays with class hamster	Assistant talks to teacher, leaves him alone

The function of Matt's challenging behavior is sensory regulation/sensory stimulation increase. Matt's challenging behavior typically produces sensory input such as movement, auditory, tactile, and oral stimulation. He engages in challenging behavior during passive and unstructured activities in which he is not actively involved or is expected to wait, sit quietly, or to listen. He also seeks very stimulating materials and activities during free-choice periods such as recess and open centers and he refuses to engage in passive activities during these free-choice periods. The sensory regulation/sensory stimulation increase function also was identified because Matt engages in appropriate behavior during activities with high levels of stimulation. For example, his behavior was appropriate when his group acted out the *Three Little Pigs* book.

In addition to seeking activities that are highly stimulating and increasing stimulation during passive activities, Matt exhibits problems with sensory regulation. For example, he was not able to calm or reduce his level of stimulation following recess (a very active activity) to the level of stimulation needed to participate in the more passive one-to-one activity with the teaching assistant.

Although Matt's challenging behavior often results in attention or interaction with a peer or adult, the function of his behavior is not positive reinforcement. If it were positive reinforcement (i.e., attention in this case) he would continue to seek attention when he is left alone. He does not consistently do this. Therefore, it is likely that the attention or interaction that he receives functions as a form of stimulation. When that form of stimulation is not available, Matt simply seeks a different form of stimulation such as rocking or running.

Negative reinforcement was not selected as the function of his challenging behavior because although Matt often left activities, this behavior consistently occurred only after he had participated in the activity for a period of time and it always followed attempts to produce stimulation through less active means such as rocking or mouthing objects. If escape from activities were the function, he would engage in challenging behavior at the start of potentially aversive activities. The activities themselves were not aversive for Matt. Rather, it was the passive stimulation level of the activities that was important (i.e., he needed higher levels of stimulation). In other words, the consistent antecedent variable was not a particular activity, but rather the level of stimulation provided by the activity. On the other side of the behavior equation, Matt's behavior did not always result in escape or termination of an activity. Rather, it resulted in a change in the level of stimulation within the activity.

In designing an intervention plan to address Matt's behavior, you should match the function of his behavior. In other words, the intervention should, in part at least, allow Matt to achieve the same function as he currently achieves through challenging behavior. Your intervention plan also should address what will happen if/when challenging behavior does occur. Finally, in addition to addressing appropriate replacement behaviors and the supports for those behaviors, you also should think about how to change antecedent conditions so that you can prevent Matt from engaging in challenging behavior. Reread the goals of intervention when the function of challenging behavior is sensory stimulation/sensory regulation in Chapters 9 and 10 as you develop an intervention plan to address Matt's behavior.

Carter

Carter is a 14-year-old student enrolled in ninth grade. He is diagnosed with attention deficit/hyperactivity disorder. Carter struggles in school and historically has received failing grades in many subjects. During interview, Carter indicates that he does not like school. His most difficult and least preferred subjects are math and science. His favorite times of the day are lunch and recess or anytime when he can "hang out with his friends." Carter indicates that health and art are okay subjects, although he does not do well in them and often receives close to failing grades for these subjects.

Carter has several teachers as he moves from class to class for different subjects. Each of his teachers has expressed concern with his behavior in terms of its effects on other students and in light of his failing grades. They feel that if his behavior cannot be changed or controlled, that he would be best served in more restrictive types of classrooms. They feel like he doesn't try hard enough to attend to lessons, stay on task, or complete in-class and homework assignments. The following list of behaviors was included on the teachers' referral for behavioral consultation:

Does not participate in classroom activities.

Often sleeps in class.

Does not complete homework.

Does not complete classroom assignments.

Does not comply with group instructions.

Does not comply with individual instructions.

Refuses redirection.

Refuses assistance with assignments.

Does not begin activities in a timely manner.

Mr. Kasuba, a member of the teacher assistance team, is assigned to work with Carter and his teachers. He first interviews Carter and then each of Carter's classroom teachers. After interviewing each teacher, Mr. Kasuba observes Carter's behavior over a 5-day period. During observations Carter walked from class to class with peers and he arrived promptly at each class. He talked with some of his teachers prior to class about his interests and activities. In other classes, Carter simply talked with peers before the class started. A sample of the observations collected by Mr. Kasuba on the ABC recording form is presented here:

Antecedents and Setting Events	Behavior	Consequence
Class lecture, students should take notes	Head down on desk, eyes closed	Told to wake up and take notes
Told to wake up and take notes	Continued to lay head on desk, eyes closed	Told he would fail the test if he slept through class
Physical education, baseball practice, batting instruction from coach	Complied with instructions	Praise
Health class, group project	Participates in group	Peer interaction
Math, lesson introduction, given worksheet	Head on desk, eyes closed, throws worksheet to floor	Reprimand, offer of assistance
Offer of assistance	Rips worksheet	Teacher leaves
Students receive homework assignment	Head on desk, eyes closed (does not copy assignment)	Teacher gives a copy of assignment
Teacher gives copy of assignment	Leaves assignment in desk	Left alone
Music period, group singing	Sings with peers	Praise to group
Science, asked to read assignment to the group	Refuses	Teacher selects another student to read
Geography, given individual work assignment	Head on desk, eyes closed	Teacher repeats instruction
Teacher repeats instruction	Refuses, argues	Argues, repeats instruction

Note: This argumentative interaction escalates to shouting for both Carter and the teacher and it continues until the end of the period. At this point, Carter moves to the next classroom and subject.

School-wide canned goods collection drive	Serves as leader of geography class team	Peer interaction, success in meeting team goal
Science test	Breaks pencil	Teacher gives new pencil
Teacher gives new pencil	Rips paper while writing name	Teacher gives new test
Teacher gives new test	Throws test in garbage	Sent to principal's office
Resource room, group discussion	Asks to go to nurse's office	Permission granted
Nurse's office, period ends	Says he is better now and leaves	Moves to next period (lunch)

The function of Carter's challenging behavior is negative reinforcement. His behavior results in escape from academic activities and assignments. The negative reinforcement function was selected because Carter only engages in challenging behavior during academic-related tasks. Carter has a long history of poor grades and failure in academic subjects. For Carter, academic activities are aversive and he engages in challenging behavior when presented with aversive academic tasks or assignments (antecedent/setting event conditions). The consequences for his behavior (e.g., arguments, and left alone) effectively terminate aversive antecedent tasks, activities, or assignments.

The negative reinforcement function also was identified for Carter because he does not engage in challenging behavior during social and nonacademic-related activities such as the canned-goods drive, transition, lunch, and physical education. During nonacademic antecedent task conditions, he engages in appropriate behavior. Thus, there are clear differences in the types of antecedent/setting events conditions that trigger appropriate versus challenging behavior. The only exception to this was health class where he works with peers on a group project. Remember, however, that Carter identifies health class as an "okay" subject. It is not an aversive activity for him. The academic activities from which he escapes all were identified as nonpreferred or aversive subjects during interview.

It may seem as though the function of Carter's behavior is sensory reduction because a frequent form of behavior that he displays is putting his head down on his desk and closing his eyes. However, Carter readily participates in active activities such as baseball practice and music. He only puts his head down on his desk during aversive or nonpreferred academic subjects. Therefore, the function of this behavior is not to reduce stimulation. The function is to escape or avoid an aversive activity. For Carter, the activity level per se is not a relevant context. Rather, the relevant context that triggers appropriate or challenging behavior is a preferred or nonpreferred activity.

Carter's behavior also is not a function of positive reinforcement. His behavior does not consistently produce or add a desired consequence to the situation (e.g., peer or adult attention, access to material, or access to peers). In fact, the consequences that followed challenging behavior are varied. For example, sometimes he is left alone, sometimes teachers argue with him, and sometimes they offer assistance. If the function of his behavior were positive reinforcement, he would not have stopped engaging in challenging behavior when he was left alone. Instead, he would have continued to seek attention, seek access to materials, or peers, and so forth. Rather than add a desired variable to the behavior equation, the consequences that followed Carter's challenging behavior consistently delayed or prevented the assigned activity or task.

In designing an intervention plan to address Carter's behavior, you typically would need to decide if it was appropriate for Carter to avoid and escape academic tasks and activities. If it was okay to escape, then the goal of your intervention plan would be to match the function of his behavior. In other words, the intervention would allow Carter to continue to avoid and escape aversive activities and tasks, but through more appropriate forms of behavior (see Chapter 8).

However, if you decided that escape and avoidance were not appropriate for Carter, then your goal should be to change the function from negative to positive reinforcement. To do this, you would need to alter both antecedent and consequence conditions so that they trigger and support appropriate behavior instead of challenging behavior and so that they prevent the occurrence of challenging behavior.

Because most school programs are not likely to agree that it is okay for Carter to escape or avoid aversive academic tasks and activities, your intervention plan should be twofold. First, you should develop strategies to allow temporary escape or avoidance using appropriate behavior. Temporary escape and avoidance contingent on appropriate behavior may be used in the initial stages of intervention and faded throughout the course of the intervention plan. Second, your intervention plan should include strategies to change the function from negative to positive reinforcement. Refer to Chapter 8 for suggestions and tips related to the negative reinforcement function.

Casi

Casi is a fourth-grade student with autism. She is enrolled in a regular education classroom with 26 other students. Casi receives occupational therapy two times per week. She also receives a combination of in-class support from the special education teacher, teaching assistant, and peer tutors.

Casi's teacher, Mr. Quelle, likes Casi a lot and is happy to have her included in this classroom. He indicates that Casi usually comes to school happy and ready to participate. She greets teachers and peers and sits quietly at her desk, waiting for all students to arrive. Unfortunately, he states that problems with Casi's behavior increase during the day. Mr. Quelle says that as the day wears on and during particular activities, Casi often screams, refuses to participate, does not attend to instructions, and can become aggressive against peers. When he attempts to guide participation through physical prompting, Casi often seems to shut down by either rolling her body into a ball while laying on the floor or by putting her head on her desk and crying.

Mr. Quelle is concerned with Casi's behavior for several reasons. First, her behavior disrupts the classroom and interferes with his teaching and student learning. Second, other students have begun to make fun of Casi and to call her names. Some also have requested that she not be placed in their work groups. Finally, Casi is not making progress on her IEP goals or in the regular education curriculum.

Mr. Quelle is afraid that Casi will have to be placed in a more segregated classroom if her behavior does not improve. This is not something that Mr. Quelle wants to happen because he believes in inclusion and he believes that Casi could benefit from the regular education curriculum and from interacting with typically developing peers. As a result, he has requested that the special educator develop a plan (in consultation with him) to address her challenging behavior. The special educator conducts functional assessment by observing in the classroom and interviewing Mr. Quelle, the occupational therapist, peer tutors, and Casi and her parents. This information led the team to identify the function of Casi's behavior as sensory regulation/sensory stimulation decrease. The following ABC recording form presents observations across 1 day, beginning with school arrival and ending with school departure. The team agrees that these observations are typical of the activities and routines that occur during each day and of Casi's behavior during these activities and routines.

Antecedents and Setting Events	Behavior	Consequence
Morning arrival	Greets teacher and peers, moves to desk, looks at comic book	Peers and teachers respond to greeting
Pledge of allegiance, announcements, review and questions about daily schedule, Casi has own picture schedule to arrange with peer assistance	Pledges with peers, listens to announcements, arranges her daily picture schedule with peer tutor	Peer interaction, schedule is in order
Expressive writing activity, working on computer	On task	Left alone, occasional praise
Partner reading	Reads with peer partner	Peer interaction, praise
Teacher writes spelling words on board	Copies spelling words	Left alone during work
Spelling bee in groups	Turns back to group, copies words again	Teacher prompts participation
Teacher prompts participation	Refuses to participate	Asks peer tutor to review words
Peer tutor reviews spelling words	Spells words for peer tutor	Peer interaction
Physical education in school gym	Lines up, moves to gym with peers	Peer interaction
Trampoline activity	Refuses to take turn on trampoline	Prompted by teacher
Teacher prompts	Screams "No!," sits on floor and refuses to move	Loss of points, next peer in line takes turn
Left alone	Sits in corner, watches peers take turns on trampoline	Left alone
End of activity	Lines up, moves to classroom, talks with peers	Peer interaction

Antecedents and Setting Events	Behavior	Consequence
Lunch	Sits with favorite peer, eats lunch	Peer interaction
Several peers join group, talk and laugh	Leaves group, sits by self, completes lunch	Reduction in peer interaction and sensory input
Bell rings, students return to classroom	Covers her ears, walks to classroom with peer	Peer interaction, decrease in auditory input
Music, students play instruments	Refuses to select instrument, sits in corner	Instructed to get an instrument
Teacher hands her the tambourine	Pushes tambourine away	Teacher leaves to work with other students
Music begins	Rolls in ball on floor, crys	Teacher asks her to join the group

Note: On a previous observation music involved listening to examples of different types of music. Casi readily participated in this activity.

Math worksheets	Works with special education teacher	Praise, completes worksheet

Note: At this point, Casi leaves the classroom and attends a half-hour occupational therapy session.

Group activity (note high noise level)	Participates with her group	Peer interaction
Team recognition at end of half-hour group activity (also high noise level)	Pushes peer next to her who is clapping and yelling for their group	Peer moves to other end of the table
Ending circle, review homework assignments, peer tutoring	Copies homework assignment, follows departure routines, says goodbye to peers and teacher	Peer and teacher interaction

The function of Casi's challenging behavior is sensory stimulation/sensory regulation decrease. Casi engages in challenging behavior during highly stimulating activities and routines. She does not generally engage in challenging behavior during passive, quiet activities and tasks.

Casi's challenging behavior functions to either decrease sensory input or it prevents her participation in highly stimulating tasks and activities. It is interesting to note that not only does Casi engage in challenging behavior during highly stimulating activities and tasks, but also her tolerance for such tasks decreases during the day. An exception to this was seen when an active group task followed occupational therapy. This is to be expected, because occupational therapy probably altered her level of stimulation (i.e., resulted in sensory regulation) so that when she returned to the classroom, she was able to respond appropriately to stimulating tasks, at least for a short period of time.

Cassi's behavior is not a function of positive reinforcement. Although it is clear that she enjoys interacting with peers and teachers, she prefers to not interact with them if they are engaged in activities that are too stimulating for Casi such as physical education and group work. For example, if the function of her behavior had been positive reinforcement, Casi would have remained with her peer tutor during lunch when additional peers joined their group. She also would have continued to participate during group recognition when her peers were clapping and shouting for their group. Instead, in these situations she engaged in behavior that effectively reduced the level of noise (i.e., stimulation).

Negative reinforcement also was not identified as the function of Casi's challenging behavior. Casi did not consistently escape or avoid particular academic or social tasks; rather, the level of stimulation within a task (antecedent/setting event context) determined whether she engaged in challenging or appropriate behavior. For example, she was appropriately engaged during the spelling activity until the activity level increased during the spelling bee. In this example, it was the activity level that changed as a result of her challenging behavior (consequence), not the activity itself (i.e., she still completed the spelling activity).

The increase in Casi's challenging behavior throughout the day is another clue as to why negative reinforcement was not the function of her behavior. Her tolerance for stimulation decreased throughout the day, probably in response to repeated or cumulative sensory stimulation. With each exposure to levels and types of stimulation that for Casi were excessive, her tolerance and ability to behave appropriately decreased. If Casi's behavior had been a function of escape, she would have been equally as likely to engage in challenging behavior at the beginning of the day as she was at the end of the day.

In designing an intervention plan to address Casi's behavior, you should match the function of her behavior. In other words, the intervention should, in part at least, allow Casi to achieve the same function as she currently achieves through challenging behavior. Your intervention plan also should address what will happen if/when challenging behavior does occur. Finally, in addition to addressing appropriate replacement behaviors and the supports for those behaviors, you also should think about how to change antecedent conditions so that you can prevent Casi from engaging in challenging behavior. You may wish to review the goals of intervention when the function of challenging behavior is sensory stimulation/sensory regulation in Chapters 9 and 10 as you develop an intervention plan to address Casi's behavior.

CASE STUDY FOUR: REDUCING RESISTANCE

This case study presents a situation in which the teacher does not wish to have you enter her classroom to do functional assessment observations and then is resistant to implementing interventions that you have recommended. However, she does want something to be done. Your job in this case study is to describe strategies that you could employ to reduce resistance, increase cooperation, and establish a collaborative relationship with this teacher. In doing this, you may refer to the sources of resistance and strategies for reducing resistance and increasing cooperation presented in Chapter 12. As you develop potential strategies, try to think about why this teacher might be resistant and try to address the sources of her resistance.

Ms. Collins, an eighth-grade teacher at John Kennedy Middle School, has referred Leon for evaluation for special education services. Leon is not doing well in his classroom and has just received failing grades in most areas. In addition, Ms. Collins indicates that he is very disruptive and distracting to other students. Her referral form lists the following challenging behaviors:

Does not listen.

Often interrupts with sarcastic comments.

Has problems getting started on activities.

Constantly asks questions or for help from peers.

Complains of too much work.

Leaves his seat.

Drums on desk top with hands.

Questions why material is important.

Off task.

Does not turn in homework.

Argues with peers.

Argues with the teacher.

Does not complete assigned work.

Does not bring materials to class.

Often is tardy and disruptive when he enters the room.

The teacher assistance team meets to review the referral form and decide to do observations in the classroom and to recommend strategies to address the student's behavior prior to recommending a full case study evaluation by the multidisciplinary team.

You are a member of the teacher assistance team and you have been assigned to work with this teacher. When you call Ms. Collins to make an appointment to conduct functional assessment observations in her classroom, she says, "I can tell you all you want to know about Leon; there is no need to disrupt my class by coming in to observe." "Besides," she continues, "I put all the information about his behavior on the referral report, didn't you read that?" Ms. Collins lets you know that she is afraid she will get nothing done with someone new coming into her class. She tells you, "You come into my class and all the students will do is look at you and talk to you. They won't be paying attention to me and this is a really critical part of the year, I have to get them ready for testing or they won't graduate eighth grade."

What would you say or do with Ms. Collins in order to reduce her resistance to observation and to get her to allow you into her classroom? In developing a plan to work with Ms. Collins, it may help to consider some of the mistakes that already have been made, which most likely helped establish her resistance. Recognition of these mistakes as well as information from Chapter 12 will guide what you do next.

Now assume that the strategies you just identified for reducing resistance to classroom observations were successful; Ms. Collins let you in her classroom. Now your observations are completed. You have been able to identify the function of Leon's behavior and have developed several strategies that you want Ms. Collins to implement in order to reduce Leon's challenging behavior and to increase his appropriate behavior.

At the meeting with Ms. Collins, you summarize your observational data, identify the function of Leon's behavior, and describe the strategies that you would like Ms. Collins to implement. At this point, Ms. Collins tells you that your suggestions won't do any good. She says, "I have tried everything there is to try, and nothing works with this kid." She says that she has tried many of the strategies that you are recommending several times and that they just don't work. She also tells you, "Besides, I don't have time to do everything that you are asking. I have twenty-six other kids in my class and it isn't fair to spend all this time on one student." She then continues, "Look, I made the referral for special education in order to get Leon out of my class. He needs to be in a special classroom that will do him some good. I didn't make the referral just so that people like you could tell me that I am a bad teacher."

What would you do or say to the teacher at this point in order to reduce her resistance and increase her cooperation? In developing your plan for future interactions with Ms. Collins, it may be helpful to identify mistakes that were made in this part of the vignette as well. These mistakes probably contributed to her continuing resistance. Analyzing these mistakes and reviewing strategies from Chapter 12 will guide the development of your plan to reduce resistance and increase collaboration with this teacher.

References

Aber, M. E., Bachman, B., Campbell, P., & O'Malley, G. (1994). Improving instruction in elementary schools. *Teaching Exceptional Children, 26*(3), 42–50.

Abrahms, B. J., & Segal, A. (1998). How to prevent aggressive behavior. *Teaching Exceptional Children, 30*(4), 10–15.

Alberto, P. A., & Troutman, A. C. (1999). *Applied behavior analysis for teachers* (5th ed.). Upper Saddle River, NJ: Merrill/Prentice Hall.

Albin, R. W., & Horner, R. H. (1988). Generalization with Precision. In R. H. Horner, G. Dunlap, & R. L. Koegel (Eds.), *Generalization and maintenance: Life-style changes in applied settings* (pp. 99–120). Baltimore: Paul H. Brookes.

Anderson, S. R., Taras, M., & Cannon, B. O. (1996). Teaching new skills to young children with autism. In C. Maurice, G. Green, & S. Luce (Eds.), *Behavioral interventions for young children with autism: A manual for parents and professionals* (pp. 195–217). Austin, TX: Pro-Ed.

Armstrong, S. W., & Kauffman, J. M. (1999). Functional behavioral assessment: Introduction to the series. *Behavior Disorders, 24*(2), 167–168.

Arndorfer, R. E., & Miltenberger, R. G. (1993). Functional assessment and treatment of challenging behavior: A review with implications for early childhood. *Topics in Early Childhood Special Education, 13*(1), 82–105.

Arndorfer, R. E., Miltenberger, R. G., Woster, S. H., Rortvedt, A. K., & Gaffaney, T. (1994). Home-based descriptive and experimental analysis of problem behavior in children. *Topics in Early Childhood Special Education, 14*(1), 64–87.

Ayllon, T., & Azrin, N. H. (1968). Reinforcer sampling: A technique for increasing the behavior of mental patients. *Journal of Applied Behavior Analysis, 1*, 13–20.

Ayres, J. A. (1972). *Sensory integration and learning disorders*. Los Angeles: Western Psychological Services.

Ayres, J. A. (1979). *Sensory integration and the child*. Los Angeles: Western Psychological Services.

Baer, D. M. (1970). A case for the selective reinforcement of punishment. In C. Neuringer & J. L. Michaels (Eds.), *Behavior modification in clinical psychology* (pp. 243–249). New York: Appleton-Century-Crofts.

Baer, D. M. (1981). *How to plan for generalization*. Lawrence, KS: H & H Enterprises.

Baer, D. M. (1982). The role of current pragmatics in the future analysis of generalization technology. In R. B. Stuart (Ed.), *Adherence, compliance, and generalization in behavioral medicine* (pp. 192–212). New York: Brunner/Mazel.

Baer, D. M., Wolfe, M. M., & Risley, T. R. (1968). Some current dimensions of applied behavior analysis. *Journal of Applied Behavior Analysis, 1*, 91–97.

Baer, D. M., Wolfe, M. M., & Risley, T. R. (1987). Some still-current dimension of applied behavior analysis. *Journal of Applied Behavior Analysis, 20*, 313–327.

Bahr, M. W., Whitten, E., Dieker, L., Kocarek, C. E., & Manson, D. (1999). A comparison of school-based intervention teams: Implications for educational and legal reform. *Exceptional Children, 66*, 67–83.

Bailey, D. B., & Wolery, M. (1992). *Teaching infants and preschoolers with disabilities* (2nd ed.). Upper Saddle River, NJ: Merrill/Prentice Hall.

Bandura, A. (1965). Behavior modification through modeling procedures. In L. Krasner & L. P. Ullman (Eds.), *Research in behavior modification*. New York: Holt, Rinehart & Winston.

Barbour, C., & Barbour, N. H. (1997). *Families, schools, and communities: Building partnerships for educating children*. Upper Saddle River, NJ: Merrill/Prentice Hall.

Barrish, H. H., Saunders, M., & Wolf, M. M. (1969). Good behavior game: Effects of individual contingencies for group consequences on disruptive behavior in a classroom. *Journal of Applied Behavior Analysis, 2*, 119–124.

Bateman, B. D., & Linden, M. A. (1998). *Better IEPs: How to develop legally correct and educationally useful programs* (3rd ed.). Longmont, CO: Sopris West.

Berg, W., & Sasso, G. (1993). Transferring implementation of functional assessment procedures from the clinic to natural settings. In J. Reichle & D. P. Wacker (Eds.), *Communication alternatives to challenging behavior: Integrating functional assessment and intervention strategies* (pp. 343–362). Baltimore: Paul H. Brookes.

Berkson, G., McQuiston, S., Jacobson, J. W., Eyman, R., & Borthwick, S. (1985). The relationship between age and stereotyped behaviors. *Mental Retardation, 23,* 31–33.

Berkson, G., & Tupa, M. (2000). Early development of stereotyped and self-injurious behaviors. *Journal of Early Intervention, 23*(1), 1–19.

Bijou, S. W., Peterson, R. F., & Ault, M. H. (1968). A method to integrate descriptive and experimental field studies at the level of data and empirical concept. *Journal of Applied Behavior Analysis, 1,* 175–191.

Billingsley, F. (1988). Writing objectives for generalization. In N. Haring (Ed.), *Generalization for students with severe handicaps: Strategies and solutions* (pp. 123–129). Seattle: University of Washington Press.

Bissel, J., Fisher, J., Owens, C., & Polsyn, P. P. (1988). *Sensory motor handbook: A teacher's guide for implementing and modifying activities in the classroom.* Torrence, CA: Sensory Integration International.

Blair, K., Umbreit, J., & Bos, C. S. (1999). Using functional assessment and children's preferences to improve the behavior of young children with behavior disorders. *Behavior Disorders, 24*(2), 151–166.

Borthwick, S. A., Meyers, C. E., & Eyman, R. K. (1981). A comparison of adaptive and maladaptive behavior of mentally retarded clients of five residential settings in three western states. In R. H. Bruininks, C. E. Meyers, B. B. Sigford, & K. C. Lakin (Eds.), *Deinstitutionalization and community adjustment of mentally retarded people* (Monograph 4, pp. 351–359). Washington, DC: American Association on Mental Deficiency.

Borthwick-Duffy, S. A., Eyman, R. K., & White, J. F. (1987). Client characteristics and residential placement patterns. *American Journal of Mental Deficiency, 92,* 24–30.

Boulware, G., Schwartz, I., & McBride, B. (1999). Addressing challenging behavior at home: Working with families to find solutions. *Young Exceptional Children, 3*(1), 21–27.

Brandenberg, N. A., Friedman, R. M., & Silver, S. E. (1990). The epidemeology of childhood psychiatric disorders: Prevalence findings from recent studies. *Journal of the American Academy of Child and Adolescent Psychiatry, 29*(1), 76–83.

Brockman, L. M., Morgan, G. A., & Harmon, R. J. (1988). Mastery motivation and developmental delay. In T. D. Wachs & R. Sheehan (Eds.), *Assessment of young developmentally disabled children* (pp. 267–284). New York: Plenum Press.

Cangelosi, J. (1993). *Classroom management strategies: Gaining and maintaining students' cooperation* (2nd ed.). While Plains, NY: Longman.

Carnegie, D. (1994). *How to win friends and influence people.* New York: Pocket Books.

Carnine, D. (1976). Effects of two teacher presentation rates on off-task behavior, answering correctly, and participation. *Journal of Applied Behavior Analysis, 9,* 199–206.

Carr, E. G. (1977). The motivation for self-injurious behavior: A review of some hypotheses. *Psych Bulletin, 84,* 800–816.

Carr, E. G. (1988). Functional equivalence as a mechanism of response generalization. In R. H. Horner, G. Dunlap, & R. L. Koegel, (Eds.), *Generalization and maintenance: Life-style changes in applied settings* (pp. 221–241). Baltimore: Paul H. Brookes.

Carr, E. G. (1994). Emerging themes in the functional analysis of problem behavior. *Journal of Applied Behavior Analysis, 27,* 393–400.

Carr, E. G., & Durand, V. M. (1985). Reducing behavior problems through functional communication training. *Journal of Applied Behavior Analysis, 18,* 111–126.

Carr, E. G., Langdon, N. A., & Yarbrough, S. C. (1999). Hypothesis-based intervention for severe problem behavior. In A. C. Repp & R. H. Horner (Eds.), *Functional analysis of problem behavior: From effective assessment to effective support* (pp. 9–31). Belmont, CA: Wadsworth Publishing Company.

Carr, E. G., Levin, L., McConnachie, G., Carlson, J. I., Kemp, D. C., & Smith, C. E. (1994). *Communication-based intervention for problem behavior.* Baltimore: Paul H. Brookes.

Carr, E. G., & Lindquist, J. C. (1987). Generalization processes in language acquisition. In T. L. Layton (Ed.), *Language and treatment of autistic and developmentally disordered children* (pp. 129–153). Springfield, IL: Charles C. Thomas.

Carr, E. G., & McDowell, J. J. (1980). Social control of self-injurious behavior of organic etiology. *Behavior Therapy, 11*, 402–409.

Carr, E. G., & Newsom, C. D. (1985). Demand-related tantrums: Conceptualization and treatment. *Behavior Modification, 9*, 403–426.

Carr, E. G., Newsom, C. D., & Binkoff, J. A. (1980). Escape as a factor in the aggressive behavior of two retarded children. *Journal of Applied Behavior Analysis, 13*, 101–117.

Carr, E. G., Reeve, C. E., & Magito-McLaughlin, D. (1996). Contextual influences on problem behavior in people with disabilities. In L. K. Koegel, R. L. Koegel, & G. Dunlap (Eds.), *Positive behavioral support: Including people with difficult behavior in the community* (pp. 403–423). Baltimore: Paul H. Brookes.

Carr, E. G., Robinson, S., & Palumbo, L. W. (1990). The wrong issue: Aversive vs. nonaversive treatment. The right issue: Functional vs. nonfunctional treatment. In A. C. Repp & N. N. Singh (Eds.), *Perspectives on the use of nonaversive and aversive interventions for persons with developmental disabilities* (pp. 361–380). Sycamore, IL: Sycamore Press.

Carr, E. G., Taylor, J. C., & Robinson, S. (1991). The effects of severe behavior problems on the teaching behavior of adults. *Journal of Applied Behavior Analysis, 24*, 523–535.

Carta, J. J., Sideridis, G., Rinkel, P., Guimaraes, S., Greenwood, C., Bagget, K., Peterson, P., Atwater, J., McEvoy, M., & McConnell, S. (1994). Behavioral outcomes of young children prenatally exposed to illicit drugs: Review and analysis of experimental literature. *Topics in Early Childhood Special Education, 14*, 184–216.

Chandler, L. K. (1991). Strategies to promote physical, social, and academic integration in mainstreamed programs. In G. Stoner, M. R. Shinn, & H. M. Walker (Eds.), *Intervention for achievement and behavior problems* (pp. 305–331). Washington, DC: National Association for School Psychologists.

Chandler, L. K. (1992). Promoting children's social/survival skills as a strategy for transition to mainstreamed kindergarten programs. In S. L. Odom, S. R. McConnell, & M. A. McEvoy (Eds.), *Social competence of young children with disabilities* (pp. 245–276). Baltimore: Paul H. Brookes.

Chandler, L. K. (1997). *Using functional assessment to prevent and remediate challenging behavior in young children with disabilities.* Preconference workshop presented at the Illinois School Psychology Association Conference, Peoria, IL.

Chandler, L. K. (1998). *Challenging behavior: A parent and provider dialogue on effective discipline for young children with special needs.* Two-day workshops and panel facilitation for the Wisconsin Personnel Development Project, Madison and Eau Claire, WI.

Chandler, L. K. (2000). A training and consultation model to reduce resistance and increase educator knowledge and skill in addressing challenging behavior. *Special Education Perspectives, 9*(1), 3–13.

Chandler, L. K., & Dahlquist, C. M. (1994). *Using functional assessment and positive intervention strategies to address the challenging behavior of young children.* Workshop presented at the Delaware Statewide Early Childhood Center, Dover, DE.

Chandler, L. K., & Dahlquist, C. M. (1995). *A team-based approach to address problem behavior through functional assessment and positive prevention and remediation strategies.* Preconference workshop presented at the Division for Early Childhood Conference, Lake Buena Vista, FL.

Chandler, L. K., & Dahlquist, C. M. (1997). *Confronting the challenging in challenging behavior through functional assessment.* Workshop presented for the State Department of Education, Colorado Springs, CO.

Chandler, L. K., & Dahlquist, C. M. (1998). *Challenging behaviors of young children: Functional assessment and positive intervention strategies.* Workshop presented for the Creche Child and Family Center and George Brown College, Toronto, Canada.

Chandler, L. K., & Dahlquist, C. M. (1999a). Integration in the preschool for children with mild or moderate disabilities. In M. J. Coutinho & A. C. Repp (Eds.), *Inclusion: The integration of students with disabilities* (pp. 206–235). Belmont, CA: Wadsworth Publishing Company.

Chandler, L. K., & Dahlquist, C. M. (1999b). The effects of functional assessment on the challenging and appropriate behavior of children in preschool classrooms. In S. Irwin (Ed.), *Challenging the challenging behaviors: A sourcebook based on the SpeciaLink Institute* (pp. 27–30, 73–79). Cape Breton Island, CA: Breton Books.

Chandler, L. K., Dahlquist, C. M., Repp, A. C., & Feltz, C. (1999). The effects of team-based functional assessment on the behavior of students in classroom settings. *Exceptional Children, 66*(1), 101–121.

Chandler, L. K., Fowler, S. A., & Lubeck, R. C. (1986). Assessing family needs: The first step in providing family-focused intervention. *Diagnostique, 11*, 233–245.

Chandler, L. K., Fowler, S. A., & Lubeck, R. C. (1992). An analysis of the effects of multiple setting events on the social behavior of preschool children with special needs. *Journal of Applied Behavior Analysis, 25*, 249–264.

Chandler, L. K., Fowler, S. A., & Stahursky, L. (1995). *Planning your child's transition to preschool: A step-by-step guide*. Champaign, IL: FACTS/LRE Project, University of Illinois.

Chandler, L. K., Frich, D. M., Hein, C., & Burke, M. (1979). *Leisure activities and their effects on the behavior of retarded individuals*. Poster presented at the Association for Behavior Analysis Conference, Dearborn, MI.

Chandler, L. K., Lubeck, R. C., & Fowler, S. A. (1992). Generalization and maintenance of preschool children's social skills: A critical review. *Journal of Applied Behavior Analysis, 25*, 415–428.

Chicago Public Schools. (1998). Attention deficit hyperactivity disorder manual: Providing successful educational interventions for students with ADHD. Chicago: Author.

Colby Trott, M., Laurel, M. K, & Windeck, S. L. (1993). *SenseAbilities: Understanding sensory integration*. Tucson, AZ: Therapy Skill Builders.

Corbett, J. A., & Campbell, H. J. (1981). Causes of self-injurious behavior. In P. Mittler (Ed.), *Frontiers of knowledge in mental retardation: Vol. 2. Biomedical aspects* (pp. 285–292). Baltimore: University Park Press.

Council for Exceptional Children. (1999, Winter). *Research connections in special education: Positive behavioral support*. ERIC/OSEP Special Project, The ERIC Clearinghouse on Disabilities and Gifted Education. Reston, VA: Author.

Cowdery, G. E., Iwata, B. A., & Pace, G. M. (1990). Effects and side effects of DRO as treatment for self-injurious behavior. *Journal of Applied Behavior Analysis, 23*, 497–506.

Crawford, J., Brockel, B., Schauss, S., & Miltenberger, R. G. (1992). A comparison of methods for the

functional assessment of stereotypic behavior. *Journal of the Association for Persons with Handicaps, 17*, 77–86.

Dahlquist, C. M., Repp, A. C., Karsh, K. G., & Chandler, L. K. (1994). *Prevention and remediation of problem behaviors in early childhood at-risk programs*. Presentation to the Aurora Head Start Program, Aurora, IL.

Davis, C. A. (1998). Functional assessment: Issues in implementation and applied research. *Preventing School Failure, 43*(1), 34–36.

Davis, C. A., Brady, M. P., Williams, R. E., & Hamilton, R. (1992). Effects of high probability requests on the acquisition and generalization of responses to requests in young children with behavior disorders. *Journal of Applied Behavior Analysis, 25*, 905–916.

Day, H. M., & Horner, R. H. (1986). Response variation and the generalization of a dressing skill: Comparison of single instance and general case instructions. *Applied Research in Mental Retardation, 7*, 189–202.

Day, H. M., Horner, R. H., & O'Neill, R. E. (1994). Multiple functions of problem behaviors: Assessment and intervention. *Journal of Applied Behavior Analysis, 27*, 279–290.

Deitz, S. M., & Repp, A. C. (1973). Decreasing classroom misbehavior through the use of DRL schedules of reinforcement. *Journal of Applied Behavior Analysis, 6*, 457–463.

Deitz, D. E., & Repp, A. C. (1983). Reducing behavior through reinforcement. *Exceptional Education Quarterly, 3*(4), 34–47.

Deitz, S. M., Repp, A. C., & Deitz, D. E. (1976). Reducing inappropriate classroom behavior of retarded students through three procedures of differential reinforcement. *Journal of Mental Deficiency, 20*, 155–170.

Derby, K. M., Hagopian, L., Fisher, W. W., Richman, D., Augustine, M., Fahs, A., & Thompson, R. (2000). Functional analysis of aberrant behavior through measurement of separate response topographies. *Journal of Applied Behavior Analysis, 33*, 113–118.

Derby, K. M., Wacker, D. P., Peck, S., Sasso, G., DeRaad, A., Berg, W., Asmus, J., & Ulrich, S. (1994). Functional analysis of separate topographies of aberrant behavior. *Journal of Applied Behavior Analysis, 27*, 267–278.

Derby, K. M., Wacker, D. P., Sasso, G., Steege, M., Northrup, J., Cigrand, K., & Asmus, J. (1992). Brief functional assessment techniques to evaluate aberrant behavior in an outpatient setting. *Journal of Applied Behavior Analysis, 25,* 713–721.

Donnellan, A. M., & LaVigna, G. W. (1990). Myths about punishment. In A. C. Repp & N. N. Singh (Eds.), *Perspectives on the use of nonaversive and aversive interventions for persons with developmental disabilities* (pp. 33–58). Sycamore, IL: Sycamore Press.

Doyle, P. M., Gast, D. L., Wolery, M., Ault, M. J., & Farmer, J. A. (1990). Use of constant time delay in small group instruction: A study of observable and incidental learning. *The Journal of Special Education, 23*(4), 363–385.

Drabman, R. S., Hammer, D., & Rosenbaum, M. S. (1979). Assessing generalization in behavior modification with children: The generalization map. *Behavioral Assessment, 1,* 203–219.

Drasgow, E., Halle, J. W., Ostrosky, M., & Harbors, H. (1996). Using behavioral indication and functional communication training to establish an initial sign repertoire with a young child with severe disabilities. *Topics in Early Childhood Special Education, 16,* 500–521.

Dunlap, G., Foster-Johnson, L., & Robbins, F. R. (1990). Preventing serious behavior problems through skill development and early interventions. In A. C. Repp & N. N. Singh (Eds.), *Perspectives on the use of nonaversive and aversive interventions for persons with developmental disabilities* (pp. 272–286). Sycamore, IL: Sycamore Press.

Dunlap, G., & Fox, L. (1996). Early intervention and serious problem behaviors: A comprehensive approach. In L. K. Koegel, R. L. Koegel, & G. Dunlap (Eds.), *Positive behavioral support: Including people with difficult behavior in the community* (pp. 31–50). Baltimore: Paul H. Brookes.

Dunlap, G., & Kern, L. (1993). Assessment and intervention for children within the instructional curriculum. In J. Reichle & D. P. Wacker (Eds.), *Communication alternatives to challenging behavior: Integrating functional assessment and intervention strategies* (pp. 177–204). Baltimore: Paul H. Brookes.

Dunlap, G., Kern-Dunlap, L., Clarke, S., & Robbins, F. R. (1991). Functional assessment, curricular revision, and severe behavior problems. *Journal of Applied Behavior Analysis, 24,* 387–397.

Dunlap, G., Koegel, R. L., Johnson, J., & O'Neill, R. E. (1987). Maintaining performance of autistic clients in community settings with delayed contingencies. *Journal of Applied Behavior Analysis, 20,* 185–191.

Dunlap, G., & Plienis, A. J. (1988). Generalization and maintenance of unsupervised responding via remote contingencies. In R. H. Horner, G. Dunlap, & R. L. Koegel (Eds.), *Generalization and maintenance: Life-style changes in applied settings* (pp. 121–142). Baltimore: Paul H. Brookes.

Dunst, C. J., McWilliam, R. A., & Holbert, K. (1986). Assessment of preschool classroom environments. *Diagnostique, 11,* 212–232.

Durand, V. M., Bertoli, D., & Weiner, J. S. (1993). Functional communication training: Factors affecting effectiveness, generalization, and maintenance. In J. Reichle & D. P. Wacker (Eds.), *Communication alternatives to challenging behavior: Integrating functional assessment and intervention strategies* (pp. 317–342). Baltimore: Paul H. Brookes.

Durand, V. M., & Carr, E. G. (1987). Social influences on "self-stimulatory" behavior: Analysis and treatment application. *Journal of Applied Behavior Analysis, 20,* 119–132.

Durand, V. M., & Carr, E. G. (1992). An analysis of maintenance following functional communication training. *Journal of Applied Behavior Analysis, 23,* 777–794.

Durand, V. M., & Crimmins, D. B. (1988). Identifying the variables maintaining self-injurious behavior. *Journal of Autism and Developmental Disabilities, 18,* 99–117.

Dwyer, K. P., Osher, D., & Hoffman, C. C. (2000). Creating responsive schools: Contextualizing early warning, timely response. *Exceptional Children, 66*(3), 347–365.

Dyer, K., Dunlap, G., & Winterling, V. (1990). Effects of choice making on the serious problem behaviors of students with severe handicaps. *Journal of Applied Behavior Analysis, 23,* 515–524.

Eber, L., Nelson, C. M., & Miles, P. (1977). School-based wrap around for students with emotional and behavioral challenges. *Exceptional Children, 63*(4), 539–555.

Ellingson, S. A., Miltenberger, R. G., Stricker, J. M., Garlinghouse, M. A., Roberts, J., Galenski, T. L., & Rapp, J. T. (2000). Effects of increased response effort of self-injury and object manipulation. *Journal of Applied Behavior Analysis, 33,* 41–52.

Elliott, S. N., Witt, J. C., & Kratochwill, T. R. (1991). Selecting, implementing, and evaluating classroom interventions. In G. Stoner, M. R. Shinn, & H. M. Walker (Eds.), *Interventions for achievement and behavior problems*. Silver Springs, MD: National Association of School Psychologists.

Epstein, R., & Skinner, B. F. (1982). *Skinner for the classroom: Selected papers*. Champaign, IL: Research Press.

Favell, J. E., McGimsey, J. F., & Schell, R. M. (1982). Treatment of self-injury by providing alternate sensory activities. *Analysis and Intervention in Developmental Disabilities, 2*, 83–104.

Favell, J. E., & Reid, D. H. (1988). Generalizing and maintaining improvement in problem behavior. In R. H. Horner, G. Dunlap, & R. L. Koegel (Eds.), *Generalization and maintenance: Life-style changes in applied settings* (pp. 171–196). Baltimore: Paul H. Brookes.

Fidura, J. G., Lindsey, E. R., & Walker, G. R. (1987). A special behavior unit for treatment of behavior problems of persons who are mentally retarded. *Mental Retardation, 25*, 107–111.

Fink, B. (1990). *Sensory-motor integration activities*. Tucson, AZ: Therapy Skill Builders.

Fisher, A. G., Murray, E. A., & Bundy, A. C. (1991). *Sensory integration, theory and practice*. Philadelphia, PA: Davis.

Flannery, K. B., & Horner, R. H. (1994). The relationship between predictability and problem behavior for students with severe disabilities. *Journal of Behavioral Education, 4*, 157–176.

Foster-Johnson, L., & Dunlap, G. (1993). Using functional assessment to develop effective, individualized interventions for challenging behavior. *Teaching Exceptional Children, 25*(3), 44–50.

Fouse, B., & Wheeler, M. (1997). *A treasure chest of behavioral strategies for individuals with autism*. Los Angeles, CA: Future Horizons.

Fowler, S. A., & Baer, D. M. (1981). "Do I have to be good all day?" The timing of delayed reinforcement as a factor in generalization. *Journal of Applied Behavior Analysis, 14*(1), 13–24.

Fowler, S. A., Chandler, L. K., Johnson, T. J., & Stella, M. (1988). Individualizing family involvement in school transitions: Gathering information and choosing the next program. *Journal of the Division for Early Childhood, 12*, 208–216.

Friend, M., & Bursuck, W. D. (1999). *Including students with special needs: A practical guide for classroom teachers* (2nd ed.). Boston: Allyn & Bacon.

Friend, M., & Cook, L. (2000). *Interactions: Collaboration skills for school professionals*. New York: Longman.

Fuchs, D., Fuchs, L. S., & Bahr, M. W. (1990). Mainstream assistance teams. *Exceptional Children, 57*, 128–139.

Gill, J. (1993). *Jim Gill sings the sneezing song and other contagious tunes*. Oak Park, IL: Jim Gill Music.

Goh, H., & Iwata, B. A. (1994). Behavioral persistence and variability during extinction of self-injury maintained by escape. *Journal of Applied Behavior Analysis, 27*, 173–174.

Goh, H., Iwata, B. A., Shore, B. A., DeLeon, I. G., Lerman, D. C., Ulrich, S. M., & Smith, R. G. (1995). An analysis of the reinforcing properties of hand mouthing. *Journal of Applied Behavior Analysis, 28*, 269–283.

Goldstein, H., & Wickstrom, S. (1986). Peer intervention effects on communicative interaction among handicapped and nonhandicapped preschoolers. *Journal of Applied Behavior Analysis, 19*, 209–214.

Golonka, Z., Wacker, D., Berg, W., Derby, K. M., Harding, J., & Peck, S. (2000). Effects of escape to alone versus escape to enriched environments on adaptive and aberrant behavior. *Journal of Applied Behavior Analysis, 33*, 243–246.

Gray, C. (1994). *The new social stories book*. Los Angeles, CA: Future Horizons.

Gray, C., & Garland, J. (1993). Social stories: Improving responses of students with autism with accurate social information. *Focus on Autistic Behavior, 8*, 1–10.

Green, G. (1990). Least restrictive use of reductive procedures: Guidelines and competencies. In A. C. Repp & N. N. Singh (Eds.), *Perspectives on the use of nonaversive and aversive interventions for persons with developmental disabilities* (pp. 479–494). Sycamore, IL: Sycamore Press.

Greenwood, C. R. (1991). Longitudinal analysis of time, engagement, and achievement in at-risk versus non-risk students. *Exceptional Children, 57*, 521–535.

Greenwood, C. R., Dinwiddie, G., Bailey, V., Carta, J. J., Dorsey, D., Kohler, F. W., Nelson, C., Rotholz, D., &

Schultz, D. (1987). Field replication of classwide peer tutoring. *Journal of Applied Behavior Analysis, 20,* 151–160.

Griffen, J. C., Williams, D. E., Stark, M. T., Altmeyer, B. K., & Mason, M. (1986). Self-injurious behavior: A state-wide prevalence survey of the extent and circumstances. *Applied Research in Mental Retardation, 7,* 105–116.

Guess, D. (1990). Transmission of behavior management technologies from researchers to practitioners: A need for professional self-evaluation. In A. C. Repp & N. N. Singh (Eds.), *Perspectives on the use of nonaversive and aversive interventions for persons with developmental disabilities* (pp. 157–174). Sycamore, IL: Sycamore Press.

Guess, D., & Carr, E. (1991). Emergence and maintenance of stereotypy and self-injury. *American Journal on Mental Retardation, 96,* 299–319.

Guevremont, D. C. (1991). Truancy and school absenteeism. In G. Stoner, M. R. Shinn, & H. M. Walker (Eds.), *Interventions for achievement and behavior problems* (pp. 581–593). Silver Springs, MD: National Association of School Psychologists.

Guevremont, D. C., Osnes, P. G., & Stokes, T. F. (1986). Programming maintenance after correspondence training interventions with children. *Journal of Applied Behavior Analysis, 19,* 215–219.

Hains, A. H., Fowler, S. A., & Chandler, L. K. (1988). Planning school transitions: Family and professional collaboration. *Journal of the Division for Early Childhood, 12*(2), 108–115.

Haldy, M., & Haack, L. (1995). *Making it easy: Sensori-motor activities at home and school.* San Antonio, TX: Therapy Skill Builders.

Halle, J., & Spradlin, J. (1993). Identifying stimulus control of challenging behavior. In J. Reichle & D. P. Wacker (Eds.), *Communication alternatives to challenging behavior: Integrating functional assessment and intervention strategies* (pp. 83–109). Baltimore: Paul H. Brookes.

Hanley, G. P., Piazza, C. C., & Fisher, W. W. (1997). Noncontingent presentation of attention and alternative stimuli in the treatment of attention-maintained destructive behavior. *Journal of Applied Behavior Analysis, 30,* 229–237.

Haring, N. (1987). *Investigating the problem of skill generalization: Literature review* III. Seattle: Washington Research Organization.

Haring, N. (1988a). A technology for generalization. In N. Haring (Ed.), *Generalization for students with severe handicaps: Strategies and solutions* (pp. 5–12). Seattle: University of Washington Press.

Haring, N. (Ed.). (1988b). *Generalization for students with severe handicaps: Strategies and solutions.* Seattle: University of Washington Press.

Haring, T. G., & Kennedy, C. H. (1990). Contextual control of problem behavior in students with severe disabilities. *Journal of Applied Behavior Analysis, 23,* 235–243.

Hendrickson, J. M., Strain, P. S., Tremblay, A., & Shores, R. E. (1982). Interactions of behaviorally handicapped children: Functional side effects of peer social initiations. *Behavior Modification, 6*(3), 323–353.

Hill, B., & Bruniks, R. H. (1984). Maladaptive behavior of mentally retarded individuals in residential facilities. *American Journal of Mental Deficiency, 88,* 380–387.

Hoff, R. (1992). *I can see you naked.* Kansas City, MO: Universal Press Syndicate.

Homme, L. E., deBaca, P. C., Devine, J. V., Steinhorst, R., & Rickert, E. J. (1976). Use of the Premack principle in controlling the behavior of nursery school children. *Journal of the Experimental Analysis of Behavior, 6,* 544–548.

Horner, R. D. (1980). The effects of an environmental "enriched" program on the behavior of institutionalized profoundly retarded children. *Journal of Applied Behavior Analysis, 13,* 473–491.

Horner, R. H. (1994). Functional assessment: Contributions and future directions. *Journal of Applied Behavior Analysis, 27,* 401–404.

Horner, R. H., & Billingsley, F. F. (1988). The effect of competing behavior on the generalization and maintenance of adaptive behavior in applied settings. In R. H. Horner, G. Dunlap, & R. L. Koegel (Eds.), *Generalization and maintenance: Life-style changes in applied settings* (pp. 197–220). Baltimore: Paul H. Brookes.

Horner, R. H., & Day, H. M. (1991). The effects of response efficiency on functionally equivalent competing behaviors. *Journal of Applied Behavior Analysis, 24,* 719–732.

Horner, R. H., Day, H. M., Sprague, J. R., O'Brien, M., & Heathfield, L. T. (1991). Interspersed requests: A nonaversive procedure for reducing aggression and self-injury during instruction. *Journal of Applied Behavior Analysis, 24*, 265–278.

Horner, R. H., Dunlap, G., & Koegel, R. L. (Eds.). (1988). *Generalization and maintenance: Life-style changes in applied settings.* Baltimore: Paul H. Brookes.

Horner, R. H., McDonnell, J. J., & Bellamy, G. T. (1986). Teaching generalized skills: General case instruction in simulation and community settings. In R. H. Horner, L. H. Meyer, & H. D. Fredericks (Eds.), *Education of learners with severe handicaps: Exemplary service strategies* (pp. 289–314). Baltimore: Paul H. Brookes.

Horner, R. H., Sprague, J., & Wilcox, B. (1982). General case programming for community activities. In B. Wilcox & G. T. Bellamy (Eds.), *Design of high school programs for severely handicapped students* (pp. 61–98). Baltimore: Paul H. Brookes.

Horner, R. H., Vaugn, B. J., Day, H. M., & Ard, W. (1996). The relationship between setting events and problem behavior: Expanding our understanding of behavior support. In L. K. Koegel, R. L. Koegel, & G. Dunlap (Eds.), *Positive behavioral support: Including people with difficult behavior in the community* (pp. 381–402). Baltimore: Paul H. Brookes.

Hundert, J., & Hopkins, B. (1992). Training supervisors in a collaborative team approach to promote peer interaction of children with disabilities in integrated preschools. *Journal of Applied Behavior Analysis, 25,* 385–400.

Individuals with Disabilities Education Act. (1997). 20 U.S.C. 1401 *et seq.*

Iwata, B. A. (1994). Functional analysis methodology: Some closing comments. *Journal of Applied Behavior Analysis, 27,* 413–418.

Iwata, B. A., Dorsey, M., Slifer, K., Bauman, K., & Richman, G. (1982/1994). Toward a functional analysis of self-injury. *Analysis and Intervention in Developmental Disabilities, 2,* 3–20. [Reprinted in *Journal of Applied Behavior Analysis, 27,* 197–209.]

Iwata, B. A., Pace, G., Cowdery, G. E., & Miltenberger, R. G. (1994). What makes extinction work: An analysis of procedural form and function. *Journal of Applied Behavior Analysis, 27,* 131–144.

Iwata, B. A., Pace, G., Dorsey, M., Zarcone, J., Vollmer, T., Smith, R. G., Rodgers, T., Lerman, D., Shore, B., Mazaleski, J., Goh, H. L., Cowdery, G., Kashler, M., McCosh, K., & Willis, K. (1994). The functions of self-

injurious behavior: An experimental-epidemiological analysis. *Journal of Applied Behavior Analysis, 27,* 215–240.

Iwata, B. A., Pace, G. M., Kalsher, M. J., Cowdery, G. E., & Cataldo, M. F. (1990). Experimental analysis and extinction of self-injurious escape behavior. *Journal of Applied Behavior Analysis, 23,* 11–28.

Iwata, B. A., Vollmer, T. R., & Zarcone, J. R. (1990). The experimental (functional) analysis of behavior disorders: Methodology, applications, and limitations. In A. C. Repp & N. N. Singh (Eds.), *Perspectives on the use of nonaversive and aversive interventions for persons with developmental disabilities* (pp. 301–330). Sycamore, IL: Sycamore Press.

Iwata, B. A., Wallace, M. D., Kahng, S. W., Lindberg, J. S., Roscoe, E. M., Conners, J., Hanley, G. P., Thompson, R. H., & Wordsell, A. S. (2000). Skill acquisition in the implementation of functional analysis methodology. *Journal of Applied Behavior Analysis, 33,* 181–194.

Jenkins, J. R., & Jenkins, L. M. (1981). *Cross age and peer tutoring: Help for children with learning problems.* Reston, VA: Council for Exceptional Children.

Jenson, W. R., Rhode, G., & Reavis, H. K. (1994). *The tough kid tool box.* Longmont, CO: Sopris West.

Johnson, D. W., & Johnson, R. T. (1995). *Reducing school violence through conflict resolution.* Alexandria, VA: Assessment for Supervision and Curriculum Development.

Johnson, J. M., & Pennypacker, H. S. (1980). *Strategies and tactics of human behavioral research.* Hillsdale, NJ: Erlbaum Associates.

Johnson, L. J., & Pugach, M. C. (1990). Classroom teachers' views of intervention strategies for learning and behavior problems: Which are reasonable and how frequently are they used? *Journal of Special Education, 24*(1), 69–84.

Johnson, R. T., & Johnson, D. W. (1981). Building friendships between handicapped and nonhandi-capped students: Effects of cooperative and individualistic instruction. *American Education Research Journal, 18,* 415–423.

Johnson, T. J., Chandler, L. K., Kerns, G., & Fowler, S. A. (1986). A conversation for families of kindergarten children: The retrospective transition interview. *Journal of the Division for Early Childhood, 11*(1), 10–17.

Journal of Applied Behavior Analysis. (1994). Special issue on functional analysis approaches to behavioral assessment and treatment.

Kahng, S., Iwata, B. A., Fischer, S. M., Page, T. J., Treadwell, K. R. H., Williams, D. E., & Smith, R. G. (1998). Temporal distributions of problem behavior based on scatter plot analysis. *Journal of Applied Behavior Analysis, 31,* 593–604.

Kalish, H. I. (1981). *From behavioral science to behavioral modification.* New York: McGraw-Hill.

Kaplan, P. S. (1996). *Pathway for exceptional children: School, home, and culture.* St. Paul, MN: West.

Katsiyannis, A., & Maag, J. W. (1998). Disciplining students with disabilities: Issues and considerations for implementing IDEA'97. *Behavioral Disorders, 23*(4), 276–289.

Kauffman, J. M., Mostert, M. P., Trent, S. C., & Hallahan, D. P. (1993). *Managing classroom behavior: A reflective case-based approach* (2nd ed.). Boston: Allyn & Bacon.

Kazdin, A. F. (1975). *Behavior modification in applied settings.* Homewood, IL: Dorsey Press.

Kazdin, A. E. (1980). *Behavior modification in applied settings* (2nd ed.). Homewood, IL: Dorsey Press.

Kazdin, A. E. (1981). Acceptability of child treatment techniques: The influence of treatment efficacy and adverse side effects. *Behavior Therapy, 12,* 493–506.

Kazdin, A. E. (1982). *Single case research designs: Methods for clinical and applied settings.* New York: Oxford University Press.

Kazdin, A. E. (2001). *Behavior modification in applied settings* (6th ed.). Belmont, CA: Wadsworth/Thomson Learning.

Keeney, K. M., Fisher, W. W., Adelinis, J. D., & Wilder, D. A. (2000). The effects of response cost in the treatment of aberrant behavior maintained by negative reinforcement. *Journal of Applied Behavior Analysis, 33,* 255–258.

Kennedy, C. H. (1994). Manipulating antecedent conditions to alter the stimulus control of problem behavior. *Journal of Applied Behavior Analysis, 27,* 161–170.

Kennedy, C. H., & Itkonen, T. (1993). Effects of setting events on the problem behavior of students with severe disabilities. *Journal of Applied Behavior Analysis, 26,* 321–327.

Kennedy, C. H., & Souza, G. (1995). Functional analysis and treatment of eye poking. *Journal of Applied Behavior Analysis, 28,* 27–37.

Kern, L., Childs, K. E., Dunlap, G., Clarke, S., & Falk, G. P. (1994). Using assessment-based curricular interventions to improve the classroom behavior of a student with emotional and behavioral challenges. *Journal of Applied Behavior Analysis, 27,* 7–20.

Kern, L., & Dunlap, G. (1999). Assessment-based interventions for children with emotional and behavioral disorders. In A. C. Repp & R. H. Horner (Eds.), *Functional analysis of problem behavior: From effective assessment to effective support* (pp. 197–218). Belmont, CA: Wadsworth.

Kern, L., Dunlap, G., Clarke, S., & Childs, K. E. (1994). Student-assisted functional assessment interview. *Diagnostique, 19,* 29–39.

Kerr, M. M., & Nelson, C. M. (1998). *Strategies for managing behavior problems in the classroom* (3rd ed.). Upper Saddle River, NJ: Merrill/Prentice Hall.

Kirby, K. C., & Bickel, W. K. (1988). Toward and explicit analysis of generalization: A stimulus control interpretation. *The Behavior Analyst, 11,* 115–129.

Koegel, L. K., Koegel, R. L., Kellegrew, D., & Mullen, K. (1996). Parent education for prevention and reduction of severe problem behaviors. In L. K. Koegel, R. L. Koegel, & G. Dunlap (Eds.), *Positive behavioral support: Including people with difficult behavior in the community* (pp. 3–30). Baltimore: Paul H. Brookes.

Koegel, R. L., Koegel, L. K., Frea, W. D., & Smith, A. E. (1995). Emerging interventions for children with autism: Longitudinal and lifestyle implications. In R. L. Koegel & L. K. Koegel (Eds.), *Teaching children with autism: Strategies for initiating positive interactions and improving learning opportunities* (pp. 1–16). Baltimore: Paul H. Brookes.

Koegel, R. L., Koegel, L. K., & Parks, D. R. (1995). "Teach the individual" model of generalization: Autonomy through self-management. In R. L. Koegel & L. K. Koegel (Eds.), *Teaching children with autism: Strategies for initiating positive interactions and improving learning opportunities* (pp. 67–98). Baltimore: Paul H. Brookes.

Koegel, R. L., & Rincover, A. (1977). Research on the differences between generalization and maintenance in extra-therapy responding. *Journal of Applied Behavior Analysis, 10*(1), 1–12.

Krantz, P. J., & Risley, T. R. (1974). Behavioral ecology in the classroom. In K. D. O'Leary & S. G. O'Leary (Eds.), *Classroom management: The successful use of behavior modification* (2nd ed., pp. 349–367). New York: Pergamon Press.

Lassman, K. A., Jolivette, K., & Wehby, J. H. (1999). Using collaborative behavior contracting. *Teaching Exceptional Children, 31,* 12–18.

LaVoie, R. (1985). FAT *City: How difficult can this be?* Washington, DC: WETA TV, National Public Television.

Lawry, J., Danko, C. D., & Strain, P. S. (2000). Examining the role of the classroom environment in the prevention of problem behavior. *Young Exceptional Children, 4*(1), 11–18.

Lazarus, B. D. (1998). Say cheese! Using personal photographs as prompts. *Teaching Exceptional Children, 30,* 4–6.

Lennox, D., & Miltenberger, R. (1989). Conducting a functional assessment of problem behavior in applied settings. *Journal of the Association for Persons with Severe Handicaps, 14,* 304–331.

Lenz, B. K., Ellis, E. S., & Scanlon, D. (1996). *Teaching learning strategies to adolescents and adults with learning disabilities.* Austin, TX: Pro-Ed.

Lewis, M. H., Baumeister, A. A., & Mailman, R. B. (1987). A neurological alternative to the perceptual reinforcement hypothesis of stereotyped behavior: A commentary on "self-stimulatory behavior and perceptual reinforcement." *Journal of Applied Behavior Analysis, 20,* 253–258.

Liberty, K., & Billingsley, F. (1988). Strategies to improve generalization. In N. Haring (Ed.), *Generalization for students with severe handicaps: Strategies and solutions* (pp. 143–176). Seattle: University of Washington Press.

Liberty, K., White, O., Billingsley, F., & Haring, N. (1988). Effectiveness of decision rules for generalization. In N. Haring (Ed.), *Generalization for students with severe handicaps: Strategies and solutions* (pp. 101–120). Seattle: University of Washington Press.

Liberty, K., White, O., Billingsley, F., Haring, N., Lynch, V., & Paeth, M. A. (1988). Decision rules in public school settings. In N. Haring (Ed.), *Generalization for students with severe handicaps: Strategies and solutions* (pp. 73–100). Seattle: University of Washington Press.

Lloyd, J. W., Landrum, T. J., & Hallahan, D. P. (1991). Self-monitoring applications for classroom intervention. In G. Stoner, M. R. Shinn, & H. M. Walker (Eds.), *Intervention for achievement and behavior problems* (pp. 201–214). Washington, DC: National Association for School Psychologists.

Luiselli, J. K. (1990). Recent developments in nonaversive treatment: A review of rationale, methods, and recommendations. In A. C. Repp , & N. N. Singh (Eds.), *Perspectives on the use of nonaversive and aversive interventions for persons with developmental disabilities* (pp. 73–87). Sycamore, IL: Sycamore Press.

Mace, F. C. (1994). The significance and future of functional analysis methodologies. *Journal of Applied Behavior Analysis, 27,* 385–392.

Mace, F. C., & Belfiore, P. (1990). Behavioral momentum in the treatment of escape-motivated stereotypy. *Journal of Applied Behavior Analysis, 23,* 507–514.

Mace, F. C., Lalli, J., & Lalli, E. (1991). Functional assessment and treatment of aberrant behavior. *Research in Developmental Disabilities, 12,* 155–180.

Mace, F. C., & Mauk, J. E. (1999). Biobehavioral diagnosis and treatment of self-injury. In A. C. Repp & R. H. Horner (Eds.), *Functional analysis of problem behavior: From effective assessment to effective support* (pp. 78–97). Belmont, CA: Wadsworth.

Mace, F. C., & Roberts, M. L. (1993). Factors affecting the selection of behavioral interventions. In J. Reichle & D. P. Wacker (Eds.), *Communication alternatives to challenging behavior: Integrating functional assessment and intervention strategies* (pp. 113–134). Baltimore: Paul H. Brookes.

Mace, A. B., Shapiro, E. S., & Mace, F. C. (1998). Effects of warning stimuli for reinforcer withdrawal and task onset on self-injury. *Journal of Applied Behavior Analysis, 31,* 679–682.

Mahur, S. R., & Rutherford, R. B. (1991). Peer-mediated interventions promoting social skills of children and youth with behavioral disorders. *Education and Treatment of Children, 14,* 227–242.

Maloney, M. (1997). *The reauthorization of* IDEA: *What are your responsibilities?* Knoxville, TN: The Weatherly Law Firm.

Malott, R. W. (1973). *Humanistic behaviorism and social psychology.* Kalamazoo, MI: Behaviordelia.

Malott, R. W., Malott, M. E., & Trojan, E. A. (2000). *Elementary principles of behavior* (4th ed.). Upper Saddle River, NJ: Prentice Hall.

Martin, G., & Pear, J. (1999). *Behavior modification: What it is and how to do it* (6th ed.). Upper Saddle River, NJ: Prentice Hall.

Mason, S., & Egel, A. (1995). What does Amy like? Using a mini-reinforcer assessment to increase student participation in instructional activities. *Teaching Exceptional Children, 28*(1), 42–45.

Mastropieri, M. A., & Scruggs, T. E. (2000). *The inclusive classroom: Strategies for effective instruction.* Upper Saddle River, NJ: Merrill/Prentice Hall.

Mazaleski, J. L., Iwata, B. A., Vollmer, T. R., Zarcone, J., & Smith, R. G. (1993). Analysis of the reinforcement and extinction components of CRO contingencies with self-injury. *Journal of Applied Behavior Analysis, 26,* 143–156.

McEvoy, M. A., Nordquist, V. M., Twardosz, S., Heckaman, K. A., Wehby, J. H., & Denny, R. K. (1988). Promoting autistic children's peer interaction in an integrated early childhood setting using affection activities. *Journal of Applied Behavior Analysis, 21*(2), 193–200.

McEvoy, M. A., & Reichle, J. (2000). Further consideration of the role of the environment on stereotypic and self-injurious behavior. *Journal of Early Intervention, 23*(1), 22–23.

McEvoy, M. A., Reichle, J., & Davis, C. A. (1995). *Proactive approaches to managing challenging behavior in preschoolers.* Minneapolis, MN: Minnesota Behavioral Support Project, University of Minnesota.

McEwan, E. K., & Damer, M. (2000). *Managing unmanageable students: Practical solutions for administrators.* Thousand Oaks, CA: Corwin Press/Sage Publications.

McGee, G. (1988). Early prevention of severe behavior problems. In R. Horner & G. Dunlap (Eds.), *Behavior management and community integration.* Monograph of proceedings of a symposium invited by Madeline Will, Assistant Secretary, Office of Special Education and Rehabilitative Services, U.S. Department of Education, Washington, DC.

McGee, G., & Daly, T. (1999). Functional assessment in preschool and school. In A. C. Repp & R. H. Horner (Eds.), *Functional analysis of problem behavior: From effective assessment to effective support* (pp. 169–196). Belmont, CA: Wadsworth.

McMahon, C. M., Lambros, K. M., & Sylva, J. A. (1998). Chronic illness in childhood: A hypothesis-testing approach. In T. S. Watson & F. M. Gresham (Eds.), *Handbook of child behavior therapy* (pp. 311–334). New York: Plenum Press.

McMahon, C. M., & McNamarra, K. (2000). *Leading a horse to water? Teacher preparation for problem-solving consultation.* Paper presented at the Annual Meeting of the National Association of School Psychologists, New Orleans, LA.

McMahon, C. M., Wacker, D. P., Sasso, G. M., & Melloy, K. J. (1994). Evaluation of the multiple effects of a social skill intervention. *Behavior Disorders, 20*(1), 35–50.

Mehas, K., Boling, K., Sobieniak, S., Sprague, J., Burke, M. D., & Hagan, S. (1998). Finding a safe haven in middle school. *Teaching Exceptional Children, 30*(4), 20–25.

Meyer, K. (1999). Functional analysis and treatment of problem behavior exhibited by elementary school children. *Journal of Applied Behavior Analysis, 32,* 229–232.

Michael, J. (1982). Distinguishing between discriminative and motivational function of stimuli. *Journal of the Experimental Analysis of Behavior, 37*(1), 149–155.

Miltenberger, R. (1997). *Behavior modification: Principles and procedures.* Pacific Grove, CA: Brookes/Cole.

Montes, F., & Risley, T. R. (1975). Evaluating traditional day care practices: An empirical approach. *Child Care Quarterly, 4,* 208–215.

Mullen, K. B., & Frea, W. D. (1996). A parent–professional consultation model for functional analysis. In R. L. Koegel & L. K. Koegel (Eds.), *Teaching children with autism: Strategies for initiating positive interactions and improving learning opportunities* (pp. 175–188). Baltimore: Paul H. Brookes.

Munk, D. D., & Karsh, K. G. (1999). Antecedent curriculum and instructional variables as classwide interventions for preventing or reducing problem behaviors. In A. C. Repp & R. H. Horner (Eds.), *Functional analysis of problem behavior: From effective assessment to effective support* (pp. 259–276). Belmont, CA: Wadsworth.

Munk, D. D., & Repp, A. C. (1994a). Behavioral assessment of feeding problems of individuals with severe disabilities. *Journal of Applied Behavior Analysis,* 27, 241–250.

Munk, D. D., & Repp, A. C. (1994b). The relationship between instructional variables and problem behavior: A review. *Exceptional Children,* 60(5), 390–401.

National Association of State Directors of Special Education (1997). IDEA *information: A reauthorized IDEA is enacted: Comparison of previous law and PL 105-17 (1997 Amendments).* Unpublished document.

Nelson, R. J., Crabtree, M., Marchand-Martella, N., & Martella, R. (1998). Teaching behavior in the whole school. *Teaching Exceptional Children,* 30(4), 4–9.

Nelson, R. J., Roberts, M. L., Mathur, S. R., & Rutherford, R. B. (1998). Ha*s public policy exceeded our knowledge base? A review of the functional behavioral assessment literature.* Unpublished manuscript.

Nelson, R. J., & Rutherford, R. B. (1983). Time out revisited: Guidelines for its use in special education. *Exceptional Education Quarterly,* 3(4), 56–67.

Nielsen, S. L., Olive, M. L., Donovan, A., & McEvoy, M. (1998). Challenging behaviors in your class? Don't react—Teach instead. *Young Exceptional Children,* 2(1), 2–10.

Northrup, J., George, T., Jones, K., Broussard, C., & Vollmer, T. (1996). A comparison of reinforcement methods: The utility of verbal and pictorial choice procedures. *Journal of Applied Behavior Analysis,* 29, 201–212.

Northrup, J., Wacker, D. P., Berg, W. K., Kelly, L., Sasso, G., & Deradd, A. (1994). The treatment of severe behavior problems in school settings using a technical assistance model. *Journal of Applied Behavior Analysis,* 27, 33–47.

O'Brien, S., & Karsh, K. (1990). Treatment acceptability: Consumer, therapist, and society. In A. C. Repp & N. N. Singh (Eds.), *Perspectives on the use of nonaversive and aversive interventions for persons with developmental disabilities* (pp. 503–516). Sycamore, IL: Sycamore Press.

Odom, S. L., Chandler, L. K., Ostrosky, M., McConnell, S. R., & Reaney, S. (1992). Fading teacher prompts from peer-initiation interventions for young children with disabilities. *Journal of Applied Behavior Analysis,* 25, 307–317.

Odom, S. L., Hoyson, M., Jamieson, B., & Strain, P. S. (1985). Increasing handicapped preschoolers' peer social interactions: Cross-setting and component analysis. *Journal of Applied Behavior Analysis,* 18, 3–16.

Odom, S. L., McConnell, S. R., & Chandler, L. K. (1994). Acceptability and feasibility of classroom-based social interaction interventions for young children with disabilities. *Exceptional Children,* 60(3), 226–236.

Odom, S. L., McConnell, S. R., McEvoy, M. A., Peterson, C., Ostrosky, M., Chandler, L. K., Spicuzza, R. J., Skellenger, A., Creighton, M., & Favazza, P. C. (1999). Relative effects of interventions supporting the social competence of young children with disabilities. *Topics in Early Childhood Special Education,* 19(2), 75–91.

Odom, S. L., Strain, P. S., Karger, M., & Smith, J. (1986). Using single and multiple peers to promote social interaction of young children with behavioral handicaps. *Journal of the Division for Early Childhood,* 10, 53–64.

Oliver, C., Murphy, G. H., & Corbett, J. A. (1987). Self-injurious behavior in people with mental handicaps: A total population study. *Journal of Mental Deficiency Research,* 31, 147–162.

O'Neill, R. E., Horner, R. H., Albin, R. W., Sprague, J., Storey, K., & Newton, J. S. (1997). *Functional assessment and program development for problem behavior: A practical handbook.* Pacific Grove, CA: Brookes/Cole.

O'Neill, R. E., Horner, R. H., Albin, R. W., Storey, K., & Sprague, J. (1990). *Functional analysis of problem behavior: A practical assessment guide.* Sycamore, IL: Sycamore Press.

O'Reilly, M. F. (1997). Functional analysis of episodic self-injury correlated with recurrent otitis media. *Journal of Applied Behavior Analysis,* 30, 165–168.

Ostrosky, M., Drasgow, E., & Halle, J. W. (1999). How can I help you get what you want? A communication strategy for students with severe disabilities. *Teaching Exceptional Children,* 31, 56–61.

Ostrosky, M., & Kaiser, A. P. (1991). Preschool classroom environments to promote communication. *Teaching Exceptional Children,* 23, 6–11.

Pace, G. M., Ivancic, M. T., & Jefferson, G. (1994). Stimulus fading as treatment for obscenity of a brain-injured adult. *Journal of Applied Behavior Analysis,* 27, 301–306.

Pace, G. M., Iwata, B. A., Cowdery, G. E., Andree, P. J., & McIntyre, T. (1993). Stimulus (demand-frequency) fading during extinction of self-injurious escape behavior. *Journal of Applied Behavior Analysis, 26,* 205–212.

Paisey, T. J., Whitney, R. B., & Hislop, P. M. (1990). Client characteristics and treatment selection: Legitimate influences and misleading inferences. In A. C. Repp & N. N. Singh (Eds.), *Perspectives on the use of nonaversive treatment of maladaptive behaviors of persons with developmental disabilities* (pp. 175–197). Sycamore, IL: Sycamore Press.

Parrish, J., Cataldo, M. F., Kolko, D. J., Neef, N. A., & Egel, A. L. (1986). Experimental analysis of response covariation among compliant and inappropriate behaviors. *Journal of Applied Behavior Analysis, 19,* 241–254.

Parrish, J., & Roberts, M. L. (1993). Interventions based on covariation of desired and inappropriate behavior. In J. Reichle & D. P. Wacker (Eds.), *Communication alternatives to challenging behavior: Integrating functional assessment and intervention strategies* (pp. 135–176). Baltimore: Paul H. Brookes.

Patterson, G. R. (1982). *Coercive family process.* Eugene, OR: Castalia Press.

Peck, J., Sasso, G. M., & Stambaugh, M. (1998). Functional assessment in the classroom: Gaining reliability without sacrificing validity *Preventing School Failure, 43*(1), 14–18.

Polloway, E. A. & Patton, J. R. (1993). *Strategies for teaching learners with special needs.* Upper Saddle River, NJ: Merrill/Prentice Hall.

Polsgrove, L., & Reith, H. J. (1983). Procedures for reducing children's inappropriate behavior in special education settings. *Exceptional Education Quarterly, 3*(4), 20–33.

Poppin, R. (1988). *Behavioral relaxation training and assessment.* New York: Pergamon Press.

Powers, R. B., & Osborne, J. G. (1975). *Fundamentals of behavior.* St. Paul, MN: West.

Premack, D. (1959). Toward empirical behavior laws: I. Positive reinforcement. *Psychology Review, 66,* 219–233.

Prizant, B. M., & Wetherby, A. M. (1987). Communicative intent: A framework for understanding social-communicative behavior in autism. *Journal of the American Academy of Child and Adolescent Psychiatry, 26,* 472–479.

Rapp, J. T., Miltenberger, R. G., Galensky, T. L., Ellington, S. A., & Long, E. S. (1999). A functional

analysis of hair pulling. *Journal of Applied Behavior Analysis, 32,* 329–337.

Reed, H., Thomas, E., Sprague, J., & Horner, R. (1997). The student guided functional assessment interview: An analysis of student and teacher agreement. *Journal of Behavioral Education, 7*(1), 33–45.

Reichle, J., McEvoy, M., Davis, C., Rogers, E., Feeley, K., Johnston, S., & Wolff, K. (1996). Coordinating preservice and inservice training of early interventionists to serve preschoolers who engage in challenging behaviors. In L. K. Koegel, R. L. Koegel, & G. Dunlap (Eds.), *Positive behavioral support: Including people with difficult behavior in the community* (pp. 227–264). Baltimore: Paul H. Brookes.

Reichle, J., & Wacker, D. P. (1993). *Communicative alternatives to challenging behavior: Integrating functional assessment and intervention strategies.* Baltimore: Paul H. Brookes.

Reid, J. B., & Patterson, G. R. (1991). Early prevention and intervention with conduct problems: A social interaction model for the integration of research and practice. In G. Stoner, M. R. Shinn, & H. M. Walker (Eds.), *Interventions for achievement and behavior problems* (pp. 715–739). Silver Springs, MD: National Association of School Psychologists.

Reisman, J., & Scott, N. (1991). *Learning about learning disabilities: Viewers guide and video.* Bellevue, WA: Therapy Skill Builders.

Repp, A. C. (1994). Comments on functional analysis procedures for school-based behavior problems. *Journal of Applied Behavior Analysis, 27,* 409–412.

Repp, A. C. (1999). Naturalistic functional assessment with regular and special education students in classroom settings. In A. C. Repp & R. H. Horner (Eds.), *Functional analysis of problem behavior: From effective assessment to effective support* (pp. 238–258). Belmont, CA: Wadsworth.

Repp, A. C., & Barton, L. E. (1980). Naturalistic observations of retarded persons: A comparison of licensure decisions and behavioral observations. *Journal of Applied Behavior Analysis, 13,* 333–341.

Repp, A. C., & Deitz, S. M. (1974). Reducing aggressive and self-injurious behavior of institutionalized retarded children through reinforcement of other behaviors. *Journal of Applied Behavior Analysis, 7,* 313–325.

Repp, A. C., Deitz, S. M., & Deitz, D. E. (1976). Reducing inappropriate classroom and prescriptive behaviors through DRO schedules of reinforcement. *Mental Retardation*, 14, 11–15.

Repp, A. C., Felce, D., & Barton, L. E. (1988). Basing the treatment of stereotypic and self-injurious behaviors on hypotheses of their causes. *Journal of Applied Behavior Analysis*, 21, 281–290.

Repp, A. C., & Horner, R. H. (Eds.), (1999). *Functional analysis of problem behavior: From effective assessment to effective support*. Belmont, CA: Wadsworth.

Repp, A. C., & Karsh, K. G. (1990). A taxonomic approach to the nonaversive treatment of maladaptive behavior of persons with developmental disabilities. In A. C. Repp & N. N. Singh (Eds.), *Perspectives on the use of nonaversive treatment of maladaptive behaviors of persons with developmental disabilities* (pp. 331–348). Sycamore, IL: Sycamore Press.

Repp, A. C., & Karsh, K. G. (1992). An analysis of a group teaching procedure for persons with developmental disabilities. *Journal of Applied Behaviors Analysis*, 25, 701–712.

Repp, A. C., & Karsh, K. G. (1994). Hypothesis-based interventions for tantrum behaviors of persons with developmental disabilities. *Journal of Applied Behavior Analysis*, 27, 21–31.

Repp, A. C., Karsh, K. G., Dahlquist, C. M., & Chandler, L. K. (1994). *Functional assessment in early childhood settings and positive intervention strategies for the prevention and remediation of challenging behavior*. Inservice workshop presented to the NSSEO, SASED, North Region School District, Roselle, IL.

Repp, A. C., Karsh, K. G., Deitz, D. E. D., & Singh, N. N. (1992). A study of the homeostatic level of stereotypy and other motor movements of persons with mental handicaps. *Journal of Intellectual Disabilities Research*, 36, 61–75.

Repp, A. C., Karsh, K. G., Munk, D., & Dahlquist, C. M. (1995). Hypothesis-based interventions: A theory of clinical decision making. In W. O'Donohue & L. Krasner (Eds.), *Theories in behavior therapy* (pp. 585–608). Washington, DC: American Psychological Association.

Repp, A. C., & Munk, D. (1999). Threats to internal and external validity of three functional assessment procedures. In A. C. Repp & R. H. Horner (Eds.), *Functional analysis of problem behavior: From effective assessment to effective support* (pp. 147–166). Belmont, CA: Wadsworth.

Reynaud, S. (1999). Behavior has no secret formula, It's just hard work. *Teaching Exceptional Children*, 31, 5.

Rhode, G., Jenson, W. R., & Reavis, H. K. (1992). *The tough kid book: Practical classroom management strategies*. Longmont, CO: Sopris West.

Rincover, A., & Devaney, J. (1982). The application of sensory extinction procedures to self-injury. *Analysis and Intervention in Developmental Disabilities*, 2, 67–81.

Risley, T. R. (1968). The effects and side-effects of punishing the autistic behaviors of a deviant child. *Journal of Applied Behavior Analysis*, 1, 21–24.

Romanczyk, R. G. (1997). Behavioral analysis and assessment: The cornerstone to effectiveness. In C. Maurice, G. Green, & S. Luce (Eds.), *Behavioral interventions for young children with autism: A manual for parents and professionals* (pp. 195–217). Austin, TX: Pro-Ed.

Rose, T. L. (1983). A survey of corporal punishment of mildly handicapped students. *Exceptional Education Quarterly*, 3(4), 9–19.

Rosenblatt, J., Bloom, P., & Koegel, R. L. (1995). Overselective responding: Descriptions, implications, and intervention. In R. L. Koegel & L. K. Koegel (Eds.), *Teaching children with autism: Strategies for initiating positive interactions and improving learning opportunities* (pp. 33–42). Baltimore: Paul H. Brookes.

Sailor, W., Goetz, L., Anderson, J., Hunt, P., & Gee, K. (1988). Research on community intensive instruction as a model for building functional, generalized skills. In R. H. Horner, G. Dunlap, & R. L. Koegel (Eds.), *Generalization and maintenance: Life-style changes in applied settings* (pp. 121–142). Baltimore: Paul H. Brookes.

Sasso, G. M., Reimers, T. M., Cooper, L. J., Wacker, D., Berg, W., Steege, M., Kelly, L., & Allaire, A. (1992). Use of descriptive and experimental analysis to identify the functional properties of aberrant behavior in school settings. *Journal of Applied Behavior Analysis*, 25(4), 809–821.

Schloss, P. J., Miller, S. R., Sedlacek, R. A., & White, M. (1983). Social performance expectations of professionals for behavior disordered youth. *Exceptional Children*, 50, 70–72.

Schloss, P. J., & Smith, M. (1998). *Applied behavior analysis in the classroom* (2nd ed.). Needham Heights, MA: Allyn & Bacon.

Schmid, R. E. (1998). Three steps to self-discipline. *Teaching Exceptional Children*, 30(4), 36–39.

Schrader, C., & Gaylord-Ross, R. (1990). The eclipse of aversive technology: A triadic approach to assessment and treatment. In A. C. Repp & N. N. Singh (Eds.), *Perspectives on the use of nonaversive and aversive interventions for persons with developmental disabilities* (pp. 403–420). Sycamore, IL: Sycamore Press.

Schreibman, L. (1988). Parent training as a means of facilitating generalization in autistic children. In R. H. Horner, G. Dunlap, & R. L. Koegel (Eds.), *Generalization and maintenance: Life-style changes in applied settings* (pp. 21–40). Baltimore: Paul H. Brookes.

Schroeder, S. R., Oldenquist, A., & Rojahn, J. (1990). A conceptual framework for judging the humaneness and effectiveness of behavioral treatment. In A. C. Repp & N. N. Singh (Eds.), *Perspectives on the use of nonaversive and aversive interventions for persons with developmental disabilities* (pp. 103–118). Sycamore, IL: Sycamore Press.

Semmel, M. I., Abernathy, T. V., & Butera, G. (1991). Teacher perceptions of the regular education initiative. *Exceptional Childern, 58,* 9–24.

Shore, B., & Iwata, B. A. (1999). Assessment and treatment of behavior disorders maintained by nonsocial (automatic) reinforcement. In A. C. Repp & R. H. Horner (Eds.), *Functional analysis of problem behavior: From effective assessment to effective support* (pp. 117–146). Belmont, CA: Wadsworth.

Shore, B., Iwata, B. A., DeLeon, I. G., Kahng, S., & Smith, R. G. (1997). An analysis of reinforcement substitutability using object manipulation and self-injury as competing responses. *Journal of Applied Behavior Analysis, 30,* 21–41.

Shore, B., Iwata, B. A., Lerman, D. C., & Shirley, M. (1994). Assessing and programming generalized behavioral reduction across multiple stimulus parameters. *Journal of Applied Behavior Analysis, 27,* 371–384.

Shores, R. E., Wehby, J. H., & Jack, S. L. (1999). Analyzing behavior disorders in classrooms. In A. C. Repp & R. H. Horner (Eds.), *Functional analysis of problem behavior: From effective assessment to effective support* (pp. 219–237). Belmont, CA: Wadsworth.

Singer, G. H. S., Singer, J., & Horner, R. H. (1987). Using pretask requests to increase the probability of compliance for students with severe disabilities. *Journal of the Association for Severely Handicapped, 12,* 287–291.

Singh, N. N., Donatelli, L. S., Best, A., Williams, D. E., Barerra, F. J., Lenz, M. W., Landrom, T. J., Ellis, C. R., & Moe, T. L. (1993). Factor structure of the Motivational Assessment Scale. *Journal of Intellectual Disabilities Research, 37,* 65–74.

Skiba, R. J., & Peterson, R. L. (2000). School discipline at a crossroads: From zero tolerance to early response. *Exceptional Children, 66*(3), 335–346.

Skinner, B. F. (1953). *Science and human behavior.* New York: Macmillan.

Skinner, B. F. (1971). *Beyond freedom and dignity.* New York: Knopf.

Skinner, B. F. (1974). *About behaviorism.* New York: Knopf.

Skinner, B. F. (1989). *Recent issues in the analysis of behavior.* Columbus, OH: Merrill.

Slaby, R. G., Roedell, W. C., Arezzo, D., & Hendrix, K. (1995). *Early violence prevention: Tools for teachers of young children.* Washington, DC: National Association for the Education of Young Children.

Smith, T. E. C., Polloway, E. A., Patton, J. R., & Dowdy, C. A. (1998). *Teaching students with special needs in inclusive settings* (2nd ed.). Boston: Allyn & Bacon.

Snider, L. M. (1991). *Sensory integration therapy: Instructors booklet.* Tucson, AZ: Therapy Skill Builders.

Sobsey, D. (1990). Modifying the behavior of behavior modifiers: Arguments for counter-control against aversive procedures. In A. C. Repp & N. N. Singh (Eds.), *Perspectives on the use of nonaversive and aversive interventions for persons with developmental disabilities* (pp. 420–434). Sycamore, IL: Sycamore Press.

Soodak, L. C., & Podell, D. M. (1993). Teacher efficacy and student problem as a factor in special education referral. *The Journal of Special Education, 27*(1), 66–81.

Sprague, J. R., & Horner, R. H. (1984). The effects of single instance, multiple instance, and general case training on generalized vending machine use by moderately and severely handicapped students. *Journal of Applied Behavior Analysis, 17,* 273–278.

Sprague, J. R., & Horner, R. H. (1992). Co-variation within functional response classes: Implications for treatment of severe problem behavior. *Journal of Applied Behavior Analysis, 25,* 735–745.

Sprague, J. R., & Horner, R. H. (1999). Low-frequency high-intensity problem behavior: Toward an applied technology of functional assessment and intervention. In A. C. Repp & R. H. Horner (Eds.), *Functional analysis of problem behavior: From effective assessment to effective support* (pp. 98–116). Belmont, CA: Wadsworth.

Sprague, J. R., & Walker, H. M. (2000). Early identification and intervention for youth with antisocial and violent behavior. *Exceptional Children*, 66(3), 367–380.

Stephenson, J., Linfoot, K., & Martin, A. (2000). Dealing with problem behavior in young children: Teacher use and preferences for resources and support. *Special Education Perspectives*, 8(1), 3–15.

Stokes, T. F., & Baer, D. M. (1977). An implicit technology of generalization. *Journal of Applied Behavior Analysis*, 10, 349–367.

Stokes, T. F., & Osnes, P. G. (1986). Generalizing children's social behavior. In P. S. Strain, M. J. Guralnick, & H. M. Walker (Eds.), *Children's social behavior: Development, assessment, and modification* (pp. 407–443). Orlando, FL: Academic Press.

Stokes, T. F., & Osnes, P. G. (1988). The developing applied technology of generalization and maintenance. In R. H. Horner, G. Dunlap, & R. L. Koegel (Eds.), *Generalization and maintenance: Life-style changes in applied settings* (pp. 5–19). Baltimore: Paul H. Brookes.

Stokes, T. F., & Osnes, P. G. (1989). An operant pursuit of generalization. *Behavior Therapy*, 20, 337–355.

Strain, P. S. (1981). Peer-mediated treatment of exceptional children's social withdrawal. *Topics in Early Childhood Special Education*, 1, 94–105.

Strain, P. S., & Hemmeter, M. L. (1997). Keys to being successful when confronted with challenging behaviors. *Young Exceptional Children*, 1(1), 2–8.

Sugai, G., Lewis-Palmer, T., & Hagan, S. (1998). Using functional assessment to develop behavior support plans. *Preventing School Failure*, 43(1), 6–13.

Sugai, G., & Rowe, P. (1984). The effect of self-recording on out of seat behavior in an EMR student. *Education and Training of the Mentally Retarded*, 19, 23–28.

Sugai, G., & Tindal, G. A. (1993). *Effective school consultation: An interactive approach*. Pacific Grove, CA: Brookes/Cole.

Sulzer-Azaroff, B., & Mayer, G. R. (1977). *Applying behavioral analysis procedures with children and youth*. New York: Holt Rinehart.

Sulzer-Azaroff, B., & Mayer, G. R. (1986). *Achieving educational excellence: Using behavioral strategies*. New York: Holt, Rinehart, and Winston.

Sulzer-Azaroff, B., & Mayer, G. R. (1991). *Behavior analysis for lasting change*. Fort Worth, TX: Holt, Rinehart, and Winston.

Symons, F. J. (2000). Early intervention for early aberrant repetitive behavior: Possible, plausible, probable? *Journal of Early Intervention*, 23(1), 20–21.

Timm, M. (1993). The regional intervention program: Family treatment by family members. *Behavior Disorders*, 19, 34–43.

Tobin, T. J., & Sugai, G. M. (1999). Discipline problems, placements, and outcomes for students with serious emotional disturbance. *Behavior Disorders*, 24(2), 109–121.

Touchette, P. E., MacDonald, R. F., & Langer, S. N. (1985). A scatter plot for identifying stimulus control of problem behavior. *Journal of Applied Behavior Analysis*, 18, 343–351.

Tremblay, A., Strain, P. S., Hendrickson, J. M., & Shores, R. E. (1980). Social interactions of normally developing preschool children: Using normative data for subject and target behavior selection. *Behavior Modification*, 5(2), 237–253.

Turnbull, A. P., & Turnbull, H. R. (1997). *Families, professionals, and exceptionality: A special partnership* (3rd ed.). Upper Saddle River, NJ: Merrill/Prentice Hall.

Turnbull, H. R., & Cilley, M. (1999). *Explanations and implications of the 1997 amendments to IDEA*. Upper Saddle River, NJ: Merrill/Prentice Hall.

Tustin, R. D. (1995). The effects of advance notice of activity transitions on stereotypical behavior. *Journal of Applied Behavior Analysis*, 21, 91–92.

Twardosz, S. A., Nordquist, V. M., Simon, R., & Botkin, D. (1983). The effect of group affection activities on the interaction socially isolate children. *Analysis and Intervention in Developmental Disabilities*, 3(4), 311–338.

Van Camp, C. M., Lerman, D. C., Kelley, M. E., Roane, H. S., Contrucci, S. A., & Vorndran, C. M. (2000). Further analysis of idiosyncratic antecedent influences during the assessment and treatment of problem behavior. *Journal of Applied Behavior Analysis*, 33, 207–223.

Vaugn, K., Hales, C., Bush, M., & Fox, J. (1998). East Tennessee State University's "Make a difference" project: Using a team-based consultative model to conduct functional behavioral assessments. *Preventing School Failure*, 43(1), 24–30.

Wacker, D. P., Cooper, L. J., Peck, S. M., Derby, K. M., & Berg, W. K. (1999). Community-based functional assessment. In A. C. Repp & R. H. Horner (Eds.), *Functional analysis of problem behavior: From effective assessment to effective support* (pp. 238–257). Belmont, CA: Wadsworth.

Wacker, D. P., Peck, S., Derby, K. M., Berg, W., & Harding, J. (1996). Developing long-term reciprocal interactions between parents and their young children with challenging behavior. In L. K. Koegel, R. L. Koegel, & G. Dunlap (Eds.), *Positive behavioral support: Including people with difficult behavior in the community* (pp. 51–80). Baltimore: Paul H. Brookes.

Wacker, D. P., & Reichle, J. (1993). Functional communication training as an intervention for problem behavior: An overview and introduction to our edited volume. In J. Reichle & D. P. Wacker (Eds.), *Communication alternatives to challenging behavior: Integrating functional assessment and intervention strategies* (pp. 1–10). Baltimore: Paul H. Brookes.

Wacker, D., Steege, M., Northup, J., Reimers, T., Berg, W., & Sasso, G. (1990). Use of functional analysis and acceptability measures to assess and treat severe behavior problems: An outpatient clinic model. In A. C. Repp & N. N. Singh (Eds.), *Perspectives on the use of nonaversive and aversive interventions for persons with developmental disabilities* (pp. 349–360). Sycamore, IL: Sycamore Press.

Wacker, D., Steege, M., Northrup, J., Sasso, G., Berg, W., Reimers, T., Cooper, L., Cigrand, K., & Donn, L. (1990). A component analysis of functional communication training across three topographies of severe behavior problems. *Journal of Applied Behavior Analysis*, 23, 417–429.

Wahler, R. G., & Dumas, J. E. (1986). Maintenance factors in coercive mother–child interactions: The compliance and predictability hypothesis. *Journal of Applied Behavior Analysis*, 19, 13–22.

Wahler, R. G., & Fox, J. J. (1981). Setting events in applied behavior analysis of behavior. *Journal of Applied Behavior Analysis*, 14, 327–338.

Walker, H. M. (1998). First steps to prevent antisocial behavior. *Teaching Exceptional Children*, 30(4), 16–19.

Walker, H. M. (2000). Reflections on a research career: Investigating school-related behavior disorders: Lessons learned from a thirty-year research career. *Exceptional Children*, 66(2), 151–162.

Walker, H. M., & Bullis, M. (1991). Behavior disorders and the social context of regular class integration: A conceptual dilemma? In J. W. Lloyd, N. N. Singh, & A. C. Repp (Eds.), *The regular education initiative: Alternative perspectives on concepts, issues, and models* (pp. 75–93). Sycamore, IL: Sycamore Press.

Walker, H. M., Colvin, G., & Ramsey, E. (1995). *Antisocial behavior in schools: Strategies and best practices.* Pacific Grove, CA: Brookes/Cole.

Walker, H. M., & Sylwester, R. (1998). Reducing students' refusal and resistance. *Teaching Exceptional Children*, 30(6), 52–58.

Walker, H. M., & Walker, J. E. (1991). *Coping with noncompliance in the classroom: A positive approach for teachers.* Austin, TX: Pro-Ed.

Walker, J. E., & Shea, T. M. (1999). *Behavior management: A practical approach for educators* (7th ed.). Upper Saddle River, NJ: Merrill/Prentice Hall.

Watkins, F. P., & Durant, L. (1992). *Complete early childhood behavior management guide.* New York: Center for Applied Research in Education.

Weeks, M., & Gaylord-Ross, R. (1981). Task difficulty and aberrant behavior in severely handicapped students. *Journal of Applied Behavior Analysis*, 14, 19–36.

Wehby, J. H., & Hollohan, M. S. (2000). Effects of high-probability requests on the latency to initiate academic tasks. *Journal of Applied Behavior Analysis*, 33, 259–262.

Wehby, J. H, Symons, F., & Shores, R. (1995). A descriptive analysis of aggressive behavior in classrooms for children with emotional and behavioral disorders. *Behavioral Disorders*, 20(2), 87–105.

White, O. R. (1988). Probing skill use. In N. Haring (Ed.), *Generalization for students with severe handicaps: Strategies and solutions* (pp. 143–176). Seattle: University of Washington Press.

White, O. R., Liberty, K. A., Haring, N. G., Billingsley, F. F., Boer, M., Burrage, A., Connors, R., Farman, R., Fedorchak, G., Leber, B. D., Liberty-Laylin, S., Miller, S., Opalski, C., Phifer, C., & Sessions, I. (1988). Review and analysis of strategies for generalization. In N. Haring (Ed.), *Generalization for students with severe handicaps: Strategies and solutions* (pp. 13–52). Seattle: University of Washington Press.

Wielkiewicz, R. M. (1986). *Behavior management in the schools: Principles and procedures.* New York: Pergamon Press.

Wilbarger, R., & Wilbarger, J. L. (1991). *Sensory defensiveness in children, ages 2–12: An intervention guide for parents and other caretakers.* Santa Barbara, CA: Avanti Educational Programs.

Will, M. C. (1984). Educating children with learning problems: A shared responsibility. *Exceptional Children,* 52, 411–415.

Williams, M., & Shellenberger, S. (1996). *How does your engine run? A leader's guide to the alert program for self-regulation.* Albuquerque, NM: TherapyWorks.

Winterling, V., Dunlap, G., & O'Neill, R. (1987). The influence of task variation on the aberrant behavior of autistic students. *Education and Treatment of Students,* 10, 105–119.

Wodrich, D. L. (1994). *Attention deficit hyperactivity disorder: What every parent wants to know.* Baltimore: Paul H. Brookes.

Wolery, M., Doyle, P. M., Ault, M. J., Gast, D. L., & Lichtenberg, S. (1991). Effects of presenting incidental information in consequent events on future learning. *Journal of Behavioral Education,* 1, 79–104.

Wolery, M., Doyle, P. M., Gast, D. L., Ault, M. J., & Lichtenberg, S. (1991). Comparison of progressive time delay and transition-based teaching with preschoolers who have developmental delays. *Exceptional Children,* 57(5), 462–474.

Wolery, M., & Gast, D. L. (1990). Re-framing the debate: Finding middle ground and defining the role of social validity. In A. C. Repp & N. N. Singh (Eds.), *Perspectives on the use of nonaversive and aversive interventions for persons with developmental disabilities* (pp. 129–144). Sycamore, IL: Sycamore Press.

Wolf, M. (1978). Social validity: The case of subjective measurement or how applied behavior analysis is finding its heart. *Journal of Applied Behavior Analysis,* 11, 203–214.

Wolfensberger, W. (1972). *Normalization: The principle of normalization in human services.* Toronto: National Institute on Mental Retardation.

Wood, F. H., & Braaten, S. (1983). Developing guidelines for the use of punishing interventions in the schools. *Exceptional Education Quarterly,* 3(4), 68–75.

Zarcone, J. R., Iwata, B. A., Hughes, C. E., & Vollmer, T. R. (1993). Momentum versus extinction effects in the treatment of self-injurious escape behavior. *Journal of Applied Behavior Analysis,* 26, 135–136.

Zarcone, J. R., Iwata, B. A., Smith, R. G., Mazaleski, J. L., & Lerman, D. C. (1994). Reemergence and extinction of self-injurious escape behavior during stimulus (instructional) fading. *Journal of Applied Behavior Analysis,* 27, 307–316.

Zarcone, J. R., Iwata, B. A., Vollmer, T. R., Jagtiani, S., Smith, R. G., & Mazaleski, J. L. (1993). Extinction of self-injurious escape behavior with and without instructional fading. *Journal of Applied Behavior Analysis,* 26, 353–360.

Zarcone, J. R., Rodgers, T. A., Iwata, B. A., Rourke, D. A., & Dorsey, M. F. (1991). Reliability analysis of the MAS: A failure to replicate. *Research in Developmental Disabilities,* 12, 349–360.

Zentall, S. S., & Zentall, T. R. (1983). Optimal stimulation: A model of disordered activity and performance in normal and deviant children. *Psychological Bulletin,* 94, 446–471.

Zhou, L., Goff, G. A., & Iwata, B. A. (2000). Effects of increased response effort on self injury and object manipulation as competing responses. *Journal of Applied Behavior Analysis,* 33, 29–40.

Zirpoli, T. J., & Melloy, K. J. (2001). *Behavior management: Applications for teachers* (3rd ed.). Upper Saddle River, NJ: Merrill/Prentice Hall.

Name Index

Subject Index